THIRD EDITION
Henretta Brownlee Brody Ware Johnson

Student Guide   America's History

Volume 1 TO 1877

Stephen J. Kneeshaw
College of the Ozarks

Timothy R. Mahoney
University of Nebraska—Lincoln

Linda Moore
Eastern New Mexico University

Barbara M. Posadas
Northern Illinois University

Worth Publishers

Student Guide by Stephen J. Kneeshaw, Timothy R. Mahoney,
Linda Moore, and Barbara M. Posadas

to accompany
Henretta, Brownlee, Brody, Ware, and Johnson:
America's History, Volume 1 to 1877, Third Edition

Printed in the United States of America

ISBN: 1–57259–215–x

Printing: 1 2 3 4 5   Year: 99 98 97

Cover: *Market Square, Germantown*, c. 1820, William Britton. Oil on canvas,
12 1/4 × 19 7/8". Philadelphia Museum of Art: Collection of Edgar William
and Bernice Chrysler Garbish. (Detail)

Worth Publishers
33 Irving Place
New York, NY 10003

Contents

To the Student

This Student Guide is designed to help you do well in the course for which you are reading Henretta, Brownlee, Brody, Ware, and Johnson, *America's History*, Volume 1.

If this is your first college-level history course, be prepared for a pleasant surprise: it will almost certainly be more challenging and more stimulating than what you experienced in secondary school.

Studies have shown that most Americans believe that history is irrelevant, that what happened in the past has little or no bearing on the present. Most Americans also believe that historical events are inevitable, that what took place in the past had to happen when and as it did.

Historians—including your instructor and the authors of *America's History* and this Student Guide—strongly disagree. We believe that one cannot understand today's American society without a knowledge of the experiences of the people from whom Americans have inherited their values, their ways of doing things, and their social, economic, political, and religious institutions. We also believe that historical events are *not* inevitable, that the development of American society has been decisively influenced by the innumerable choices of individuals and groups. It is impossible to understand race relations in late twentieth-century America, for example, unless you know why slavery came into existence in colonial America and how the slave system functioned for two centuries. Slavery grew and flourished, not merely because of the climate and the cotton gin, but because thousands of people decided for specific reasons to organize their labor system in that way. Relations between the races in modern America would be significantly different if other choices had been made in early American history.

Of course you must form your own opinions about these important issues. Is the past irrelevant or indispensable to understanding the present? Are past events inevitable or the result of choices? But don't answer these questions until you have read *America's History* and this Student Guide.

How to Study History

Gerald J. Goodwin
University of Houston

The key to effective study of any history textbook is to keep in mind that historical analysis always contains two elements: *facts*—American independence was declared on July 4, 1776—and *interpretations*—statements about the reasons why the colonists declared independence. It's usually pretty obvious what the facts are, and basic facts are seldom in dispute. But what are interpretations? They are broad general statements about cause and effect and the relationships between and among events. It is in their interpretations, and the topics they choose to emphasize, that historians differ.

Your central concern should be to understand how an interpretation gives meaning to discrete facts and how concrete bits of information support the interpretation. The two elements—interpretations, sometimes called the main themes or main ideas, and the specific details about people, places, and events—always go together. The relationship between the two is central to understanding *America's History* or any other work of history.

Using This Student Guide

For each chapter in *America's History*, there is a corresponding chapter in this Student Guide. And the material in each Student Guide chapter is arranged in exactly the same order throughout.

It goes without saying that you should use this Student Guide in whatever way is most helpful to you. But here are some suggestions.

Reading the Parts

America's History has been organized to make it easy for you to see the main developments in each period. This volume of the textbook is divided into three chronological Parts:

> Part 1 1450–1775
> Part 2 1775–1820
> Part 3 1820–1877

Before beginning the reading assigned in a particular part, read the two-page introduction to that Part. On the left-hand page a Thematic Timeline lists the main events and developments (facts) in political, diplomatic, economic, social, and cultural history. The text on the right-hand page then provides an interpretation by explaining the general significance of these events. Don't worry if you don't yet understand everything in the introduction. It is only a framework—a very sketchy outline—for the pages of information that follow.

Then, for additional help in understanding the Thematic Timeline and the Part introduction, consult the corresponding Part introduction in the Student Guide. It explains how to read the Timeline and how to relate the facts in it to the interpretations of the Part introduction. It also poses a half dozen or so questions on the main ideas of the Part. Once you have read the chapters in that Part, you should return to the Part introduction of the Student Guide and make sure you can answer all the Part questions.

Reading the Chapters

It is best to study chapter-size chunks, unless your instructor gives you a different assignment. Use the chapter structure to guide your initial reading: *preview* the chapter by reading (1) the chapter introduction, (2) the section introductions, and (3) the Summary.

1. *Chapter Introduction.* Each chapter begins with a two- to four-paragraph interpretive introduction. In most cases it reminds the reader where the last chapter left off, then previews the principal significance of the events in the chapter. *Do not skip it.*

   For example, Chapter 1 of *America's History* begins with a broad, general assertion in the very first sentence:

   > The United States had its origins in two great historical events—first, the settlement of the Western Hemisphere over thousands of years by various native American peoples and, second, the emergence of a dynamic commercial sector in the traditional agricultural society of Western Europe.

   From this you now know that the chapter will be largely devoted to explaining these two developments in some detail. Well-known events, such as the voyages of the Portuguese and Columbus, are to be seen as part of the transformation of Europe. And the Spanish conquest of the Aztecs is one of the major episodes in the confrontation between Europeans and native Americans.

2. *Section Introductions.* There are usually three sections in each chapter: they are headed by the largest-size titles (for example, "Native American Worlds" on page 4). Each of these section headings is followed by a one- or two-paragraph section introduction. Like the chapter introductions, the section introductions are largely interpretive, though they focus on only a portion of the chapter.

3. *Summary.* The summary at the end of each chapter restates the main themes of the chapter. It generally repeats the points made in the chapter introduction but adds more details. Sometimes it will look ahead to the next chapter.

After previewing the chapter in this way, you should have a clear idea of what its main topics are and the interpretation or framework the author will use to explain them.

Now go back and read the chapter. If you cannot read the whole chapter in one sitting, try to break off at the end of one of the main sections. As you read, take note of the smaller heads, which will alert you to the topics being covered. In addition, pay particular attention to the maps, figures, and tables. They frequently contain information that is *not* in the chapter text but which you will be expected to know. And they often clarify difficult text passages. For ex-

ample, you will have a clearer idea of the military campaigns of the American Revolutionary War and the Civil War if you refer to the maps as you read the chapter text. Take special note of tables that conveniently collect in one place facts scattered in the chapter, such as the lists of North American colonies in Tables 2.1 and 3.1. These should be particularly helpful when you are reviewing for an exam.

You can mark up the text as you read or write notes. It may be necessary to go over some paragraphs or a section of a chapter more than once.

Now turn to the corresponding chapter in this Student Guide, working through the seven sections in order.

1. *Chapter Précis.* The first section briefly summarizes the central ideas of the textbook chapter, restating the key generalizations so you can make sure you understand them all. If you missed any main point, use the page references in the Student Guide to go back to the appropriate section of *America's History*. As you read through the Chapter Précis, answer the accompanying fill-in questions. (The answers are provided at the end of the Student Guide chapter.) How well you do will provide a rough measure of how well you understand and remember the textbook chapter.

2. *Expanded Timeline.* This is an expansion of the Timeline that appears at the end of the text chapter. The events and facts listed are the same, but the Expanded Timeline also provides interpretations of those facts, explaining the significance of the various events. This will help you understand why these particular events and developments are the most important in the chapter. Careful study of the Expanded Timeline will also help you keep events and developments in chronological order. The sequence of events often exposes connections, such as cause and effect, among persons and events. It is advisable to memorize some important dates; used in exam essays, accurate dates can make a positive impression on the grader.

3. *Glossary.* The Glossary defines and explains selected terms from the text chapter. Use the page references to see how the glossed terms are used in the text. (Terms should be relatively easy to find there since when first used they are usually italicized or capitalized.) If there are any unfamiliar terms used in the chapter that are not glossed in the Student Guide, look them up in a dictionary or encyclopedia.

4. *Identification.* These fill-in-the-blank questions are the first part of the informal chapter self-test. Fill in all the answers of which you are reasonably certain. Use the page references to *America's History* to find the answers to those you do not know. (The correct answers are at the end of the Student Guide chapter.)

5. *Skill-Building Exercise.* The second part of the self-test is an exercise involving a map, a table, or a fig-

ure. Follow the instructions and work through the exercise. This kind of exercise allows you to work with visual and numerical information. It will help you to develop your map- and chart-reading skills and encourages analytical thinking. (Check your answers at the end of the Student Guide chapter.)

6. *Document Exercises.* The last part of the informal self-test is an exercise based on the American Voices documents and either the American Lives or New Technology essay in the textbook chapter. If you skipped these on your first reading of the chapter, go back and read them now. Then turn to the Student Guide, where you will find additional information and a series of questions on each piece. Write brief answers to each of the questions, rereading the passages in the textbook as needed. These exercises have been designed to encourage analytical reading; they also help show how each excerpt or essay illustrates one or more of the general themes developed in that chapter.

7. *Self-Test.* The final section is a formal, two-part Self-Test. Before you attempt this, take a break. Test your-

self several hours later or the morning after you have studied a chapter using both the textbook and the Student Guide. The brief delay will indicate how well you are retaining the material. You should expect factual information to pass out of memory sooner than interpretations. The latter, once thoroughly understood, will be retained for long periods, sometimes for a lifetime. You will need to retain both facts and interpretations at least for the duration of the course. After answering the multiple-choice questions and writing a three- or four-sentence answer to each of the short-answer questions, check your responses against the answers at the end of the chapter. If you get most of them right, you are probably studying with the required care and thoroughness. Use the page references to find the pages in the textbook you need to reread in order to correct any misunderstandings or errors.

There is no substitute for patient, studious reading that self-consciously isolates the text's interpretations and links persons, places, and events to those interpretations. Using *America's History* and this Student Guide together will facilitate that kind of reading.

What History Is

Gerald J. Goodwin
University of Houston

★   ★   ★

What accounts for the popular view that history is irrelevant? Part of the explanation can be found in the distinctive historical experiences of the American people. Many of the Europeans who migrated to the lands that would become the United States deliberately distanced themselves from an Old World whose economic and religious institutions they found corrupt or restrictive. So Americans tended to exaggerate the differences between their New World society and European societies. In time it seemed an advantage not to carry the past around on one's shoulders. Europeans seemed to be burdened by their history, whereas Americans seemed to have been freed from its heavy load. The Africans who were forced to come to the New World were gradually cut off from their communal histories by the slave trade and the slave system that developed in America. When the Europeans overwhelmed native Americans, they all but obliterated the cultures of those peoples as well. So Americans seemed historyless.

Another part of the explanation for the popular view about the past's irrelevance can be found in the understandable confusion about what the word *history* means. In common English usage, *history* refers to all the events of the human past. Thus, we correctly speak of Columbus's voyages and the war in Vietnam as historical events. A brief moment of reflection makes it clear that these events, having once taken place, cannot happen again. True, we can recreate them using replicas of Columbus's ships and actors to reenact the battles that took place in Vietnam. But no one would confuse these recreations with the original events. Each historical event is unique.

So the word *history* properly designates past events that have taken place and cannot take place again. Used in this sense, *history* does seem to suggest that the events of the past are finished, "over and done with." This sense of *history* also implies that writing history means simply compiling factual statements about past events, making history seem inert, dead, irrelevant.

In common English usage, the word *history* has another meaning—written studies of the human past. We describe as histories books about Columbus's voyages or the war in Vietnam. Just as no one would confuse a reenactment of the voyages with the actual events, so no one would confuse a book about the voyages with the original explorations. Yet we use the same word to refer to both the event and to studies written about the event.

Understandably, confusion results from carelessness about which meaning of *history* a writer or speaker intends. Each of us has heard many times that "history teaches" this or that lesson. But it makes a great deal of difference whether the history teaching us the valuable lesson is an actual past event or a book about that event. In the first case, the lesson seems to possess a special kind of authority, coming as it seems out of an unalterable past. In the second case, however, the lesson comes merely from the author who wrote the study, and "history teaches" is the equivalent of "a historian teaches." When people are involved, the lesson is much less authoritative, since people are, as we well know, prone to error and misjudgment.

Where does this leave us? You can avoid a good deal of confusion simply by being careful about which meaning of *history* you intend. *America's History* is a history in the second sense; it is a study of the American past. Another point to keep in mind is that events themselves are mute and cannot communicate any message without being analyzed by someone who subjects them to systematic scrutiny. So the familiar refrain "history teaches us" can only mean "historians tell us." And just what can historians tell us that we ought to listen to?

What Historians Do

A historian is anyone who uses the historical method to study one or another aspect of the human past. Archeologists, anthropologists, paleontologists, and other scholars also study the human past. But historians differ because they rely heavily, although not exclusively, on written materials: letters, diaries, journals, newspapers, magazines, books, laws, government reports, census figures. For nonliterate social groups—for example, most of the native groups of the New World before 1492—there can be, at best, only partial histories derived from the writings of others. Historians supplement the written record with other primary sources, including paintings, drawings, photographs, motion pictures, tape recordings, videotapes, and oral interviews.

What do historians do with these sources, the raw materials of their craft? They ask the sources two questions about their topic: What happened? Why did it happen? They then subject their sources to a systematic analysis to extract credible testimony that can be used to answer the two questions. A historian writing a study of the Battle of Gettysburg, for example, would examine all the available first-hand accounts of the event, such as letters, diaries, journals, and the recollections of participants and other witnesses. He or she would examine contemporary newspaper accounts and the battle reports of Union and Confederate commanders. By analyzing these materials, the historian extracts believable evidence, which is then used to construct an account of the battle. This will almost always take the form of a story, a narrative that will answer the two questions at the same time. The history will tell the reader what took place, as best as can be determined, on those three July days in 1863 at Gettysburg. But the narrative will also attempt to explain the events. It will answer such subsidiary questions as why the Union and Confederate armies collided at that particular time near that particular town, why the battle developed as it did, why the Confederate army withdrew from the field, and why the Union army did not pursue it. A history of the battle might try to do more, but this would be the barest minimum. The result then, this *history*, would be an explanatory story, full of facts to be sure, but facts related to an explanatory framework.

Now that we have taken a look at what historians do, it will be easier to understand how profoundly history as the study of the human past differs from history as the events of the human past. Historical studies are undertaken by individuals who do the analyses and write the narratives. And these historians bring to the study of the past diversity, variety—and controversy. All historians use essentially the same method to extract credible testimony from the primary sources. But the judgments they make about what is believable and the arguments they use to construct their explanations will necessarily be influenced by their own life experiences and value systems. This means that historians will often disagree with one another in their explanations of the same event. History as events may be over and done with, but history as study is an ongoing intellectual activity, because historians continue to examine past events from new perspectives. We should expect a history of the European settlements in the New World written by a descendant of the Aztecs to differ from a history of the same subject written by a descendant of the Spanish *conquistadores*. A history of North American slavery written by a person convinced of black inferiority would differ from a study of the same subject by someone convinced of racial equality.

For these and other reasons, the study of history is a dynamic enterprise. And it is the scholarly discipline most accessible to nonspecialists. The historical method—the rules used to extract believable testimony from the sources—is simple and practical. Historians avoid jargon and technical terms, and most American histories are written in straightforward English. So the only requirements to gain access to this body of scholarship are the ability to read, intellectual curiosity, and a willingness to think analytically.

The Two Histories

A society's group identity is organized around its understanding of its own history in much the same way as an individual's identity is structured by accumulated memories. You are what you remember, and a society is what it remembers about its group experiences. At any given time there are two histories—sets of stories about the group past—in circulation at the same time.

One of these histories consists of folk beliefs, myths, legends, and popular assumptions. Folk history is usually connected to real historical events, but the stories are frequently altered or adapted to provide emotional satisfaction. Every American is familiar with one of the classic myths of folk history. As the story goes, young George Washington chopped down a cherry tree. When his father asked the boy if he was the culprit, George replied that he could not tell a lie and that, yes, he had cut down the tree with his hatchet. Historians know that there is no evidence for such an incident, that one of Washington's first biographers (one not bound by the requirements of the historical method) invented it. Yet some teachers still tell this myth to children in the lower grades (usually in February) even when the teachers know it is not true. Their intent, of course, is to illustrate the virtues of one of the nation's heroes. Nothing better illustrates the essential function of folk history, to satisfy the emotional needs of society's members.

The other history in circulation is "scientific": its practitioners use the historical method and make a sustained effort to determine their data accurately and to test the interpretive generalizations they construct. In short, they follow the procedure outlined above in "What History Is." The object of scientific history is intellectual, not emotional, satisfaction. Historians try to find out what happened and why, and they make a self-conscious effort not to be influenced by their desires about what would be satisfying conclusions. They try to be objective. The intellectual satisfaction comes from finding out what happened and being able to explain it.

Henretta, Brownlee, Brody, Ware, and Johnson's *America's History* is a synthesis of the best and most recent scholarly studies of the nation's past. *America's History* and this Student Guide are based on the conviction that any society is more likely to deal effectively with the present if its members possess an understanding of the past founded on accurate information and sober judgment, that is, on scientific history.

PART 1

The Creation of American Society
1450–1775

As "Using This Student Guide" (p. 1) explains, the Thematic Timeline and Part introduction present, respectively, the most important events and the main interpretive generalizations for each period. The Thematic Timeline for Part 1 organizes the most important developments from 1450 to 1775 topically and chronologically. The topical categories are the economy, society, government, religion, and culture. On page 1, the Part introduction summarizes the generalizations that will be developed in the following chapters. Read the Timeline and the Part introduction together, beginning with the left-hand Timeline column.

First, the principal economic development highlighted in the Timeline is the change "from staple crops to internal growth." The specific entries list the steps in this process: the American economy developed from one dependent on exporting fish, furs, tobacco, and other staples to a mature subsistence economy with a rudimentary manufacturing sector. The third paragraph of the Part introduction explains the significance of this development.

The second column lists the ethnic, racial, and class divisions and conflicts that were so central to colonial society, from chronic warfare between English settlers and Indians and the enslavement of Africans to upris-

ings by backcountry farmers. The first and fourth paragraphs of the introduction interpret these developments.

Third, the most dramatic change in colonial government was the emergence of a relatively open and free political system that led Americans to abandon monarchy and embrace republican principles. Paragraph five of the Part introduction outlines the reasons for this fundamental change.

Fourth, the religious lives of the colonists evolved "from hierarchy to pluralism," from a general acceptance of clerical authority toward greater toleration and religious diversity. These developments are summarized in paragraph six of the Part introduction.

Fifth, despite their varied backgrounds, people living in the colonies began to create a distinct American identity. Some features of this new identity are discussed in paragraphs seven and eight of the Part introduction.

Now read the Timeline columns across from left to right. This will help you see which events and developments occurred at approximately the same time, perhaps influencing each other. For the period 1760–1775, for example, many factors are shaking up the old order—from backcountry uprisings to Enlightenment ideas of popular sovereignty.

Part Questions

After you have completed studying the chapters in this Part you should be able to answer the following questions:

1. Compare the subsistence agricultural societies of medieval Europe and the Eastern Woodlands Indians of North America, including agricultural technology, social structure, gender roles, and religion.

2. Describe the impact of European conquest and settlement on native Americans from the fall of the Aztecs to 1775.

3. Trace the rise of representative political institutions in the English mainland colonies from 1607 to 1775.

4. When and why was African slavery established in the English mainland colonies? What were the consequences up to 1775?

5. Compare and contrast the economic and social development of New England, the mid-Atlantic region, and the southern colonies. Did most whites achieve their dream of a freeholding society?

6. What was the impact of the Enlightenment and the Great Awakening in America, especially on religious beliefs and practices and political ideology?

CHAPTER 1

Worlds Collide: Europe and America 1450–1630

★　　　★　　　★

CHAPTER PRÉCIS

Native American Worlds   pp. 4–11

The First Americans

The first people in the Western Hemisphere crossed from Asia to America more than 14,000 years ago. These nomadic people were hunters and gatherers who spread in all directions throughout North and South America in search of wild game. In time, some of the wanderers began to farm the land and laid the foundation for settled societies in the Americas.

1. When native American groups settled into farming, they cultivated wild grasses, notably teocentli, which over time they developed into
_____. (p. 4)

The Maya and the Aztecs

At least seven centuries before Christ (B.C.), several sophisticated native societies and civilizations developed across Mesoamerica, beginning with the Olmecs, eventually stretching from the lowlands along the Gulf of Mexico to the highlands and the central Valley of Mexico. Skilled in agriculture, engineering, writing, and astronomy, these native Americans built great cities and huge monuments to honor their gods.

2. The Aztec capital city of Tenochtitlán is the site of present-day
_____. (p. 5)

The Indians of North America

Perhaps ten million native people lived north of the Rio Grande by the turn of the fifteenth century, running from the Southwest to the Atlantic coast. These native groups varied greatly in social and cultural patterns, each having a distinct language and customs. But many drew heavily from older Mesoamerican cultures whose influences can be seen in architecture, artistry, and religion. Some of these North American groups

3. Around 100 A.D. a vigorous native culture known as the _____ established itself through trade as the dominant force in the Mississippi Valley, from Louisiana on the Gulf of Mexico to Wisconsin in the North. (p. 6)

mixed farming with hunting and gathering to sustain themselves; others engaged in handcraft and artistic activities to supplement agriculture. By the time white Europeans arrived in the Americas, these native groups were well established as settled people with complex cultures.

Traditional European Society in 1450   pp. 11–15

The Peasantry

More than 90 percent of Europe's population lived in the countryside until the Industrial Revolution, usually in isolated communities. Life for these peasants was hard and demanding, both physically and emotionally. Their lives had little variety: planting in the spring, harvesting and preparing for winter during the summer and fall, threshing grain and weaving cloth during winter. Most peasants lived life on the edge, simply trying to survive from one year to the next.

4. For most European peasants their greatest dream was to earn enough money to become _____ , or farmers who owned enough land to support their families in some degree of comfort. (p. 12)

Hierarchy and Authority

Life in Europe, especially for peasants, was tightly structured and highly disciplined. Family life, directed by the father, was authoritarian, with position and opportunity dictated by gender and birth order. Discipline was also demanded at the community level, where the common good took precedence over individual freedoms. Over the whole of society stood the king and the nobility, who held land and power, making an egalitarian society virtually impossible.

5. In European society a woman surrendered virtually all of her rights and property to her husband under a legal system known as_____ . (p. 12)

The Power of Religion

After A.D. 1000 the Catholic Church emerged as one of the most powerful forces in Europe, rivaling kings and nobles for control of the people. Religion provided a framework for life and for daily living among rich and peasant populations. Having won control of Europe, the Church attempted to crush those who held other religious beliefs, including Muslims and Jews. The religious wars that followed ushered in an age of change for Europe, not just in religion but also in commerce and agriculture.

6. Between A.D. 1095 and 1272 Christian armies fought a series of religious wars called _____ against the Muslim "infidels" who held territories in the Holy Land. (pp. 14–15)

Europe and the World, 1450–1630   pp. 16–26

Renaissance Beginnings

In the fourteenth century, a rebirth of learning and culture swept across Europe. This Renaissance grew in part out of European contacts with the eastern world—including the Crusades—and the commercial revolution that followed. A new moneyed elite that traded in the goods of Asia came to prominence. These powerful merchants and bankers joined with monarchs to break the dominance of the landed elite and lay the foundation for modern nation-states in Europe.

7. The Renaissance began in _____ in about A.D. 1300 and then spread to other areas of Europe. (p. 16)

8. During the Renaissance, Moorish scholars reacquainted the people of Europe with their classical heritage when they translated the works of Aristotle, Ptolemy, and others into _____ . (p. 16)

Portugal Penetrates Africa and Asia

The European leader in the race for overseas exploration was Portugal, a small state on the Atlantic edge of the continent. With a long tradition of seafaring, a commitment to compete with Muslim and Italian merchants, and the ambition to be a world leader, Portugal extended its reach into the far corners of the world, from Europe to West Africa and from India to the East Indies and the coast of Asia. They traded food items such as salt and fish, precious goods such as ivory and gold, and humans, who were brought as slaves to Atlantic islands and to the West Indies.

9. Portugal's ambitious plans to explore widely and open trade routes around the world were largely the work of a Portuguese prince known as
_____ . (p. 18)

Spain and America

After Portugal had reached the Indies by sailing south and east, Spain planned a voyage westward across the Atlantic to reach Asia. Christopher Columbus received royal backing to undertake this challenge to open new trade routes and find new lands. In the fall of 1492 he "discovered" a New World (*nuevo mundo*) and opened the way for Europe to extend its influence into another corner of the globe.

10. In 1492, Spanish forces ousted African Moors from Spain at the battle of Granada, capping a century-long campaign known as _____ . (p. 19)

The Conquest

Following the first wave of Spanish explorers and adventurers, Spanish conquistadors arrived in the Americas in the early 1500s with plans to conquer as well as colonize. Armed with superior weaponry and bearing Old World diseases, these Spaniards ran quickly through great native civilizations, reducing them to ruins in a matter of years. The native people were stripped of their wealth, their land, their culture, and their dignity.

11. Some Spanish explorers were drawn into the heart of the North American mainland in hopes of finding the legendary cities of gold known as
_____ . (p. 22)

The Protestant Reformation and the Rise of England, 1500–1630   pp. 26–33

The Protestant Movement

After enjoying religious control over Europe for a millennium, the Catholic Church came under fire in the early 1500s during the Protestant Reformation. Critics protested the Church's abuse of power and challenged Catholic doctrines, preparing the way for new churches to rise to prominence. The Reformation enjoyed its greatest strength in northern Europe, especially in Germany; southern Europe remained solidly Catholic. The Reformation produced more than a century of social turmoil and warfare and caused many persecuted Europeans to look to the Americas for religious freedom and personal safety.

12. The Protestant Reformation began when the German monk
_____ nailed his Ninety-five Theses to the door of Wittenberg Cathedral. (p. 26)

Spain's Rise and Decline

For the first century after entering the New World, Spain rode the crest of its American successes to become the most powerful state in Europe. Philip II wanted more: He hoped to impose Spanish power and Catholi-

13. In 1588 Spain assembled a great fleet known as the _____ to challenge England on the seas, only to fail when the English navy and a fierce storm decimated the fleet. (p. 28)

cism on all of Europe. Countered by England and challenged by the newly independent Netherlands, Spain's dreams turned to nightmares, and Spain fell into decline as a European and world power.

Social Change and Migration from England

Dramatic changes across the European continent, including the Protestant Reformation and the price revolution, led to economic upheaval in England after 1550. Inflation pushed prices to higher levels, creating opportunities for some groups, such as the gentry and yeomen farmers, and causing an economic downturn for others, including the landed aristocracy. Peasants and farm laborers were driven to the brink of poverty. For many of these groups, migration across the Atlantic became an attractive alternative in the early 1600s as they dreamed of a new and better life.

Mercantilist Expansion

England's entry into the race for colonies was delayed until the late 1500s, when the Crown began to subsidize merchants who wanted to open new trade routes. State support for manufacturing and trade promoted national power and wealth and encouraged merchants to invest some of their new profits in overseas adventures. After some feeble attempts at colonization, all proving to be miserable failures, by the early 1600s England was ready to compete for colonies in America.

The English Reformation and the Puritan Exodus

The Protestant Reformation reached England in the 1530s, when Henry VIII broke away from the Catholic Church, but the new Church of England retained much traditional Catholic dogma, organization, and ritual. During the next century, many English Protestants rejected these Catholic connections, creating tensions within England. Religious persecution became the fate of Presbyterians, Puritans, and Catholics, all out of step with the Church of England. Seeking an opportunity and a place to practice their beliefs freely, many of these dissenters looked across the Atlantic to new English colonies.

14. The program in England to fence open fields and then use the land for grazing sheep rather than for farming was called ＿＿＿＿＿＿＿＿＿ . (p. 30)

15. The economic system of state support of manufacturing and trade, with an emphasis on domestic production for export trade, is known as ＿＿＿＿＿＿＿＿＿ . (p. 31)

16. During the reign of Elizabeth I, the Church of England—with the queen's approval—adopted a Protestant confession of faith known as the ＿＿＿＿＿＿＿＿＿ . (p. 32)

EXPANDED TIMELINE

30,000–12,000 B.C.   **Settlement of eastern North America**
Over a span of centuries, ending at the close of the last great Ice Age, thousands of migrants from Asia crossed into North America. They spread across the Americas, from the Arctic to the eastern woodlands, from the Rocky Mountains to the tropics of Mesoamerica, from the Gulf of Mexico to the tip of South America. These were the "native" people who greeted the white Europeans who arrived in America after 1492.

3000–2000 B.C.   **Cultivation of crops begins in Mesoamerica**
The nomadic people who came to America from Asia became settled groups when they learned how to tame wild grasses. Giving up their ways as hunters and gatherers, they were no longer at the mercy of the wild game they had hunted. This change allowed them to develop a stable economic basis for society and establish more complex cultures.

1200 B.C   **Olmec culture appears**
The "mother culture" that gave rise to the great civilizations of Mesoamerica, including the Mayas

and Aztecs, developed along the Gulf of Mexico more than one thousand years before the birth of Christ. The Olmec peoples overcame the challenges of tropical rainforests to flourish for about 800 years until they divided into a series of smaller, regional culture groups.

100–
400   **Hopewell culture in Mississippi Valley**
Around 100 A.D. a complex culture known as Hopewell evolved out of the Adena peoples in the central regions of North America. For three centuries the Hopewell flourished in the Ohio, Illinois, and Mississippi River valleys. In time, remnants of the Hopewell culture blended with ideas working their way north from Mesoamerica, giving birth to the Mississippian culture that rose around 800 A.D.

300   **Rise of Mayan civilization**
The first great native civilization to emerge in Mesoamerica from the Olmec "mother culture" was known as Maya. Developing in the hot and steamy junglelands of present-day Guatemala, the Maya flowered as a culture for about six centuries in what is called their "Classic Period." Their skills in artistry, astronomy, and writing set a high standard for other Mesoamerican cultures in later centuries.

500   **Zenith of Teotihuacán civilization**
In the subtropics of Mesoamerica, great societies developed more than two millennia ago. The Maya and the people of Teotihuacan built on their knowledge of agriculture, engineering, and mathematics, and for hundreds of years they enjoyed thriving civilizations. Then suddenly, for a variety of reasons that are open to speculation (possibly long droughts or invasions by aggressive neighbors), they fell into decline and gave way to other native societies.

600   **Emergence of Pueblo cultures**
In what is now the American Southwest, three important cultures developed between 600 and 1250 A.D. One of the common features of the Hohokam, Mogollon, and Anasazi was a system of architecture that involved the construction of complex villages built into steep cliffs. This pattern for villages, called pueblo (Spanish for "town"), characterized these cultures. Eventually the word pueblo came to be used to describe many of the village-dwelling cultures of the Southwest, including the Zuni of western New Mexico and the Hopi of northeastern Arizona, who followed in later times.

700–
1100   **Spread of Arab Muslim civilization**
After the death of their prophet, Muhammad, Muslims set out to convert and conquer the world. They carried their ideas into Africa, India, and parts of Europe, winning some converts but also threatening traditional cultures and religions. In the Crusades that followed, the Christian people of Europe tried to reclaim lands that had been lost to the Muslims.

800–
1350   **Mississippian culture**
Native groups in the lower Mississippi Valley had frequent contact with Indian civilizations in Mexico and Central America. This created a mixed culture that blended regional and out-of-area ideas into new social institutions and religious beliefs.

1096–
1271   **Crusades bring Europeans into contact with Islamic civilization**
The Crusades, holy wars between Christians and Muslims to control the Holy Land of the Middle East, introduced western Europeans to advanced learning in the Islamic world and to the riches of Asia, including spices such as cinnamon and pepper. The initial contacts inspired further travels by curious Europeans who craved both knowledge of this new world and the luxury goods that the Orient offered.

1212–
1492   **Spanish *reconquista***

The presence of African Moors in Spain throughout most of the Middle Ages—and the resultant religious wars between Catholics and Muslims—made it difficult for Spain to get an early start in the race for empire. Finally, after an extended campaign marked by religious feuding and violent warfare, Spanish forces reclaimed full control of their state in the battle of Granada (1492). This capped the Reconquest—in Spanish, *reconquista*—and opened the way for Spain to send Columbus across the Atlantic in search of the Indies.

1300–
1450   **Italian Renaissance**
The age of the Renaissance (rebirth) opened the eyes of Europe to a world of new opportunities. A revolution in knowledge and the acquisition of luxury goods and spices from the East inspired wanderlust among the peoples of Europe. The appearance of a new moneyed elite, whose wealth was based on commerce, and the rise of nation-states helped usher in a new age of exploration and discovery.

1325   **Aztecs establish their capital at Tenochtitlán**
One of the great civilizations of Mesoamerica arose in the central Valley of Mexico when people called Aztecs entered the region. From their capital city of Tenochtitlán (now Mexico City) they controlled the valley by repression and force of arms. These brutal ways pushed other groups in the region to side with

the Spanish in the early 1500s, when they drove the Aztecs from power and forced them out of Tenochtitlán.

1415–
1500   **Portuguese establish maritime empire**
With much of Europe involved in religious feuding and general wars, Portugal jumped into the lead to open new trade routes and explore new territories in the fifteenth century. Portuguese mariners sailed around Africa to India, the East Indies, China, and Japan. Their successes inspired Spain to follow.

1440s   **Portugal enters trade in African slaves**
In their quest for wealth through trade, Portuguese captains and sailors added humans to the list of cargo that they would carry for trade and sale. Beginning in the 1440s, Portuguese ships began to transport Africans from Senagambia and other points in West Africa first to Atlantic Islands, such as the Azores, and later to Brazil and the West Indies. Portugal was the first European state to enter the slave trade.

1492   **Christopher Columbus's first voyage to America**
After the expulsion of the Moors in the *reconquista* of 1492, Spain was ready to join Portugal in the race for colonies. An Italian mariner from the city-state of Genoa, Christopher Columbus, won support from King Ferdinand and Queen Isabella to test his plan to reach Asia by sailing westward. Columbus never reached Asia. Instead he found a New World in the Americas, laying the basis for a Spanish empire stretching across two continents.

1513   **Juan Ponce de Leon explores Florida**
As Spanish explorers entered the New World and made contact with native people, they heard a variety of rumors of great riches that could be found on the American mainland. One of these stories purported to describe a "fountain of youth," whose waters could keep people forever young. Spanish adventurer Juan Ponce de Leon sought this treasure—along with gold and slaves—in what is now Florida. Ironically, Ponce de Leon's search for the fountain of youth cost him his life at the end of an arrow from a Calusa Indian.

1517   **Martin Luther starts Protestant Reformation**
Growing concern about corruption and abuse within the Catholic Church culminated with Luther's challenge to church authority. Luther's broad attack on Catholic doctrine inspired religious revolution across northern Europe. In time, the Reformation spawned social change, often through wars, across all of Europe.

1521   **Hernando Cortés leads Spanish conquest of Mexico**
In the early 1500s, Spanish adventurers known as conquistadors swept across the New World to break the great native civilizations that had developed. Cortés in Mexico and Pizarro in Peru

overwhelmed the Indian tribes, leaving their societies in ruin and their people in bondage. This exploitative system laid the basis for a Spanish empire across the Americas and for the "Black Legend" of the Spanish conquest.

1534   **Henry VIII establishes Church of England**
During the early stages of the Reformation, Henry VIII resisted the spread of Protestantism to England. But when the Catholic Church rejected the king's request for a divorce from his first wife, who had not given him a son, Henry broke away from Rome and established the Church of England. This schism between the Catholic Church and the English Crown signaled the onset of religious and political conflicts that inspired civil war in England and encouraged religious dissenters to migrate from England to America.

1536   **John Calvin's *Institutes of Christian Religion***
French theologian John Calvin built upon the challenges to church doctrine introduced by Martin Luther and offered a harsher version of Protestantism. Calvinist theology, specifically the doctrine of predestination, had a profound impact in Europe and in America, to which Puritans and Presbyterians who followed Calvin's thinking migrated in search of religious freedom.

1539–
1543   **Hernando de Soto invades southeastern region of America**
Following the first wave of invaders and conquerors, such as Cortés and Pizarro, Spanish explorers moved into the interior of North America in the late 1530s and 1540s. In the Southwest, Francisco de Coronado sought the fabled golden cities of Cibola. At the same time, in the southeast, Hernando de Soto traveled from Florida across the southern Mississippi River Valley into Arkansas and Texas. Neither Coronado nor de Soto found the riches they sought, but they did open up new lands for Spain to settle later in the sixteenth century.

1550–
1630   **Price revolution**
            English mercantilism
            Enclosure movement
After 1550, dramatic economic changes created turmoil in much of Europe. Inflation sent prices into an upward spiral (e.g., wheat prices increased by 300 percent), furthering the decline of Spain but enhancing rising economic states such as England. Within England this price revolution worked to the advantage of merchants and some landholders but to the detriment of many of the English citizenry. The enclosure movement shut off land that had formerly been farmed cooperatively and added to the economic pressures on the lower classes. They looked for alternatives and discovered a viable option in migration across the Atlantic where they could settle a new land.

1556 Philip II becomes king of Spain
When Philip II ascended the Spanish throne, Spain was the most powerful state in Europe. Philip proposed to expand Spanish power and reestablish the Catholic Church across the continent. His plans were dashed by England and the Netherlands, which emerged to replace Spain as the dominant political and commercial powers in Europe.

1558–
1603 Elizabeth I, queen of England
The age of Elizabeth was one of the brightest periods in English history for literary and artistic development. It was also the time when Protestantism, in the form of the Church of England, was established as the state religion. Elizabeth's resistance to radical religious reforms led to a persecution of dissenters that continued well into the 1600s.

1560s English Puritan movement begins
Opposition to continuing Catholic influences in the Church of England and a push to purify the church led to the rise of Puritanism. The marked disagreement of Puritans with Anglican doctrine resulted in persecution of the Puritans and their eventual migration out of England.

Pedro Menéndez de Avilés plans North American empire
Spanish explorers came into the New World with several goals, perhaps best summarized in three words: God, Glory, and Gold. They hoped to promote their Catholic faith and enhance the prestige of their Crown and themselves, while they got rich plundering the wealth of native civilizations. One of the most ambitious of these Spanish *adelantados* was Pedro Menéndez de Avilés, who hoped to conquer and control the east coast of North America. His goal proved unattainable, but his vision reflected the grand plans that brought many people from Spain to America.

1603–
1625 James I, first Stuart king of England
Queen Elizabeth's passing brought James I to the English throne and ushered in a new era for the state. James put aside Elizabeth's long feud with Spain and promoted England as a colonial as well as a commercial and political power. James saw myriad benefits in the establishment of colonies in America. Not only would he increase his power and reputation as king of an imperial state, but by letting persecuted people migrate to America to settle the new colonies, he would rid the country of troublemakers.

GLOSSARY

were-jaguar Among the pre-Columbian groups of Mesoamerica and South America, the jaguar had special meaning in culture and religion. The great cat that roamed the jungles was accorded a semi-god-like status, and figures based on the look and shape of jaguars (often mixed with the features of a human) appeared on larger-than-life stone monuments. The jaguar remained a popular symbol for centuries and provides an important link among native cultures of the Americas. (p. 5)

chinampas The Teotihuacán people devised an agricultural plan, called *chinampas*, to get the best use from their surroundings. They cultivated crops on small artificial islands in natural and man-made lakes. This method was adopted by the Aztecs, who raised vegetables and flowers on floating islands in Lake Texcoco, the site of their capital city, Tenochtitlán. (p. 5)

pochteca Toward the close of the twelfth century a wandering people who came to be called Aztecs appeared in the central Valley of Mexico. Using a variety of methods, including brute force and skillful trading practices (organized in the form of guilds or trading groups known as *pochtecas* for protection and support), they seized control of the region and dominated the valley until the arrival of Spanish conquistadors in the early 1500s. (p. 6)

wampum North American Indian tribes often used wampum (shells made into beads) as money, giving them a method of paying for the goods or services they needed. The beads could also be used for decorative purposes; strung together, they were worn as bracelets or necklaces. (p. 8)

ishki chito According to Choctaw legend, the *ishki chito*, or "great mother," a temple mound in present-day Mississippi, was the site where the Great Spirit created the first Choctaw peoples. This was one of the sacred places for Indians of the Mississippian culture. Most native groups pass on creation stories, or myths, from one generation to another as a time-honored way to make connections across the ages. (p. 9)

clan and **matrilineal** Many native peoples organized their societies around clans, which were made up of groups of related families who usually shared a common ancestor. Descent typically was traced through female lines, making clans matrilineal (descended from the mother). Clan members supported one another socially and economically. Representatives of the clans often provided political leadership for the tribe as a whole, a tribe being a collection of clans. (pp. 10–11)

yeoman In medieval England, yeoman (a word that can be used as either noun or adjective) designated a farmer below the level of gentry. A yeoman was a freeholder, that is he owned his own land, which freed him from economic connections to either the king or a feudal lord. For many European peasants, becoming a yeoman farmer was a dream to follow and a goal to seek. (p. 12)

coverture   In traditional European society, most decisions were made by men. Women enjoyed few rights, and after marriage became totally dependent on their husbands, even surrendering title to their personal possessions. In a legal condition known as coverture, a married woman only had use—-not possession—of personal items. Even if her husband died, a woman could not hope to regain title to her belongings, receiving only a dower, a small portion of the husband's estate for use during her life. (p. 14)

parlement   In French, *parler* means "to speak." *Parlement*—the French equivalent of the British Parliament—was a legislative institution (sometimes with the power to act as a court, too) in which French noblemen could challenge the authority of kings and princes and address public or national issues. This sort of institution gave people an opportunity to criticize collectively rather than simply as individuals. (p. 14)

civic humanism   Although Niccolò Machiavelli (1469–1527) is probably best known for authoring *The Prince*, for American history his more important work was *The Discourses* (1513–1521—English trans. in 1636) in which he advocated service to the state in order to promote the good of the nation and its people. This idea of service, sometimes referred to as civic humanism, was critical in a republic where control was vested in a politically active and committed citizenry. (p. 17)

reconquista   Through much of the fifteenth century, African Moors, who practiced the Muslim faith, presented a religious and political challenge to Spain and its Catholic majority. After a long effort to recover control of their country, the Spanish drove these outsiders back to Africa at the battle of Granada in 1492. This marked the Reconquest (*reconquista*) of Spain and the restoration of religious and civil harmony. (p. 19)

nuevo mundo **and conquistadors**   The conquistadors (from the Spanish word meaning "conquerors") followed the first wave of Spanish explorers in the *nuevo mundo*, or "new world," of the Americas. Their plan was to get rich quickly by stripping native people of their gold and jewels. For the conquistadors, the Indians were "the dung and filth of the earth" without any standing as human beings (see the American Voices selection on text p. 23). The conquerors did not hesitate to overrun the native civilizations in this *nuevo mundo* that Europeans intended to control as their own. (p. 20)

adelantados   As Spanish explorers began to open up the New World of the Americas, the Spanish Crown commissioned a number of *adelantados* (translated as "advance agents") to extend the outer limits of the empire and to promote the Catholic faith among native groups. In return, these adelantados were titled as nobles and had the Crown's permission to acquire land and riches. (p. 20)

mestizo   The *mestizos*, literally people of mixed blood, were the offspring of intermarriage and sexual liaison between white Europeans and native people, usually a white man and an Indian woman. With so few European women available in the early years of colonization, the settlers in this *nuevo mundo* chose to marry native women. Today *mestizos* form the majority of the population in most Latin American nations. (p. 23)

simony and **indulgences**   In the Catholic Church during the Middle Ages, simony involved abuses of power and the selling of favors for money by Church officials. Specifically, simony referred to the sale of spiritual services or offices; a widespread practice that generated a great deal of revenue for the Church. The sale of indulgences, meaning the remission of punishment owed for sin after absolution by a priest, was one form of simony. Selling indulgences to wealthy people frequently funded a wide range of charitable activities sponsored by the Church. In his Ninety-five Theses, Martin Luther railed against the misuse of indulgences. (p. 26)

predestination   When Swiss theologian John Calvin joined Martin Luther and others in fostering the Protestant Reformation, he brought in the rigid concept of predestination. According to this Calvinist doctrine, a person's destiny—salvation or damnation in hell—is determined by God before birth without regard to an individual's worth or good works. This harsh belief became a fundamental tenet of Puritan theology. (p. 27)

price revolution   When Spanish economic and political power began to decline in Europe in the late sixteenth century, in part because Philip II had compromised his treasury, a murderous rate of inflation gripped much of Europe. During this so-called price revolution the cost of food and homemade goods skyrocketed. These dramatic changes in Europe's economy benefited England, France, and the Netherlands—all rising economic powers—but caused further decline for Spain. (pp. 29–30)

gentry   In English society during the Middle Ages, three groups laid claim to most of the land: the aristocracy at the top of the economic scale followed closely in line by the gentry (or landed gentry) and the yeomen. The gentry lacked the social privileges and titles of nobility that marked the aristocracy but they still wielded a great deal of economic clout because they generally managed their lands efficiently. (p. 30)

enclosure and **cotters**   In sixteenth century England, sheep-raising capitalists secured the right to fence their lands to keep villagers from sharing and farming what traditionally had been open lands. This enclosure movement guaranteed sheep owners a kind of monopoly on wool, but it also dispossessed many of England's poor. Instead of being farmers with access to open land, they became a new class of landless laborers, called cotters, who depended on others for their daily work and wages. Many cotters joined in transatlantic migrations in the 1600s in search of land they could call their own and farm freely. (p. 30)

outwork Rather than depend on European countries, especially France and the Netherlands, for good textile products, after 1500 English merchants began investing in domestic textile manufacturing. They supported the production of goods through an outwork system, using people in the countryside to produce textiles that the merchants could in turn sell at market. By selling directly, English merchants could maximize their profits. This gave employment to cotters and other landless people whose livelihood depended on opportunities provided by others. (p. 31)

mercantilism As nation-states arose in Europe, their rulers sought to control economic development to their advantage. Mercantilism, the approach preferred in England, involved strict state regulation of the economy, with colonies serving as sources of raw materials and markets, and the home country monopolizing manufacturing and export. British colonies in America were organized to fit this economic philosophy. (p. 31)

joint-stock companies European colonization in the Americas proved to be a demanding and costly enterprise. When royal benefactors could not be found to support colonial adventures, the burden fell on individual investors, who usually could not manage more than a small-scale effort. Joint-stock companies provided a workable alternative for financing colonization and settlement. Merchants banded together as stockholders, sharing the risks and profits in proportion to their part of the total investment. Large sums of money could be accumulated without any one person having to put too much at stake. (p. 31)

divine right The concept of divine right affirms the supremacy of the Crown, rejecting the idea of accountability to subjects or to political bodies, such as the Parliament in Great Britain. English political philosopher Robert Filmer is often seen as the leading theorist on divine right, but the idea was also described from a king's perspective in James I's *The True Laws of Free Monarchy*. James I and Charles II often used divine right to justify their actions. (p. 33)

IDENTIFICATION

Identify by filling in the blanks.

1. In the mid-fifteenth century, the most dynamic region of Europe was in the city-states of _____ , which had established themselves as thriving centers of trade. (p. 3)

2. The dietary staple of most native American groups was _____ . (pp. 4 and 8)

3. The Mayan and Aztec civilizations of Mesoamerica drew heavily on the older culture known as _____ that rose around 1200 B.C. along the Gulf of Mexico. (p. 5)

4. The people of Teotihuacán built the huge Pyramid of the Sun to honor the sun god in what is now the country of _____ . (p. 5)

5. The greatest city of the Mississippian culture was _____ , at the site of present-day East St. Louis. (p. 9)

6. Agricultural "slaves" in Western Europe who, until 1450, were legally bound to the land were known as _____ . (p. 11)

7. In his political treatise titled _____ (1513), Niccolò Machiavelli suggested a variety of ways for European monarchs to strengthen their hold on power. (p. 16)

8. The most important spice that traders brought into European markets from the Orient was _____ , which was in demand for flavoring and preserving meat. (p. 16)

9. The _____ were Arabs who had invaded Spain around 700 A.D. and controlled its southern region until the late 1400s. (p. 17)

10. Christopher Columbus won backing for his voyages to the New World from the rulers of Spain, King _____ of Aragon and Queen _____ of Castille. (pp. 19–20)

11. Spanish adventurers who arrived in the Americas in the early 1500s with the intention of overpowering native civilizations by force and stripping away their riches were known as _____ . (p. 20)

12. In the Catholic Church during the Middle Ages, the selling of favors for money by Church officials was a practice known as _____ . (p. 26)

13. John Calvin's most important contribution to the Protestant Reformation was the doctrine of _____ , holding that salvation or damnation for every person is determined by God. (p. 27)

14. The famous "lost colony" of _____ began with great hopes of success but then suddenly vanished without a trace or apparent cause. (p. 31)

SKILL-BUILDING EXERCISE

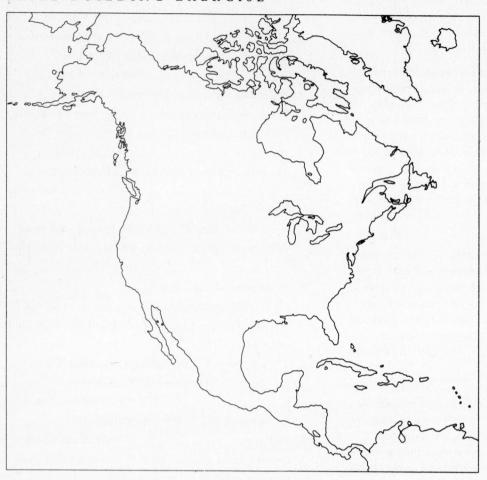

1. Identify and locate the regions where these major Indian societies and civilizations developed before the appearance of white European explorers and conquerors: Maya, Aztec, Iroquois, and the Civilized Tribes (the Creek, Chickasaw, and Cherokee).

2. Locate the sites of these Spanish colonies: Cuba, Santo Domingo (Hispaniola), and Puerto Rico.

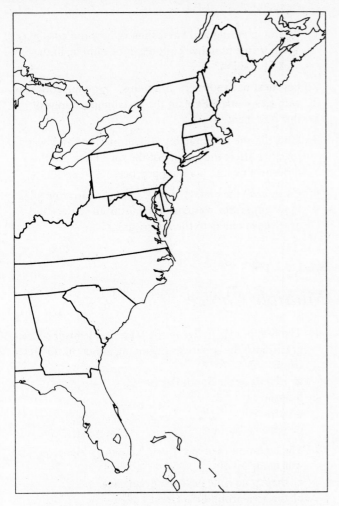

3. Identify and locate the first English colonies in the New World established by these individuals and groups:
   a. Sir Ferdinando Gorges
   b. Sir Walter Raleigh
   c. Virginia Company of London
   d. Pilgrims (Separatists)
   e. Puritans (non-Separatists)
   f. English Catholics

DOCUMENT EXERCISES

American Voices

The Customs of the Natchez— Father le Petit

The motivations for Europeans to control the New World after the first round of discovery were manifold. But three goals dominated: God, Glory, and Gold, each of which could take different forms. Many of the early Spanish and French immigrants were Catholic missionaries who hoped to convert native groups to their Christian faith. A good number of the natives accepted these new religious ideas, but others resisted. In "The Customs of the Natchez," a French Jesuit describes some of his impressions of the native people and their customs.

As you read "The Customs of the Natchez," ask yourself the following questions:

1. According to Father le Petit, in what ways was the Natchez religion similar to that of ancient Romans? What does he say that might suggest they had some beliefs similar to those of Christians?

2. How does Father le Petit describe the Natchez temple? What does he see in the temple that might suggest that he viewed the Natchez to be a "savage" people?

3. Many native groups in the Americas worshipped the Sun. In fact, the Incas of Peru believed themselves to be the "Children of the Sun." What role did the Sun play in Natchez religion? How did this affect Natchez views about their leader?

4. Many native American cultures used a matrilineal-based system in politics. Did this hold true for the Natchez? Explain.

The Spanish Conquest Condemned— Bartolomé de Las Casas

The conquistadors who traveled to the Americas in the early 1500s planned to conquer rather than colonize; their intention was to get rich off the native people. Cortés, Pizarro, and others plundered the land; they brought down great civilizations; and they stripped the Indians of their wealth, their power, and their dignity. They laid the foundation for Spanish-speaking nations across the Americas but at the same time created the "Back Legend" (actually more fact than legend) in Spanish and Latin American history.

As you read "The Spanish Conquest Condemned," ask yourself the following questions:

1. How did the Spaniards deal with the native men? With the women? With the children?

2. What were the Spaniards' motives for decimating the native groups?

3. Legend has it that on landing in the New World, Columbus fell on his knees and then fell on the Indians. How did the Spaniards justify their treatment of the Indians, especially since the Spaniards considered themselves to be good Christians?

American Lives

Luis de Velasco/Opechancanough/ Massatamohtnock: Multiple identities

In the face of European invasion, native American groups often tried to learn as much as they could of these invaders, to understand their cultures, their religious and political customs, and anything else that might help them keep control of their own lives and destinies. On occasion, the native groups engaged in subterfuge, working their way into the trust of the Spanish, French, or English. No one seems to have done these things better than the Pamunkey leader who bore at least three names in his lifetime. To the Spanish, he was Luis de Velasco; to his own people, he was Opechancanough and later, when he became the Powhatan, he was called Massatamohtnock. He had many names and he played many roles in his efforts to defend the native ways of life.

As you read "Luis de Velasco/Opechancanough/Massatamohtnock: Multiple identities," ask yourself the following questions:

1. What actions in his life—both as a young man among the Spanish and as a Pamunkey elder in contact with the English—lead you to believe that Opechancanough converted from his native origins to become a man "whose soul [was] white"?

2. Despite his frequent hostility toward Europeans, in what ways did Opechancanough help to foster good relations between native Americans and European colonizers?

3. What actions on Opechancanough's part suggest that despite his connections to the Spanish and English, in the end he was a "native American patriot"?

New Technology

Indian Women and Agriculture

Historians often talk about the "Columbian Exchange" of the sixteenth century, meaning the transfer of ideas and goods across the Atlantic—in both directions. European colonizers brought a good part of their world with them, including metal implements for home and farm, horses, weaponry, and some food products. (Though not intentionally, they also brought diseases.) Native Americans in turn introduced European settlers to their culture, notably to tobacco and to foods that grew well in the Americas; the most important of the native foods was corn, which became a staple of the settlers' diet.

As you read "Indian Women and Agriculture," ask yourself the following questions:

1. Beyond planting and harvesting it, how did corn play a major role in native cultures, for example, in the area of religion?

2. For most native American groups, "growing corn was women's work." Explain the social implications of this statement.

3. How did the Indian habit of planting corn and beans together affect the quality of the soil? How did this differ from white planting practices?

4. Corn was "the dietary staple" of most native people. How important was corn for European settlers and other newcomers to the Americas?

SELF-TEST

Multiple Choice

1. The first people to live in the Western Hemisphere migrated into the Americas beginning about 30,000 B.C. from:
   a. islands in the South Pacific.
   b. Asia.
   c. Africa.
   d. western Europe.

2. The region of the New World known as Mesoamerica was made up of:
   a. the Arctic zone near the Bering Sea.
   b. the area around the Great Lakes.
   c. present-day Mexico and Guatemala.
   d. Peru and Bolivia in South America.

3. The most brutal of the native American civilizations, based in part on the practice of human sacrifice, was that of the:
   a. people of Teotihuacán in the highlands of Mexico.
   b. Maya in the Yucatan Peninsula.
   c. Olmec peoples along the Gulf of Mexico.
   d. Aztecs in the central Valley of Mexico.

4. The people of Teotihuacán had as a major deity and a prime object of worship the feathered serpent they called:
   a. Tenochtitlán.   c. Toltec.
   b. Quetzalcoatl.   d. Tuscarora.

5. Between 600 and 1250 A.D. *all* of the following native cultures developed in the American Southwest *except*:
   a. Hohokam.   c. Anasazi.
   b. Mogollon.   d. Choctaw.

6. In many eastern woodland tribes, notably the Iroquois, important decisions were made by the senior women, and inheritances—including rights to land and other property—passed from mother to daughter.

This sort of society would be described as:

a. matrilineal.   c. intergenerational.
b. patriarchal.   d. hierarchical.

7. The traditional language of scholarship in Europe that was preserved by Catholic priests and monks was:

a. Italian.   c. Latin.
b. German.   d. Greek.

8. The first Europeans to engage in African slavery, by trading, transporting, and selling humans into bondage, were the:

a. Spanish.   c. Dutch.
b. Portuguese.   d. English.

9. The Portuguese were able to outmaneuver and outgun their Arab rivals on the seas because they sailed a small but swift type of ship known as a:

a. musketeer.   c. malabar.
b. caravel.   d. clipper.

10. Spanish entrepreneurs who were licensed by the Crown to acquire and manage land in the New World in return for promoting Spanish control were known as:

a. *adelantados*.   c. florentines.
b. *conquistadors*.   d. caravels.

11. In the 1520s, Francisco Pizarro began a long trek into the mountains of Peru that resulted in the Spanish conquest of the empire of the:

a. Incas.   c. Arawaks.
b. Aztecs.   d. Toltecs.

12. The notion that Spain's primary goal in the New World was to conquer native peoples in cruel and violent fashion is known as:

a. *Reconquista*.   c. the Black Legend.
b. the Reckoning.   d. Moctezuma's Revenge.

13. One of the abuses of the Catholic Church that led to protests by critics was the selling of religious offices, a practice known as:

a. indulgences.   c. nepotism.
b. simony.   d. anticlericalism.

14. *Institutes of the Christian Religion* (1536), a book that depicted God as an awesome sovereign and emphasized the corruption of the human race, was written by:

a. Martin Luther.
b. Cardinal Thomas Wolsey.
c. John Calvin.
d. St. Thomas Aquinas.

15. The "Royal Fifth" was the term used to describe:

a. special indulgences given the Spanish monarch by the pope.
b. the great fleet launched by Spain against England.
c. territories controlled by Spain in northern Europe.

d. the percentage of treasure taken from America that went directly to the Spanish crown.

16. Which of the following groups did *not* benefit from inflation and the price revolution that hit England in the mid 1500s?

a. the aristocracy   c. yeomen farmers
b. the landed gentry   d. wool merchants

Short Essays

Answer the following in a brief paragraph.

1. According to our best knowledge, how did native Americans first come into the Americas, and where did they settle? (pp. 4–11)

2. What made the life of European peasants so difficult and demanding? (pp. 11–13)

3. What was the status of women in European society during the 1500s and 1600s? (pp. 13–14)

4. Why did the Catholic Church have such a strong hold on the population of Europe after 1000 A.D.? (pp. 14–15)

5. What changes occurred in Europe during the Renaissance, from the 1300s into the 1500s, to help prepare European states for the age of exploration and discovery? (pp. 16–18)

6. What enabled the small state of Portugal to seize the lead in the great surge of European expansion? (p. 18)

7. Why did the Spanish find it so easy to conquer the native groups of the Americas in the early 1500s? (pp. 20–22)

8. In what four major areas did Martin Luther's teachings differ from Roman Catholic doctrine? (pp. 26–27)

9. What three great historical changes in England in the 1500s resulted in transatlantic migration and English settlement in North America in the 1600s? (pp. 26–33)

ANSWERS

Chapter Précis

1. maize or Indian corn
2. Mexico City
3. Hopewell
4. yeoman
5. coverture
6. the Crusades

7. Italy
8. Latin
9. Henry the Navigator
10. *reconquista* or Reconquest
11. Cibola
12. Martin Luther
13. Spanish Armada
14. enclosure
15. mercantilism
16. Thirty-nine Articles

Identification

1. Italy
2. maize or corn or Indian corn
3. Olmec
4. Mexico
5. Cahokia
6. serfs
7. *The Prince*
8. pepper
9. Moors
10. Ferdinand; Isabella
11. conquistadors
12. simony
13. predestination
14. Roanoke

Skill-Building Exercise

1. See map 1.1, text p. 7.
2. See map 1.3, text p. 21.
3. a. Gorges—Maine
   b. Raleigh—Roanoke Island
   c. Virginia Company—Jamestown
   d. Pilgrims—Plymouth
   e. Puritans—Massachusetts Bay
   f. Catholics—Maryland

Self-Test

Multiple Choice

1. b	5. d	9. b	13. b
2. c	6. a	10. a	14. c
3. d	7. c	11. a	15. d
4. b	8. b	12. c	16. a

Short Essays

1. Anthropologists and archaeologists suggest that native groups came to America from Asia during the last great Ice Age. They crossed a land bridge into America and then spread across North America and into Central and South America in the centuries that followed. Some of the wanderers moved into the eastern woodlands of North America, where they mixed farming with hunting and gathering; others traveled into Mesoamerica, and some established great civilizations that rivaled the most advanced in Europe; still others crossed into South America, going all the way to the tip of the continent.

2. Until the Industrial Revolution most Europeans lived as peasants in isolated communities. They were at the mercy of kings and aristocrats who set the rules for society. Diseases and malnourishment threatened their lives, and bad weather threatened livelihood. With only primitive farm implements and machines, peasants had to do all work by hand over long and exhausting months.

3. In European society, women's lives were hedged about with numerous constraints established by tradition and law. As a daughter, a woman was bound to follow the orders of her father. She could expect a small dowry upon marriage, but most property would pass to her brothers. As a wife, a woman surrendered her personal identity and property to her husband. Women were dependent beings, subordinate to the men in their lives.

4. The Church was an integral part of daily life, using a calendar that reflected the cycle of agriculture, and blending Christian and pagan traditions to join the new with the old. Priests provided spiritual guidance for both rich and poor, and the sacrament of Holy Communion gave everyone an opportunity to touch the divine. In addition, the Church, with its hierarchical doctrines, fitted well into the disciplined society to which Europeans were accustomed.

5. According to its definition Renaissance means rebirth. In fact, the Renaissance was a time of birth—for new

ideas, for inventions, for innovation, and for adventure. Europeans who had traveled to the East, as Crusaders and as traders, brought back to Europe a rich variety of goods from Asia that inspired interest in Asia and the Indies and promoted the development of new trade routes toward the East. Innovations in astronomy and geography—some developed in China and Egypt—stimulated interest in travel. And the rise of new economic groups, such as merchants and bankers, whose wealth was dependent on trade, created a demand for opening new parts of the world for markets and for sources of goods that could be sold back in Europe at good profit.

6. Bogged down in internal turmoil, religious feuding, and external wars, most European states in the fifteenth century were unprepared to strike out in search of new lands. This opened the way for Portugal to take the lead. Geography had blessed Portugal: Its situation on the edge of Europe was perfect for exploring the Atlantic. With a long history of seafaring, a strong merchant fleet that used the new ship design called the caravel, and determined leadership—most notable that of Prince Henry the Navigator—Portugal was well suited to become a major player in the race for commerce and colonies.

7. The conquistadors came to the Americas well armed and prepared to reduce to ruin the great societies they found there. Cortés's way into Mexico was facilitated by the Aztec legend of Quetzalcoatl, a great god whose return had been predicted. Believing Cortés to be that god, the Aztecs welcomed the Spanish with great pomp and ceremony. The Spanish overwhelmed the native people with their advanced weaponry, protective body armor, and horses—all of which were new to the Indians. Disease was another important weapon that decimated native Americans, who lacked immunity to Old World diseases. With these advantages, hundreds of Spanish easily defeated hundreds of thousands of native people.

8. In the early stages of the Protestant Reformation, Martin Luther launched a broad attack on Catholic dogma, ritual, and practices. First, he rejected the notion that Christians could win salvation either by faith or by good works, arguing that salvation came by faith alone. He rejected the spiritual authority of the pope as the head of the Church. He proclaimed the priesthood of all believers rather than giving special standing to priests. Finally, Luther considered the Bible to be sole authority in matters of faith.

9. England, in company with the rest of Europe, was reshaped by major changes sweeping the continent. The English monarchs, whose power and influence were based on colonies and commerce, encouraged the expansion of shipping and trade, which required the establishment of overseas empires. The Protestant Reformation created religious divisions within England and led to the persecution of Catholics and some Protestants. The price revolution and the accompanying inflation altered traditional landholding patterns and put economic pressure on many groups in England. Unhappy English people grew tired of the troubles at home and looked across the Atlantic for new opportunities for themselves and their families.

CHAPTER 2

Invasion and Settlement 1565–1675

★   ★   ★

CHAPTER PRÉCIS

Spanish, French, and Dutch Goals   pp. 38–43

Imperial Rivalries and American Settlements

In the last half of the sixteenth century, the American mainland became a battleground involving native peoples and European states. Spain's early hold on the continent came under challenge on several sides. Spanish settlements in the Southeast—notably Florida—and the Southwest frequently engaged in conflict with native groups and with European rivals, the latter attempting to make inroads where Spain had established permanent colonies or fledgling settlements. On the seas, too, Spain came under fire, as French corsairs and English "sea dogs" plundered Spanish ships carrying bullion from the Americas.

New Spain: Territory and Missions

The Catholic Church, through its priests and monks, was the prime force in developing New Spain, especially in the area north of the Rio Grande. Besides bringing Christianity to native Americans, these missionaries introduced European culture and agricultural techniques. In the face of imposed religious beliefs and forced labor by the Spanish, some native groups rebelled. The Spanish generally overcame these uprisings, but in time they allowed the natives to practice traditional religions and they excused them from forced labor.

1. The first permanent European settlement in what is now the United States was established by Spain in Florida at a fort called _____ . (p. 38)

2. When Spanish *adelantados* moved into new territories they often established their presence in military garrisons known as _____ . (p. 38)

3. In New Spain most of the Spanish missionaries were Catholic priests (friars) from the _____ religious order. (p. 40)

New France: Furs and Souls

As with England, France was slow to establish permanent colonies in the New World. In the early 1600s, beginning with the settlement at Quebec, French explorers and priests laid the foundation for New France, whose economic strength came from fur trading. French policies at home and poor weather in New France discouraged migration and kept the population of the colony small. Although French missionaries converted few Indians to Christianity, they established good relations with the natives.

New Netherland: Commerce

Dutch expansion into the Americas was based primarily on commerce, with minimal interest in promoting religion or founding an empire. Dutch traders established outposts along the middle Atlantic coast, but their colonies attracted only small numbers of permanent settlers. Dutch traders concentrated their attention on territories outside the North American mainland, leaving Dutch holdings easy prey for the English, who took control of the colonies in 1664.

Social Conflict in the Chesapeake pp. 43–52

The English Invasion

Colonization of the Chesapeake region marked the successful entrance of English migrants into the New World. After dismal failures in the late 1500s, England in the early 1600s established permanent colonies at Jamestown (Virginia) and St. Mary's City (Maryland). The cultivation of tobacco provided an agricultural base for the Chesapeake colonies and promised economic success. However, tobacco demanded both land and labor. The former meant conflict with native groups who held the land; the latter meant the importation of Africans. The consequence was economic vitality at a high social and moral cost.

Tobacco and Disease

Tobacco became the economic mainstay of the Chesapeake colonies soon after its introduction. This "vile Weed" enriched Virginia and Maryland and filled the royal treasury in England. The mild climate also facilitated the spread of diseases that shortened the life span of Chesapeake settlers and disrupted traditional patterns for families and communities.

Indentured Servitude

During the seventeenth century, thousands of English men and women escaped poverty and persecution in their home country by migrating to America as indentured servants. They received passage from Europe in return for four or five years of service. For those who held the contracts, indentured servitude provided cheap labor with virtually no restrictions under law. For the servants, life was hard: About half died before they

4. After exploring the Mississippi River and claiming the region for France, in 1681 La Salle named the area _____ in honor of the king of France. (p. 41)

5. Wealthy Dutch traders who were granted large estates along the Hudson River became landed proprietors known as _____ . (p. 43)

6. The early years of settlement in Jamestown, marked by malnutrition and disease that threatened the survival of the colony, are known as the "_____ ." (p. 44)

7. Maryland was established as a proprietary colony in 1634 under the leadership of the _____ family. (p. 45)

8. Of the various diseases that affected communities in the Chesapeake, the worst was _____ , which was spread by the bite of mosquitoes. (p. 48)

had fulfilled their contract obligations, and most who survived remained poor even as free people.

The Seeds of Revolt

After boom times for tobacco in the early 1600s, by mid-century tobacco prices had plummeted on the world market. Overproduction, restrictive trade laws, and high duties on tobacco coming into England drastically reduced the market price for the Chesapeake region's staple crop. Problems with land and labor caused tensions between planters on one side and yeomen and tenant farmers on the other, a forewarning of the social and political unrest that was about to explode.

Bacon's Rebellion

Class tensions came to the front in Virginia in the 1670s, pitting wealthy landowners and merchants along the coast against farmers along the frontier. The issue involved the seizure of Indian lands to be used by the growing white population in inland frontier regions. Under the leadership of Nathaniel Bacon, the western settlers waged war against Indian groups and then against the royal government. The rebellion persuaded planters and merchants to distribute political power more equitably and contributed to the emergence of slavery as a new labor system in the Chesapeake region.

Puritan New England   pp. 52–63

The Puritan Migration

Religious persecution and economic turmoil in England in the early seventeenth century pushed many men and women out of their home country. Beginning in 1620, thousands of Pilgrims and Puritans joined the exodus from England to America, hoping to settle in a place where they could purify the Church of England and find opportunities for economic advancement. Puritan leaders sought to create a religious commonwealth that blended representative government with a state-supported religion.

The Puritans and the Pequots

Just as settlers in Virginia opened the frontier at the expense of native groups, in New England settlers stripped land away from the Indians, whom they regarded as inferior and degenerate. In the most famous confrontation, Puritan militiamen killed some five hundred Pequot villagers, virtually committing genocide on that Indian nation. A few of the native Americans who survived European diseases and colonial arms eventually came to live peacefully under Puritan supervision.

Religion and Society, 1630–1670

The Puritans contended that the Church of England could be purified from within, in part by breaking free of Catholic influences. Drawing

9. During William Berkeley's governorship in Virginia, a corrupt political oligarchy, the _____ faction, doled out favors to themselves and to friends to the detriment of yeomen and landless freeholders. (p. 51)

10. The political elite in Virginia, whose policies of exploitation of western farmers prompted Bacon's rebellion, were known as the _____ . (p. 51)

11. The first "constitution" adopted in North America, providing a frame of government for settlers in the Plymouth colony, was known as the _____ . (p. 53)

heavily on the teachings of John Calvin, the Puritans created rigid standards for membership in their churches. They believed that their members were special in the eyes of God, who had infused them with grace, and that God would continue to bless them individually and collectively as long as they followed his laws.

For this reason, Puritan magistrates shut off all criticism, especially on matters of doctrine. Dissenters suffered banishment from the Bay colony. Forced to relocate out of Massachusetts, some of these critics established new colonies with more liberal policies than Puritan leaders would have ever sanctioned. By the mid-1600s religious and political troubles in England climaxed with the overthrow of the monarchy, which also undercut Puritan power. After the restoration of the Crown in 1660, fearing that their great experiment might collapse, Puritan authorities loosened their restrictions on church membership, making salvation easier to obtain.

The Puritan Imagination and Witchcraft

For all their devotion to religion, many Puritans were intrigued by supernatural forces, trying to read divine messages into any strange occurrence. Ironically, this attitude led some devout Puritans into pagan practices, such as using astrology to determine the right time for planting crops or making significant decisions. Fearing challenges to their authority, Puritan leaders condemned people who were different, to the point of alleging witchcraft and wizardry. Hysteria swept through several towns in the 1690s, leading to the execution of some suspected witches.

A Freeholding Society

For the Puritans, their "just society" required that settlers have the opportunity to acquire their own land, free of restraints or encumbrances. Reflecting their religious views that congregations should make decisions for themselves, in the political arena Puritans wanted freeholders to control their own towns and villages. This push for democratic rule allowed towns to develop their own identities and gave New England a rich diversity.

The Indians' New World   pp. 63–65

Metacom's War

Increasing pressure from white settlers, combined with European diseases, took a heavy toll on native populations in New England. As the colonists pushed deeper into the interior, conflict with Indian nations was inevitable. Racial hatred on both sides led to bloody confrontations. In two centuries the native population in New England was cut by 90 percent. Along the Atlantic Coast, too, conflict between white settlers and native people virtually destroyed the traditional Indian way of life.

12. The first major challenge to Puritan solidarity came from _____, a minister in Salem who urged his congregation to break completely from the Church of England rather than attempt reform from within. (p. 54)

13. Many Puritan colonists expected that the settlement of New England would mark the onset of the _____, Christ's thousand-year reign on earth as forecast in the book of Revelation. (p. 55)

14. The most famous episode of witch hunting in Massachusetts occurred in the town of _____ in 1692. (p. 60)

15. Throughout Puritan New England the main instrument for local government was the _____, through which the male heads of households ran the community. (p. 61)

16. Among the Puritans, Chief Metacom of the Wampanoag tribe was better known as _____ . (p. 64)

The Fur Trade and the Inland People

In the interior, Indians managed a little better for a time, but eventually these people also fell victim to white expansion. The fur trade that brought them European goods through barter caused them to neglect their traditional crafts. These contacts also compromised their traditional religious and cultural beliefs and altered the character of their society.

EXPANDED TIMELINE

1560s   **English and French attack Spanish treasure ships**
Through the sixteenth century, Spain commanded the mainland of the Americas as wells as islands on the periphery. But the English and French found ways to profit from Spain's territorial control and economic good fortune. English "sea dogs" and French corsairs—in a word, pirates—often attacked Spanish ships crossing from America to Europe. This set the stage for conflict over territories in the Americas in the1600s.

1565   **Spain establishes St. Augustine, Florida**
Spain followed its initial rush into the New World by establishing towns and outposts in Mexico and the Caribbean islands, but not until 1565 did Spain found a permanent colony in what is now the United States. St. Augustine in Florida provided a foothold that Spain used to control the Florida peninsula for the next two centuries and, with Indian allies, put pressure on British settlers along the Atlantic coast.

1573   **Spanish Comprehensive Orders for New Discoveries**
After encountering problems with native groups in Florida and the Southwest, the Spanish adopted a more peaceful approach toward natives. The Comprehensive Orders for New Discoveries of 1573 gave Catholic missionaries primary responsibility for "pacification" of new lands. The resulting calm was shortlived. By the end of the century, tensions again marked Spanish relations with native populations.

1580s   **Failure of Roanoke and other English colonies**
In the late 1500s, English efforts to establish colonies in the Americas were dismal failures. Queen Elizabeth I preferred to let loose her "sea dogs" to gain New World revenue by stealing from Spanish ships rather than to underwrite voyages of discovery and settlement. The most famous early English venture, Sir Walter Raleigh's colony at Roanoke (along the Outer Banks of North Carolina), literally became "lost" in the 1580s, souring English expansionists on New World settlements.

1598   **Acoma War in New Mexico**
Despite Spanish promises of peaceful dealings with native peoples under Comprehensive Orders for New Discoveries, Spanish leaders could not always control their *adelantados* in the field. Spanish attacks on Pueblo peoples led to retaliation by the Acoma, at great cost to both sides. The Acoma lost some 800 people in the fighting, and the Spanish for a time withdrew from the Southwest to the safety of their protected settlements in New Spain.

1603– 1625   **King James I of England**
Ascending to the throne in 1603, James I put aside England's long feud with Spain in order to promote England as a colonial as well as a commercial and political power. The establishment of permanent colonies increased James's power and reputation as king of an imperial state. Other benefits accrued to James and those who followed him as king: The English treasury was enriched, and by encouraging persecuted peoples (for example, the Pilgrims who established Plymouth) to migrate to America and settle the new colonies, he rid England of troublemakers and threats to the Crown.

1607   **English adventurers settle Jamestown, Virginia**
Under a charter from James I, the Virginia Company of London established the first permanent English colony at Jamestown in the spring of 1607. Seeking a quick path to fame and fortune—expecting to find large stores of gold—the colony almost died a swift death during the "starving time," when disease and hunger claimed more than half of the settlers. The introduction of tobacco provided an economic base and saved the colony from failure.

1608   **Samuel de Champlain founds Quebec**
The first permanent French colony in the Americas was established at Quebec. From this position, French explorers moved into the heart of the continent, led by fur traders and Jesuit missionaries. But New France never attracted enough settlers to give France a large number of permanent settlements and a guaranteed hold on the region.

1613   **Dutch set up fur-trading post on Manhattan Island**
Dutch enterprises on the American mainland centered on Manhattan Island, where organizers established New Amsterdam as the capital of the colony. From this base, the Dutch began fur trading along the length of the Hudson River. However, their emphasis on commerce rather than permanent settlement deprived the colony of a strong foundation.

1619   **First Africans arrive in Chesapeake**
        Virginia House of Burgesses convened
        As the first permanent English colony in the
        Americas, Virginia could be counted on to establish
        a number of "firsts." In 1619, two important firsts
        occurred. The cultivation of tobacco required great
        time and care. Virginia settlers did not want to work
        that hard at farming, and the native Americans did
        not adapt well to forced labor. Africans, first as
        indentured servants and later as slaves, provided the
        labor supply that the South needed. In the same
        year, Virginia became the first English colony to
        elect its own representative assembly, the House of
        Burgesses, to make laws and levy taxes. Thus,
        bondage and democracy came to America in the
        same year.

1620   **Pilgrims found Plymouth colony**
        The "separatist" Puritans, known as Pilgrims, fled
        England for America in hope of spreading the
        gospel and purifying their church. Against all odds
        their faith and endurance stood the test, and they
        survived to establish the first permanent English
        colony in New England. Their commitment set an
        example for other settlers to follow.

1620–
1660   **Tobacco boom in Chesapeake colonies**
        Growing demand in England for American tobacco
        sent market prices into an upward spiral. The boom
        caused planters to increase their investments in land
        and labor while the market stayed strong. However,
        the boom turned into a bust in the 1660s, when
        overproduction and restrictive economic policies
        imposed by England lessened demand and cut prices
        disastrously.

1621   **Dutch West India Company chartered**
        During the seventeenth century, the Dutch became
        major players in the competition among European
        nations to control commerce and colonies. They
        worked chiefly though two trading groups, the
        Dutch East India Company and the Dutch West
        India Company. The latter was given priority for
        establishing Dutch holdings in the Americas. The
        main achievement of the early 1600s was gaining
        control of lands that would become New
        Netherland, opening up a commercial enterprise on
        the mainland of North America.

1622   **Opechancanough's uprising**
        Between 1617 and 1622 Virginia flourished as a
        settler colony, creating a rush for good land to farm.
        Colonists coveted land that Indian groups had
        cleared for their own use, making conflict between
        settlers and native Americans inevitable. One of the
        most famous conflicts occurred when an alliance of
        Indian tribes, led by Chief Opechancanough,
        attacked white settlers, setting in motion a
        continuing sequence of raids and counterattacks
        that would mark Indian-white relations throughout
        the colonial era.

1624   **Virginia becomes a royal colony**
        Economic troubles and Indian tensions in Virginia
        forced James I to dissolve the Virginia Company
        and convert Virginia to become the first royal
        colony under a governor appointed by the Crown.
        This move gave the king tighter political control
        over the colony and a greater opportunity to profit
        from the potentially bountiful tobacco trade.

1625   **Jesuits undertake missionary work in Canada**
        For the French, in the race for American colonies,
        Catholic missionaries often played the role of
        advance agents. The lead group was the Jesuit
        order—the "Black Robes" to native peoples—who
        wanted to bring their Catholic faith into the
        wilderness of New France (Canada) at the same
        time that they opened the way for permanent
        French settlers to follow.

1625–
1649   **King Charles I**
        The death of James I in 1625 brought his son to the
        throne as Charles I. The new king's commitment to
        maintain strong royal support for the Church of
        England—a by-product of which was persecution of
        religious dissenters—and his arbitrary rule caused
        hardships for many English people. First Puritans
        and then Catholics—both outsider groups in
        Anglican-dominated England—sought a haven in
        the American colonies, improving the chances of
        success for English attempts at permanent
        settlement.

1627   **Company of New France urges migration to Quebec**
        In the first two decades after the founding of a
        permanent French settlement at Quebec, French
        numbers grew slowly because of French policies at
        home and poor soil and harsh weather conditions in
        New France. Hoping to entice more settlers into the
        colony, the French Crown chartered the Company
        of New France to encourage migration. But even
        this was not enough to overcome people's hesitation
        to move to America. And, in fact, most of the early
        French migrants to the American colonies eventually
        returned home to France.

1630   **Puritans found Massachusetts Bay colony**
        Unhappy with life in England and concerned about
        their economic and religious future in the home
        country, thousands of Puritans migrated to Massa-
        chusetts after 1629 as part of the Great Migration
        of Pilgrims to the New World. Their goal was to
        establish a "City upon a Hill" as an example for all
        to follow. They expected to find good land and
        opportunity for themselves and their children. Good
        land was limited, but they made their way and
        prospered as a colony and as a people.

1634   **Maryland settled**
        Maryland differed in some important ways from its
        Chesapeake neighbor, Virginia. Where Virginia was
        a royal colony with an established Anglican Church,
        Maryland was a proprietary colony founded to

provide refuge for Catholics. This contrast showed that the British Crown was willing to try a variety of models for colonization until one or another of the approaches proved most successful.

1635–
1637 Pequot War
Throughout the colonial era, white settlements usually expanded from the coast into the frontier, at a great cost to native populations. No Indian tribe paid a higher price than the Pequots of the Connecticut River Valley. Holding fertile territory that the Puritans wanted cost the Pequots their land and their lives. In one of the most brutal episodes of Indian-white conflict, some five hundred Pequots were massacred and the survivors sold into slavery, resulting in virtual annihilation of the tribe.

Roger Williams banished, settles Rhode Island
Anne Hutchinson expelled from Massachusetts Bay
After fleeing persecution in England, the Puritans became persecutors themselves once they settled in Massachusetts, demanding strict compliance with their theology. Banishment was the fate for dissenters such as Roger Williams and Anne Hutchinson, both of whom were charged with heresy. Williams, who left the Bay colony to found Rhode Island, reversed the emphasis on conformity demanded by Puritan magistrates, insisting on political and religious freedom. Rhode Island prospered as a democratic-minded enterprise.

1640s Five Iroquois Nations go to war over fur trade
Using the strength of their confederation, known as the Five Nations, the Iroquois of New York attempted to gain command of the fur trade in the regions between the Atlantic coast and the Great Lakes. In the early stages, they were successful, routing several native tribes in battle and forcing some to relocate to new areas. By the 1670s a counter-alliance that tied itself to the French had weakened the Iroquois, who were forced to give up plans to monopolize the fur trade.

1649–
1660 Puritan Commonwealth in England
Charges of arbitrary rule against Charles I and of religious pressure against William Laud, the archbishop of Canterbury, prompted political and religious revolution in England. Out of these civil troubles emerged a Puritan-controlled common-wealth. The change of government reflected dissension that had been building among the people, but the new system enjoyed only a short life. What had the early look of a democracy turned to dictatorship, and by 1660 the monarchy had been restored.

1651 First Navigation Act passed
The Act of Trade and Navigation marked the first attempt by Parliament to regulate the economic life of the American colonies. By setting restrictions on trade—shutting European rivals out of American ports and prohibiting Americans from trading directly with non-English merchants—Parliament initiated a system that hurt the colonies economically and eventually inspired political revolt.

1660 William Berkeley Governor of Virginia until 1678
William Berkeley's second term as royal governor of Virginia coincided with a dramatic downturn in the world tobacco market. Already suffering from a collapse in the market for tobacco, Virginians now had to endure corruption, patronage, and cronyism on the part of Berkeley and his "Green Spring" faction. Berkeley's policies exacerbated class tensions between rich and poor in Virginia and invited social and political unrest.

1660–
1720 Poor tobacco market
After four decades of boom times, the tobacco market declined dramatically in the 1660s. Overproduction of the "vile Weed" and increasing taxes on imports into England combined to cut market price and demand. The consequences for the Chesapeake colonies were profound: a weakened economy, social and class conflict (e.g., Bacon's rebellion), and a loss of reputation as a colonial leader. The revival of the tobacco market eventually solved some of these problems, but it also ensured that slave labor would remain an integral part of American life.

1662 Connecticut receives royal charter
After a short time in America, some Puritans began to question the strict standards demanded by authorities in Massachusetts. Critics left the Bay Colony to settle in Rhode Island and Connecticut where self-government was guaranteed by a charter from the Crown. These colonies offered an alternative to the harsh demands in Massachusetts and led some Bay Puritans to fear that their mission in America might fail.

Halfway Covenant revises Puritan theology
To counter a decline in church membership and energize their congregations, Puritan leaders devised the Halfway Covenant. This compromise in traditional standards allowed baptism for the children of baptized Puritans. Parents no longer had to be "saved" to merit baptism for their offspring. The Halfway Covenant meant that Puritan churches would stay strong in numbers, but it also required Puritans to rethink their sacred mission in America.

1664 English conquer New Netherland
Even after forty years of Dutch control, New Netherland lacked political and economic vitality. During this period of Dutch control, English settle-ments along the Atlantic coast were beginning to prosper. By 1664 the Dutch could not resist or halt the movement of English forces into New Nether-land; rather than risk bloodshed and certain military defeat, the Dutch ceded their colony to the English.

1670s   **Indentured servitude declines**

For poor Europeans who dreamed of a better life in America, indentured servitude seemed a blessing. Many were quick to trade four or five years of service for passage to the colonies. But as servants their lives were hard and tightly regulated. Most servants died before the end of their indenture (contract), and few of the survivors realized a better life. These problems and the rise in population—through birth and migration—meaning less of a need for indentured servants, caused a decline in this system by the 1670s.

1673   **Marquette and Joliet travel down Mississippi**

French colonial ventures in North America revolved primarily around the work of missionaries and fur traders. The pairing of Jacques Marquette, a Jesuit priest, and Louis Joliet, a trader, is reflective of this French approach. Traveling together from Quebec in 1673, Marquette and Joliet reached the Mississippi River and floated hundreds of miles south on the great waterway. This venture marked the first step in France claiming the Mississippi River Valley that would run through a territory that the French would call Louisiana.

1675–
1676   **Bacon's rebellion**

By the late seventeenth century class warfare threatened to split Virginia apart. Wealthy planters and merchants found themselves and their power under fire from western settlers. Following the lead of Nathaniel Bacon, farmers along the frontier challenged the colonial authorities, setting in motion a sequence of events that would bring increased power to the lower classes and provide a model for the American break from England a century later.

Metacom's uprising

In Virginia, Nathaniel Bacon and his followers seized native lands in bloody confrontations. In New England, the story was repeated when Puritan settlers faced a challenge from an alliance of Indian groups led by Metacom of the Wampanoag tribe. The Indian uprising was crushed in all-out warfare. Racial conflict thus reared its ugly head from New England to the South.

Expansion of African slavery in the Chesapeake

In 1619, slavery—at first disguised as servitude—came to the Chesapeake when "a Dutch man of war . . . sold [Virginians] twenty Negars." Over the next half century indentured servitude for Africans evolved into permanent slavery in the Chesapeake colonies of Virginia and Maryland where slave codes were adopted in law. Slavery was deemed economically necessary to assure that tobacco crops would prosper; socially and politically slavery proved valuable too, as a way of limiting the number of white indentured servants and thus forestalling unrest by freed white servants.

1680   **Popé's Rebellion in New Mexico**

For the first century and a half of Spanish control in the Americas, native groups suffered greatly under Spanish policies. Even the *encomendia* that was designed to uplift the Indians was abused by some *encomenderos*. For some Pueblo people the pressure of forced labor, inclement weather, and raids by hostile neighbors threatened their existence. In 1680, under a shaman called Popé, a sizable number of Southwest Indians rose up against Spanish rule. The uprising eventually was broken, but the natives gained the right to follow their own religions and to avoid forced labor under Spanish *encomenderos*.

1681   **La Salle claims Louisiana for France**

In 1673 Marquette and Joliet opened up the Mississippi River valley for France. Less than a decade later René Robert Cavelier, Sieur de La Salle, extended those efforts as he attempted to identify the best areas along the river to take fur-bearing animals. Along the way La Salle claimed the whole of the Mississippi basin for France from the northern stretches near the Great Lakes to the mouth of the river where France later would establish a great city called New Orleans.

1692   **Salem witchcraft trials**

In response to some Puritans' attraction to the supernatural, Puritan ministers struck out at anyone who claimed to possess special powers as a healer or prophet. They hunted for witches and wizards in their midst, trying many for witchcraft and executing some. The most famous episodes of witch hunting occurred in Salem, pitting poor farmers against wealthy church members. Class conflict was a fact of life in the Bay Colony, just as it was in the South.

GLOSSARY

pueblos   In the American Southwest, Pueblo Indian groups became a dominant cultural force that proved difficult for Spain to control. They lived in impressive multistory structures called pueblos—after the people themselves—that were constructed of brick or adobe and built into cliffs, often near rivers or other water sources. From these elevated positions, the Pueblos could see into the distance to provide early warning of outsiders approaching. (p. 38)

presidios   As the Spanish moved into California and the American Southwest, they established their presence in military garrisons (or forts) from which Spanish authorities and troops could command the surrounding area. Along the California coast, these *presidios* stretched from San Francisco south to San Diego. (p. 38)

encomenderos The Spanish transported many of their social and cultural institutions from Europe to the Americas when they began to establish colonies. One of these was the *encomienda*, literally "the entrustment." At one time used to control the Moors in Spain—before the *reconquista*—the *encomienda* became one means for the *adelantados* to exploit natives under the guise of uplifting them from their "savage" state. In return for teaching Indians about Christianity and the basics of European civilization, the *encomenderos* (those who received an *encomienda*) could exact tribute and forced labor from the natives. (p. 40)

repartimiento In Spanish American colonies, *repartimiento* developed as a labor institution to replace the *encomienda*. *Repartimiento* involved the temporary allotment of Indian workers for a specific task. A colonist who needed laborers for a short time applied to royal officials for a specific number of Indian workers for a set amount of time. In theory, officials of the Crown were required to see that fair payment was made, but, in fact, the *repartimiento* became another way to exploit the native populations. (p. 40)

coureurs de bois Fur trading provided the economic foundation for New France in the seventeenth and eighteenth centuries. The *coureurs de bois* (runners of the woods) charted the French advance into the heart of the North American continent. They opened up the western stretches of the St. Lawrence River and the Great Lakes in their search for fur-bearing animals. Their role was similar to that of the mountain men who initiated American movement into the Rockies in the nineteenth century, opening the way for others. (p. 41)

manitou The belief in manitou—strong spirits or supernatural forces—manifests itself in many native religions, especially among the Algonquin. Manitou were generally viewed as representatives of nature, often as animals, although they could take human form. Among native Americans, representatives of the Church, including missionaries, sometimes were thought to be incarnations of manitou. (p. 42)

patroon Hoping to guarantee some permanency to settlements in New Netherland, the Dutch authorities invited migrants into the Hudson River Valley with the lure of huge landed estates. The proprietors (patroons) of these estates (patroonships) were promised full and clear title if they brought fifty tenants onto an estate within four years. The program failed—only one patroon fulfilled the requirements—leaving the Dutch with few permanent settlers in the important region north of New Amsterdam. (p. 43)

corporate colony Exploration and settlement were expensive undertakings that required a wealthy royal patron or creative financing. In the early 1600s, English bankers and merchants introduced the concept of joint-stock companies, which shared the risk and profit of establishing colonies and led to the founding of corporate colonies. This device was used extensively by England; for example, Virginia was a corporate colony under title of the Virginia Company of London. (p. 43)

headright To attract settlers to Virginia and enhance the colony's chances for success, the Virginia Company introduced the headright system. This program granted the head of a household 50 acres of land for himself and 50 additional acres for every adult family member or servant brought into the colony. Land-hungry English peasants jumped at this opportunity and helped boost the population of Virginia to levels that made success inevitable along the Chesapeake. (p. 44)

royal colony and proprietary colony Royal colonies were established under the direction of the Crown, with three institutions always present. Beginning with Virginia, every royal colony had a royal governor, an elected assembly, and Anglicanism as the religion. This pattern was duplicated from New England (Massachusetts and New Hampshire) to the South (Virginia, the Carolinas, and Georgia). Proprietary colonies were founded on different political and religious bases. A proprietary colony was owned by a proprietor, usually a wealthy individual or family granted land by the Crown. The proprietor, whose rights were hereditary, controlled the land and the politics of the colony. Some proprietary colonies were established to provide a haven for persecuted religious groups, such as Catholics in Maryland and Quakers in Pennsylvania. (p. 47)

indentures The lure of life in America, with the promise of good land and economic opportunity, drew thousands of English migrants across the Atlantic. People who could not pay for their passage frequently bartered four or five years of service for the price of a ticket by signing labor contracts called indentures and binding themselves to a planter. The system was especially popular in the Chesapeake region, where laborers were required in large numbers to work the tobacco fields. Indentured servants figured that a few years of labor was a small price to pay for the chance to acquire land in America. In fact, most of them died before the end of their indenture, and only a few who completed their contract ever escaped poverty. (p. 49)

Act of Trade and Navigation Under a mercantilist system, colonies exist for the benefit of the home country. The Act of Trade and Navigation passed by Parliament in 1651 was meant to give England an economic advantage over its European rivals, especially the Netherlands. This act, and later revised versions of it, prohibited Americans from trading with non-English merchants in certain "enumerated" categories of goods and banned non-English ships from American ports. In time, colonists viewed this act and other laws that limited their economic freedom as unjust. (p. 50)

patent   Among its other meanings, a patent is an instrument by which a government can convey legal title to public lands in fee simple. In the colonial era, the authorities frequently distributed land as grants or patents, for example, under the headright system in Virginia, as a way to increase population and settlement. (p. 50)

Congregationalists   Puritans proposed to cleanse and simplify the Church of England by removing all vestiges of Catholicism. Among many concerns, they opposed the hierarchical structure of the Catholic Church. Rather than depend on authority figures such as bishops for guidance, the Puritans preferred a church structure directed by the laity, the ordinary members of each individual church or congregation. As Congregationalists, they set their own rules rather than relying on outsiders for direction. (p. 56)

covenant   According to Puritan theology, Puritans were special people in the eyes of God, who had sent them on a mission into the wilderness of America to spread his word and set an example for others to follow (the "City upon a Hill" concept). They believed they had a covenant, or contract, with God and would be blessed with his grace—and be "saved" from damnation—as long as they followed his laws. If they broke this covenant, they risked damnation as individuals and collapse as a community. (p. 57)

antinomian   The most serious religious crisis in Puritan Massachusetts was the antinomian controversy that centered on Anne Hutchinson. During Bible study meetings in her home, Hutchinson criticized ministers who, she claimed, preached a false message that could lead people to believe that good deeds and outwardly holy lives were signs of salvation. She countered that salvation could come only through a "covenant of grace" between God and believer. As an antinomian—one who claimed that grace freed her from the bonds of church rules—Hutchinson was charged with heresy and banished from Massachusetts. (p. 58)

millennium   In the Bible, the book of Revelation predicts that Christ will reign over the earth for a thousand years before the end of the world. This prediction of the millennium—with no specific time set for Christ's return—filled Puritan believers with hope and anxiety. Many believed that the Puritan Revolution heralded the onset of the millennium. However, their hopes were dashed by the restoration of the monarchy in 1660, and some feared that their church would decline unless it was revitalized. The Halfway Covenant and a new design for their mission into

the wilderness grew out of the Puritans' fear for their church's future. (p. 58)

proprietors   Puritan leaders planned a society based on freeholding to prevent a few wealthy individuals from dominating property in the New England colonies. Thus, they rejected the headright system that allowed planters to accumulate large areas of land. Instead, they granted land titles to groups of township settlers, known as proprietors, who in turn determined how the land would be apportioned. The large tracts of land often went to men of high status, although the Puritan leaders had hoped that this system would inspire greater equality among landholders. (p. 61)

town meeting and selectmen   The concept of town meetings as a means of decision making in communities grew out of the Puritan plan for land to be apportioned among township settlers. Just as they shared the land, the settlers shared political power in town meetings in which everyone in the community had a voice. Voting rights were restricted to adult male householders. Each year the town meeting would choose selectmen to oversee community affairs; typically these were men of wealth and property. Although this was not a fully democratic system—women had a voice but no vote, and selectmen were usually gentlemen of means—it gave settlers in New England a greater say in organizing their affairs than their counterparts in the South had. (p. 61)

fee simple and quitrent   Under feudal customs in Europe, landholders were required to pay an annual fee, known as a quitrent, to the government or an aristocrat. In many of the American colonies (across New England and in Pennsylvania) the quitrent system was replaced by fee simple, which meant that landholders owned their property outright, without encumbrance or obligation. This system allowed American colonists to break European patterns that vested large amounts of property in the hands of a few wealthy individuals. Instead, Americans moved toward the establishment of a freeholding society that allowed most male adults to acquire and hold their own land. (p. 61)

totem   By definition, a totem is an object in nature, usually an animal, that stands as the symbol of a clan, tribe, or nation and often represents its founding ancestors. The prevalence of clan totems among native Americans is related to the Indian belief that everything in nature has a soul or spirit that merits respect—a belief that helps to maintain a balance in the environment. The totem chosen by a clan or tribe—such as the fox, deer, bear, or eagle—carries special meaning for that group. It plays a leading role in original tales and oral histories; it can be displayed as a means of identification; and it holds a place of honor in ceremonies. (p. 65)

IDENTIFICATION

Identify by filling in the blanks.

1. French claims to territory in North America were established in the 1530s, when _____ sailed into the Gulf of St. Lawrence to find a northwest passage. (p. 38)

2. Spanish voyages of discovery along the Atlantic coast included expeditions into a waterway the Spanish called Bahia de Santa Maria. To the English this came to be known as _____ . (p. 38)

3. When Jesuit missionaries first arrived in New France, the Indians welcomed them as _____ , powerful spiritual beings with magical powers. (p. 42)

4. The capital of New Netherland was _____ , which is present-day New York City. (p. 43)

5. John Rolfe introduced _____ into Virginia when he imported seeds from the West Indies and began to cultivate the crop. (p. 44)

6. Cecilius Calvert's plans for Maryland included having the colony become a refuge for followers of the _____ Church. (p. 45)

7. In 1649 the Maryland assembly passed legislation known as the _____ , which granted religious freedom to all Christians. (p. 45)

8. In the mid-seventeenth century, in an attempt to prevent the Dutch from cutting into English trade and interfering with English colonies, Parliament passed a series of laws known as the _____ . (p. 50)

9. Puritan "Separatists," better known as _____ , founded the first permanent English community in New England in 1620 at Plymouth. (p. 53)

10. The highly regarded country gentleman who led the Puritan exodus from England to Massachusetts Bay in 1630 was _____ . (p. 53)

11. In Puritan Massachusetts, church members, who were known as _____ , set rigorous standards for membership, making it difficult for most people to affiliate fully with a church. (p. 56)

12. Among the more prominent dissenters in Massachusetts, a Puritan wife, mother, and midwife, _____ , was accused of heresy and banished from the Bay colony. (p. 58)

13. Freeholders who held title to their land outright, free from feudal obligations or feudal dues, were said to hold their land in _____ . (p. 59)

14. To keep their churches strong and their authority intact, Puritan ministers designed the _____ , under which the children of baptized Puritans could be presented for baptism even if their parents could not prove that they had won salvation. (pp. 59–60)

15. Many native Americans worshipped an animal such as the fox or beaver as their _____ , or symbol, even seeing themselves as descendants of that animal. (p. 65)

SKILL-BUILDING EXERCISE

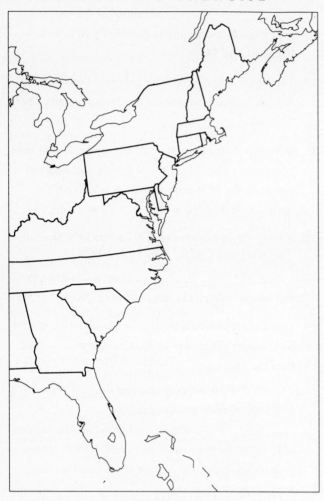

1. On the map, locate and identify the English colonies founded in the early seventeenth century:
    (a) Virginia,
    (b) Plymouth,
    (c) Massachusetts,
    (d) Connecticut,
    (e) Maryland, and
    (f) Rhode Island.
    Also locate and identify other European settlements:
    (g) New France, and
    (h) New Netherland.

2. Map 2.3 (see text p. 48) shows that Virginia planters often settled along the James River. In fact, in most colonies early settlements were found along waterways. Using the maps in this chapter and drawing on your reading, explain why colonists tended to settle along waterways. What were the advantages? What were the particular advantages in Virginia? What were the drawbacks?

3. Figure 2.1 (see text p. 49) gives a comparison of life expectancy in Virginia and New England. The accom-

panying text tells why life span was short in Virginia. Drawing on your reading, why might New Englanders have enjoyed a longer life span than their contemporaries in the South?

4. Using Table 2.1 on "European Colonies in North America before 1660" (see text p. 59) and drawing on your reading, explain why the English colonies were more likely to succeed and even to prosper than the colonies of New France, New Netherland, and New Sweden.

DOCUMENT EXERCISES

American Voices

A Franciscan Reflects on Spain's Policies in New Mexico

Jut as the French in Canada used Jesuit missionaries and fur traders as twin forces for expansion, so, too, did the Spanish in the American Southwest rely on Franciscans and *adelantados* to extend the boundaries of their empire. Despite some occasional differences of opinion and action, the missionaries and advance agents usually worked together well. In the situation described in this selection from "American Voices" that was not the case. One of Spain's *adelantados* in the Southwest, Juan de Oñate, who also was an *encomendero*, had violated his entrustment from the Crown, with doleful consequences for both the natives and the Spanish.

As you read "A Franciscan Reflects on Spain's Policies in New Mexico," ask yourself the following questions:

1. According to this Franciscan friar, how did Juan de Oñate violate the provisions of the *encomienda* that he had received? What was he entitled to receive from the Indians? What did he demand of them?

2. How else might Spain have taken control of the region with more positive results than the uprisings and wars that resulted from Oñate's actions?

3. According to this friar's lament, why was Spain having such a difficult time with the natives? Why did he deem it important to stay the course in the Southwest and not abandon the region?

The Life Story of a Puritan Tailor— John Dane

For most Puritans, both in England and in the American colonies, life was a constant battle between good and evil to control one's mind and life. Temptation was everywhere, and even if a Puritan avoided "folly" or some other sin in action, some believed that the very thought of wrongdoing was equivalent to sin. Although Puritan doctrine included a strong belief in predestination—meaning that good actions would not help win salvation, a devout Puritan did not want to tempt fate and live a profligate life.

As you read "The Life Story of a Puritan Tailor," ask yourself the following questions:

1. What sort of temptation does John Dane describe in the opening passage? How did he avoid falling into "folly" in this situation?

2. Although Dane had avoided "folly," he still believed that he had committed a sin and that he was suffering punishment. How was it that he could equate the insect sting with punishment from God?

3. Why did Dane migrate to the American colonies? What did he expect to find? Was life any different for him in America than it had been in England?

4. Dane came close to suicide, but he resisted at the last minute. Why did he change his mind? Did that decision to live rather than to die have an effect on him and the way he would live in the future?

Captivity Narrative—Mary Rowlandson

A frequent theme of American western movies is the story of young white boys and girls, occasionally adult women as well, falling captive to Indians during raids on settlements (for example, John Ford's classic *The Searchers* or the Kevin Costner film *Dances with Wolves*). In time, these white captives usually fit in with the native people and adopted their ways. In this account by a white woman taken captive in 1675, we find an outcome similar to that of many Hollywood films. Tensions between white settlers and native Americans ran high in the 1600s with a great cost on both sides. That fact makes Mary Rowlandson's story—and her eventual release—an important piece of history.

As you read "Captivity Narrative," ask yourself the following questions:

1. How did Mary Rowlandson react when she was first taken captive by the Indians? How did she change after the first couple of weeks?

2. What was her attitude toward Indian food? Toward tobacco? Do these attitudes surprise you? Why or why not?

3. How was Mary able to fit in so quickly with her captors? Did their attitudes toward her change?

4. According to this narrative, what was native life like for the Indian men? For the Indian women? Did any of this surprise Mary?

5. In your opinion, why did the Indians release Mary from captivity? Would they have been better off keeping her or even killing her?

American Lives

Margaret Brent: A Woman of Property

Henry VIII's break from the Catholic Church in Rome in the 1530s brought the Protestant Reformation from the European mainland to England. In the decades to follow, Catholics came under a cloud of scrutiny and suspicion and fell victim to religious persecution. In the early 1600s their situation worsened as Puritans joined the Anglican majority to condemn Catholics and their faith. In the 1630s, the Calvert family tried to remedy the situation by establishing Maryland as a haven for Catholics in the Americas.

Maryland prospered under the Calverts' proprietorship, with Catholic settlers migrating in large numbers to the Chesapeake region. But by 1647 Protestants outnumbered Catholics in Maryland, and the newcomers began to pressure the Calverts for changes in the colony. This "American Lives" episode describes the events that followed, including the efforts of Margaret Brent, a single Catholic woman of some standing in Maryland, to support the Calvert family in their attempts to hold the colony together and to protect Catholic settlers from renewed persecution.

As you read "Margaret Brent: A Woman of Property," ask yourself the following questions:

1. Why did Leonard Calvert entrust his personal holdings to Margaret Brent rather than to someone else, perhaps the new governor or his brother?

2. Why was Margaret Brent so intent on settling Maryland's problems? What sort of personal skills did she bring to these efforts?

3. Why did Lord Baltimore propose the Toleration Act? Who had the most to gain from this legislation? Why?

4. How did Lord Baltimore react to Margaret Brent's plans to pay the mercenaries? Why?

5. Why might you describe Margaret Brent more as a "soldier of fortune" than as an early representative of women's rights in the colonies?

SELF-TEST

Multiple Choice

1. Among the English "sea dogs" (that is, pirates) who attacked Spanish ships to steal gold bullions being shipped from the Americas to Spain was:
   a. Walter Raleigh.   c. Juan de Oñate.
   b. Francis Drake.   d. William Kieft.

2. In New Spain, the Spanish Crown often allowed privileged settlers to collect tribute from the natives through a system of forced labor called:
   a. *adelantado.*   c. *repartimiento.*
   b. *presidio.*   d. *encomendero.*

3. Most French missionaries in North America came from the religious order known as:
   a. Franciscans.   c. *Coureurs de Bois.*
   b. Jesuits.   d. Huguenots.

4. In 1609, Henry Hudson found and named the Hudson River while exploring the Atlantic coast under the flag of:
   a. England.   c. the Netherlands.
   b. France.   d. Spain.

5. After founding New Netherland, the Dutch West India Company established trading posts in *all* of the following places *except*:
   a. Connecticut.   c. Pennsylvania.
   b. New Jersey.   d. Virginia.

6. In "Kieft's War" of the 1640s, the Dutch authorities tried to rid New Netherland of potential enemies by sending armed bands against:
   a. the Algonquian tribes.
   b. the Iroquois nations.
   c. patroons in the Hudson River Valley.
   d. English settlers in Massachusetts.

7. After some tensions between Virginia settlers and his native people, in 1609 Powhatan accepted the presence of the English by giving his daughter Pocahontas in marriage to:
   a. Henry Hudson.   c. John Rolfe.
   b. John Smith.   d. Walter Raleigh.

8. The colonial land system that provided 50 acres of land to the head of a household for every family member or servant brought to America was known as:
   a. freehold.   c. fee simple.
   b. headright.   d. quitrent.

9. The Act of Trade and Navigation (1651) was intended to cut colonial trade with non-English states, with the primary impact to be felt by the:
   a. Spanish.   c. French.
   b. Portuguese.   d. Dutch.

10. The "Manifesto and Declaration of the People" (1676) that advocated the death or eviction of all native Americans from Virginia and proposed an end to rule by the wealthy elite was written by:
    a. William Berkeley.
    b. Nathaniel Bacon.
    c. the Green Spring faction.
    d. John Winthrop.

11. When Puritans declared that they wanted to "be as a City upon a Hill," their intention was to:
    a. build their first church on the highest point in the Massachusetts Bay colony.
    b. found their community on a hill to provide better defense against hostile native Americans.
    c. give American settlers an understanding of their special destiny as a people and a nation.
    d. be able to look down with scorn on other religious groups that settled in New England.

12. In the 1630s, the Puritans of Massachusetts waged "war" and virtually eliminated the native people known as:
    a. Iroquois.   c. Pequot.
    b. Huron.   d. Anasazi.

13. Puritan theology in England and America drew mainly on the teachings of:
    a. John Calvin.   c. Martin Luther.
    b. John Winthrop.   d. Jacob Arminius.

14. In 1635 Massachusetts Bay Puritans expanded the scope of education in the colonies when they founded:
    a. Salem College.   c. Covenant College.
    b. Mather Seminary.   d. Harvard College.

15. Under feudal landholding traditions, individuals had to pay the government or an aristocrat a token sum of money to hold the land. This annual payment was known as:
    a. fee simple.   c. headright.
    b. quitrent.   d. land grant.

16. The fur trade between whites and Indians along the frontier region of the Atlantic colonies involved *all* of the following animals *except*:
    a. buffalo.   c. fox.
    b. beaver.   d. deer.

Short Essays

Answer the following in a brief paragraph.

1. How did the Spanish and French differ in their efforts at colonization in North America? (pp. 38–42)

2. What three institutions distinguished a royal colony from other types of English colonies in America? (p. 45)

3. Why was indentured servitude such a profitable system of labor for planters in the Chesapeake colonies? (pp. 49–50)

4. Why were four decades of boom times for Chesapeake tobacco growers followed by a bust in the mid-1600s? (p. 50)

5. Why did the Puritans flee England for America in the early 1600s? (pp. 52–54)

6. Compare Bacon's rebellion in Virginia and the Salem witch trials in Massachusetts for evidence of growing class conflict in the American colonies. (pp. 51–52, 60–61)

7. In what ways did white Europeans cause social upheaval and compromise the traditional way of life among native groups during the colonial era? (pp. 38–42, 45, 51–52, 54–55, 63–65)

ANSWERS

Chapter Précis

1. St. Augustine
2. presidios
3. Franciscan
4. Louisiana
5. patroons
6. starving time
7. Calvert
8. malaria
9. Green Spring
10. grandees
11. Mayflower Compact
12. Roger Williams
13. millennium
14. Salem
15. town meeting
16. King Philip

Identification

1. Jacques Cartier
2. Chesapeake Bay
3. manitou
4. New Amsterdam
5. tobacco
6. Catholic
7. Toleration Act
8. Navigation Acts
9. Pilgrims
10. John Winthrop
11. Elect or Saints
12. Anne Hutchinson
13. fee simple
14. Halfway Covenant
15. totem

Skill-Building Exercises

1. Locate on map 2.2, text p. 42, and map 2.4, text p. 55, and map 2.5, text p. 62.

2. In most of the English colonies, settlements were located on or near waterways (the Atlantic coast, bays, or rivers) for practical reasons, such as ease of trade and transportation, quick escape from hostile natives, and, in the case of rivers, a source for drinking water. In Virginia the tobacco economy demanded easy access to water to allow quick shipment of tobacco after picking and curing. In Virginia the main drawback to settling along waterways was problems with diseases carried by insects that inhabited wet lands.

3. Many European settlers in America fell victim to disease or lost their lives in conflicts with native groups. In New England, where cold weather meant less likelihood of epidemic diseases spreading, fewer colonists died from illnesses than in the Chesapeake, where a milder climate prevailed. Despite some famous wars in New England between whites and native Americans, such as the Pequot War and Metacom's War, in general there were fewer instances of Indian-white conflict in the North than in the South where the search for farmland was constant, leading to regular hostile contact with native Americans.

3. The first several columns on this chart give little information to indicate reasons for the success or failure of colonies. The last column, "Chief Export or Economic Activity," gives good clues. The French, Dutch, and Swedish colonies were based on the fur trade. The methods of trapping used during the colonial era—trapping out an area and then moving on—meant that there would be little economic stability or continuity of population in colonies that depended on the fur trade. In contrast, agriculture—farming and raising livestock—provided a renewable and ongoing source of income and a greater likelihood of success. In addition, farm families were more stable as settlers than were fur traders, who needed to be on the move in their search for fur-bearing animals.

Self-Test

Multiple Choice

1. b	5. d	9. d	13. a
2. c	6. a	10. b	14. d
3. b	7. c	11. c	15. b
4. c	8. b	12. c	16. a

Short Essays

1. Time and geography provide the first points of difference. The Spanish entered the New World in earnest in the early 1500s with settlements in the American Southeast and Southwest as well as in Mexico and the Caribbean. The French established their first permanent colony in 1608 in present-day Canada and then moved southward into the Mississippi Valley. Both Spain and France sought wealth: The Spanish hoped for quick riches by finding gold; the French emphasized fur trading. Spanish policies toward native groups were coercive, including efforts to use Indians as forced labor. The French, in contrast, lived among the Indians in a more cooperative fashion.

2. Following the example of Virginia, which became the first royal colony in the 1620s, royal colonies were

distinguished by three institutions. A royal governor, appointed by the Crown, directed the political fortunes of the colony with the advice of a small advisory council. Royal colonies were allowed to choose members for an elected assembly—in Virginia, this was the House of Burgesses. Finally, royal colonies had an established Anglican church, meaning that tax revenue was used to pay the clergy in the Church of England.

3. Indentured servitude provided tobacco planters in Virginia and Maryland with a cheap and stable supply of labor in the seventeenth century. In return for paying a servant's cost of passage from England to America and providing him or her with food, clothing, and shelter for the period of indenture, the planter received four to five years of labor. With tobacco commanding a good price on the world market, a planter could make up his costs in a few months and then have several more years of "free" labor. Colonial law also favored the planters, who had full control over the conduct of their servants. This ensured the planters a stable labor supply in their tobacco fields.

4. In the 1620s, tobacco commanded two shillings a pound on the world market; by the 1660s the price had fallen by more than 90 percent. The main problem was overproduction, spurred by the good market and increasing numbers of planters. Political decisions also contributed to the decline. The Act of Trade and Navigation (1651) prohibited Chesapeake planters from selling tobacco to Dutch traders, who traditionally paid the highest prices for tobacco. At about the same time, England raised import duties on tobacco entering the home country, and this reduced demand and profits.

5. The Puritan migration from England to America was the outgrowth of religious turmoil, political strife, and economic pressures. King Charles I reaffirmed state support for the Church of England, placing Puritans outside the mainstream and subjecting them to persecution. Puritans also resented the king's arbitrary rule, which included higher taxes and the dissolution of Parliament, denying the English citizenry a voice in their government. Finally, Puritans fled England in search of good land and economic opportunities for themselves and their children, which they expected to find in America.

6. After decades of hardship and suffering, with the colonies struggling to survive, by the late 1600s life was better from New England to the South. In the Chesapeake colonies, especially in Virginia, settlers began moving into the interior. Their quest for good land set them at odds with native groups and, in time, with colonial leaders. Bacon's rebellion in the 1670s pitted western farmers against wealthy merchants and royal representatives along the coast and showed growing discontent among the common people toward the upper classes. Similarly, the witch trials in Salem pitted poor Puritan farmers against wealthy church members and their families and threatened to tear apart Salem and the surrounding communities. Class warfare became a fact of everyday life in many of the colonies as the lower classes tried to seize a share of political and economic power from the elite.

7. For native groups who had lived free and prospered for centuries, the arrival of white Europeans signaled the beginning of the end of their traditional way of life. As settlers moved from the Atlantic coast into the interior, they seized Indian lands by guile and force. Armed conflict took a heavy toll on Indian lives. Other natives died from European diseases. Missionaries and ministers introduced European religions and compromised native beliefs. Rum brought drunkenness and sapped the vitality of tribal life. Through the fur trade, natives acquired a variety of European goods, including ironware and hoes, and lost their talent for working with clay and flint. They became dependent on Europeans for basic necessities.

CHAPTER 3

The British Empire in America 1660–1750

★ ★ ★

The Politics of Empire, 1660–1713   pp. 69–76

The Restoration Colonies

The Restoration of the Stuart monarchy in 1660 led to the founding of additional English colonies along the Atlantic seaboard. Charles II gave generous land grants to friends and supporters to establish the Carolinas, New York, and New Jersey as proprietorships. Pennsylvania became the most prosperous of these new colonies because of its liberal religious and political policies.

1. The scheme of government for the Carolinas, outlined in the Fundamental Constitutions of Carolina (1669), was written by English political theorist _____ . (p. 70)

The New Mercantilism

To increase the value of the empire and raise revenues for the Crown, Charles II placed strict controls on colonial trade. A series of Navigation Acts regulated trade involving the colonies, the home country, and other European states that posed an economic threat to England. As a consequence of this new mercantilism, England broke Dutch supremacy in world trade.

2. The exporting of _____ , a deep violet-blue dye extracted from a subtropical plant, was regulated by the Navigation Act of 1660. (p. 72)

The Dominion of New England

England profited immensely from the new mercantilism but faced widespread unrest among colonists who resented unprecedented intervention in their internal affairs. To increase royal authority, James II and the Lords of Trade revoked colonial charters and merged several colonies into one huge colony known as the Dominion of New England, stretching from New York and New Jersey to Maine.

3. Before he ascended to the English throne in 1685, James II had been known by the title _____ . (p. 73)

The Glorious Revolution of 1688

Because of his arbitrary rule and Catholic sympathies, James II was driven into exile in 1688 in a bloodless coup known as the Glorious Revolution. Protestant parliamentary leaders replaced James with his daughter Mary and her Dutch husband, William of Orange. The Glorious Revolution sparked popular uprisings in the American colonies from New England southward into Maryland. One of the consequences of this unrest was the breakup of the Dominion of New England. Beyond these troubles, following the Glorious Revolution, ethnic strife, class tensions, and political instability rocked New York for several years. The political and economic strength of Dutch artisans in New York City was destroyed by a bloc of wealthy English merchants who did not want too much power left in the hands of the common people.

The Empire in 1713

After a long series of wars in Europe and North America with European rivals, England dominated the American landscape by 1713. The British reigned supreme in both commercial enterprises and colonial holdings. But the Crown could not establish a single set of rules to govern all the colonies because of opposition from colonists and Parliament. Despite British successes, both France and Spain maintained a presence in North America and remained threats to British control of the continent.

The Imperial Slave Economy, 1660–1750

pp. 78–94

The African Background

In the centuries before contact with white Europeans, the tribes of West Africa developed thriving economies and cultures and organized themselves into complex states. In some ways their cultures resembled those of Europe (e.g., stratified social structures directed by princes), and in other ways they resembled those of the Americas (e.g., some states organized themselves by family and lineage, and some worshipped a large number of gods). By the sixteenth century, European traders had made their way into West Africa, at first through contacts that were mutually beneficial. These relationships changed dramatically once Europeans began trading people, a practice that already was thriving among West Africans themselves but that took on a decidedly different and more sinister look when Europeans started transporting slaves across the Atlantic.

The South Atlantic System

During the 1600s Europeans revolutionized both agriculture and commerce by establishing links between the continent and the Western Hemisphere. Using slave labor, they grew crops such as sugar and tobacco on huge plantations. The resulting oceanic trade between the Americas and Europe was known as the South Atlantic system, which

4. The unrest that followed the Glorious Revolution resulted in the elimination of the Catholic Church as a prominent political force in the colony of _____ . (p. 75)

5. In the Treaty of Ryswick, at the end of King William's War, France won assurances that it would control that part of Santo Domingo now known as _____ , and thus have access to rich sugar-growing areas on the island. (p. 76)

6. The first European contacts with West African states were made by European traders out of _____ . (p. 79)

7. Beginning about 1650 English merchants developed the island of _____ as England's first sugar colony in the Caribbean. (p. 81)

England dominated. This economic system, combined with the mercantilist policies of the Navigation Acts, made England a wealthy nation. But the South Atlantic system had tragic consequences for the countries and people of Africa. A growing demand for cheap labor to work on the sugar plantations in the Caribbean created a market for slave labor that involved some 15 million Africans between 1550 and 1870. European merchants and American planters reaped huge profits at great economic and human cost to Africans.

Slavery and Society in the Chesapeake

Africans first appeared in Virginia in 1619, but slavery as a legal institution was slower to arrive. For about fifty years blacks could avoid enslavement by converting to Christianity. But by the 1660s conditions changed as Virginia adopted a series of laws that bound black laborers in permanent and hereditary bondage, thus creating a society based on slave labor. In this new Chesapeake society a number of changes appeared in relations between men and women and between the gentry and the poor. The landed elite, who often tried to model themselves after the English aristocracy, used their economic and political power to take control of the Chesapeake region, even at the expense of the king's representatives.

The Expansion of Slavery

The demands of growing labor-intensive crops and the desire to reap huge profits with the cheapest possible labor inspired the buying and trading of slaves throughout the Caribbean and the American southern colonies. The arduous passage across the Atlantic, intense labor under subtropical sun, and the epidemic spread of disease, especially in the sugar islands, claimed many African lives. Slavery supported the power of wealthy planters and merchants, and prompted whites to develop an exploitative, slave-based society.

The Creation of an African-American Community

In the early years of slavery in the American colonies, Africans tried to maintain their identity as members of specific tribes and language groups. In time, they changed their views and developed an African-American culture that blended their traditional African heritage with the realities of their American lives. This distinctive culture was based on common language, family bonds, community patterns, and religious practices.

Oppression and Resistance

In the West Indies and throughout the southern colonies slaves were kept under control by various methods ranging from whipping to branding to castration. Slaves resisted in different ways, by working slowly, stealing, or escaping—usually without success—but seldom resorted to outright rebellion. On those few occasions when slaves rose up against their masters, they suffered severe punishment, and slave owners reacted by tightening their grip on the slaves.

8. In law, the ownership of one human being by another, in the fashion of slavery in the American South, is known as _____ slavery. (p. 82)

9. In the early 1700s, many Virginia gentry sent their sons to England to be educated as gentlemen at the training ground for English lawyers known as _____ . (p. 84)

10. The perilous voyage of Africans to the New World on overcrowded, disease-ridden ships was known as the "_____ ." (p. 84)

11. In the lowlands of South Carolina, slaves created the _____ dialect, a common language that incorporated English and African words. (p. 89)

12. The first major slave revolt in American history took place in the late 1730s when South Carolina blacks fled to Florida in the _____ Rebellion. (p. 91)

The Northern Economy

The South Atlantic system had broad impact across the American colonies, providing opportunities for economic growth among the wealthy, notably for a growing merchant class, and giving access to a wide variety of goods for all of the colonists. Both the mainland colonies and the sugar islands gained in a developing economic exchange. The sugar islands needed northern foodstuffs and lumber; West Indian trade stimulated shipbuilding in the North. Mercantile activities, fishing, and lumbering meant further diversity within the economy. The South Atlantic system provided markets for farmers and economic opportunities for merchants, artisans, and workers in rural areas and seaport cities.

Seaport Society

Social patterns in seaport cities of the North mirrored southern society. Merchants (rather than the landed elite) stood at the top of the economic scale in cities such as Boston, New York, and Philadelphia. Artisans and their families formed a large middle sector; they were butchers, bakers, masons, and carpenters, among other specialists. Day laborers, white indentured servants, and black slaves formed the lower ranks of the social order. But, regardless of social or economic standing, everyone in the American colonies felt the impact of the South Atlantic system.

The New Politics of Empire, 1713–1750

pp. 94–101

The Rise of the Assembly

Politics in the American colonies went through upheaval after the Glorious Revolution. Power shifted from Puritan magistrates, merchants, and landed gentry to the colonial assemblies. Still, the system was hardly democratic because prominent families continued to pass wealth and political influence to succeeding generations. But these family dynasties usually were responsive to the will of the people, who increasingly opposed imperial governors and bureaucrats.

Salutary Neglect

In the mid-1700s royal bureaucrats relaxed their control of internal affairs in the colonies, preferring to emphasize military defense and expansion of trade. During this period of "salutary neglect," the colonies began to enjoy greater freedom from British control. The appointment of mediocre officials to colonial posts and their inability to counter increasing unrest widened the gap between colonies and home country.

Consolidating the Mercantile System

The founding of Georgia marked the last English colonial expansion along the Atlantic Coast. The colony's founders intended to experiment with new ideas, for example, outlawing slavery, but Britain viewed Geor-

13. By 1776 the largest colonial city was _____ , with a population estimated at 30,000. (p. 92)

14. Following the Glorious Revolution in England, the fight for a constitutionally limited monarchy rather than an absolute one was led by the political group known as the _____ . (p. 95)

15. The system of "salutary neglect" that allowed the colonies to prosper with lessened interference from the British was facilitated by the political system under Prime Minister _____ . (p. 96)

gia primarily as a buffer colony to protect the Carolinas from Spanish and Indian threats out of Florida. By the mid-eighteenth century Britain had reaffirmed its military and commercial power, allowing British mercantilists to strengthen their policy by prohibiting the colonies from manufacturing or trading goods available from the home country. But American shippers still prospered from intercolonial and transatlantic commerce. Eventually British and American enterprises came into conflict. The British then became determined to replace "salutary neglect" with a stricter system to control the colonies.

16. During the War of the Austrian Succession, British forces captured the powerful French naval fortress of Louisbourg on Cape Breton Island, which commanded the entrance to the

_____ River and access

to New France. (p. 98)

EXPANDED TIMELINE

1651   **First Navigation Act**
The Navigation Acts provided underpinnings for the English mercantilist system. The first trade act, passed in 1651, was intended to cut into Dutch trade in the Americas that had provided competition for British traders. Over the next century many other Navigation Acts followed, all intended to enrich British shippers and merchants. When they were enforced, the system worked. But they raised the ire of colonists who resented too much control by the home country.

Barbados becomes sugar island
When the English finally established a successful colony in the Americas, they quickly sought ways to make their enterprises pay. The Atlantic coastal colonies emphasized tobacco and other agricultural goods as well as commerce. In the West Indies, where tropical sun and rich soils created a number of options, the English concentrated on sugar, with Barbados the most prized sugar-rich island. Sugar would be one of the most enriching commodities that Great Britain would produce in the Americas. Sugar also helped to inspire a slave-based labor system that had profound impact on the Americas and on Africa.

1660   **Restoration of Charles II**
After a decade of bloody civil war in England, the restoration of the monarchy promised a return to order. While the restoration inspired the establishment of several new colonies, it also meant that England generally had less interest in the American colonies while it paid greater attention to problems and policies at home.

1660s   **Virginia moves toward slave system**
The first Africans arrived in the Chesapeake colonies in 1619 as indentured servants whose labor was needed in the expanding tobacco economy. Slowly, but steadily, indentured servitude for Africans evolved into a heinous system of slavery. By the 1660s slave codes were in place in Virginia, with other colonies to follow. The slave codes

authorized under law the permanent and hereditary bondage of African people in America.

New Navigation Acts
After the first Navigation Act of 1651 helped Great Britain successfully combat European economic rivals, the British Parliament enacted several other trade laws that benefited British shippers and merchants to the detriment of American colonists. Some of the Navigation Acts, such as the Woolens and Hat Acts, prohibited Americans from producing goods that might compete with British manufacturers. Others placed restraints on American shippers. The result was ill feelings between the American colonists and their home country.

1663   **Carolina proprietorship granted**
Following the Restoration of the Crown, Charles II rewarded his supporters with sizable grants of land in America. Beginning with Carolina, named in honor of the king, these new colonies allowed for expansion of English settlements along the Atlantic coast.

1664   **New Netherland captured; becomes New York**
When the Dutch West India Company established the colony of New Netherland, the plan of investors was to get rich quickly from the fur trade rather than to develop a settled colony. New Netherland grew and prospered as a trading center, attracting people from many countries. But the colony never displayed the vigor and vitality needed for permanence. By the mid-1600s, British settlements had begun to surround New Netherland, to a point that the British regarded the Dutch as trespassers. In 1664, the Duke of York (later to become James II) took control of the colony in the name of the Crown and turned New Netherland in to the British colony of New York.

1669   **Fundamental Constitution of Carolina**
The Carolinas were established in 1663 as the first of the Restoration colonies, with control in the hands of wealthy proprietors. They wanted their new colony to follow traditional English models in which power and ranks were determined by the amount of land a person owned. To implement this

model, they asked John Locke to design the colony's scheme of government, later known as the Fundamental Constitution of Carolina. The plan backfired because most Carolina settlers tended to come from lower economic levels. These farmers—hardly a landed elite—eventually came into control of the colony, forcing the original proprietors to abandon their claims and their dream of an aristocratic colony.

1681   William Penn founds Pennsylvania
From the outset, Pennsylvania—"Penn's Woodland"—was a prosperous colony that attracted a mixed racial, ethnic, and religious population. William Penn's first intention was to use Pennsylvania as a haven for Quakers who frequently suffered persecution in England. But Penn's liberal social and economic policies ensured Pennsylvania's success and a prominent place for it in colonial America.

1685   James II becomes king of England
The Duke of York, who seized New York from the Dutch in 1664, ascended the throne as king intending to strengthen his hand at home and in the colonies. His enemies, faced with loss of their power and prestige, plotted his overthrow before he could implement his plans.

1685–
1689   Dominion of New England
James II and his supporters, who wanted to enforce royal authority in the colonies, revoked charters in Connecticut, Rhode Island, New York, and New Jersey and established one large colony known as the Dominion of New England. Colonists protested vigorously and soon joined with James's enemies in England to support his overthrow and exile.

1688   Glorious Revolution
Threatened by James II's grasping for power and fearful that he would restore Catholicism as the state religion, Protestant leaders in Parliament schemed to drive him from the throne. A bloodless coup brought James's daughter, Mary, and her husband, William of Orange, to the throne and guaranteed a Protestant monarchy.

1689   Rebellions in Massachusetts, Maryland, and New York
The Glorious Revolution and the fall of James II from the throne prompted widespread upheaval in the American colonies. In Massachusetts colonists advocated the break-up of the Dominion of New England; in Maryland there was bitter religious feuding between Catholics and Protestants. In New York, the Glorious Revolution inspired ethnic strife between Dutch and English colonists. Jacob Leisler rode the crest of Dutch rebellion against English authority until a new governor with wealthy merchant friends forced Leisler from power. The Leisler rebellion showed that ethnic groups resented

too much English control over their positions in colonial society.

1689–
1702   Mary II and William III
Brought to the throne by the Glorious Revolution, William and Mary agreed to abandon the traditional concept of divine right and rule as constitutional monarchs, with greater power in parliamentary hands. This lessening of royal political power also loosened the Crown's hold on commerce and overseas enterprises, increasing the power of merchants and bankers.

1689–
1713   Intermittent war in Europe and America
In the aftermath of the Glorious Revolution, peace between England and France gave way to a series of "world wars" that involved fighting in both Europe and North America. The causes were complex, owing to political and religious differences as well as economic and imperial rivalry. These wars continued for about 75 years, finally closing with the Great War for Empire that ended in 1763 (see Chapter 4).

1696   Board of Trade created

English leaders tried to strengthen their control over colonial economies through the Board of Trade, made up of officials familiar with colonial affairs. This marked another in a line of Navigation Acts intended to keep the colonies under close supervision.

1699   Woolens Act
The mercantilist economic system required that colonies serve the needs of the home country and not challenge English manufacturers or merchants. The Woolens Act filled a gap in the system, prohibiting intercolonial sale of American-made textiles. This prohibition raised one more point of protest among Americans who resented increasing interference in their economic lives.

1705   Virginia statute defines slavery
Beginning in 1619, slavery evolved slowly in the Chesapeake colonies. A series of slave codes passed in the last four decades of the seventeenth century gradually consigned Africans into bondage, with a capstone law in 1705 that formally defined slavery by using religion rather than race as the prime determinant of slavery. If an individual came into the American colonies without Christian beliefs, he or she "shall be accounted and be slaves." Slavery, by the early eighteenth century, was entrenched in the South as a key part of social and economic life.

1713   Treaty of Utrecht
At the end of Queen Anne's War (also called the War of the Spanish Succession), Great Britain exacted territorial concessions from France and Spain. In the Americas, Great Britain gained control

of much of northern and eastern Canada and in Europe control of Gibraltar, a point that commanded entrance into the Mediterranean. In the Treaty of Utrecht, Great Britain consolidated its position as the controlling force in both American and European politics.

**1714–
1750**
British policy of "salutary neglect"
Rise of American assemblies
British "reexport" trade in sugar and tobacco
During the reigns of George I and George II, British authorities relaxed their supervision of internal colonial affairs. This "neglect" allowed colonists an opportunity to act more freely than ever before and gave them a taste of independence. They exercised this right principally in the political realm. Colonial assemblies grew stronger under "salutary neglect," gaining some power that previously had been in the hands of royal governors or proprietors. At the same time, however, Great Britain continued to wield command of economic matters through Navigation Acts. As an example, British law required the "reexport" of valuable colonial commodities such as sugar and tobacco. All American goods were required under law to be sent to England before they could be distributed to world markets, greatly magnifying the profits for English merchants without similar gain for American producers.

Dahomey becomes "slaving" state
Even before the arrival of European slavers in Africa, a number of West African states engaged in the slave trade, selling and trading their own people and others who were captured out of neighbor states. In some countries—with Dahomey the best example—the royal families profited immensely from the slave trade. This financial gain, in turn, could be used to purchase guns that could be used to take more slaves, creating a vicious cycle of exploitation that brought ruinous conditions to many African cultures.

1718
Spanish missions and garrison in Texas
By the early 1700s, the Spanish began to feel threatened by the presence of the French to their north and east in Louisiana. To solidify their hold on the northern stretches of New Spain, the Spanish established permanent settlements—with Franciscan missions and military garrisons—in Texas, the first at San Antonio in 1718.

**1720–
1742**
Sir Robert Walpole chief minister
British policies during the Walpole tenure led to milder colonial programs and the emergence of "salutary neglect" toward the colonies. Imperial rule was weakened as a result of Walpole's reliance on patronage, which brought mediocre people into office and undermined British authority in America.

This allowed the colonies to move closer to genuine independence.

**1720–
1750**
Black natural increase
African-American society created
By the early eighteenth century, American slaves tried to establish their own culture, blending old (African) with new (American) traditions to help them face the rigors of bondage. In South Carolina, slaves created a new language known as Gullah, when used both English and African words. In the Chesapeake region cultural development included promoting kin relationships as living conditions improved and slaves were able to establish families. For slave owners this meant a supply of young people born and reared as slaves, which was preferable to continued dependence on the importation of slaves.

Rice exports from Carolina soar
Planter aristocracy in Southern colonies
In South Carolina the presence of large numbers of Africans from rice-growing cultures meant the addition of a new and enriching commodity for the colony's economy. As more rice was grown for export, South Carolina investors saw their investments soar. This was the same phenomenon that had visited the Chesapeake region where tobacco had been the principal crop. The planter aristocrats who used slave labor to work their lands, whether it be in rice or tobacco, rose to economic and political power and became the dominant force in the South.

Expansion of seaport cities on mainland
The growth of colonial economies added greatly to the physical expansion of the colonies and the development of cities as trade centers. In all parts of colonial America, from New England, where factories and farms shared attention, to the South, where tobacco and rice dominated, seaport cities blossomed in size and numbers. Boston, Newport, New York City, Philadelphia, and Charleston all thrived on trade, and they became centers for cultural and social expansion as well as economic and political power.

**1732–
1733**
Georgia colony chartered; Spain protests
The last of the original thirteen colonies to be founded by England along the Atlantic coast, Georgia provided a natural buffer to protect the Chesapeake colonies and the Carolinas from attacks by the Spanish or their Indian allies out of Florida. The Spanish resented what they regarded as British intrusion into their sphere of influence, creating the possibility of war between Great Britain and Spain.

Hat Act and Molasses Act
For a full century (1651–1751) the British tried to

tighten their economic hold on the colonies by a series of restrictive acts of trade. By prohibiting the intercolonial trade of hats and by putting a high duty on non-British molasses, royal bureaucrats tried to restrict the colonies even further.

1739   **Florida governor encourages slave desertions**
Stono Rebellion
War of Jenkins' Ear
Spanish Florida, at the doorstep of the American colonies, frequently caused problems for British authorities. In 1739, for example, the Spanish governor in Florida invited runaway slaves to move southward where they could find good land for themselves. The resulting Stono Rebellion and the War of Jenkins' Ear in that same year showed that Spain could pose a major threat to British colonial authority as long as Spain held control of Florida. These troubles with Spain continued until 1819, when the independent United States gained title to Florida in a treaty with Spain.

1740   **Veto of Massachusetts land bank**
To assure an adequate supply of money, colonies often printed paper currency on their own. After accepting this practice for some time in different colonies, in 1740 British officials refused to allow Massachusetts to issue currency. This was another sign that the British government, after years of salutary neglect, intended to crack down on the colonies and reassert control.

1740–1748   **War of the Austrian Succession**
Between 1688 and 1763 the British fought a series of wars with European rivals, with the conflicts always reaching into America. Until the last of the wars (the French and Indian War), little territory changed hands, but the British always seemed to gain some advantage in each war. The War of the Austrian Succession (also called King George's War) reinforced British military control in the southeast region of the American mainland and allowed British commerce to expand at Spain's expense.

1750   **Iron Act**
By the middle of the eighteenth century, American colonists had fallen victim to a whole series of Navigation Acts that placed limits on American production of some goods—e.g., the Hat Act and Woolens Act—and restricted American trade. The Iron Act of 1750 added to these limiting laws, prohibiting Americans from turning out finished iron products that might compete with British wares. The British justified these limitations within the mercantilist system, but American critics condemned them as unjust intrusions of their rights.

1751   **Currency Act**
The last of the acts of trade, the Currency Act marked another British effort to tighten the economic hold on the colonies. On the American side the law meant one more British mistake in dealing with the colonies and one more step toward pushing for independence.

GLOSSARY

fee simple   According to feudal tradition a landholder was required to make ongoing payments (known as quitrent) to authorities for the right to hold land. By introducing a fee simple system, which gave an individual clear title to the land without encumbrance or obligation to the government, colonial leaders such as William Penn made their colonies more attractive to settlers and more likely to prosper. The fee simple system gave individual landholders greater freedom to control their own destinies. (p. 72)

chattel slavery   By definition, a "chattel" is a possession that is movable. In colonial times this included slaves, who could be moved or sold at will by the owner or master. In time the word chattel became synonymous with slave. (p. 82)

lugars   West African groups carried to the American colonies in bondage brought with them working knowledge of the growing and harvesting of rice. They had learned these skills in the lugars, or rice fields, in their home countries. Rice became one of the most important cash crops in colonial America, especially in South Carolina, where rice grew well in marshy lowlands along the coast. (p. 88)

Guiny   Africans sold into slavery in the sugar islands of the Caribbean and in the Atlantic coastal colonies came originally from the west coast of Africa. All of the countries in this region, stretching from around Cape Mount or the Sierra Leone River to the Bight of Benin, came to be known generically as the Guinea coast, Guinea, or "Guiny." (p. 89)

Whigs   In British politics the Whigs won a reputation as supporters of liberal principle and reform. They favored "mixed government" in which common people would have some voice in shaping policies, notably the power of taxation. In Great Britain today, Whigs are known as the Liberal party. The term Whig also came to identify American colonists who supported reform, even to the point of seeking independence from Great Britain. (p. 95)

Court (or Crown) party   Within most democratic political systems elected leaders traditionally trade in favors, offering appointed positions to friends and followers (patronage) or endorsing legislation favorable to one or another group in return for support for the elected officials' own policies. The resulting "Court party" can be counted on for loyalty and votes on matters of importance. (p. 96)

Country party Robert Walpole was accused of currying favor with a select group in Parliament, thus creating a Court party, to ensure that his policies would win support and votes when needed. Across the political aisle was aligned a conservative group known as Tories, which supported the status quo. The Tory members of Parliament, who saw themselves as putting Great Britain and high principles above petty partisan politics, formed what they called a "Country party." In fact, they feared the loss of the personal and political power that had been vested in them for many generations as a landed class. (p. 96)

placemen To ensure loyalty to the government in power, British prime ministers filled administrative and parliamentary positions with friends and cronies. These placemen (literally, men with a "place" in government) helped to create a Court party that owed allegiance to the prime minister and his government rather than to the country. (p. 97)

land bank Under the mercantilist system, most of the gold and silver that American merchants received for overseas trade was sent to Great Britain as payment to British manufacturers for their goods, thus keeping the cash in British hands. American assemblies tried to create their own money supply by establishing "land banks" to assist colonists—farmers, artisans, and others—who needed money to purchase goods or to expand their holdings. Banks lent money to land or property holders in return for a mortgage on the property. Land banks gave the colonists greater control over their individual economic standing and helped break dependence on Britain. (p. 99)

IDENTIFICATION

Identify by filling in the blanks.

1. Prior to 1664, when it fell into English hands, New York had been a Dutch colony known as _____ . (p. 70)

2. Proprietors in North Carolina continued a feudal tradition that required landowners to pay an annual fee known as _____ to continue to hold a deed. (p. 72)

3. The Frame of Government guaranteed political liberty and religious freedom in the colony of _____ . (p. 72)

4. In the late 1680s James II and the Lords of Trade revoked the corporate charters of Connecticut and Rhode Island as a first step toward the creation of a new royal province called the _____ . (p. 73)

5. The political tract *Two Treatises on Government* (1690), proposing that legitimacy of government rests on the consent of the governed, was written by _____ . (p. 74)

6. The first permanent Spanish settlement in Texas was established in 1718 at _____ . (p. 76)

7. During the early colonial era, five native American tribes—the Mohawk, Oneida, Onondaga, Cayuga, and Seneca—joined in the _____ confederation, which stretched from the Hudson River to the Great Lakes. (p. 77)

8. In West African states, secret societies—the _____ for men and the _____ for women—provided a variety of social needs, including sexual education for children and enforcement of codes governing conduct and morality. (p. 79)

9. The various economic connections that developed among the four continents of Europe, Africa, North and South America in the eighteenth century came to be known as the _____ . (pp. 80-81)

10. South Carolina was first settled in the 1680s by land-hungry whites from the sugar island of _____ . (p. 85)

11. As early as 1690, an Englishman named John Steward was actively promoting production of _____ in South Carolina, both for export and for cheap food for his slaves. (p. 88)

12. During the colonial period, the only major southern seaport was_____ , South Carolina. (p. 92)

13. During the Walpole ministry, reliance on patronage brought to political office a number of mediocre appointees known as_____ , who held office but did little work. (p. 97)

14. The founder of Georgia, _____ , hoped that the new colony could become a colony of small farms where England's poor could find safe haven. (p. 97)

15. In 1739, Great Britain and Spain became involved in hostilities called _____ , fought over British rights to trade with the Spanish West Indies. (p. 98)

SKILL-BUILDING EXERCISE

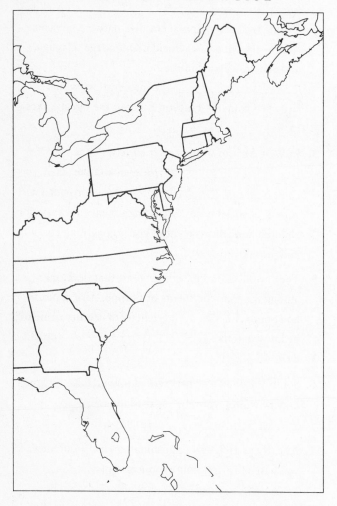

1. On this map locate and identify: (a) the British colony started by Swedish settlers; and (b) the mainland colony first settled by the Dutch West India Company.

2. Locate and identify the six Restoration colonies established after 1660.

3. Mark the location of the most important seacoast town in the southern colonies.

4. Using Map 3.2 on 77, ask yourself why there was such a wide disparity in the population figures between white and black populations in British colonies in the West Indian Islands in comparison to mainland colonies?

DOCUMENT EXERCISES

American Voices

The Brutal "Middle Passage"—Oloudah Equiano

Africans along the "Guiny" coast lived in constant fear of being sold into slavery by other Africans. Even in their worst nightmares these new slaves could not have imagined the horrors of the "middle passage" that would take them from their homeland to New World colonies. In this selection from his memoirs, Oloudah Equiano gives a vivid description of the start of his passage to America.

As you read "The Brutal 'Middle Passage,'" ask yourself the following questions:

1. As he arrived at the Guiny coast, what sorts of feelings filled Equiano?

2. What conditions on board ship did the Africans face as they crossed the Atlantic?

3. Why would Equiano refer to death as a "friend"?

4. What alternatives did the Africans envision for themselves during this "middle passage" to America?

The Waning of British Authority—Governor George Clinton

The British policy of "salutary neglect" inspired American opposition to colonial authority and made it difficult—sometimes impossible—to enforce British law in the colonies. Because of Prime Minister Walpole's use of patronage, unqualified men filled many of the leadership roles in the colonies. George Clinton, who received his appointment through family connections, was not a strong governor. He chafed at his inability to control New York.

As you read "The Waning of British Authority," ask yourself the following questions:

1. Specifically what "incroachments" did the colonial assembly make on royal authority?

2. What did Clinton believe to be the most important power of the assembly for undercutting British authority? Why?

3. What did Clinton propose as a solution to these problems?

4. Does anything in this selection suggest that Clinton is fearful of losing his appointment? Or does he appear to be higher-minded and truly concerned for British authority?

American Lives

William Byrd II (1674–1744) and the Maturation of the Virginia Gentry

When the first permanent English settlers arrived in Jamestown in 1607, they expected to get rich quickly and return to their home country amid riches and glory. Fate ordained that they would have to endure suffering in a hard land that challenged them at every turn. After a century in this new land of America, others still dreamed of discovering that same path to wealth and power that the Jamestown settlers had expected but never found. Achieving success in the American colonies was quite possible, but translating that New World good fortune into a high life in England was not so easy. As a second-generation American, William Byrd II expected that family wealth from Virginia and an English education would bring him a hearty welcome into English society as a gentleman. After years of finding success in America but frustration in England, Byrd began to understand what it meant to be a son of the colonies.

As you read "William Byrd II and the Maturation of the Virginia Gentry," answer the following questions:

1. In William Byrd's time, what were the basics of a good English education? What did Byrd hope to gain from this sort of schooling?

2. What was "the stigma of birth" that Byrd suffered? How did this hamper him in his efforts to move higher in the English social and political order?

3. William Byrd described Virginia as a "lonely . . . silent country" that often made him feel "like being buried alive." What did he mean by these disparaging remarks? How did Byrd overcome these difficulties? What sort of success did he achieve in Virginia? Explain with specific detail.

4. Despite his great successes, Byrd also encountered some notable setbacks—politically, economically, and personally. What troubles did he suffer? Were the setbacks of his own making or determined by others and by outside influences?

5. Why did Byrd finally "renounce his quest to be an English gentleman"? What kind of life did Byrd live after realizing that he would never become an English gentleman or a governor of the Crown?

6. Drawing on your reading in the text as well as this "American Lives" segment, ask yourself whether William Byrd II was unique or similar to other second-generation Americans of his social and economic level. Explain.

New Technology

Rice: Riches and Wretchedness

African people, first as indentured servants and then as slaves, had a profound and lasting impact on the economic and social life of the American colonies. Typically we read about the work of Africans in the tobacco fields through the 1700s and at a later time in the cotton fields of the South before the Civil War. Less frequent is discussion of the role of Africans in the development of rice as a staple food and cash crop in colonial America. But in the production of rice, no less than in the growing of tobacco and cotton, Africans made crucial contributions, not just with their labor but also with their knowledge of the planting, tending, and harvesting of rice.

As you read "Rice: Riches and Wretchedness," ask yourself the following questions:

1. Why were Africans successful in planting and harvesting rice in the colonies where European newcomers had failed?

2. What was the value of rice to the colonial economy, especially in South Carolina?

3. Why was African knowledge vital to the hulling of rice, that is, for the preparation of rice for use as food, just as it had been for planting and harvesting?

4. Why is the subtitle of this section—"Riches and Wretchedness"—such an appropriate description of the impact of rice on the social and economic life of the colonies?

SELF-TEST

Multiple Choice

1. In the mid-seventeenth century England's most prized overseas possessions were:
   a. the Chesapeake colonies.
   b. the New England colonies.
   c. Pennsylvania and New York.
   d. the West Indian sugar islands.

2. The Restoration colonies included *all* of the following *except*:
   a. New York.   c. Maryland.
   b. New Jersey.   d. North Carolina.

3. William Penn established the colony of Pennsylvania as a refuge for:
   a. Catholics.   c. Anglicans.
   b. Quakers.   d. Puritans.

4. Because of outspoken opposition to the new mercantilism and violations of the Navigation Acts, royal officials in the Dominion of New England aimed their harshest actions against:
   a. Connecticut.   c. Massachusetts.
   b. Rhode Island.   d. New York.

5. Jacob Leisler guided a political rebellion against English rule in New York with the support of:
   a. Dutch artisans.
   b. wealthy merchants.
   c. Puritan leaders who had relocated from Massachusetts.
   d. Irish-Catholic settlers.

6. Texas received its name from the "Kingdom of Tejas," one of the confederacies of the native American people known as:
   a. Anasazi.   c. Caddo.
   b. Pueblo.   d. Tiajuanas.

7. In the Treaty of Utrecht (1713), the British received *all* of the following French territories in North America *except*:
   a. Newfoundland.
   b. Acadia.
   c. the Hudson Bay region.
   d. Louisiana.

8. Which of the following was a corporate colony rather than a royal or proprietary colony?
   a. Rhode Island   c. Pennsylvania
   b. Massachusetts   d. Virginia

9. When Europeans opened commercial contacts with West Africa, they often fell victim to tropical diseases that included *all* of the following *except*:
   a. yellow fever.   c. malaria.
   b. polio.   d. dysentery.

10. The most important foods brought into Africa from the Americas were:
    a. millet and yams.
    b. coconuts and oranges.
    c. maize and manioc.
    d. salt and palm nuts.

11. At the height of the slave trade—between 1700 and 1810— the majority of Africans transported to the Americas were sold to:
    a. tobacco farmers in the Chesapeake region.
    b. cotton planters in the deep South.
    c. sugar planters in the West Indies.
    d. coffee growers in Brazil.

12. One West African state that steadfastly opposed the slave trade, while other neighboring states were trading and selling their own people, was:
    a. Dahomey.   c. Barsally.
    b. Benin.   d. Asante.

13. During the colonial era, rice was grown as the most important cash crop in:
    a. South Carolina.
    b. Georgia.
    c. Maryland.
    d. Rhode Island.

14. In West Africa, where many of the American slaves had learned to grow rice, the rice fields were known as:
    a. huskes.
    b. guerards.
    c. lugars.
    d. paddies.

15. Among the African peoples in America, "Gullah" was a:
    a. rice dish that was a favored food in Africa.
    b. new language that mixed English and African words.
    c. secret slave society that plotted escapes.
    d. corruption of the word "girl" that was used for house servants.

16. British leaders supported the founding of the colony of Georgia in the early 1730s because:
    a. Georgia's founders proposed to outlaw slavery.
    b. Georgia's founders wanted to provide refuge for the English poor.
    c. Georgia provided a buffer between the Carolinas and Spanish Florida.
    d. they hoped Georgia would develop into a good source of sugar products.

Short Essays

Answer the following in a brief paragraph.

1. What was the relationship between England's sugar colonies in the Caribbean and the mainland colonies in North America in the seventeenth century? (p. 69)

2. What policies and practices allowed Pennsylvania to develop into a model colony marked by peace and prosperity? (pp. 71–72)

3. In what ways did the South Atlantic system stimulate the English economy? (pp. 80–81)

4. Why was life expectancy for slaves so short in the sugar islands of the Caribbean? (p. 85)

5. How did southern slaves create a uniquely African-American culture in the American colonies? (pp. 89–91)

6. In what ways did the South Atlantic system stimulate the economy of the northern colonies? (pp. 92–93)

7. Compare economic activity in the interior towns and rural regions with the towns and cities along the Atlantic coast. (pp. 92–94)

8. How did Britain crack down on the American colonies at the end of the era of "salutary neglect"? (p. 99)

ANSWERS

Chapter Précis

1. John Locke
2. indigo
3. Duke of York
4. Maryland
5. Haiti
6. Portugal
7. Barbados
8. chattel
9. the Inns of Court
10. middle passage
11. Gullah
12. Stono
13. Philadelphia
14. Whigs
15. Sir Robert Walpole
16. St. Lawrence

Identification

1. New Netherland
2. quitrent
3. Pennsylvania
4. Dominion of New England
5. John Locke
6. San Antonio
7. Iroquois
8. Poro; Sande
9. South Atlantic system
10. Barbados
11. rice
12. Charleston or Charles Town
13. placemen
14. James Oglethorpe
15. the War of Jenkins' Ear

Skill-Building Exercise

For locations, see the endpaper map in the textbook.

1. a. Delaware; and b. New Netherland/New York
2. New York, New Jersey, North and South Carolina (Carolina as original colony), Pennsylvania, and Georgia
3. Charleston or Charles Town, South Carolina
4. The West Indian Islands are generally small in size, meaning that they cannot sustain too large a population. But because of their rich soil and the subtropical climate, these islands were perfectly suited for growing of rich crops such as sugar. The English developed these islands for their economic value—rather than as settlement colonies—and they imported large numbers of Africans to do the draining work in the sugar fields. On the mainland colonies, on the other hand, large numbers of white Europeans arrived to establish settlement colonies. Slaves were important in the South for the growing of tobacco and rice, but their numbers did not rival those of the white colonists.

Self-Test

Multiple Choice

1. d	5. a	9. b	13. a
2. c	6. c	10. c	14. c
3. b	7. d	11. c	15. b
4. c	8. a	12. b	16. c

Short Essays

1. In the seventeenth century, sugar produced with slave labor in the West Indian colonies brought wealth and power to England. The mainland colonies added revenue through export of cash crops such as rice and tobacco. They also provided the sugar colonies of the Caribbean with needed supplies, such as foodstuffs (for example, rice), that these islands could not provide for themselves.

2. From the beginning, William Penn provided liberal political and economic freedoms to settlers in Pennsylvania. The "Frame of Government" that he drew up in 1681 promised that there would be no established church or religious taxes and that male Christians of all faiths—not just Quakers—would enjoy the right to vote and hold office. In addition, to attract a wide range of settlers, Penn sold land at low prices and in fee simple.

3. The English economy was enriched in several ways by the South Atlantic system. The direct profits of sugar production returned to England, where most planters lived as absentee landowners. The requirement that all staple crops from America be exported via England (i.e., reexported) raised the quantity and value of English exports. Shipyards won orders for more ships for use in Atlantic commerce. Transatlantic commerce created jobs within England, for example, in the construction of port facilities and warehouses.

4. Sugar can be grown only in a subtropical climate. Successful growing and harvesting required long days of intensive labor that allowed slaves too little time for physical recovery. Epidemics of yellow fever, smallpox, and measles ran swiftly through the densely populated sugar islands, taking a heavy toll of those slaves who had survived the ordeal of the sugar fields.

5. Although they came from different tribes and from many regions of West Africa, slaves in the American colonies tried to transcend their tribal identities and create a common culture to help them survive the rigors of bondage. Acquisition of a common language, usually English, was a necessary first step. (In South Carolina, slaves created their own dialect called Gullah that provided a shared experience.) Improved conditions encouraged stable family relationships, with some notable success in the Chesapeake region. Religion and music also contributed to the creation of a new culture.

6. The plantations of the sugar islands depended on the New England and middle colonies for bread, meat, fish, and lumber. Trade with the Caribbean also encouraged industry; New Englanders built factories to process raw sugar into refined sugar and to turn molasses into rum. Mercantile activities and shipbuilding also enriched the northern economy.

7. In the interior regions of the colonies, emphasis was placed on producing foodstuffs and raw materials (for example, lumber) that could be sent to coastal cities for sale or trade. In small towns artisans worked their trades, and even small cities located on rivers engaged in some shipping. Seaport towns, such as Boston and Philadelphia, offered a wider range of occupations, from coastal to transatlantic commerce, from sawmills to shipyards, from fishing to manufacturing.

8. When colonial economic growth threatened Britain's financial interests, British leaders determined to enforce the various Navigation Acts more carefully. New legislation was enacted to control production of currency and to prohibit the colonies from manufacturing and selling goods available from the home country. Duties were placed on molasses imported from non-British colonies. Overall, the British renewed their efforts to keep the colonies under direct control and in line with British policies.

CHAPTER 4

Growth and Crisis in American Society 1720–1765

★   ★   ★

CHAPTER PRÉCIS

Freehold Society in New England   pp. 104–108

The Farm Families: Women's Place

In New England society men played the dominant role in politics and in domestic matters. Women were subordinate to their husbands and had few rights under law. Daughters typically had a lesser position than sons. A woman's place was in the home, serving as a dutiful daughter to her father or as a helpmate to her husband. Women were kept in check by cultural expectations, colonial laws, and religious restrictions.

Farm Property: Inheritance

For many colonists, the most important reason for migrating to America was the availability of land. In America most land was held by common people who passed the land to their children to ensure that the family's needs would be met from one generation to another. New England farmers were able to create communities composed of independent property owners.

The Crisis of Freehold Society

Dramatic increases in population and overcrowding of the land threatened freehold society in New England where good land was difficult to find. Farm communities responded to this crisis by asking the government to open new land along the frontier, planting crops with better yields, and sharing labor and goods.

1. Women who helped prepare expectant mothers for childbirth, helped with delivery, and assisted mother and child after the birth were known as
_____ . (p. 105)

2. Under the English legal device called
_____ , a father could preserve his land in the family name by willing the land to a son with specific requirement that the land stay in the family forever. (p. 107)

3. One way that Massachusetts farmers responded to economic problems was to petition their provincial government to create a _____ that could issue paper currency and make loans that might help encourage trade and stimulate the economy. (p. 108)

The Mid-Atlantic: Toward a New Society, 1720–1765   pp. 108–116

Opportunity and Equality

For the first century after their founding, the middle colonies offered fairly equal economic opportunities to settlers. By the 1760s, in Pennsylvania, New York, and New Jersey, the landed gentry and merchants had grown rich, while yeomen farmers had fallen behind economically; there were increasing numbers of tenant farmers and poor people without any property. Changes in the international market for wheat led to social as well as economic divisions in these colonies.

4. To harvest grain crops more easily, many farmers cut and arranged wheat by using long-handled scythes known as _____ . (p. 109)

5. The Dutch manors of the Hudson River Valley, created by the Dutch West India Company, were known as _____ . (p. 110)

Ethnic Diversity

From its founding, Pennsylvania attracted a mixed religious and ethnic population, with Quakers as the dominant social group. Quaker teachings were quite different from those of other Protestant denominations. For example, Quakers believed that all men and women—not just a small group of the "elect"—could be saved, emphasized religious equality for women, and advocated peaceful relations with native Americans. Liberal social and religious policies in Pennsylvania attracted thousands of Europeans who were fleeing war, religious persecution, and poverty in their homelands. The largest ethnic migrations to Pennsylvania in the 1700s involved Germans and Scots-Irish. Most immigrants from these two groups settled along the frontier, where they kept alive the social patterns and traditions they had brought from Europe.

6. The more proper name for the religious group, popularly known as Quakers, who settled Pennsylvania was the Society of _____ . (p. 111)

A Pluralistic Society

The mid-Atlantic colonies, especially Pennsylvania, were marked by religious and ethnic diversity. Religious differences actually enhanced stability because the churches enforced a strict code of behavior among their members. By the 1750s, however, ethnic differences that found Scots-Irish and Germans opposing Quaker leadership were causing tension and creating political conflict.

7. The only other religious denomination in Pennsylvania that endorsed the Quakers' belief in pacifism was the _____ . (p. 115)

The Enlightenment and the Great Awakening, 1740–1765   pp. 116–123

The Enlightenment in America

In the mid-eighteenth century, the European Enlightenment and the "new learning" it engendered swept across the American colonies, affecting politics, education, science, and many other areas of life. By challenging traditional religion-centered views and emphasizing the power of human reason to shape the world, the Enlightenment revolutionized thought and action in both Europe and America.

8. The writing of *Poor Richard's Almanac*, the founding of the American Philosophical Society, and the invention of bifocal lenses for eyeglasses were all the work of American Enlightenment thinker _____ . (p. 117)

Pietism in America

Where the Enlightenment emphasized human reason and caused some followers to abandon traditional religions, the Pietist movement of the mid-1700s stressed emotion and mystical union with God. Pietism—being devout—appealed principally to the lower social groups. Across the colonies ministers promoted Pietism through forceful, emotional sermons intended to restore a spiritual commitment among the colonists.

George Whitefield and the Great Awakening

Revivalism spread across the American colonies through the preaching of wandering evangelists. The most important of them was George Whitefield, a young English minister who traveled throughout the colonies from the South to New England. His emotional sermons helped turn local revivals into the Great Awakening.

Religious Upheaval in the North

The Great Awakening created tensions and caused divisions in many traditional colonial denominations, including Congregational churches in New England and Dutch Reformed churches in New York and New Jersey. The Awakening challenged long-held beliefs and questioned religious taxes, the idea of established (that is, tax-supported) churches, and the authority of ministers. At the same time, it injected new enthusiasm into other areas of colonial life, such as education.

Social and Religious Conflict in the South

The Great Awakening caused religious turmoil within the southern colonies, especially in heavily Anglican Virginia. New Light Presbyterians posed a challenge to the established Church of England in both the Tidewater and the backcountry, and Baptist revivalists made inroads among poor whites and black slaves, threatening the political and economic power of the landed gentry. The strong reaction of the gentry to these challenges to traditional thinking reflected the growing class antagonisms that had developed in many parts of the South.

The Mid-Century Challenge: War, Trade, and Land pp. 124–133

The French and Indian War

By the middle of the eighteenth century British colonists, principally Virginians, began looking westward toward the Ohio Valley in search of land for new settlements. The French, who were active in the region as fur traders, viewed the colonists' movements as a threat to their economic and territorial interests. By 1754, Virginians were engaged in hostilities with France that soon spread across the Atlantic into a full-scale war between Great Britain and France.

9. The Dutch minister _____ spread Pietism among German settlers in many Pennsylvania communities, delivering sermons and organizing private prayer meetings. (p. 118)

10. George Whitefield's enthusiastic preaching attracted a large following among people known as _____ who pledged to follow in his footsteps. (p. 118)

11. Under the influence of the Great Awakening, Baptists established the College of Rhode Island that today is known as _____ . (p. 122)

12. _____ were church members who controlled lay organizations that helped ministers oversee church affairs, especially finances. (p. 122)

13. As a colonel in the Virginia militia, _____ was sent into the Ohio Valley in 1754 to establish British rights in the region. (p. 124)

The Great War for Empire

Under the leadership of William Pitt, Great Britain escalated the French and Indian War into the Great War for Empire, attempting to finish France as an economic and colonial rival in America. British victories across New France and on battlefronts around the world confirmed the triumph of British arms. France was forced out of almost all of North America, leaving Great Britain to expand its territorial holdings and consolidate control of its Atlantic coast colonies.

British Economic Growth

By the mid-eighteenth century, Great Britain was experiencing the Industrial Revolution, which resulted in the production of more and better goods at lower prices. Among the prime markets for these goods were the American colonies. To pay for these manufactured wares and textiles, Americans increased their production and export of tobacco and foodstuffs and borrowed heavily from British merchants, who were generous with credit.

Land Conflicts

As the population increased in the Atlantic colonies, especially in land-poor New England, colonists looked to the West, pushing land claims to the maximum. Colonies began to squabble over boundaries and land grants along the frontier. A "feudal revival" in the proprietary colonies threatened the freehold system and the status of yeomen farmers.

Uprisings in the West

As more settlers moved from the crowded eastern seaboard into frontier regions, tension and armed conflict arose between settlers and colonial authorities. The most serious problems occurred in the backcountry of Pennsylvania, North Carolina, and South Carolina. Western settlers, especially the Scots-Irish, resented what they regarded as arbitrary government, unjust taxation, and insufficient political representation. Their concerns reflected the attitude of many Americans toward Great Britain.

14. As a sideshow to Pontiac's uprising of 1763 against the British in North America, another native American prophet, _____ of the Delaware tribe, urged native groups to reject all ties to European states and return to their traditional ways of life. (p. 127)

15. The region of rolling plains and hills inland from the Tidewater counties of Virginia is known as the _____ . (p. 129)

16. In the 1750s, farmers in Connecticut formed the _____ to assist them in opening up lands along the frontier, including western sections of Pennsylvania. (p. 130)

17. In the Pennsylvania backcountry, Scots-Irish farmers tried to push Indians off the land by forming a vigilante group known as the _____ . (p. 131)

EXPANDED TIMELINE

1700   **Freehold ideal in rural communities**
Household mode of production
One of the greatest attractions of the American colonies in the early years of settlement was the availability of good land for farming, especially in rural areas where virgin land could be acquired cheaply by colonists who dreamed of becoming yeomen freeholders. Land became less available with each passing generation, but fathers often passed at least part of their land to their children. As a way of conserving monetary resources, many families engaged in a system that allowed them to share and exchange goods and services. This so-called "household mode of production" meant that farmers, laborers, and artisans could help each other without having to pay in cash for work that was done.

Arranged marriages common
Woman's "place" as subordinate helpmate
During the colonial era, American women enjoyed few rights under law. Their traditional role—maintained, even demanded, in the colonies—was to be dutiful daughters at home and, after marriage, be subordinate "helpmeets" to their husbands. In some families, fathers or older brothers went so far as to arrange marriages for their daughters or sisters. For fathers, arranged

marriages were especially important if they had no male heir. A strong son-in-law, with good farming skills, would be welcomed as a son, and within the concept of the stem family would inherit the farm after the father's passing.

Female literacy in New England expands
In the early 1700s, women in America found that the doors to education were opening a bit. College training remained limited to young men, but grade-level schooling became available to many girls. The main roles for women continued to be those of daughter and wife, but there were indications that their standing in society would gradually improve.

1700–1714

New Hudson River manors created
Old-line Dutch families with property rights along the Hudson River opened land to new tenants in the early 1700s as a way to increase revenues without selling off their estates. Unlike areas of the middle colonies where freeholders were predominant, the Hudson River Valley of New York contained a mix of wealthy Dutch patroons and tenant farmers.

1720s

German migrants settle in middle colonies
Scots-Irish migration grows
The frontier regions of the middle colonies attracted large numbers of non-English settlers. In the early 1700s the largest of these ethnic groups were Germans and Scots-Irish, who settled mostly in the backcountry of Pennsylvania. They tried to retain their own cultures and identities as German and Scots-Irish people, countering the usual trend toward assimilation and adoption of English ways. At first they fit well into Pennsylvania society, but over time their views came into conflict with the Quaker leadership.

Enlightenment ideas spread to America
The Enlightenment, or Age of Reason, changed the way people looked at the world by challenging the status quo in science, mathematics, religion, and government. In the American colonies, the Enlightenment loosened the bonds with the home country, laying the foundation for unrest and revolution.

Frelinghuysen holds revivals
Pietism came to the colonies when Dutch minister Theodore Jacob Frelinghuysen brought revivalism to German settlers in the backcountry of Pennsylvania and New Jersey. Revivalism and the Great Awakening soon spread through the colonies and revolutionized religious life and thought.

1730s

Tennents lead Presbyterian revivals
Following the lead of Frelinghuysen, who spread Pietism among German settlers, William and Gilbert Tennent fostered revivalism among Scots-Irish congregations in Pennsylvania and New Jersey. Their work expanded the denominational scope of revivalism in America.

Jonathan Edwards preaches in New England
The Puritan preacher Jonathan Edwards delivered pietistic "hellfire and damnation" sermons in Congregational churches in the Connecticut River Valley. Edwards's work brought revivalism into the New England colonies and to English colonists much as Frelinghuysen and the Tennents had done in the middle colonies among non-English settlers.

1739

George Whitefield and the Great Awakening
Whitefield was perhaps the most important of the itinerant evangelists who carried their message out to the people directly by going on the road from Massachusetts to Georgia. He contributed to the Great Awakening by spreading revivalism into the southern colonies and transforming local revivals into a broader awakening among the people.

War of Jenkins' Ear
Spain's control of Florida, the doorstep of the American colonies, frequently caused problems for the British. The War of Jenkins' Ear showed that Florida posed a major threat to British colonial authority. These troubles continued until 1819, when the United States gained title to Florida.

1740–1760s

Population pressure in New England
Smaller family size; more premarital pregnancies
Rapidly increasing population growth in New England—partly caused by an increase in premarital pregnancies—threatened to overcrowd long-settled areas. Colonial leaders tried to relieve the population pressure by opening new land grants along the frontier, expanding colonies toward the West, and creating new communities.

Women active in religion and market activities
Beginning in the 1740s, a number of social and economic changes affected Great Britain's mainland colonies. One of the most critical changes—certainly for its long-term consequences—was an expanded role for women in American society. Following the lead of religious groups such as Quakers and Baptists, which preached equality of men and women, other denominations slowly began to allow women a more active role in religious life. At the same time, women also became more active players in the American economy, frequently producing goods at home, such as yarn, cloth, or cheese, to sell at market and to enhance their family's income.

Ethnic pluralism in middle colonies
No region of colonial America enjoyed a greater mix of race, religion, and ethnicity in its population than the mid-Atlantic colonies. The Dutch heritage of New York, the Swedish foundation of Delaware, and the variety of people lured into New Jersey and Pennsylvania by liberal Quaker policies (e.g., Germans and Scots-Irish) assured that the middle colonies would have a rich pluralism to broaden the social, cultural, and religious life of Great Britain's mainland colonies.

Rising grain and tobacco prices

Population growth in Europe combined with European wars to create a greater need for American goods. European farmers—men who had been called to war—simply could not produce enough to support the expanding population of the continent. The resulting higher prices for American agricultural goods brought a boom to the colonies, followed by a quick bust when peace returned.

Increasing rural inequality

The growing number of settlers in the American colonies began to stretch resources, especially land, thin by the middle of the eighteenth century. Many families no longer could parcel out land to their children in plots large enough to make a decent living. In some colonies, large numbers of landless people known as inmates began to settle at the bottom of the social and economic scale. For many colonists the dream of a better life vanished amid the realities of an increasing population and thinning resources.

1740s Old Lights versus New Lights
Religious establishment questioned

The Great Awakening created tension and caused splits in religious denominations between traditionalists (Old Lights) and supporters of revivalism (New Lights) by questioning the views of established churches. These divisions tore into the fabric of society and caused many settlers to question the status quo, first in religion and then in other areas, including political life.

1740s New colleges founded

The influences of the Great Awakening were felt in many aspects of American life, including education. Under the leadership of the New Lights, a number of religious denominations promoted their beliefs through newly established colleges, including Princeton (originally the College of New Jersey), which was founded by Presbyterians. Other colleges, such as Brown and Rutgers, appeared in the 1750s and 1760s.

Newspapers increase
Enlightenment ideas (Locke, Newton) spread

Just as the American colonies attracted European immigrants, they also provided fertile ground for the new learning of the Enlightenment. The ideas of John Locke, Isaac Newton, and other Enlightenment thinkers spread across the Atlantic to influence the work of such divergent colonists as Cotton Mather and Benjamin Franklin. The Enlightenment worked its way into American life through churches, schools, clubs, magazines, and newspapers. The number of newspapers and the number of readers increased dramatically between 1740 and 1765 when most colonies could boast of regularly published newspapers.

1743 Franklin founds American Philosophical Society

In the 1740s, Philadelphia became the intellectual center of the Enlightenment in America. A key institution for the spread of the new knowledge of the Enlightenment was the American Philosophical Society that Benjamin Franklin helped establish in that city in 1743.

1749 Ohio Company formed
Susquehannah Company in Connecticut

Prominent Virginia planters organized the Ohio Company as the first step toward opening new lands for settlement in the Ohio Valley. To the north, Connecticut settlers formed the Susquehannah Company to help them claim lands in northwestern Pennsylvania. Increasing pressure by Anglo-American settlers on French posts in the Ohio Valley led to war by 1754.

1750s Proprietary resurgence

The establishment of the Ohio Company and the Susquehannah Company encouraged other landowners to revive long-standing land claims that had lain dormant for some time. Proprietary families, such as the Calverts in Maryland and the Penns in Pennsylvania, watched their wealth increase many times over as they gained new lands that could be sold for profit or leased to tenants.

Industrial Revolution begins in England
Consumer "revolution" raises American debt

By the 1750s, British artisans began to produce a variety of goods (e.g., textiles, wood pieces, and iron ware) by steam- and water-powered machines. The result was greater output of goods sold at lower prices. This transition from human- to machine-produced goods revolutionized the British economy with an immediate echo effect on the American colonies. American consumers enjoyed better and cheaper goods from the home country but often went into debt to buy those goods. Some colonial farmers were hard pressed to improve or expand their holdings without going deeper into debt or going into tenancy. Resentment against British merchants and colonial proprietors began to build.

Indian "play-off" system breaks down

Into the mid-eighteenth century, Native Americans held a firm grip on the Ohio Valley by melding tribes together in covenant chains for greater strength and threatening hostile action against white settlers. When this intricate system broke down, American colonists along the seaboard cast covetous eyes toward the fertile Ohio Valley and began to plan a series of migrations out of both the North and South into the interior of the continent.

1754 French and Indian War begins

The last of the wars for empire between England and France began in America when Virginians moved into the Ohio Valley, where France had been active in the fur trade. Within two years the war spread to Europe and then became world-wide in scope. This Great War for Empire resolved forever the competition between Great Britain and France to determine which country would be the dominant European power in North America.

Albany Congress

Shortly after the French and Indian War began, representatives of the northern colonies and the Iroquois Nations met to discuss possible courses for the war. The Albany "Plan of Union" that grew out of their discussions proposed a cooperative arrangement to oversee trade and defense. The plan floundered because of concerns from both colonial governments and British leadership.

1755 ### French Acadians deported

In order to assure British control of eastern Canada in the early stages of the French and Indian War, the British expelled some 6,000 Acadians from Nova Scotia (Acadia). Many of the Acadians sought refuge in the southern regions of France's mainland colonies, principally in Louisiana, where they eventually came to dominate as "Cajuns."

1759 ### Fall of Quebec

William Pitt's imperial strategy in the French and Indian War was to take control of French strongholds in the St. Lawrence Valley. The capture of Quebec opened the way to control the valley and ensured the removal of France from the American mainland. When Montreal fell to British arms in 1760, the outcome of the Great War for Empire was sealed.

1760s ### New York and New England border conflicts
Regulator movements in the Carolinas

By the middle of the eighteenth century major political, economic, and social changes in the colonies were causing tension between western settlers and colonial authorities along the seaboard. These tensions in both the North and the South pointed toward the future and to imminent conflict between the colonies and their home country.

Evangelical Baptists in Virginia

During the Great Awakening, traditional ways of thinking and acting frequently came under challenge. Nowhere was this more apparent than in Virginia where Baptist ministers drew large numbers of supporters and converts from the poor white and black populations of the colony. In fact, slaves were welcomed at Baptist revivals where a message of equality often was preached. This threat to long-standing beliefs and actions deepened the growing gap between the landed gentry on one side and poor whites and blacks on the other.

1762 ### Treaty of Fontainbleau gives Louisiana to Spain

With the end of the Great War for Empire near, the British made plans for the takeover of France's mainland colonies and Spanish Florida. Rather than see everything transferred to Great Britain, in 1762 France ceded a part of Louisiana to its good friend and frequent ally, Spain. Spain received title to all of Louisiana west of the Mississippi River to add to its other holdings in the West, Southwest, and Mesoamerica. Louisiana remained under Spanish control until the early nineteenth century, when Spain receded the territory to France.

1763 ### Treaty of Paris ends Great War for Empire
Florida and Canada ceded to Britain
Postwar colonial recession

The Treaty of Paris removed France as a threat to England in America by stripping away from France its mainland colonies. In a secondary deal, Great Britain also assumed control of Spanish Florida. Americans believed that these territorial changes would allow them to move freely into the interior of the continent without fear of French opposition. However, the end of the war also brought a downturn to an American economy that had prospered from wartime spending by British troops in America.

Pontiac leads Indian uprising

Tensions between Native Americans and Europeans were a staple of life in colonial America. The Indians often fell victim to fraud and abuse on the part of Europeans. Chief Pontiac of the Ottawa rose up against Anglo-American settlers moving out of New England and New York into the area of the Great Lakes. The rebellion ultimately failed—the British kept control—but the episode offered another reminder of ill feelings between native Americans and European "invaders."

Paxton Boys in Pennsylvania

As colonists established new settlements along the frontier, conflict with native Americans was inevitable. In Pennsylvania, the Scots-Irish Paxton Boys massacred Indians who stood in the way of their settlement, creating a political crisis for the Pennsylvania leadership.

GLOSSARY

marriage portion   In return for years of work on the family farm, parents frequently gave their children a parcel of land or farm equipment as a marriage gift to help them start life on their own. Parents hoped that the children would repay this marriage portion by caring for their aged parents. (p. 106)

dower rights   In English and colonial law, women had limited rights to hold and manage property. Upon a husband's passing, his widow was entitled under law to the use of one-third of the estate during her lifetime. She surrendered her share if she married again. (p. 107)

entail   In British law, entailment was a method of limiting inheritance, especially of landed estates, to guarantee that the holdings would stay in the family. Some colonists adopted this restrictive practice rather than risk losing family lands that fell into the hands of a ne'er-do-well child. (p. 107)

stem family   Another way to preserve family lands from one generation to the next was the stem family. A married son or son-in-law would work the land (as the "stem") alongside his or his wife's parents and inherit the land after the father's passing. (p. 107)

cradle   This tool was a long-handled scythe with wooden fingers that arranged wheat for easy bundling. The cradle marked a major improvement over the hand sickle, more than doubling the amount of work a farmer or field hand could do. This and other labor-saving devices increased output and freed some workers to do other chores that would benefit the farmer economically. (p. 109)

trenchers and noggins   Most colonial families did not have much money to spend on frills. Wealthy families could afford pewter or ceramic ware for their dining tables, but most American colonists made do with wooden implements that they could buy cheaply or whittle. These included trenchers (wooden plates or platters), noggins (wooden cups), and spoons. (p. 110)

capitalists   During colonial times, some farmers, shopkeepers, and merchants generated enough funds to purchase land, equipment, and goods in quantity and then sell them to newcomers at a profit. These capitalists reached a level of wealth where they could stand comparison to the owners of landed estates and begin to create class distinctions based on wealth in the towns and cities. (p. 110)

inmates   As the population expanded in the colonies, particularly among non-English groups, increasing numbers of people could not find good land at affordable prices. These single men and families without property came to be known as inmates, and they formed a new class of the poor. Finding it impossible to acquire land, they became tenant farmers or day laborers without much hope of earning economic freedom. (p. 110)

redemptioners   An indentured servant who crossed from Germany or Switzerland to the colonies with a contract running two to seven years was referred to as a redemptioner or "free willer." At the end of the service (average time was about four years), he could "redeem" himself, that is, become free to take up an independent life in the colonies. Good estimates put indentured servants at 60 percent or more of all immigrants to the American colonies up to 1775. (p. 112)

Enlightenment   Sweeping first through Europe and then America, the Enlightenment, also known as the Age of Reason, revolutionized patterns of thought in science, mathematics, and government, by stressing the power of human reason. In rejecting the divine right of kings as a basis for government, Enlightenment thinkers laid the foundation for American independence. (p. 116)

Pietism   Developing at the same time as the Enlightenment, Pietism was a movement stressing emotion in religion that had great success among American farmers, laborers, and slaves. Revivalists spread Pietism across the colonies during the Great Awakening, turning people back to God with passionate sermons that sounded themes of hellfire and damnation. Like the Enlightenment, Pietism struck at the heart of the status quo and opened a path to independence. (p. 116)

social compacts   Enlightenment thinkers such as John Locke, who rejected the notion of the divine right of kings as a basis for government, offered "social compacts" (sometimes called social contracts) as their alternative. They proposed that government arose from agreement among the people, who set their own rules for the government to follow. Because authority flowed from the people, they could also decide when they wanted to change their form of government, even through revolution. This concept is at the heart of the American Declaration of Independence. (p. 116)

deists   One result of Enlightenment thinking was deism, a religious movement that countered emotion and revivalism—Pietism—by emphasizing reason. Deists rejected orthodox Christianity in favor of a God who revealed himself through nature and reason. For deists, God was a rational being who created the universe and then, indifferent to human affairs, left it alone. The most notable American deist was Thomas Jefferson. (p. 117)

IDENTIFICATION

Identify by filling in the blanks.

1. When the sons and daughters of colonial farmers reached marriageable age, their parents usually gave them what was called a _____ of land and livestock to help them get an economic start. (p. 106)

2. In Pennsylvania, Scots-Irish settlers who had little if any taxable property were called

   _____ . (p. 110)

3. In Pennsylvania backcountry towns such as Bethlehem and Nazareth, German sectarians known as

   _____ added to the colony's religious diversity. (p. 111)

4. The first religious group in the American colonies to advocate the abolition of slavery was the _____ . (p. 112)

5. The "new learning" of the Enlightenment inspired Puritan minister Cotton Mather to develop a new technique of inoculation to fight _____ , a virulent disease that reached epidemic proportions in the colonies. (p. 117)

6. An author, inventor, and scientist, _____ was the model of an Enlightenment thinker in America. (p. 117)

7. Developing in Europe at the same time as the Enlightenment, _____ was a movement stressing emotion in religion that enjoyed great success in the American colonies. (p. 118)

8. Critics of the Great Awakening who feared that revivalism might destroy established churches were known as _____ . (p. 119)

9. Under the banner of the Great Awakening, New Light Presbyterians established the College of New Jersey, later known as _____ , in 1747. (p. 122)

10. In the middle of the eighteenth century, the main French settlements on the American mainland were the trading centers of Montreal and Quebec along the _____ River. (p. 124)

11. The British prime minister who determined that the French and Indian War would become the Great War for Empire to crush France as a colonial rival was _____ . (p. 126)

12. "I am French, and I want to die French." With these words, the Ottawa Indian chief _____ committed himself and his people to an alliance with France in the French and Indian War. (p. 127)

13. In the feudal land system brought from Europe to America and applied by wealthy proprietors, tenants had to pay the landowners fees known as _____ . (p. 131)

SKILL-BUILDING EXERCISE

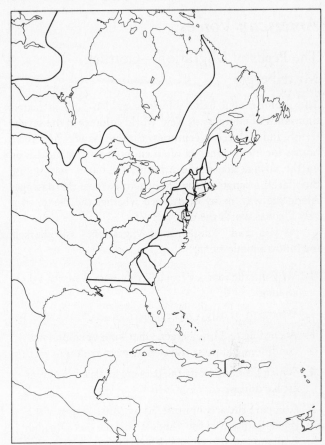

On this map:

1. (a) Locate the four middle colonies, and (b) mark the area where German immigrants preferred to settle in this region.

2. Locate the St. Lawrence River and identify the two major French settlements in Canada.

3. Mark the extent of the British Empire on the mainland of North America under the terms of the Treaty of Paris (1763).

4. Take a careful look at map 4.4 on text p. 125. Why was the Ohio River Valley south of the Great Lakes a critical region for both France and Great Britain? Why would it become a source of controversy between the two colonial powers?

DOCUMENT EXERCISES

American Voices

The Perils of Migration—Gottlieb Mittelberger

The promise of a better life in a golden land attracted thousands of migrants to New World colonies in the seventeenth and eighteenth centuries. Europeans who left their homes for life in America often endured terrible hardships on the voyage across the Atlantic. Crammed into ships, they faced a lengthy struggle just to survive the passage. Along the way, many questioned whether the dream of a new life was worth the risk.

As you read "The Perils of Migration," ask yourself the following questions:

1. Why did the journey from Germany to America take so long?

2. What sort of cargo was carried?

3. According to Mittelberger, what kind of shipboard conditions did these travelers have to endure?

4. Which groups among the passengers faced the greatest hardships?

5. Compare the account offered by Mittelberger with the description of the "middle passage" by Olaudah Equiano (see text p. 82). What similarities and what differences can you find in these two selections?

The Paxton Boys March on Philadelphia— Henry Melchiot Muhlenberg

The liberal social and economic policies that William Penn introduced in Pennsylvania attracted a rich variety of ethnic and religious groups into "Penn's Woodland." The largest of the ethnic groups, the Scots-Irish, usually shunned urban areas to settle along the frontier. At first, they accepted Quaker policies, such as pacifism. After a time, however, they decided that they could not abide by this non-violent philosophy and still live in the backcountry where native groups were strong. The most famous of the Scots-Irish groups to oppose Quaker views was a vigilante force known as the Paxton Boys. This segment of "American Voices" describes their coming into Philadelphia to bring attention to their demands.

As you read "The Paxton Boys March on Philadelphia," ask yourself the following questions:

1. According to rumors in Philadelphia at the time, why were "backwoods settlers" marching toward the city?

Did they have the numbers needed to carry out their plan?

2. How did the citizens of Philadelphia plan to protect themselves against the invaders from the frontier? Why did these preparations seem "strange" to some people?

3. What actions by the Quakers—leading to the march on the city and during preparations for defense—surprised their neighbors? Were these actions in line with traditional Quaker beliefs or different?

American Lives

Jonathan Edwards: Preacher, Philosopher, Pastor

Of all the Puritan ministers, Jonathan Edwards perhaps has the greatest reputation as both preacher and philosopher. He added his own touches and interpretations to traditional Puritan doctrine, and mixed in ideas from the Enlightenment, to inspire the New England phase of the Great Awakening. His most famous sermon, *Sinners in the Hands of an Angry God*, stirred his congregation and wider audiences in the Connecticut River Valley to break from their apathy and lethargy and recommit themselves to a vengeful God who demanded conversion and commitment. Differences of opinion on doctrine and interpretation between Edwards and his congregation—with some political implications—led to his dismissal from his church. But this fact does not detract from his overall impact on Puritan thought and life.

As you read "Jonathan Edwards," ask yourself the following questions:

1. According to Edwards, what would be the fate of someone who died without undergoing a conversion experience?

2. How did the ideas of the Enlightenment affect Edwards's life and his intellectual development as a philosopher and minister?

3. How did Edwards build on the Enlightenment ideas of John Locke to make it easier for common people to understand their world?

4. Over what issue did Edwards break with his congregation and suffer dismissal as minister from his Northampton pulpit?

5. Within the context of Pietism and revivalism, how might you classify Edwards? As an Old Light? As a New Light? Or as something else? Why?

Multiple Choice

1. Under English and colonial law, a widow was allowed to hold and use one-third of the family's estate during her lifetime. This was known as:
   a. the widow's portion.
   b. entailment.
   c. dower rights.
   d. marital freehold.

2. During the colonial period the only prominent religious denomination that gave women an active role in church matters was the:
   a. Puritans.   c. Methodists.
   b. Congregationalists.   d. Quakers.

3. In order to ensure that a family's property stayed under family control, parents in New England often chose a son or son-in-law to work the land with them and then to inherit that farm after the father's death. This system was known as:
   a. dower rights.
   b. the stem family.
   c. marriage portion.
   d. freehold insurance.

4. To make better use of their land, after 1750 many New England farmers replaced traditional English crops with one that provided a greater yield per acre. This new crop was:
   a. wheat.   c. barley.
   b. potatoes.   d. rice.

5. The largest group of new migrants to British North America in the mid-eighteenth century was the:
   a. Scots-Irish.   c. Dutch.
   b. Germans.   d. Welsh.

6. French Calvinists who suffered expulsion from their home country and then settled in the American colonies, usually in New York or in seaboard cities, were known as:
   a. Redemptioners.
   b. Lapsed Catholics.
   c. Huguenots.
   d. the Society of Friends.

7. In the early 1700s, the middle colonies grew prosperous primarily because:
   a. a population explosion in Western Europe created a demand for more wheat.
   b. artisans in New York and Philadelphia began to mass-produce their products.
   c. the fishing banks off New England were played out, causing Massachusetts fishermen to move southward.
   d. British soldiers began to buy their products.

8. Unable to afford expensive pewter plates and utensils at their dinner tables, many colonial families used wooden ware, including:
   a. reapers and mugs.
   b. cradles and scythes.
   c. trenchers and noggins.
   d. ceramics and kilns.

9. By the 1750s. Quaker policies in Pennsylvania had come under fire from all of the following religious groups *except*:
   a. Lutherans.
   b. Presbyterians.
   c. Reformed churches.
   d. Mennonites.

10. According to John Locke, one of the great Enlightenment thinkers, at birth a child's mind was a *tabula rasa*, meaning a:
    a. table raised for learning.
    b. blank slate.
    c. tablet to be inscribed by God.
    d. magical cosmos.

11. Which of the following groups was *not* likely to support Enlightenment ideas in the colonies?
    a. merchants in seaport towns
    b. yeomen farmers
    c. urban artisans
    d. planters in the South

12. During the colonial era, *all* of the following magazines were aimed at a readership of wealthy gentlemen *except*:
    a. the *New York*.
    b. the *Massachusetts*.
    c. Franklin's *General*.
    d. the *American Philosopher*.

13. Before bringing his religious message to America, George Whitefield became a disciple of John Wesley, best known as the founder of:
    a. Methodism.   c. Congregationalism.
    b. Presbyterianism.   d. Quakerism.

14. The notion that conversion and knowing God's grace, rather than education in theology and knowledge of the Bible, were needed to qualify to be a minister was argued in *The Dangers of an Unconverted Ministry* by:
    a. Jonathan Edwards.   c. Martin Luther.
    b. Gilbert Tennent.   d. Solomon Stoddard.

15. At the onset of the French and Indian War, George Washington and his command of Virginia militia were captured by French troops at a site in the Ohio Valley known as:
    a. Fort Duquesne.   c. Fort Necessity.
    b. Point Pittsburgh.   d. Fort Allegheny.

16. The Albany "Plan of Union," which proposed cooperation between the American colonies in the North and the Iroquois nations to oversee trade and defense, was principally the work of:
    a. William Pitt.
    c. George Washington.
    b. Benjamin Franklin.
    d. Edward Braddock.

Short Essays

Answer the following in a brief paragraph.

1. In colonial New England, what were the responsibilities and rights of women? (pp. 104–107)

2. How did William Penn's social and religious system in Pennsylvania differ from that of many other colonies? (pp. 111–114. Also see Chapter 3)

3. In what ways did the growth and development of Philadelphia reflect the basic concepts of the Enlightenment? (pp. 117–118)

4. Why were revivalists in Virginia—New Light Presbyterians and Baptists—seen as a threat to the status quo? (pp. 122–123)

5. In addition to the crises associated with the Enlightenment and the Great Awakening, what events in the mid-eighteenth century transformed American colonial life and redefined the British empire in North America? (pp. 124–130)

6. How did the French and Indian War mark the end of France as an imperial power in North America? (p. 128)

7. In what ways did the Industrial Revolution in Great Britain affect the American colonies? (pp. 128–130)

ANSWERS

Chapter Précis

1. midwives
2. entail
3. land bank
4. cradles
5. patroonships
6. Friends
7. Mennonites
8. Benjamin Franklin
9. Theodore Jacob Frelinghuysen
10. New Light

11. Brown
12. Vestrymen
13. George Washington
14. Neolin
15. Piedmont
16. Susquehannah Company
17. Paxton Boys

Identification

1. marriage portion
2. inmates
3. Moravians
4. Quakers
5. smallpox
6. Benjamin Franklin
7. Pietism
8. Old Lights
9. Princeton
10. St. Lawrence
11. William Pitt
12. Pontiac
13. quitrents

Skill-Building Exercise

1. (a) Middle colonies: New York, Pennsylvania, New Jersey, and Delaware. See map 4.2, text p. 109.
   (b) Pennsylvania (Note: There were other concentrations of German settlers along the frontier in Virginia and Maryland and in central South Carolina.) See map 4.2, text p. 109.

2. Mark the St. Lawrence River, and locate Quebec and Montreal. See map 4.5, text p. 125.

3. In 1763, the British Empire covered the eastern half of North America, from Canada on the north to Florida on the south, and stretched westward to the Mississippi River.

4. For both Great Britain and France the Ohio Valley was a desirable territory to acquire if there was any hope of expanding their empires on the North American mainland. Blocked from expansion to the east by the Atlantic Ocean, Great Britain needed the Ohio Valley if it hoped to break away from the coast where it had established colonies and expand into the inte-

rior of the continent. For the French, the Ohio Valley was needed to tie together New France to the north and Louisiana to the south. Without the Ohio Valley, France's primary mainland holdings would be split apart.

Self-Test

Multiple Choice

1. c	5. a	9. d	13. a
2. d	6. c	10. b	14. b
3. b	7. a	11. b	15. c
4. b	8. c	12. d	16. b

Short Essays

1. In colonial New England women had few rights under the law. Theirs was a subordinate role, first to their fathers and later to their husbands. In fact, a woman's right to hold property was less than that of her children. She surrendered her property when she married, and even if widowed she could not recover full title to her own goods. According to a legal system known as dower rights, a widow was able to use one-third of her husband's estate for her life, surrendering even that if she remarried. In contrast, a woman had significant responsibilities as a helpmate to husband, working with him on the farm or in the business while managing the household, and as a mother, bearing and raising children.

2. From the beginning, William Penn proposed policies and programs for Pennsylvania that differed from those of the other colonies. The Quaker faith was different from that of other Protestant denominations—offering equality to women, propounding that all people were capable of being "saved," and refusing to defer to superiors—and these differences influenced the development of political, social, and religious patterns in Pennsylvania. For example, Pennsylvania supported pacifism and opposed slavery. In addition, there was no established church or taxes to support a church.

3. Among its basic tenets, the Enlightenment emphasized a belief in the power of human reason and stressed the concept that people can improve their societies. In Philadelphia these ideas became realities in several ways. Philadelphia boasted a circulating library through which ideas from Europe and the other

colonies could be introduced, including new scientific theories. The first American medical school was founded there in 1765, the American Philosophical Society was established in 1743, and Philadelphia also attempted to help the sick and poor by providing hospitals and shelters for the aged and disabled.

4. In Virginia the landed elite, who were members of the established Church of England, feared that revivalism would undermine their position, including their long-time hold on political power. Presbyterians, who appealed to skilled workers and farmers, were a minor nuisance; Baptist revivalists posed a more important threat because they appealed to poor whites and black slaves with talk of democratic principles. Prominent Virginians were appalled to think that their slaves might learn about ideas such as equality and liberty, which might encourage them to try breaking free from bondage. Baptists also condemned many of the social activities of the gentry, including gambling, horse racing, and drinking.

5. Three events had a major impact on American life and the state of the British Empire. The French and Indian War, which began in America in 1754, quickly spread to Europe as the last great Anglo-French war for empire. Expansion of transatlantic trade increased American prosperity, but at the price of heavy debt to British creditors. The Treaty of Paris and the end of war between England and France opened the West to rapid American settlement and eventually led to tensions between the colonies and their home country.

6. The Treaty of Paris of 1763 eliminated France as an imperial power in North America. France surrendered to the British control of all of New France: Canada and the territory of Louisiana south of the Great Lakes to the Mississippi River. France's New World empire was reduced to some sugar islands in the West Indies and two small islands off the coast of Newfoundland.

7. By 1750, the Industrial Revolution was in full flower in Great Britain. Water- and steam-driven machines produced goods faster and cheaper than human labor could. Better goods at lower prices found a ready market in the American colonies. Shopkeepers and merchants expanded their inventories, and settlers bought equipment for their farms, resulting in a consumer revolution. To cover the cost of these goods, many Americans received credit from British merchants. Americans enjoyed a higher standard of living, but they also became dependent on overseas creditors.

CHAPTER 5

Toward Independence: Years of Decision 1763–1775

★   ★   ★

CHAPTER PRÉCIS

The Reform Movement, 1763–1765   pp. 138–144

Tensions in the Imperial System

Victory in the Great War for Empire made Britain the dominant military and imperial power in Europe. After years of neglecting its colonies in America, Great Britain decided to use some of that power to bring the colonies back into line. Stronger enforcement of the Navigation Acts, the passing of more restrictive laws, and the permanent stationing of troops in America showed British determination to keep the colonies in check. The colonies, on their part, were growing weary of British oppression.

The Financial Legacy of the War

Military victory in the Great War for Empire came at a high cost to Great Britain. The national debt almost doubled in less than a decade, requiring higher taxes to pay the debt and interest on the debt. British governmental bureaucracy grew larger, in part to have sufficient officials to collect these new taxes, despite protests in both the colonies and in the home country.

British Reform Strategy

After 1763 British leaders were determined to reform the imperial system to ensure British dominance over the colonies, in part by maintaining taxes on imports, especially molasses and sugar, and by restructuring the court system. The colonists resented the growing authority of the British state and what they regarded as their second-class status under British law.

1. To control colonial printing and passing of paper money, Parliament passed the _____ in 1764, banning the use of paper money as legal tender. (p. 139)

2. Much of the burden of devising and enforcing new tax laws after the Great War for Empire fell on _____ , who replaced William Pitt as prime minister in 1761. (p. 140)

3. The high point of Lord Bute's ministry was his successful negotiation of the _____ in 1763, which ended the Great War for Empire between Great Britain and France. (p. 141)

The Stamp Act

To increase British revenue and force the colonies to pay a portion of the cost of maintaining the British army in the colonies, Parliament passed the Stamp Act in 1765, which placed a tax on legal documents and paper items, including newspapers and playing cards. Once again this raised the twin issues of taxation to support the British presence in America and taxation without representation, and brought forth an outcry of opposition from angry colonists.

4. The _____ required colonists to provide food and housing for British troops stationed in the colonies. (p. 143)

The Dynamics of Rebellion, 1765–1766

pp. 144–150

The Crowd Rebels

Resistance to the Stamp Act in the colonies was strong and immediate. Despite some appeals from prominent merchants in major port cities for peaceful resistance, angry Americans took to the streets to protest the tax; they threatened the tax collectors and boycotted British goods. Enforcement of the Stamp Act proved to be impossible. The protests that grew out of opposition to the Stamp Act reflected increased hostility to British authority, but also displayed developing colonial support for an American identity that would allow the colonies to step out from the shadow of Great Britain.

5. The most active of the Patriot groups opposing the Stamp Act, even to the point of mob violence, was a group of colonists who called themselves _____ . (p. 145)

Ideological Roots of Resistance

Resistance to British authority after 1763 centered in seaboard cities, where restrictive policies had a quick and profound effect on the income of merchants, artisans, and lawyers. Eventually colonial concerns worked their way into rural communities. Undergirding the resistance was concern about English common law, the rationalism of the Enlightenment, and the British political tradition. Emotion and ideology combined to turn tax protests into broader resistance.

6. When prominent Boston merchant John Hancock was accused of smuggling, his defense was based on common-law principles at the insistence of his lawyer, _____ . (p. 147)

The Informal Compromise of 1766

American protests over the Stamp Act won support in some corners of Great Britain. Some British political leaders agreed with the colonists that taxation without representation was unconstitutional. British merchants feared that they would suffer economically if boycotts continued and might lose American markets if colonial protests turned into full-scale resistance. By 1766 a compromise was devised: The Stamp Act was repealed and the sugar tax was reduced, but Parliament applied the sugar tax to British as well as foreign imports and reasserted its right to bind colonies "in all cases whatsoever."

7. In Great Britain a political faction known as _____ supported American protests against the Stamp Act and even argued that it was unconstitutional to tax the colonies. (p. 149)

The Growing Confrontation, 1767–1770

pp. 150–156

The Townshend Initiatives

Under the direction of Charles Townshend, British policies became harsher and more repressive toward the colonies after 1767. New taxes were levied on paper, paint, glass, and tea, with part of the revenue to be used to pay the salaries of British officials in the colonies. Townshend also forced New Yorkers to quarter troops under threat of dissolving its assembly.

8. In 1767 Townshend pushed the _____ through Parliament, suspending the New York assembly until the colony agreed to quarter troops. (p. 151)

America Again Resists

Americans continued to protest the passage and enforcement of tax laws as unconstitutional infringements on their rights. The Townshend duties inspired a new round of protests and another call for boycotts and non-importation of British goods. Colonists increased the domestic production of goods such as paper and cloth to lessen their dependence on British sources. After some opposition, the boycotts gained momentum. The British authorities responded by sending troops to America as a first step toward military coercion of the colonies.

9. In an effort to divide the colonists and to split off the most vocal critics of the Townsend duties from the rest of the colonists, Lord Hillsborough called for repeal of the duties in all colonies except _____ . (p. 154)

The Second Compromise

As had happened in 1765–1767 when American protests led to repeal of the Stamp Act, in 1770 the British conceded to American protests. Most of the Townshend duties were repealed, except for the tax on tea, which was retained to underscore Parliament's ultimate control over the colonies. Most Americans accepted the compromise rather than push Britain to the point of a full-scale confrontation. However, a growing interest in redefining the role of the colonies within the British empire showed that the compromise had brought only a truce, not a settlement of American problems with Britain.

10. The most famous confrontation between colonists and British troops over taxes and British occupation of the colonies came in Massachusetts in 1770 in an event known as the _____ . (p. 155)

The Road to War, 1771–1775   pp. 156–163

The Tea Act

After relative quiet for three years, troubled relations between the colonies and the home country erupted again in 1773. Parliament's passage of the Tea Act once more raised the question of taxes. Colonial leaders urged their people to resist paying the tax, and generally they accomplished this end peacefully. Boston was an exception. In December 1773, Patriots destroyed 342 chests of tea aboard a British ship in Boston harbor. The Boston Tea Party brought a prompt and repressive response in the form of the Coercive Acts, which were intended to make Boston pay for its tea party and bring Massachusetts into line as an example to all the colonies.

11. In an incident that foreshadowed the destruction of British property in the Boston Tea Party, in 1772 Patriots in Rhode Island burned the British ship _____ to protest enforcement of the Navigation Acts. (p. 156)

12. The tea that was destroyed in the Boston Tea Party was the property of the _____ , a British trading group operating under royal charter. (pp. 156–157)

The Continental Congress Responds

The Coercive Acts convinced colonial leaders that they needed to consider taking more direct action against Great Britain. The First Continental Congress called for resistance aimed at economic pressure, including boycotts and nonimportation of British goods. Despite some pleas in Great Britain for compromise, the ministry and Parliament were committed to forcing the colonies to accept British rules on British terms.

The Rising of the Countryside

The Patriot movement was slow to win support in rural areas of the colonies. Many farmers and planters felt little personal connection to the troubles suffered in seaport cities. As taxes increased to pay for quartering British troops and prices rose to cover import duties, rural Americans shifted to the Patriot side. Some people of property—large landowners and wealthy merchants—opposed Patriot overtures in favor of continued support for the Crown; but they constituted a small minority without enough influence to turn the colonies away from resistance and the inevitable march toward independence.

The Failure of Compromise

With Massachusetts in the lead, colonial resistance to British authority stiffened in 1774–1775. Britain responded with more troops and raids on Patriot storehouses. Six months of stalemate ended in the spring of 1775 with the outbreak of fighting. Economic skirmishes and constitutional debate between the colonies and the home country finally reached the point of open war.

13. To display their deep contempt for the Coercive Acts, Patriots began to refer to these punitive measures as the
"_____ ." (p. 161)

14. Colonial militiamen who pledged themselves to be ready to take up arms against British troops on short notice were known as _____ . (p. 163)

EXPANDED TIMELINE

1754–	**Salutary Neglect ends**
1763	**British national debt doubles**
After decades of letting the colonies have their own way in most matters, British authorities decided to bring the colonies back into line. Great Britain's wars against France to control North America and determine their standing in Europe had created a severe drain on the British treasury. The king and cabinet, with backing from Parliament, determined that the colonies would have to start paying a fair share of the cost of the empire. On their side, after a century of virtual freedom, American colonists were unwilling to accept new controls.

1760	**George III becomes king**
Upon his ascension to the throne, George III put close friends in positions of power and reasserted the power of the monarchy at the expense of Parliament. His ministers fought financial crisis by proposing new laws to raise revenue from the colonies.

1761	**Lord Bute becomes prime minister**
Two years before the end of the Great War for Empire, Lord Bute rose to the position of prime minister, replacing William Pitt, who engineered the British victory in war with France. It fell to Bute to deal with the heavy financial burden that Great Britain faced after many years of war. The programs that he supported, many of which required greater numbers of bureaucrats, drew criticism in Great Britain and in the American colonies.

1762	**Revenue Act reforms customs service**
Royal Navy stops trade with French islands
Colonial circumvention of the Navigation Acts, sometimes by bribing officials not to collect duties on imports, caused Britain to require that officeholders manage the customs department in person. The British hoped to end corruption and at the same time increase the collection of revenue. British officials also ordered the Royal Navy to become tougher in blocking trade with French colonies in the West Indies that had been restricted under the acts of trade. The main purpose was to assure Britain the advantages of their mercantilist system, but one of the consequences was angering American colonists who protested any restrictions on free trade.

1763   Treaty of Paris ends Great War for Empire
Spanish evacuate Florida
Proclamation Line restricts western settlement
Peacetime army in America
Grenville becomes prime minister
John Wilkes demands reform of Parliament
The close of the French and Indian War with the
Treaty of Paris marked the end of a proximate
French threat to colonists on the mainland of North
America when France lost control of both New
France and Louisiana. At about the same time, the
Spanish threat out of Florida diminished when most
Spanish settlers migrated to Cuba. But what might
have been a high time in the colonies quickly turned
to frustration and anger with the onset of new trou-
bles between the colonies and the home country.
The British, under the Grenville ministry, tried to
crack down on the colonies with a variety of restrictive laws, including the Proclamation of 1763 and
new revenue acts. The British also decided that they
would station a permanent armed force in the
colonies to maintain order in the face of possible
threats from the French in Quebec, Indians in the
Ohio Valley, and colonials along the Atlantic coast.
Some colonists hoped that a change in British policies might result from the election of John Wilkes to
Parliament. Wilkes wanted to reform Parliament,
but his efforts were blocked, leaving the colonies
without much hope of political change in London.

1764   Currency Act
Sugar Act
Colonists oppose vice-admiralty courts
Franklin proposes American representation in
Parliament
To keep the colonies in line, Parliament passed several laws to maintain control of the economy and
raise new revenues to pay for the costs of empire.
Through the Sugar Act, Parliament also increased
the powers of vice-admiralty courts, which could
operate outside the bounds of English common law.
On their side, Americans protested that these laws,
which had been passed without their having any
voice or vote in Parliament, violated their traditional rights as English citizens. Benjamin Franklin
suggested that the British government allow the
colonies to have representation in Parliament. But
British leaders rejected this idea out of hand.

1765   Stamp Act
Quartering Act
Patrick Henry and Virginia Resolves
Stamp Act Congress
Riots by Sons of Liberty
The British continued to press their position on tax-
ation and control of the colonies. Passage of a
Stamp Act (a new tax plan) and a Quartering Act
intensified colonial anger. No British measure to
control the colonies or raise revenue caused greater
turmoil than the Stamp Act. Some Americans
openly challenged the new legislation, including the
Virginia House of Burgesses that adopted a resolu-

tion from Patrick Henry to condemn the act. A
Stamp Act Congress representing nine colonies
questioned the constitutionality of the stamp tax.
Patriot groups, led by the Sons of Liberty, refused to
pay the tax, threatened tax collectors with violence,
and called for a boycott of British goods. This repudiation of British authority also pushed Americans
closer to a break with Great Britain.

1765–
1766   First nonimportation movement
In response to the Stamp Act, colonial merchants in
major cities such as New York, Boston, and
Philadelphia called for a boycott of British goods.
This action cut into British profits and led
merchants in Great Britain to join Old Whigs in a
call for repeal of the Stamp Act.

1766   First Compromise: Rockingham repeals Stamp Act
and Declaratory Act
Colonial protests against the stamp tax forced the
British authorities to compromise with the colonies.
Parliament repealed the Stamp Act but then passed
the Declaratory Act to reassert its authority to
control the colonies and even to levy taxes. This
action—it was giving with one hand but taking back
with the other—brought about a temporary truce
between the colonies and the home country.

1767   Townshend Duties
Increased illegal imports of Dutch tea
"Restraining Act" in New York
Charles Townshend was committed to restructuring
British colonial policy. He pushed new taxes
through Parliament, including a tax on tea.
Colonists showed contempt for these taxes in
various ways. To counter the tax on tea, for
example, they smuggled larger quantities of Dutch
tea into the colonies, to a point that Dutch tea
accounted for ninety percent of the tea consumed by
colonists. Other laws promoted by Townshend
expanded the reach of vice-admiralty courts and
tried to force compliance with existing laws that
previously had been enforced only minimally. In an
effort to coerce the New Yorkers, he threatened
suspension of their assembly unless they agreed to
quarter troops. This hard line brought forth
renewed protests and aggressive action by the
colonies.

Second nonimportation movement begins
Daughters of Liberty make homespun cloth
The Townshend duties triggered a new round of
protests, including another call for boycotts and
nonimportation of British goods. Americans
promoted domestic production to make up for the
loss of cloth, paper, and other wares from England.
These moves caught British attention and pushed
tensions to a higher level.

1768   British army occupies Boston
Support for boycott grows
Allegedly to guarantee the collection of the
Townshend taxes, but more likely to provoke a

confrontation with colonial protestors, the British ordered army regulars into Boston. Lord Hillsborough hoped to break colonial resistance by force of arms if necessary. In fact, these British actions merely intensified colonial anger, bringing greater support to the boycott.

1770   **Second Compromise: North repeals most Townshend Duties**
Golden Hill riots in New York
Boston Massacre
Continued colonial protests, combined with a downturn in the British economy, persuaded British leaders to seek a compromise on the tax problem. Tensions eased, but in some areas, notably Boston, unrest continued to the point of confrontation between colonists and British troops. The Golden Hill riots and the Boston Massacre were previews of things to come in the next few years.

1772   **Gaspée burned in Rhode Island**
Colonial Committees of Correspondence
When Patriots burned the British ship Gaspée in 1772 to protest enforcement of the Navigation Acts, British officials intensified their actions against the colonies. In a counter-effort to unify protest movements across the colonies, Massachusetts Patriot leader Sam Adams organized a Committee of Correspondence to contact the other colonies. The idea spread from New England into the South, showing that colonial unity could be achieved in the face of British repression.

1773   **Tea Act**
Boston Tea Party
On the surface, to provide economic assistance to the British East India Company but also to reaffirm British authority, Parliament passed a Tea Act. The colonies protested peacefully until Patriots dumped tons of tea into Boston Harbor in a blatant slap at British policy. The Boston Tea Party brought a quick and decisive response from Parliament, which wanted to punish Boston severely.

1774   **Coercive Acts punish Massachusetts**
Quebec Act
The Boston Tea Party marked a turning point in British policy toward the colonies. After several attempts to compromise with the colonies—but always reasserting its right to control them—Parliament decided not to compromise but to coerce. The Coercive Acts (known as the Intolerable Acts among colonists) were directed at Massachusetts and especially at Boston but included a message for all the colonies. Any colony that openly challenged British authority could expect to face punitive actions. The colonies also resented British passage of the Quebec Act, which granted special favors to French Catholics who had come under British control after the Great War for Empire ended.

First Continental Congress
Third nonimportation movement
Loyalists organize
Passage of the Coercive Acts inspired colonial leaders to offer a unified front against British authority. Representatives from the mainland colonies met in Philadelphia to plan their response. Another call for nonimportation of British goods stepped up the economic pressure but did not force a change in British policies. The British ministry had committed itself to coercion rather than compromise. Growing talk of independence among the Patriots caused some Loyalists to rally to the British side and voice their discontent. But generally these supporters of the Crown were too few in number to make any significant impact or to slow down the fervor of colonial patriotism.

1775   **Battles of Lexington and Concord**
By the spring of 1775, Massachusetts was in open defiance of British authority, with other colonies rallying to the call for resistance. On April 19, Massachusetts militiamen faced off against British regulars outside Boston. "The shot heard 'round the world" began a war for independence that promised to turn the British Empire upside down.

GLOSSARY

excise levies   Under the British system of taxation forced upon the British citizenry at home, two basic types of taxes were assessed. External taxes included taxes or tariffs on products being imported into the country, such as tobacco and sugar. Internal taxes included excise levies—or sales taxes—that were placed on certain commodities that were popular with the people, including salt, beer, and distilled spirits. In this way the burden of taxation was spread throughout the population, although the common people resented everyday products being priced higher because of taxes. (p. 140)

pensioners and **placemen**   To ensure loyalty to the government in power, British prime ministers filled administrative and parliamentary positions with their friends and cronies. The pensioners (hirelings who held office) and placemen (literally people with a place in government) helped create a Court party that owed allegiance to the prime minister and his government rather than to the country. (p. 141)

rotten boroughs   In eighteenth-century Britain the distribution of seats in Parliament was very uneven. Rotten boroughs were small districts containing relatively few inhabitants whose votes were easily controlled by the wealthy and powerful merchants and aristocrats of the district. (p. 141)

vice-admiralty courts   To strengthen its hand in the colonies and guarantee that import duties would be paid,

Great Britain under provisions of the Sugar Act shifted suits over customs offenses from colonial courts to vice-admiralty courts. Awaiting judgment before a Crown-appointed judge, rather than a lenient jury composed of colonists or an American-born judge, and with a presumption of guilt rather than innocence, defendants could be assured of harsh treatment. The use of vice-admiralty courts by the British authorities became a major grievance in the colonies. (p. 142)

homespun As the British authorities tightened their hold on the colonies, resistance spread throughout the population. American women played an important role by producing homespun, which involved the spinning of wool into yarn and then weaving it into fabric for clothes, blankets, and other items. The production of this rough material helped free the colonies from dependence on British textile manufacturers. (p. 152)

minutemen As tensions between the American colonists and British forces built to fever-pitch proportions, some colonies organized voluntary militia units, who would be ready to face British redcoats in battle. These units, which operated outside legal bounds, were composed of the minutemen, who could respond immediately ("at a minute's warning") in any emergency. The minutemen formed the core of the citizen army that met the British at Lexington when the War of Independence began in April 1775. (p. 163)

IDENTIFICATION

Identify by filling in the blanks.

1. Under the _____ , the British prohibited white settlement west of the Appalachians and regulated the fur trade with native Americans in the region. (p. 139)

2. Although France lost most of its North American colonies in 1763 at the close of the French and Indian War, the sugar islands of _____ and _____ remained under French control. (p. 139)

3. The prime minister who presided over British attempts to reform the colonial system in America after the Great War for Empire was _____ . (p. 141)

4. Legislation that required the colonies to pay a tax on legal papers, newspapers, playing cards, and other printed items was called the _____ . (p. 143)

5. Americans who openly defended American rights and protested British measures to restrict the colonies with both voice and violence were known as _____ . (p. 144)

6. In 1766, in the _____ , Parliament proclaimed its "full power and authority" to "bind the colonies and people of America in all cases whatsoever." (pp. 149–150)

7. Parliament authorized duties on paper, paint, glass, and tea imported into the colonies under new tax legislation known as the _____ . (p. 151)

8. Under the Restraining Act of 1767, Parliament suspended operations of the colonial assembly of _____ until the colony complied with demands of the Quartering Act. (p. 151)

9. To support British authority and ensure collection of taxes on imports, Lord Hillsborough in 1768 stationed four regiments of British troops in the city of _____ , raising the specter of military coercion. (p. 153)

10. Outside the northern colonies, probably the most outspoken critic of British policies and advocate of American resistance was _____ of Virginia. (p. 155)

11. The _____ of 1774 extended legal recognition to Roman Catholics in French regions of Canada, stirring old religious hatreds between Catholics and Protestants, especially in New England. (p. 160)

12. Conservative Americans who stayed faithful to Britain and denounced Patriot schemes for independence were called _____ . (p. 162)

SKILL-BUILDING EXERCISE

1. Figure 5.1, text p. 140, shows the fluctuation of British spending for its military services between 1690 and 1780. There are four high points shown on the chart—1710, 1750, 1760, and 1780. Using your text—with Chapters 3, 4, and 5—and your understanding of the colonial era, ask yourself why these years marked the high points for spending. How do you explain the increases leading to these years?

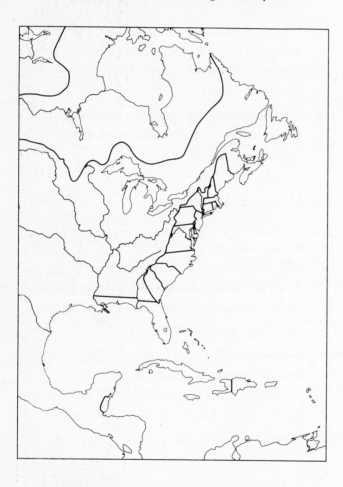

On the map above:

2. Identify the locations of the four vice-admiralty courts created under the Revenue Act of 1767.

3. Locate and mark the line of settlement mandated under the Proclamation of 1763; locate the Ohio River; locate the Ohio River Valley.

DOCUMENT EXERCISES

American Voices

A Stamp Act Riot—William Almy

Resistance to British colonial policies grew powerful in the mainland colonies in the 1760s, especially in New Eng-

land, which became the center of protest. The Sons of Liberty set themselves up as defenders of American freedoms, with a willingness to use any means, including violence, to emphasize their position. They raided the shops and homes of merchants who opposed boycotts, and made personal attacks on representatives of the Crown, among them individuals who were commissioned to sell stamps under the hated Stamp Act.

As you read "A Stamp Act Riot" ask yourself the following questions:

1. What sort of "mind games" did Patriot mobs play on those who supported England and their families?

2. How much physical damage did the mobs cause to the homes and property of British colonial authorities?

3. According to the letter, what effect did the mob actions have on the stamp master? Do you think the man could have responded in any other way to the mob's threats? Why or why not?

The Wedding of George III, 1762—Eliza Lucas Pinckney

During the colonial period, many well-to-do Americans maintained close contacts with British society. Through commercial dealings and other connections born out of trade, political associations, educational opportunities for children, and leisure travel, they often visited with their British friends. Eliza Lucas Pinckney, prominent in her own right and through her husband, often stayed in touch with friends through letters. In this segment from "American Voices" we get a glimpse of Eliza Pinckney's "curiosity" about affairs in Great Britain.

As you read "The Wedding of George III, 1762," ask yourself the following questions:

1. Why did the letter and enclosures Eliza Pinckney received from her friend please her so much? What does Pinckney mean by words such as "impatience" and "curiosity"?

2. How does Pinckney express her loyalty to the Crown? Why might this assurance matter to her correspondent?

3. This letter was written in 1762. Why might Pinckney have been so concerned about the troubles of war and the prospects for peace at that time?

American Lives

George R. T. Hewes and the Meaning of the Revolution

Following a century of neglecting the American colonies, after 1763 British authorities tried to reassert control by enforcing the long-neglected Navigation Acts and passing new laws to control trade and raise revenue. These policies, supported by British troops in the colonies, invited resistance and led to occasional confrontation between angry colonists and redcoats. The most famous episodes of violence before the outbreak of war were the Boston Massacre (1770) and the Boston Tea Party (1773). George R. T. Hewes, a common man who aspired to become more, played a part in both of these critical events, coming under fire at the massacre and leading a band of rebels at the tea party.

As you read "George R. T. Hewes and the Meaning of the Revolution," ask yourself the following questions:

1. Why did George Hewes have such a strong aversion to brutality and violence? Why do you think he began to change his views on this?

2. In what ways did the Boston Massacre mark a turning point in Hewes's life?

3. Why was Hewes's role in the Boston Tea Party so out of character? What did that event mean to him?

4. Many Americans paid dearly for their involvement in the War of Independence. What did the war cost Hewes?

5. Why is George R. T. Hewes such a good representative of the "meaning" of the American Revolution?

SELF-TEST

Multiple Choice

1. The Currency Act of 1764 was enacted by Parliament because a plan for deficit financing—printing money in a sufficient amount to pay bills without imposing taxes to support the money—had been approved in:
   a. New York.
   b. Pennsylvania.
   c. Virginia.
   d. South Carolina.

2. During the Great War for Empire, British forces won control of the rich subcontinent of Asia by routing French armies in:
   a. India.
   b. Pakistan.
   c. Siam (Thailand).
   d. Vietnam.

3. In 1763 Radical Whigs launched a campaign to reform Parliament by abolishing tiny districts that were controlled by wealthy aristocrats and merchants. These districts were known as:
   a. dirty districts.
   b. rotten boroughs.
   c. corrupt counties.
   d. pensioners' places.

4. The Treaty of Paris (1763), which brought an end to the French and Indian War, was negotiated during the ministry of:
   a. Thomas Pownall.
   b. Thomas Whatley.
   c. William Pitt.
   d. Lord Bute.

5. The tax on molasses imported into the American colonies from the French West Indies was reduced to 3 pence per gallon under terms of the:
   a. Sugar Act.
   b. Molasses Act.
   c. Declaratory Act.
   d. Proclamation of 1763.

6. Among British political leaders the only one who openly supported a proposal for American representation in Parliament was:
   a. George Grenville.
   b. Lord Bute.
   c. Charles Townshend.
   d. William Pitt.

7. Every November 5 the British celebrate Guy Fawkes Day to commemorate:
   a. the Puritan migration to New England that rid England of a large number of religious and political dissenters.
   b. the failure of Catholic rebels to overthrow the British government in 1605.
   c. the capture of the French flag at Quebec in the Great War for Empire.
   d. the call by Fawkes in Parliament to suppress colonial resistance to the Stamp Act at any cost.

8. In an effort to criticize the Crown as part of their resistance to the Stamp Act, some colonists tried to revive antimonarchical sentiment associated with the Puritan revolution in England by signing protest letters with the name of:
   a. John Winthrop.
   b. Roger Williams.
   c. Oliver Cromwell.
   d. Guy Fawkes.

9. Educated colonists drew on three intellectual traditions to justify their opposition to British policies. These included *all* of the following *except*:
   a. English common law.
   b. rationalism.
   c. English political tradition.
   d. accommodationism.

10. In 1765, delegates from nine American colonies gathered to protest British taxes on the colonies. This meeting was called the:
    a. Stamp Act Congress.
    b. Committee of Correspondence.
    c. Colonial Congress.
    d. Albany Assembly.

11. The one major colonial city that objected to a new call for the boycott of British goods after passage of the Townshend duties was:
    a. Boston.
    b. New York City.
    c. Philadelphia.
    d. Charleston.

12. British soldiers charged for their involvement in the Boston Massacre were defended in a Boston court by the prominent American Patriot:

    a. John Adams.   c. Crispus Attucks.
    b. Benjamin Franklin.   d. Patrick Henry.

13. The Coercive Acts included *all* of the following *except* the:
    a. New Tea Tax.
    b. Boston Port Bill.
    c. Quartering Act.
    d. Administration of Justice Act.

14. The one section of colonial America that held out for a political compromise with Great Britain after the enactment of the Coercive Acts was:
    a. New England.   c. the frontier regions.
    b. the middle colonies.   d. the South.

15. The only mainland British colony not represented at the First Continental Congress was:
    a. Rhode Island.
    b. New Jersey.
    c. North Carolina.
    d. Georgia.

16. The onset of war between Great Britain and the mainland colonies began with a skirmish between British troops and American colonials at:
    a. Philadelphia.
    b. Baltimore.
    c. Lexington.
    d. Portsmouth.

Short Essays

Answer the following in a brief paragraph.

1. Why did Great Britain decide in 1763, after the Great War for Empire, to station a large peacetime army in the American colonies? (p. 139)

2. What British policies enacted shortly after the Great War for Empire led Americans to believe that they were "second-class" citizens rather than English citizens with full rights? (pp. 141–142)

3. How did Americans show their opposition to the Stamp Act in 1765? (p. 143)

4. What three intellectual traditions provided an ideological basis for colonial resistance to British authority after 1763? (pp. 147–148)

5. Did any support exist in Great Britain for Americans who protested the Stamp Act? If so, of what kind was it? (pp. 148–150)

6. In what ways did the British authorities give in to American protests over taxes during the years 1765–1770? (pp. 149–150, 154–156)

7. Why did rural sections of colonial America finally join seaport cities in support of the Patriot push for independence? (pp. 161–162)

ANSWERS

Chapter Précis

1. Currency Act
2. Lord Bute
3. Treaty of Paris
4. Quartering Act
5. Sons of Liberty
6. John Adams
7. Old Whigs
8. Restraining Act
9. Massachusetts
10. Boston Massacre
11. *Gaspée*
12. British East India Company
13. Intolerable Acts
14. minutemen

Identification

1. Proclamation of 1763
2. Guadaloupe; Martinique
3. George Grenville
4. Stamp Act
5. Patriots (also acceptable—Sons of Liberty)
6. Declaratory Act
7. Townshend Act
8. New York
9. Boston
10. Patrick Henry
11. Quebec Act
12. Loyalists

Skill-Building Exercise

1. Each of these four years coincides with British involvement in war or finds war near at hand. In 1710, the British were engaged in Queen Anne's War (or the War of the Spanish Succession) that ended with the Treaty of Utrecht in 1713. In 1750, King George's War (or the War of the Austrian Succession) was two years past, ending in 1748 with the Treaty of Aix-la-

Chapelle. In 1760, the British and French were nearing the close of the French and Indian War (or the Seven Years War in Europe); a downturn in British military spending after 1760 can be explained by the fact that the outcome of the war on the battlefield had been determined by that time. All that remained was negotiating the peace accord. And finally, the buildup from the mid-1770s to 1780—with more spending ahead—came with the onset of the American War for Independence.

2. The four vice-admiralty courts were located in Halifax (Nova Scotia), Boston, Philadelphia, and Charleston. See map 5.2, text p. 153, to check the locations.

3. The Proclamation Line runs from northeast to southwest along the chain of the Appalachian Mountains; the Ohio River begins at the confluence (joining) of the Monongahela and Allegheny Rivers and flows westward; the Ohio Valley is located along the Ohio River to the north and south. See map 5.3, text p. 160.

Self-Test

Multiple Choice

1. c	5. a	9. d	13. a
2. a	6. d	10. a	14. b
3. b	7. b	11. c	15. d
4. d	8. c	12. a	16. c

Short Essays

1. Britain's decision to station a permanent army in America was based on three factors. British officials wanted to discourage rebellion in newly captured territories such as Canada and Florida where French and Spanish settlers still had some prominence in numbers. They also wanted to establish a military presence that would prevent new Indian wars, especially in the Ohio Valley. Finally, British leaders hoped that a large standing army would deter the American colonists from making any moves toward independence.

2. American colonists resented British efforts to control their lives without their having any say in the matter in Parliament and other British circles. The Proclamation of 1763 prohibited them from establishing settlements in the West where they hoped to expand; the Currency Act limited their control over money in the colonies; the Sugar Act maintained a tax on molasses and sugar without allowing the colonies to have a voice in the matter; and expansion of the jurisdiction of vice-admiralty courts limited colonial control over British officials. Americans believed that they were being denied the "rights of Englishmen" and their interests were being subordinated to the needs of the British state.

3. American opposition to the Stamp Act was vocal and violent. Mobs directed by Patriot groups such as the Sons of Liberty threatened collectors with physical force, burning effigies of the stamp masters and attacking their homes and property. Newspaper editorials and letters to newspapers played on memories of the English civil war by reviving the memory of Oliver Cromwell as a threat to the British Crown. Colonial merchants called for a boycott of British goods. Enforcement of the Stamp Act proved impossible.

4. The roots of American resistance to British rule can be found in three intellectual traditions. First, the colonies placed trust in common law—rules and procedures that had been used for centuries in the courts of Great Britain and that colonists believed had been transferred to America. The Enlightenment encouraged questioning of the past and proposed that people could work together to improve society. Finally, the English political tradition, including opposition to taxes and to standing armies, inspired resistance to new British efforts to tighten control over the colonies.

5. In Great Britain, support for American protests of the Stamp Act came principally from two groups. Old Whigs in Parliament believed that the American colonies were more important as a source of trade than as a source of tax revenue; they also were of the opinion that Britain did not have the right to tax the colonies without giving them representation in Parliament. And British merchants favored the American cause because they feared that pushing for tax revenues might force Americans to continue their boycotts of British goods with devastating consequences for British trade and for the health of the economy at home.

6. Most Americans refused to recognize the British right to tax them. Their protests often involved nonimportation agreements and boycotts of British goods that caused a dramatic drop in the sale of imported goods in the colonies. To get these markets reopened, British authorities on two separate occasions repealed hated tax laws. In 1767, Parliament overturned the Stamp Act, and in 1770, Parliament repealed most of the Townshend duties. But the British took back even as they gave: Passing the Declaratory Act of 1767 and

retaining the tax on tea reaffirmed Britain's claim that the colonies would remain under the control of the king and Parliament.

7. In the early years after the Great War for Empire, resistance to British policies centered in seacoast cities rather than in rural regions of America; by the 1770s the countryside had joined the Patriot movement. Higher taxes to support British armies in the colonies and higher prices for imported goods cut deeply into the already limited resources of farm families. Many farmers believed that the British authorities would expand their reach and enact taxes specifically focused on rural areas. They also believed that the Coercive Acts that applied to Massachusetts might be extended to other regions.

P A R T 2

The New Republic

1775–1820

Part 2 treats the period from the American Revolution to 1820. The Thematic Timeline (page 166) lists the main developments topically in five columns: government, diplomacy, economy, society, and culture. Read the Timeline and the Part introduction together, beginning with the left-hand Timeline column.

First, the most fundamental change in this period was the creation of republican institutions, especially state and national governments. Paragraph two of the Part introduction explains these developments.

Second, the period was marked by a series of conflicts and entanglements with European powers, most notably two wars with Great Britain. The third paragraph interprets these events.

The third Timeline column charts the expansion of American commerce and manufacturing in these years. Economic growth and westward expansion laid the foundations for an integrated national economy, as summarized in paragraph four of the Part introduction.

Fourth, Americans had to decide what their republican society would be like, what the ideals of liberty and equality should mean in practice. The Timeline lists the key advances in male suffrage, religious liberty, and other areas. But, as paragraph five of the Part introduction explains, women and African-Americans were excluded from participating as equals in republican society.

Fifth, the citizens of the new republic strived to establish a national cultural identity. And, despite their di-

versity, by 1820 a distinctive American character had emerged, as the last paragraph of the Part introduction explains.

Now read the Timeline across to find out which events were occurring at about the same time. Note, in the period 1810–1820, for example, that the decision to go to war against Britain in 1812 was made while the federal government was dominated by the Jeffersonian Republican party.

Part Questions

After you have completed studying the chapters in Part 2, you should be able to answer the following questions:

1. How did the state constitutions and the Constitution of 1787 embody republican principles?

2. What are the most important differences between the Constitution of 1787 and the Articles of Confederation? What accounts for these differences?

3. Describe the role the United States played in the struggles among the European powers during this period. In particular, examine cases in which the United States was able to exploit Great Power rivalry, as in concluding the French alliance in 1778, as well as instances when European conflicts, such as the Napoleonic Wars, damaged American interests. And

explain why foreign policy so sharply divided Federalists and Republicans in this era.

4. How did the American Revolution and the War of 1812 influence the nation's economy? How did Federalists and Republicans differ in their visions of America's economic future?

5. How did Americans implement republican principles in their homes and families during and after the American Revolution?

6. Describe the emergence of an American national identity from the Revolution to the time of Tocqueville's travels in 1831. Evaluate the role of the following events in forging that identity: the Revolutionary War and the War of 1812, republican ideology and government institutions, westward expansion, economic development, and the Second Great Awakening.

7. What were the key decisions and developments that affected the status and role of native Americans and African-Americans from 1775 to 1820? What role did these peoples have in shaping the emerging American identity?

CHAPTER 6

War and Revolution 1775–1783

★ ★ ★

Toward Independence, 1775–1776   pp. 170–173

Civil War

After the outbreak of fighting, a divided Second Continental Congress organized a Continental Army in May 1775 and initiated economic sanctions against Great Britain. Even as the fighting continued in Massachusetts, Congress sent contradictory resolutions to the King, one requesting that he repeal the offending legislation that had begun the crisis, the second stating their case for taking up arms. Rather than exploiting these divisions, King George responded by declaring the colonists to be in rebellion and vowed to crush it. These threats, coupled with aggressive efforts of governors in Virginia and the Carolinas to put down the rebellion, inflamed local activists to call special conventions to declare themselves independent.

Common Sense

Even as patriots condemned Parliamentary legislation and eroded public acceptance of Parliamentary supremacy, most colonists remained loyal to the monarchy. Recognizing this hesitation to resist further, politicians, ministers, and intellectuals began to focus on shifting public support away from the monarchy. In January 1776, recent immigrant Thomas Paine argued in his pamphlet *Common Sense* for Americans to reject the arbitrary powers of the king, as well as the mixed government of Great Britain and move toward an independent republican government.

1. In the summer of 1775 the Second Continental Congress, seeking reconciliation with King George III, passed the _____ , which the king rejected. (p. 170)

2. _____ , in response to the House of Burgesses seizing authority in Virginia, formed two military forces, one white, and one black, composed of slaves whom he offered freedom if they would join the British side. (p. 170)

3. Among the Philadelphia intellectuals who began to question the legitimacy of the king in 1775, and the same man who Thomas Paine had a letter of introduction to upon his arrival in Philadelphia in 1774, was _____ . (p. 172)

Independence Declared

The shift of focus to the king is evident in Thomas Jefferson's Declaration of Independence. By enumerating the incidents in which the king had failed to restrain Parliament, the Declaration showed him to be a tyrant, thus justifying the Revolution both to Americans and to others. Establishing a republican tradition, the Declaration radicalized many Americans overnight and spread support for the Revolution.

The Perils of War and Finance, 1776–1778

pp. 173–179

War in the North

With a larger population and a larger, more professional army, the British had superiority in the field. This became apparent when in 1776 British forces invaded and occupied New York City and the surrounding area, pushing the Continental army into Pennsylvania. Realizing the advantage the British had, Washington shifted his strategy in late 1776 from confrontation in the open field to surprise attacks, thus achieving small victories against superior forces.

Armies and Strategies

The British sought to negotiate with the Americans or force them to surrender, rather than to destroy them. Washington's strategy, in response, became increasingly defensive, seeking to draw the British away from the coast and sap their morale. Having an inexperienced, underfinanced, and undersupplied army of short-term enlistees, Washington had little choice.

Victory at Saratoga

The British grand strategy to isolate New England culminated in the 1777 campaign. But an overcomplicated plan, overconfidence, generals working at cross-purposes, and leisurely troop movements undermined the effort. While Howe moved slowly to take Philadelphia, troops heading north were bogged down. Without reinforcements, the British were left exposed to the thousands of American militiamen who converged on them at Saratoga, New York. The British defeat at Saratoga was a turning point in the war because it encouraged the French to join the Americans in their fight against the British. The British defeat also left the Indians who had allied with the British isolated and they were forced to fight the Americans across New York on their own.

Wartime Trials

Reluctant to impose taxes for fear of weakening its authority, Congress sought to finance the war by borrowing money, by selling Continental loan certificates, and by issuing paper money. This policy touched off the most rapid inflation in American history and, by setting self-interest

4. In both the Declaration of Independence and his earlier _____ , Thomas Jefferson made a case for blaming the king for the crisis, thereby allowing him to declare George III a _____ and, thus, unfit to be the ruler of a free people. (p. 172)

5. The Battle of _____ , which the Continental army won on Christmas night in 1776, raised American hopes. (p. 174)

6. Washington's primary opponent and the formulator of the cautious British strategy in the early years of the war was General _____ . (p. 174)

7. General Howe again defeated Washington by outflanking him at the Battle of _____ , south of Philadelphia in September 1777. (p. 176)

8. The Iroquois, who allied with the British to protect their land against American encroachment, were lead by the Mohawk chief known to the whites as _____ . (p. 176)

against patriotism, undermined support for the Revolution. In the winter of 1777–1778 the army was caught between congressional insolvency and popular demoralization. Unable to acquire supplies from either Congress or the local population, the army suffered horribly. By winter's end, almost 3,000 soldiers had died and another thousand had deserted. Amid the gloom, Baron von Steuben imposed a standardized drill system and trained the survivors into a leaner, tougher professional army.

The Path to Victory, 1778–1783   pp. 179–187

The French Alliance

Seeking revenge for their defeat in the French and Indian War, the French, early supporters of the American Revolution, formally entered into an alliance with the Americans and infused the Patriot cause with new life and money. As a result of both the French alliance and the growing costs of the war, the war became increasingly unpopular in England. Initially, the British sought a compromise, but it was too late. Most Americans had, by 1778, embraced the Revolution and republican ideas. Instead, the British were compelled to fight on, spreading many of their troops across the West Indies to protect them from French invasion, while shifting their strategy away from New England and toward winning back the more valuable southern colonies.

War in the South

After reconquering Georgia, the British moved from one victory to another, until they were stopped by local militia forces in North Carolina. Marching into Virginia, the British forces were eventually encircled—by American and French troops on land and the French fleet at sea—and compelled to surrender at Yorktown.

The Patriot Advantage

Though weak, the American army had the advantage of fighting on its own territory and receiving continual support from local militias and the majority of the population, who usually provided aid at critical moments. To succeed, the British not only had to win battles, they also had to win over the American population—something that was beyond their ability. George Washington provided confident, stable military leadership and always deferred to civilian authority. He also recruited outstanding men to transform the Continental army into an efficient fighting force.

Diplomatic Triumph

Maneuvering between British and French interests, the Americans won a major victory at the bargaining table. Not only did the Treaty of Paris formally recognize the independence of the United States, it also ceded all the land east of the Mississippi River to the Americans, thus setting the stage for the opening of the West to American expansion. The treaty was signed in September 1783.

9. Patriots in towns across the North organized _____ to collect taxes, send food and clothing to the Continental army, and impose fines on or jail Loyalists. (p. 178)

10. The winter that the American army spent at _____ was graphic proof of the inability of the Congress to raise sufficient money to supply its needs. (p. 179)

11. The British general who surrendered to the Americans at Yorktown in October 1781 was _____ . (p. 182)

Republicanism Defined and Challenged

pp. 187–193

Republican Ideals and Wartime Pressures

Although the Declaration of Independence articulated the individual freedom and civil rights of every citizen, republican theory argued that each individual owed certain duties and responsibilities to the common good and should selflessly contribute to public virtue. The Revolutionary War increased this tension by setting patriotism against individual self-interest. Soldiers, though lauded for their self-sacrifice, were condemned and punished for attempted mutinies motivated by their frustration over harsh conditions and lack of material rewards from Congress. Officers wanted lifetime pensions; soldiers, back pay and clothes. Among civilians, economic opportunities for short-term profit, amid the general economic distress and deprivation created by the war, prompted many Americans to reexamine the nature of republican virtue. In most cases, self-interest triumphed. In response to the desperate need for clothing and supplies, American women dramatically increased their production of cloth. Many others filled in for their absent men by assuming farm production as well. Taught from childhood to be selfless, few women suffered from tension between civic virtue and self-interest.

Meanwhile, the currency issued by the government depreciated, forcing Congress to redeem it and remove it from circulation. Many speculators had bought up the Continental bills from farmers and artisans who were unable or unwilling to hold the depreciating currency and unwilling to pay a "tax" every time they spent it. Speculators used the currency to pay their taxes, making a substantial profit. Again, self-interest triumphed over virtue and patriotism, boding ill for the republican form of government.

The Loyalist Exodus

The war disrupted the lives of tens of thousands of people. Armies marching back and forth across states caused people to live in fear and polarized public opinion. Both Loyalists and Patriots were active, depending on which troops were in their area. Loyalists were forced to migrate. Although Loyalist land, buildings, and goods were seized, many public officials opposed the confiscation and redistribution of Loyalist property. In the cities republican merchants and professionals replaced the departing Loyalists, whose exodus thus did not constitute a major change in society.

The Problem of Slavery

The republican agenda of the Revolution generated an intense debate over slavery. Thousands of slaves responded to Lord Dunmore's offer of freedom if they fought with the British, while thousands more evacuated with the British when they left Charleston. Other slaves who were Loyalists fled to Canada. Still others negotiated with their masters, staying

12. In 1779 the Philadelphia Committee on Prices invoked traditional ideas of a _____ to prevent profiteering by city merchants. (p. 188)

13. Cloth produced by American women in their homes was called _____ . (p. 189)

14. In 1800 a Virginia slave, _____ , who planned a slave uprising that was discovered and prevented, was executed along with thirty of his followers. (p. 191)

loyal during the war in return for their freedom after the war. In the northern states, thousands of free blacks fought with the Patriots.

In the debate that followed, many northern states moved toward abolishing slavery, while several southern states permitted masters to manumit their slaves, resulting in the freeing of about ten thousand slaves. But these developments were short-lived. Whites feared and did not want a biracial society. Meanwhile, economic developments reinvigorated the institution slowing the emancipation of those slaves who were working for their freedom. When, in response to growing frustration, a planned slave revolt was discovered and prevented in Virginia in 1800 and its leaders executed, southern governments reconfirmed their commitment to slavery and property rights, no matter how much it contradicted republican ideals.

A Republican Religious Order

Republican theory affected religious life as Anglicans renounced their allegiance to the king, the head of the Church of England. Some state legislatures passed laws to establish religious freedom, making all churches equal by supporting none financially. Established churches remained in a few states. But everywhere, freedom of religion spread, republican principles liberalized religious ideas, and religious participation was viewed increasingly as a voluntary activity.

15. In 1786 the Virginia legislature passed a Bill for Establishing Religious Freedom written by _____ . (p. 193)

EXPANDED TIMELINE

1775   **Second Continental Congress meets in Philadelphia**
Olive Branch Petition
The Second Continental Congress was divided between Patriots who wanted independence and conservatives who preferred reconciliation with Great Britain. They expressed this view in the Olive Branch petition to King George. Nevertheless, Congress did organize a Continental Army, name Washington as commander, and authorize the invasion of Canada.

Battle of Bunker Hill
The Continental Army thus took over the waging of the war, which, through early summer 1775 had been fought by militiamen from Massachusetts. They had withstood three assaults from British troops before giving up their position outside Boston at Bunker Hill in June 1775.

Lord Dunmore's Proclamation to slaves
When Patriots took over the Virginia Assembly, the governor, Lord Dunmore, took refuge on a ship and organized two military forces, one of which he hoped to fill with slaves who, in a special proclamation, he offered freedom to if they would come and join the Loyalist cause.

American invasion of Canada

British Prohibitory Act

1776   **Patriots Skirmish with Loyalists in South**
Thomas Paine's *Common Sense*
Early in 1776 Thomas Paine's pamphlet *Common Sense* gave a boost to the efforts of Patriots to move for independence and encouraged some Patriots in Virginia to call for the consideration of independence at the Continental Congress.

Declaration of Independence (July 4)
In the Declaration of Independence, Jefferson put the king at fault for not restraining Parliament from abridging the rights of his subjects and declared him a tyrant, thus giving the Americans the legal right to declare themselves an independent nation.

Howe defeats Washington in New York
Through New York and New Jersey, the British moved from one victory to another against the inexperienced American army, pushing Washington's troops into Pennsylvania late in the year.

Virginia Declaration of Rights

American victories at Trenton (December 26) and Princeton (January 3, 1777)
In need of a boost in morale, Washington launched two successful surprise attacks on British outposts in New Jersey and reenergized the Patriot cause.

1777   **Patriot women assist war economy**
Howe occupies Philadelphia
The British launched a new campaign in 1777 to invade Canada and cut off New England from the other colonies. Howe, however, leisurely went south

and, after defeating Washington's troops yet again at Brandywine Creek, occupied Philadelphia.

Horatio Gates defeats Burgoyne at Saratoga
Howe's occupation of Philadelphia left Burgoyne, who was bogged down in the Hudson Valley, without support. Burgoyne was forced to surrender to Horatio Gates and thousands of American militiamen at Saratoga, New York.

Continental army suffers at Valley Forge
Patriot paper currency creates inflation
Congress, reluctant to raise taxes, issued paper currency to finance the war. But the money quickly depreciated, making it nearly impossible to acquire supplies just as Washington's army went into winter camp at Valley Forge, leaving them without provisions and forcing them to endure incredible hardship.

1778   **Franco-American Alliance (February 6)**
Lord North seeks negotiated settlement
Congress grants officers half-pay pensions
British begin "southern" strategy by capturing Savannah
The American victory at Saratoga reassured the French that the British could be beaten and encouraged them to sign a treaty of alliance with the Americans. Lord North, eager to forestall such an alliance, tried one last time to negotiate a settlement with the Americans, but it was far too late. As a result, the British, now wary of French designs on the rich West Indies colonies, spread out their troops and concentrated on trying to recover the rich southern colonies, were they believed there was considerable Loyalist sentiment and a good chance for victory. Congress meanwhile, buoyed by French support and access to European loans, responded to officers' demands by offering them lifetime half-pay pensions.

1779   **Confrontation in Philadelphia over price regulation**
Seizure and sale of Loyalist property begins

1780   **General Clinton captures Charleston**
French army lands in Rhode Island
Greene's forces harass Cornwallis's army
Patriots prevail at King's Mountain
Continental currency continues to depreciate
In response to the successful British capture of Charleston and Camden, American militia and regular forces intensified their efforts to defend the south. While American forces increased their harassment of British forces and eventually prevailed at King's Mountain, North Carolina, the French landed in Rhode Island, which, by posing a threat to British troops in New York, forced the British to again shift their strategy. The French presence also allowed the Americans to acquire loans that improved support for American forces.

1780s   **Debate over religious establishment: general assessment laws and freedom of conscience**

1781   **Cornwallis invades Virginia; surrenders at Yorktown**
Large-scale Loyalist emigration to Canada and Britain
Cornwallis, stymied in North Carolina, headed northeast into Virginia. Meeting little opposition, his forces and those led by Benedict Arnold ransacked the countryside. But the arrival of French troops, combined with that of the French fleet from the West Indies, enabled Washington to march his troops south against Cornwallis and surround him at Yorktown, forcing him to surrender. All the while, wartime conditions polarized opinion and increased Patriot harassment of Loyalists, forcing many to leave the country by 1781.

Partial redemption of Continental currency
Escaped slaves depart with British

1782   **Slave manumission act in Virginia (reversed in 1792)**
The presence of British troops in the South increased the number of slaves who sought refuge behind British lines and escaped to freedom. Some masters, seeking the loyalty of their slaves, traded that loyalty for the promise of future freedom. Others sensed the implications of republican theory and freed their slaves or let them work to free themselves. In 1782 the Virginia legislature passed an act that allowed masters to free their slaves, leading to the manumission of at least 10,000 slaves by 1792.

1783   **American officers at Newburgh, New York, plot against Congress**
Treaty of Paris (September 3)
Maneuvering around French delaying tactics and taking advantage of British political interest in signing a treaty quickly, American diplomats managed to acquire both recognition and land rights to all the territory between the Appalachians and the Mississippi River, thus establishing the basis for a large and powerful nation.

1784   **Ethan Allen publishes *Reason: The Only Oracle of Man***

1786   **Virginia Bill for Establishing Religious Freedom**
Republican theory swept across American life, changing people's attitudes toward religion. Many state legislatures passed laws separating church and state and making all churches equal before the law by providing no government support for any denomination.

1799   **New York enacts Gradual Emancipation Act**
Both the Enlightenment and Republican theory put slavery on the defensive in the North, where there were few slaves. Following the lead of Massachusetts, which had abolished slavery in 1784, and Pennsylvania, Connecticut, and Rhode Island, which passed laws enacting its gradual abolition, New York passed a law in 1799 freeing the children of slaves when they reached age twenty-five.

1800   **Gabriel Prosser's rebellion in Virginia**
By the 1790s the tide had turned against emancipation of slaves in the South. When Virginia officials discovered plans for a slave rebellion led by Gabriel Prosser, they suppressed the planned uprising and executed Prosser and thirty of his followers, thus reaffirming the southern commitment to slavery and white supremacy.

GLOSSARY

mercenary   Someone, such as a soldier or a farmer, who cares nothing for principles or values and will fight or trade for money. (pp. 174, 180)

outflanked   When two armies face each other in battle, one of them may send forces to the right or left of the opposing lines. If the first army then successfully attacks from the side, it has outflanked its opponent. The British troops routinely outflanked the Americans because the British were better-trained soldiers and able to move more quickly in large numbers. (p. 176)

redeeming currency   Before modern times, when a government issued currency, the currency represented a certain actual amount of gold and silver. To redeem a currency, the government would purchase the notes for gold or silver, or for some other paper money backed by another source. This maintained the value of the currency by creating confidence that people who held the notes could, if they wanted, actually get the promised amount of gold or silver for it. Also, the government would accept this currency in payment of taxes due, thus giving it value. (p. 178)

republican virtue   This is a trait that is embodied in individuals who act collectively in the interests of all. Thomas Paine, Benjamin Rush, and other Patriots believed that each citizen had a responsibility to contribute to the good of the republic. (p. 187)

classical liberal   Classical liberals argued that each individual should be free to act in an enlightened manner according to his or her self-interest. As a result, they believed government should not restrain trade, control prices, or have any right to take away personal property. (p. 188)

manumission   When masters set their slaves free, they literally "let go from the hand," or manumitted, them. (p. 190)

self-purchase   One way for slaves to gain their own freedom was to work for wages and then use that money to buy themselves from their masters. (p. 191)

deists   Deists believed that God created the universe and set it in motion, then let it run without interference and according to natural laws. (p. 193)

IDENTIFICATION

Identify by filling in the blanks.

1. When the assembly seized control of Virginia, the governor, Lord Dunmore, took refuge on a warship, declared martial law, and offered freedom to any slave who would serve against the Americans in the _____ . (p. 170)

2. Thomas Paine was the author of _____ , a political pamphlet that encouraged Americans to break their ties with the king and declare their independence as a republic. (p. 172)

3. When they attacked Trenton on Christmas night in 1776, Washington and the Americans encountered German mercenaries, called _____ , who had long fought for the British. (p. 174)

4. The "financier of the Revolution" who tried to keep the financial system of Congress afloat was _____ , a Philadelphia merchant. (p. 178)

5. The Prussian military officer who instituted a standardized system of drilling and maneuver at Valley Forge was _____ . (p. 179)

6. One of the three American diplomats who negotiated the Treaty of Alliance with France in 1778 was _____ , who was already famous in the new United States as a publisher, scientist, Enlightenment thinker, and politician from Philadelphia. (p. 179)

7. The British Minister who had initiated the war in 1775, launched England's initial grand strategy to defeat the Americans in 1776, then attempted to negotiate a constitutional settlement in 1778 in order to forestall the Treaty of Alliance was _____ . (p. 180).

8. The French aristocrat who aided the Continental army as a member of Washington's staff, encouraged the French to offer stronger military support, and then led forces in Virginia against Cornwallis was _____ . (p. 182)

9. The British troops under General Cornwallis surrendered to American and French troops in October 1781 at _____ . (p. 182).

10. In 1783 Washington had to use his personal authority to thwart a potentially dangerous mutiny among his officers at _____ . (p. 187)

11. Opponents of the Patriot cause were called either Loyalists or _____ . (p. 189)

12. After thousands of slaves had been freed or escaped to freedom in the Revolutionary Era, a reaction occurred when a planned slave revolt under the leadership of _____ was discovered and prevented. (p. 191)

SKILL-BUILDING EXERCISE

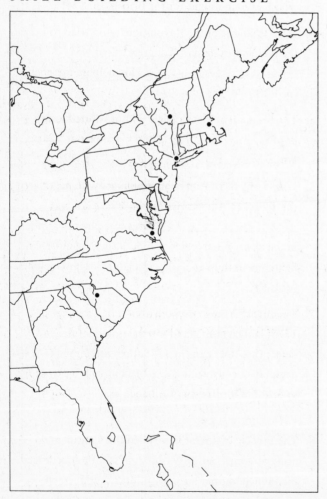

On the map locate the following places: Boston, New York, Philadelphia, Saratoga, Brandywine Creek, Camden, and Yorktown.

DOCUMENT EXERCISES

American Voices

Partisan Warfare in the South—Moses Hall

As the British pushed their campaign to take the South, an ongoing struggle between Loyalists and Patriots erupted into a brutal civil war. In this account, an American officer describes violations against the rules of war, and outright brutality and criminal behavior that occurred in the southern campaign. The internecine guerilla character of the war, fought among families, neighbors, and sometimes brothers—many of whom were amateur soldiers—on different sides over who was right and moral inflamed the passions of both sides and contributed to the loss of control over the troops. Once the fighting began, however, it took on the self-justifying dynamics of a blood feud.

As you read "Partisan Warfare in the South," ask yourself the following questions:

1. What were or are some of the traditional conventions of war that were disregarded or violated in this case?

2. How does one explain the degree of brutality here?

3. How did the issues and the nature of the war intensify feelings and make it harder to control emotions?

African-American Freemen from North Carolina Petition Congress

In this remarkable document, three African-American citizens of the United States, disregarding the prejudice against them, go over the heads of the state legislature and petition the Federal Government in 1788 to protect their rights. Though the right to petition was an accepted right of all citizens—that after all is what the colonists did against Great Britain—the actual process by which this was to be done remained unclear. By implication the Federal Government, through the Bill of Rights, was to safeguard the individual liberty of every citizen of the country. But the role of the legislature or the judiciary in this process remained, in 1797, woefully unclear. Nevertheless, Congress would have accepted the petition, and perhaps formulated legislation to protect free blacks had not political pressure from southern representatives compelled Congress to refuse to accept it.

As you read "African-American Freemen from North Carolina Petition Congress," ask yourself the following questions:

1. How do the tactics, arguments, and presentation of evidence by these former slaves reflect the political and legal awareness of free African-Americans in the 1780s?

2. What outlet did the freemen have to redress their grievances?

3. What do the efforts of three former slaves say about self-identity and opportunities for free blacks in the South? How did they respond?

4. How did the officials of North Carolina expect such a policy to "safeguard the institution of slavery"?

American Lives

The Enigma of Benedict Arnold

Throughout the war, many Patriots—from farmers and merchants to soldiers and officers in the Continental army—struggled with the conflict between civic duty and private self-interest. By 1778, Benedict Arnold had established a distinguished record of service in the Patriot cause, rising to be a major general in the Continental army. He then fell into debt and became involved in shady financial schemes. Facing congressional investigation and a possible court martial, he switched sides and sought fame and fortune in the service of the British army. Arnold committed treason not because he thought the British cause the right one or because he was disgusted with Congress and embittered at his lack of recognition; rather, he selfishly sought his own material advancement. For him, self-interest prevailed over civic duty, earning him the disdain and contempt of both sides in the war.

As you read "The Enigma of Benedict Arnold," ask yourself the following questions:

1. What were Benedict Arnold's military achievements for the Patriot cause? What does his behavior reveal about his character?

2. What hint does his behavior as commander in Philadelphia in 1778 provide as to the real reason behind his subsequent treason?

3. What constitutes Benedict Arnold's specific act of treason?

4. What does Benedict Arnold's career as a British general tell you about his military skills? Why, in spite of his success, was he never popular among the British?

SELF-TEST

Multiple Choice

1. King George responded to the Olive Branch Petition by:
   a. sending diplomats to America to begin negotiations.
   b. receiving the petition, considering it carefully, and deciding that he must continue the military effort to put down the rebellion.
   c. ceasing hostilities while trying to figure out what to do.
   d. refusing to receive the petition and issuing a Proclamation for Suppressing Rebellion and Sedition.

2. The British had an advantage over the Americans in *all* of the following areas *except*:
   a. professionally trained soldiers.
   b. supplies and weaponry.
   c. support of the local population.
   d. financial resources.

3. The Articles of Confederation are best characterized as a:
   a. failure in foreign affairs.
   b. success in managing western lands and establishing the framework of a dynamic society.
   c. success in managing the financial affairs of the nation.
   d. success in negotiating grievances among states.

4. Despite overwhelming superiority, the British failed to win during the first year of the the war for *all* of the following reasons *except* that:
   a. General William Howe had the authority to negotiate and wanted the surrender of the rebels rather than their defeat.
   b. they were restrained by distance from their source of supplies.
   c. they evaded the rebels, hoping to wear them down.
   d. they failed to encourage Loyalists to support the British army.

5. General Howe advanced on Philadelphia in 1777 rather than reinforcing Burgoyne up north because he:
   a. believed that by taking the capital he would draw Washington into a battle and end the war with a major victory.
   b. believed that if Philadelphia were taken, the middle colonies would fall and divide New England from the South.
   c. believed that by going to Philadelphia he would force Washington to keep some troops in the middle colonies, and thus limit those that could be sent against Burgoyne in the north.
   d. preferred Philadelphia to New York because it had a larger Loyalist population.

6. The British lost the Battle of Saratoga for *all* of the following reasons *except*:
   a. they failed to receive support from Howe's army.
   b. the Iroquois joined the Americans.
   c. they traveled with a heavy baggage train and became bogged down in the wilderness.
   d. they faced the large forces of the American militia.

7. To finance the war, Congress did *all* of the following *except*:
   a. levy heavy taxes against the people.
   b. issue Continental loan certificates.
   c. borrow from the French and Dutch.
   d. print paper money.

8. The French alliance affected the American cause in *all* of the following ways *except*:
   a. it provided badly needed funds and improved the supply of goods to the army.
   b. the French officers and advisers eclipsed Washington as commander of the Continental army.
   c. the extra funds allowed Congress to give pensions to the officers.
   d. the French provided manpower and a navy, enabling the American-French forces to outnumber and overpower the British.

9. The military defeat of Cornwallis's troops involved *all* of the following strategies *except*:
   a. Cornwallis moved north into Virginia and then marched east onto the York peninsula.
   b. Washington's and Rochambeau's armies marched south from New York in the fall.
   c. the Americans won a great pitched battle outside of Yorktown.
   d. the French fleet gained control of the waters of Chesapeake Bay, cornering the British by sea.

10. The terms of the treaties of Paris and Versailles in 1783 included *all* of the following *except*:
    a. the return of Canada to the French.
    b. the granting to the Americans of control over the land between the Appalachians and the Mississippi River.
    c. recognition of the United States of America by Britain.
    d. the transfer of Florida from Britain to Spain.

11. American women contributed to the war effort by doing *all* of the following *except*:
    a. supervising hired laborers and slaves.
    b. producing increased amounts of homespun.
    c. making clothing for the troops.
    d. involving themselves in politics.

12. During the Revolution thousands of slaves gained their freedom in *all* of the following ways *except*:
    a. seeking refuge behind British lines.
    b. striking bargains with their masters that if they remained loyal they would be freed after the war.
    c. manumission by their masters, who felt slavery was a contradiction of republican ideals.
    d. escaping to Canada.

13. Which of the following did *not* characterize the new republican religious order?
    a. attempts to separate church and state
    b. the increased prevalence of deism

c. the increase of secularism across society
d. elimination of religious requirements for voting or political office.

Short Essays

Answer the following in a brief paragraph.

1. Why did Thomas Paine write the pamphlet *Common Sense*, and what did he argue in it? (pp. 171–172)

2. Why did the first year of the war go so badly for the Americans? (pp. 173–175)

3. How did the victory at Saratoga perfectly manifest British weaknesses and American strengths in the war as a whole? (pp. 176–178)

4. Why was the Continental Congress so unsuccessful in financing the war? (pp. 178–179)

5. What were France's motives in deciding to join the Americans in the war against Great Britain? Which motive was most important? (pp. 179–180)

6. Compare and contrast how the military and civilians tried to live up to the ideals of republicanism. (pp. 187–189)

7. How did republican ideals affect the role of women in American society? (pp. 188–189)

8. How were Loyalists treated by Patriots and state governments during the war? (pp. 178, 189–190)

9. Was the American Revolution radical, moderate, or conservative? (pp. 189–193)

10. Did the Revolution increase or decrease the power of organized religion in the United States? (pp. 192–193)

A N S W E R S

Chapter Précis

1. Olive Branch Petition
2. Lord Dunmore
3. Benjamin Franklin
4. *A Summary View of the Rights of British America;* tyrant
5. Trenton, New Jersey
6. William Howe
7. Brandywine Creek
8. Joseph Brant
9. Committees of Safety
10. Valley Forge

11. Lord Cornwallis

12. "just price"

13. homespun

14. Gabriel Prosser

15. Thomas Jefferson

Identification

1. Ethiopian Regiment

2. *Common Sense*

3. Hessians

4. Robert Morris

5. Baron von Steuben

6. Benjamin Franklin

7. Lord North

8. the Marquis de Lafayette

9. Yorktown

10. Newburgh, New York

11. Tories

12. Gabriel Prosser

Skill-Building Exercise

For New York, Philadelphia, Saratoga, and Brandywine Creek, see Map 6.1 (text p. 175). For Camden (N.C.) and Yorktown, see Map 6.2 (text p. 181). For Boston, see Map 5.3 (text p. 160).

Self-Test

Multiple Choice

1. d	6. b	10. a
2. c	7. a	11. d
3. b	8. b	12. d
4. c	9. c	13. c
5. a		

Short Essays

1. Thomas Paine sensed that the American people needed to be convinced of the legitimacy of breaking from the Crown. Paine equated monarchy with tyranny and argued that the people should rule themselves in a republican system.

2. Washington had had no time to train the ragtag, militia-based Continental army. As a result, the Americans were no match for the professionally trained army that the British were able to put in the field. Time and time again Washington's forces were outflanked and forced to retreat. Only their speed of retreat and luck kept them from being caught and forced to surrender. At this time Washington had also not yet formulated his defensive and evasive strategy.

3. The British command was timid and slow in bringing the war to the Americans. The British easily outflanked the Americans at Fort Ticonderoga but failed to capture the army. Overelaborate strategy and the need to wait for slow baggage trains hindered the British effort. The Americans relied on surprise, fighting from the forest, and the participation of local militia to increase the size of their force.

4. Having initiated a revolutionary war based on the grievance of unjust taxation, Patriot politicians were reluctant to tax the people directly. Instead the Continental Congress requisitioned funds from the states but received little. The Congress borrowed money from the French and the Dutch and sold loan certificates to wealthy Americans. But as costs escalated beyond available funds, their resources ran out and Congress was forced to print paper money to finance the war effort.

5. The French sought revenge against Great Britain for their defeat in the Seven Year's War, which resulted in the loss of Canada and some islands in the Caribbean. They wanted to regain lost territory and reestablish a naval presence on the North Atlantic. In strengthening the challenge to British rule in North America and severing its lucrative Empire, the French also sought to spread British forces thin and reduce Great Britain's power in international affairs. Revenge was their primary motive.

6. Many Americans considered private property to be the basis of happiness and self-interested action to be healthy behavior. Republicanism argued that for government by the people to work, the people had to exercise public virtue by acting selflessly and contributing to the public good. For men, this conflict between self-interest and public virtue existed in both civilian and military life. Hardships in the field led many soldiers to mutiny, and officers demanded pensions. Economic hardship convinced many civilians to act in their own self-interest rather than contribute to the war. Used to self-sacrifice, women experienced little tension between self-interest and republican virtue.

7. Women were not included in the Founding Fathers' discussions of liberty and justice for all. Women were expected to continue to carry out traditional family roles and defer to their husbands or male relatives in matters of politics and public life. Nevertheless, they

were affected by the war and contributed to the war effort. During the war women organized drives to gather goods for the army, produced homespun cloth and clothes for the soldiers, supervised workers, and ran the farms in their husbands' or sons' absence. These extra efforts increased women's self-confidence and self-esteem.

8. Committees of Safety forced people to take loyalty oaths or face penalties, fines, and jail terms. Some formed Patriot groups and engaged in direct actions against Tories, forcing many to leave their homes. Governments often rented out or confiscated and resold Loyalist property, though in most places property was confiscated only to the extent that creditors needed to be paid off, and the rest reverted to widows or kin of the Loyalists.

9. After the exodus of the Loyalists the court system maintained the respect for property rights, and thus confiscated a limited amount of property. There was, therefore, no significant redistribution of wealth. Those Loyalists who left were replaced by others who rose up from the middling classes who were more entrepreneurial in their outlook. Likewise, women and slaves mostly remained where they had been before the war. Nevertheless, the new focus on rights, and the new republican language of social interaction assured that the new governments would be republican. These ideas, which were radical for the day, would in time radically transform American society. In the 1780s, they only had a moderate effect on American society.

10. The effect of the Revolution on organized religion varied from state to state. In general, though, state legislatures passed laws that made all churches equal before the law and gave support to no particular church. This decreased the role of established churches.

CHAPTER 7

The New Political Order 1776–1800

★   ★   ★

CHAPTER PRÉCIS

Creating New Institutions, 1776–1787

pp. 198–207

The State Constitutions: How Much Democracy?

While the Revolutionary War raged, politicians within the new states debated over how democratic the new republican state constitutions should be. Radical Patriots wanted state government to directly reflect the people. They formed extremely democratic governments, such as that in Pennsylvania in which there was universal suffrage for white males and a unicameral legislature. Moderates and conservatives, lead by John Adams, feared that too much democracy would lead to democratic legislative tyranny and sought to develop institutions that would provide a mix of functions and interests, which would check and balance each other, and thus prevent the tyranny of one group over others. In various states, suffrage restrictions based on property, direct election of a governor with veto power, the division of legislatures into two bodies, and government into three branches thwarted the unchecked power of democracy. In doing so, they established democratic republican governments, which would become a model for the federal Constitution.

While the Revolution democratized American governments by broadening suffrage and making representation more proportional, it did little to change traditional gender assumptions that maintained government and law as the domain of men. Elite women were quick to see the contradictions in republicanism, and argued for increased public rights and equality before the law, while challenging the assumptions

1. John Adams sought to make state government less democratic by making its power and functions more

_____ . (pp. 198–199)

2. _____ argued in "On the Equality of the Sexes" that women are intellectually equal to men and need only training and education to show it. (p. 201)

upon which women's secondary status was based. Some women even argued that women should play the important role of establishing the moral basis of social order through the education of their children. Nevertheless, though some states liberalized property laws for women and expanded access to public schools for young women, women remained second-class citizens unable to participate in the political life of the nation.

The Articles of Confederation

The Articles of Confederation, ratified in 1781, cautiously established the first national government by confirming the operations of the Confederation Congress, which, since its formation as the Continental Congress, had formed an Army and Navy for defense, declared independence and war, established diplomatic relations with other countries, and adjudicated disputes among states. The Congress lacked, however, the power to tax, and had no power to enforce financial requisitions from the states to support their operations. Faced by bankruptcy and lacking any national domain, the Articles innovatively exerted the power they had to create and control the national domain of western lands as a means to enhance its power and ease its fiscal difficulties. By means of the Treaty of Paris and various land cessions from the states, Congress acquired control over the public lands west of the Appalachians and then established a land sale and territorial system, which facilitated the sale of western lands, western settlement, the creation of new territories, and their admission as equal new states into the Confederation. In doing so, the Articles of Confederation laid the groundwork for the creation of a dynamic expanding society and polity.

3. The _____ established a grid system to facilitate land sales and provided for the creation of three to five states north of the Ohio River. (pp. 202–203)

The Postwar Crisis

After the war, worthless currency, large state debts, and the disruption of trade plunged America into a recession. Creditors urged politicians to pass laws that would limit the use of paper money and impose higher taxes to accelerate debt repayment. In some states the debtors resisted such measures, which created even more difficult conditions for them, and prodebtor legislation was passed. However, in Massachusetts, where such legislation was not enacted, merchant and land-owner creditors in the east pressed farmer debtors in the west to the brink of bankruptcy. The farmers resisted, and a popular movement coalesced into a full-scale uprising, in which an army of disgruntled farmers challenged state authority. Though it was put down, this movement provided evidence of growing discontent.

4. In response to a postwar economic recession many states were forced to raise taxes to meet wartime indebtedness, which pressed hard on many farmers and debtors. For relief they advocated the passage of _____ legislation, which protected them from eastern creditors and increased the supply of money. (p. 206)

The Constitution of 1787 pp. 207–214

The Rise of a Nationalist Faction

In response to Shays's Rebellion, the lack of power of the central government, and the financial weakness and prodebtor policies of several states, a group of nationalists decided to take action. Many had been

5. In 1786 a group of nationalists called for reform of the Articles of Confederation at a commercial convention in _____ . (p. 207)

military officers, government officials, or diplomats during the Revolution and had a national rather than state view of politics. They wanted a national tariff and taxation policy. Though only a few delegates showed up, those present proposed that a new convention be called to revise the Articles of Confederation.

The Philadelphia Convention

At the Constitutional convention, which met in Philadelphia in 1787, James Madison introduced the Virginia Plan, which argued for a republican government in which three separate branches checked and balanced each other in order to maintain order and limit democracy. After a series of compromises concerning representation, the plan was approved and offered to the people for ratification.

6. In opposition to the Virginia Plan, delegates from small states at the Philadelphia Convention supported the New Jersey Plan, which was introduced by _____ . (p. 209)

The Debate over Ratification

The debate between Federalists and anti-Federalists over ratification glossed over and left unresolved not only fundamental questions concerning the real relationship between the federal government and state governments (although Madison clearly stated that the federal government would have supremacy), but also a number of procedural issues concerning functions, operations, and power of the three branches. The Federalists, who were supported by many nationally known leaders who had been active in the Revolution, argued for a stronger federal government and assured opponents that the checks and balances within the system would safeguard liberty. The anti-Federalists were a diverse group who distrusted central power and mercantile elite rule and feared that it would encroach on state powers. After a series of very close votes the Constitution was ratified by nine of the thirteen states and the new national government went into effect in 1789.

7. Supporters of the Constitution such as James Madison, John Jay, and Alexander Hamilton published a series of articles called _____ . (p. 211)

The Constitution Implemented

As the first president, George Washington established precedents for how the executive branch would operate. He set up executive departments under the control of secretaries; they were members of his cabinet, his body of advisers. The organization of the judicial department into a Supreme Court, three circuit courts, and thirteen district courts was clarified in the Judiciary Act of 1789. A Bill of Rights, as demanded by the anti-Federalists, was also passed, ensuring broad political support for the new government.

8. The first secretary of state, an experienced diplomat, was _____ . (p. 214)

The Political Crisis of the 1790s   pp. 214–225

The general wording of the new Constitution, however, still left it open to different interpretations concerning critical national powers. When, at the beginning of the Washington administration, Alexander Hamilton moved to establish a national financial policy, a series of increasingly acrimonious political disagreements ensued. These divisions, based on different opinions of how democratic the new republic should be, were exacerbated by conflicting opinions on the French Revolution, which broke out in 1789.

Hamilton's Program

Alexander Hamilton believed, like other supporters of the Constitution, that strong central government must rest on a solid financial foundation. He sought to do this by redeeming the credit of the Confederation, creating a national debt, and establishing a national bank that could regulate or stimulate the economy. In particular he hoped the government would stimulate manufacturing so that the United States could achieve economic self-sufficiency. These powers, he argued, were implied by the Constitution when it empowered Congress to make all laws "necessary and proper" to run the country. Hamilton articulated a "loose" interpretation of the Constitution.

Jefferson's Vision

To many observers, these actions exceeded the powers articulated by the Constitution. Arguing that Congress could only do what the Constitution specifically said it could do, "strict" constructionists opposed Hamilton's schemes. Initially, southern opponents accepted Hamilton's plan only in return for relocating the new national capitol on the Potomac River. But as Hamilton's programs were instituted, his opponents began to disagree not only on how to interpret the Constitution, but also on what kind of republic of yeomen farmers who ruled themselves though the state governments. Democracy, he believed, flourished when economic activity and political power was dispersed and abundant land was available for western settlement. Jefferson feared that a strong central government run by a ruling elite would corrupt and endanger democracy by contracting a national debt and increasing taxation of citizens, both of which would undermine individual autonomy and liberty.

War and Politics

War in Europe increased prices for grain and cotton and set in motion a boom in farming and trade. The American merchant fleet quickly became one of the largest in the world. However, this increase in trade brought more Americans directly in contact with the belligerents, threatening to embroil the United States in a war. Americans generally favored the republicanism of the French Revolution, but conservative Federalists were appalled by the execution of the king, political terror against members of the aristocracy, and the abandonment of Christianity. The Federalists increasingly favored a pro-British neutrality, whereas the Republicans favored neutrality with a French bias. For five years American politicians maneuvered between pro-British and pro-French policies. In response to their apparently pro-French actions, the British began seizing American ships. To avert war, Jay's Treaty was negotiated, securing a pro-British policy, with considerable criticism from Democratic-Republicans.

Meanwhile, a domestic rebellion against new taxes imposed on whiskey erupted in Pennsylvania. Justifying their actions with the ideas of the French Revolution, armed rebels resisted government tax collec-

9. Hamilton's three-tiered program to revive the finances of the United States involved the paying off of old government securities, the _____ of state debts incurred during the war, and the chartering of a national bank. (pp. 215–216)

tors. To uphold the power of the federal government, Washington raised an army and suppressed the rebellion.

The Rise of Parties

Before the election of 1796, parties formalized their organization and mobilized support among voters. This marked the emergence of two political parties: the Federalists, who supported a strong central government and a pro-British foreign policy, and the Republicans, a diverse coalition of farmers and southerners who supported the rights of states and a limited central government. In the national elections, a flaw in the electoral college process resulted in the election of John Adams, a Federalist, as president and Thomas Jefferson, a Republican, as vice-president, creating a divided administration.

After the election of 1796, French arrogance toward diplomats of the Adams administration increased the danger of war against France, but Adams maintained neutrality while allowing American ships to help the British attack French shipping. Thus, America found itself in a quasi-war against France.

The Crisis of 1798–1800

To prevent partisan debate, the Adams administration repressed free speech and deported foreigners, actions that alienated many Federalist supporters and increased Republican support in the election of 1800. A tie in the electoral college between Thomas Jefferson and Aaron Burr threw the election into the House of Representatives. Not until Alexander Hamilton, who was more opposed to Burr than to Jefferson, persuaded key Federalists not to vote for Burr did the election finally go to Jefferson. In spite of party strife and threats of civil war, constitutional procedures ultimately worked, allowing a peaceful transfer of power. The success of the Republicans and their desire to return to the promises of the Declaration of Independence and a strict interpretation of the Constitution amounted to, as Jefferson called it, the "Revolution of 1800."

10. John Adams was incensed when three agents of the French government attempted to solicit a bribe from American diplomats. Since Adams wished to keep the identities of the agents secret, he referred to the incident as the _____ . (p. 224)

11. In 1798 the Adams administration, through the _____ , abridged the rights of free speech by prohibiting malicious criticism of administration policies and limiting the rights of foreigners. (pp. 224–225)

EXPANDED TIMELINE

1776   Declaration of Independence
        Pennsylvania's democratic constitution
        Although popular sovereignty was established in the Declaration of Independence and everyone assumed that the national government of the new United States would be republican, it was up to the states to decide how their own governments would be constitutionally organized. Radicals in Pennsylvania offered the most democratic plan, creating a unicameral assembly that ruled without a council or governor.

        John Adams, *Thoughts on Government*
        John Adams offered a more conservative system,

which was republican but less democratic. He wanted to emulate the mixed system of the British by establishing three separate branches of government, each with a single function; these branches would use checks and balances to restrain each other and maintain liberty. This system was instituted in Massachusetts and some other states because it was similar to the government the people were used to and limited the excesses of direct democracy.

1777   Articles of Confederation (ratified 1781)
        The Articles of Confederation created a national government centered in Congress. The Articles did not grant to the federal government the right to tax, form a judiciary, control interstate commerce, or compel the states in any way. However, they were

effective in terms of diplomacy and organizing the acquisition, surveying, and sale of western lands.

New York's conservative constitution

1779   **Judith Sargent Murray, "On the Equality of the Sexes"**
Judith Sargent Murray challenged contemporary assumptions about the inferiority of women. Women were, she argued, intellectually equal to men, but their training was less rigorous, resulting in apparent inequality. Women's equality made them fit to assume an equal position in society.

1780   **Postwar commercial recession**
Burdensome debts and
creditor-debtor conflicts in states
The loss of monopolies and of the protection of the Navigation Acts left Americans with few markets after the war. In addition, states were overburdened by debts accumulated during the war years. This compelled them to raise taxes and limit paper money, putting the squeeze on debtors. As creditors pressured debtors for payment, the debtors sought and sometimes received legal protection from the state.

1781   **Robert Morris superintendent of finance**
Bank of North America
Rhode Island vetoes national import duty
Robert Morris became superintendent of the finances of the Articles of Confederation and, shocked at its financial weakness, sought to undertake a program to improve the financial stability and authority of the national government. His plan, which outlined Alexander Hamilton's program of a decade later, was stymied, however, by Congress's inability to raise revenues from taxes. When Morris sought to raise revenues by a national import tariff or duty, Rhode Island rejected the plan, thus preventing the program from being implemented. The Articles of Confederation, as a result, continued to lack any financial basis upon which to establish authority.

1784   **Ordinance outlines policy for new states**
In its search for funds, the Articles of Confederation government turned to western lands. After considerable efforts, it gained control of western lands from individual states, initiated a policy to acquire lands from the native Americans, organized and supervised the sale and settlement of western lands to generate revenue, and provided for the orderly organization of western territories and their admission as equal states into the Union.

1785   **Land Ordinance sets up survey system**
The Land Ordinance of 1785 establishes the grid system of surveying western lands and legal rules to facilitate land sales.

Jefferson's Notes on the State of Virginia

1786   **Annapolis commercial convention**
Shays's Rebellion

Organized resistance to procreditor policies occurred in Massachusetts, where prodebtor legislation was not passed. Farmers and artisans, unable to pay their debts, refused to let creditors foreclose on debtors and organized meetings and an army to resist efforts by the state to enforce procreditor laws. Shays's rebellion, under the leadership of Daniel Shays, was overwhelmed by cold weather and political pressure. The rebellion did, however, convince some nationalist observers of the chaos that could result from a weak central government. To amend the Articles of Confederation, they convened a commercial meeting at Annapolis, Maryland, and then called for a constitutional convention in Philadelphia the following summer.

1787   **Northwest Ordinance**
Following up on the Land Ordinance of 1784, the Northwest Ordinance provided for the sale of lands, the establishment of territories, and admission of three to five free states north of the Ohio River.

Philadelphia convention
Madison's "nationalist" Virginia Plan
At this meeting to reform the Articles of Confederation, the Virginians offered a comprehensive restructuring of the government in a proposal known as the Virginia Plan. The Virginia Plan gave the national government supremacy over the states, and it called for three branches of government that would balance and keep one another in check. This radical revision was reshaped by numerous amendments designed to placate various interest groups.

1788–
1789   **Ratification conventions**
The nationalists, who called themselves Federalists, argued that a powerful central government would strengthen the United States and restore public credit and property rights. Their opponents, who called themselves anti-Federalists, feared central power, the control of government by mercantile elites, and the weakening of state governments.

The Federalist (Jay, Madison, Hamilton)
Many of these fears were answered by the supporters of the Constitution in *The Federalist*. James Madison argued that fears of central government were unfounded. The system of checks and balances would control government, thus preserving liberty, and the size and diversity of America would require the formation of factions, which would be numerous and prevent any one from gaining dominance. In a series of very close debates at ratification conventions, the Constitution passed and became law.

1789   **George Washington becomes first president**
Washington established executive departments and appointed secretaries of foreign affairs, finance, and war to run them.

Judiciary Act establishes federal court system

The Judiciary Act set up federal judicial districts in each state.

Outbreak of the French Revolution

The French Revolution, inspired in part by the American Revolution, overthrew the monarchy in France, a development with which most Americans sympathized.

National tariff; aid to American shipping

1790 **Alexander Hamilton's program: redemption and assumption**

Alexander Hamilton, secretary of the treasury, offered a three-part program to restore public finances. The federal government would pay off Revolutionary Era securities and bonds, assume the debts of the states, and establish a national bank with the power to tax and issue currency.

1791 **Bill of Rights ratified**

The first ten amendments to the Constitution were passed to mollify anti-Federalist fears that the central government would encroach on the liberties and rights of the people.

1792 **Debate over Bank of United States**
Mary Wollstonecraft, *A Vindication of the Rights of Woman*

Women remained a marginal group, as men ignored the comments of Judith Sargent Murray. A more radical critique, written by the Englishwoman Mary Wollstonecraft, argued for the legal and political equality of women. Though she gained a widespread hearing, many Americans were shocked by Wollstonecraft's sexually free lifestyle. Most men did not understand her argument.

First French Republic declared; Louis XVI executed (1793)

1793 **Democratic-Republican party founded**
War between Britain and France
Washington's Proclamation of Neutrality

In France, the change from a constitutional monarchy to a republican Directory that executed the king polarized American opinion. Federalists agreed with the British that this went too far toward anarchy. Meanwhile, Republicans under Madison and Jefferson remained sympathetic, though concerned about the radical direction of the Revolution. When Britain went to war against France, Washington and the Federalists tried to remain neutral; this became difficult when the British began seizing American ships.

1794 **Whiskey Rebellion**

While national politics became polarized, some people in Pennsylvania reacted to the passing of national taxes by forming an assembly and arming themselves. President Washington raised an army and put down this rebellion.

1795 **Jay's Treaty**

To avert war with Britain, John Jay was sent to negotiate a treaty that established American neutrality in exchange for allowing the British to seize French goods on American ships and compensating the British for losses during the Revolution. In return the British agreed to withdraw their troops from forts in the Northwest, stop supporting the Indians, and redress American merchants' losses incurred through illegal British seizure of their goods.

1796 **John Adams elected president**

Two organized parties offered slates of candidates in the 1796 election. The Federalist John Adams was elected president, but Thomas Jefferson, a Republican, was elected vice-president, creating a divided administration.

1797 **XYZ Affair**

1798 **Undeclared war against France**

In response to America's pro-British policy, the French began to attack American shipping. John Adams's attempts to negotiate were rebuffed, and the Americans incensed at French arrogance, as exposed in the XYZ affair, joined the British in attacking French shipping. Though Adams averted full-scale war, the United States was involved in a quasi-war against France for two years.

Alien, Sedition, and Naturalization acts Kentucky and Virginia resolutions

Adams sought to quell opposition by pushing through the Alien and Sedition Acts, which restricted foreigners and limited free speech by prohibiting criticism of the administration's policies. The Republicans attacked these acts as encroachments on states' powers and asserted the rights of the states in the Kentucky and Virginia resolutions.

1800 **Jefferson elected in "Revolution of 1800"**

Taking advantage of the opposition to the Alien and Sedition Acts and Federalist war policies, the Republicans carried the election of 1800. However, Aaron Burr of New York and Thomas Jefferson of Virginia tied in the electoral college vote for president, throwing the election into Congress. After numerous votes and a growing threat of civil war, Alexander Hamilton convinced several Federalists to let Jefferson be elected. Constitutional procedures thus led the nation through a political stalemate and permitted the peaceful transfer of power. Jefferson called this "the Revolution of 1800" because the ascendancy of the Republicans ensured a return to the initial principles of the Declaration of Independence and the Constitution.

GLOSSARY

unicameral A one-house assembly in which legislators are elected who directly represent the people is referred to as unicameral. Considered efficient and democratic, this type of assembly can pass legislation more quickly and do so with less consideration. Pennsylvania had a unicameral assembly during the Revolution; only Nebraska has such a state legislature today. (p. 198)

mixed government   John Adams's plan called for three branches of government, with each representing one function: executive, legislative, or judicial. Their interaction would maintain a balance of power and ensure the legitimacy of governmental procedures. (p. 198)

bicameral   A bicameral congress or assembly has two houses, usually a house of representatives and a senate. Different qualifications, procedures, term lengths, and means of election differentiate the two and ensure that each piece of legislation is reviewed and debated by two different groups. (p. 199)

checks and balances   Vesting different functions and procedures in different branches of government allows each branch to limit the actions of the others. This ensures an equal balance of governmental functions and maximizes liberty. (p. 199)

franchise   In the early national period, the franchise, the right to vote, was limited by property restrictions, but later all white men over age twenty-one were given the vote. The term *suffrage* also refers to the right to vote. (p. 201)

tariff   A tariff is a tax added to the cost of an imported item, raising its price and making local products more desirable. Tariffs are intended to give a price advantage to domestic producers over foreign producers. (p. 202)

electoral college   As set forth in the Constitution, the president was to be elected indirectly. A group of electors, usually politicians, were appointed each election year, to vote for the president and vice-president. This was done to give the states some power in the choosing of a president and to make the vote more indirect. Because the president would be elected by state votes, rather than by the popular vote, even close popular votes would become clear majorities in the electoral college. (p. 209)

cabinet   Washington organized bureaucratic departments to carry out the work of the executive branch and appointed secretaries to run those departments. These secretaries, who constituted a small group of the president's close advisers on matters of policy, is called his cabinet. (p. 214)

national debt   By borrowing money from the people through the sale of bonds, a government goes into debt. Hamilton believed that drawing on this source of capital to finance government would create ties of loyalty between the government and the financial community. (p. 215)

assumption   Hamilton wanted the federal government to assume the debts of the states by buying the debts and repaying the creditors. The national government quickly acquired a national debt while relieving the state governments of their debts. (p. 216)

strict interpretation   In a strict interpretation of the Constitution, the national government can do only what is explicitly stated in the Constitution, leaving to the states all powers not expressly mentioned. Jefferson and Madison argued for this interpretation. (p. 217)

loose interpretation   In a loose interpretation, all powers that are necessary and proper to carry out the functions of government are implied in the Constitution. Hamilton argued for this interpretation. (p. 217)

laissez faire   *Laissez faire* means "leave alone" in French. Adam Smith argued that traditional mercantilist intervention in the economy supports inefficiency and inhibits personal enterprise. A government should let the economy operate according to the principles of open competition, prices being determined by supply and demand. He also believed in free trade between nations. Hamilton and subsequent American policymakers argued against free trade and sought to protect American manufacturing from competition from the British. They advocated tariffs to protect American markets and governmental investment to stimulate development. (p. 217)

faction   A faction is a small political group or alliance organized around a single issue or person. Factions often become the basis for political parties. In the eighteenth century factions were considered dangerous. (p. 217)

yeomen farmers   Jefferson believed that American society was based on the work of the independent yeomen farmers who owned their land and planted crops for a market. (p. 219)

party   A party is an organized political movement that establishes a platform, holds caucuses to select a slate of candidates, and runs campaigns. (p. 223)

judicial review   The idea that the Supreme Court has the power to review laws passed by Congress and determine whether they are constitutional is referred to as judicial review. In the first years of the republic this aspect of the Supreme Court's powers was untested. (p. 225)

states' rights   This is an interpretation of the Constitution which argues that the states hold the ultimate sovereignty and have power over the federal government. It was expressed in the Virginia and Kentucky resolutions and formed the basis for resistance by the South against attempts to control slavery. (p. 225)

IDENTIFICATION

Identify by filling in the blanks.

1. The author of *Thoughts on Government*, a treatise on the formation of state constitutions, was

   _____ . (p. 199)

2. A 1776 law inadvertently gave the vote to widows and single women of property in the state of _____ until it was rescinded in 1807. (p. 201)

3. A radical view of women's rights was articulated by the English republican author _____ in *A Vindication of the Rights of Woman*. (p. 201)

4. _____ tried to organize the national government's finances under the Articles of Confederation by creating a national debt and establishing a national bank. (p. 202)

5. The Ordinance of 1784, which made provisions for the admission of new states in the western territories, was written by _____ . (p. 202)

6. In 1786, _____ led a prodebtor revolt against the government of Massachusetts. (p. 206)

7. Thomas Jefferson missed the Philadelphia convention of 1787 because he was serving as the American minister to _____ . (p. 208)

8. People who opposed the ratification of the new Constitution because they feared a strong central government called themselves _____ . (p. 210)

9. As part of the constitutional compromise over slavery, Congress was denied the power to ban the slave trade for _____ years after ratification of the Constitution. (p. 210)

10. _____ of Massachusetts, who had been an influential leader of the patriot movement in Boston before and during the Revolutionary War, joined the Shaysites in opposing the new Constitution. (p. 212)

11. The author of the "Report on the Public Credit" in 1790 and first secretary of the treasury was _____ . (p. 215)

12. The Scottish economist who advocated a government policy of *laissez faire* in his famous book of 1776, *The Wealth of Nations*, was _____ . (p. 217)

13. Those who adopted a _____ interpretation of the Constitution based their argument that Congress should make "all laws which shall be necessary and proper" on Article I, Section 8. (p. 217)

14. When three agents of the _____ government insulted American diplomats by soliciting a loan and demanding a bribe, Adams dubbed the episode the XYZ affair. (p. 224)

15. The man who was prevented from becoming president after he had tied with Thomas Jefferson in the electoral college in 1800 was _____ . (p. 225)

SKILL-BUILDING EXERCISE

This map shows the geographic pattern of votes at the district level for and against ratification of the Constitution and suggests that delegates from seaboard areas near commercial cities supported it while those from rural backcountry areas were against it. Aside from regional large and small state frictions, what other factors account for the pervasive opposition of backcountry people to the Constitution? Drawing from previous maps in the text that showed the patterns of ethnic diversity, land disputes, or military action in colonial America, examine the various motives which fueled this backcountry opposition (see Maps 4.1, 4.3, 4.6, 6.1, 6.2).

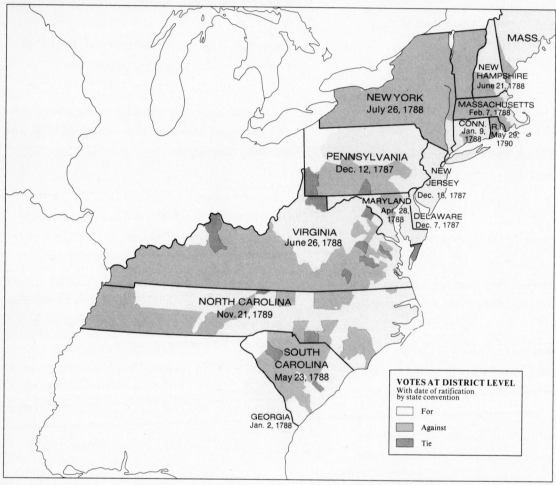

DOCUMENT EXERCISES

American Voices

A Farmer Praises the Constitution— Jonathan Smith

Concerned about the implications of Shays's Rebellion, this farmer expresses his support for the Constitution, which he hopes will cure the disorders of excessive democracy. For Smith, the ratification of the Constitution is the fruition of the effort that was begun by sending delegates to the constitutional convention in 1787.

As you read "A Farmer Praises the Constitution," ask yourself the following questions:

1. What aspect of Shays's Rebellion worried this farmer?

2. On what previous civic experience was the farmer basing his judgment of the new Constitution?

3. Is Smith aware that he is supporting a position not held by the majority of farmers? What arguments does he use to persuade other farmers to support the Constitution?

Hamilton's Funding Scheme Attacked, 1790—A Pennsylvania Farmer

Alexander Hamilton's argument that those who owned certificates and bonds issued by the Revolutionary government should be allowed to redeem them at face value draws the ire of this farmer. For Hamilton, these are simply free-market transactions in which individuals act according to self-interest. The farmer argues that the certificates were meant for the soldiers and farmers who bought them and that the reason many later sold them was that the government's financial policies had impoverished the people. The government, therefore, had a moral obligation to reimburse the farmers rather than enriching those who had taken advantage of the farmers' distress by buying the certificates. Thus, for this farmer the course pursued by Hamilton is unjust.

As you read "Hamilton's Funding Scheme Attacked," ask yourself the following questions:

1. What different sets of ethics are in conflict here?

2. What does the farmer imply about citizenship and duty? Is he a Republican?

3. What strategy for changing Hamilton's policy does the farmer suggest?

A Federalist Attacks French Republicanism—Peter Porcupine (William Cobbett)

William Cobbett responds in this essay to an inflammatory comment in which one's loyalty to the republican cause was based on whether or not one supported the French Revolution. What angers Cobbett is the notion that any individual can determine who is and is not a republican. In doing so, such critics are moving toward the arbitrary demagoguery, which Cobbett argues is the mindset that led directly to the abuses of the French Revolution. Such a view of politics, Cobbett argues, sees all those who disagreed slightly with one as "enemies," and condemns even men like George Washington, without whose sacrifice and duty there would probably have not been a United States.

As you read "A Federalist Attacks French Republicanism," ask yourself the following questions:

1. What precipitated this strong emotional comment by Cobbett?

2. What did Cobbett argue were the dangers of radical republicanism?

3. How were the French radicals able to act in this way?

American Lives

Gouverneur Morris: An Aristocratic Liberal in a Republican Age

The career and life of Gouverneur Morris, son of a New York aristocrat, indicates how members of the colonial elite responded to the Revolution and republican social theory by shifting the basis of their leadership from lineage to personal achievement. Having good connections, Morris was able to make a considerable fortune in business, which allowed him to live like an aristocrat. Only now he claimed elite status not on the basis of who he was, but rather because he had earned it through work and achievement. His ideas reflected the values of emergent capitalism, which emphasized the free individual in the economy and promised to provide a new theory of social order based on individualism.

As you read "Gouverneur Morris," ask yourself the following questions:

1. How does one reconcile Gouverneur Morris's aristocratic beliefs and his willingness to support the Revolution?

2. What other founding fathers shared Morris's political and social views?

3. How can someone who is suspicious of majority rule and requires property to vote or act in politics advocate freedom or equal rights for all?

New Technology

Technology and Republican Values

Thomas Jefferson believed in the moral superiority of independent yeomen farmers and argued that they were the best hope for a successful democratic republic. Yet he recognized that the lack of industrial development in America threatened to make Americans subject to foreigners and became convinced of the need to develop American manufacturing. He sought to develop manufacturing without its negative consequences—the concentration of power in the hands of a few, the the impoverishment of the workers, and their living and working in horrible conditions—all of which would undermine democracy. He argued that the household, farm, and plantation could become small manufactories, providing everything that Americans needed. How slave labor on a plantation worked to support democracy Jefferson did not explain. Nor was he able to explain how a small-scale system of household production using primarily manual power could compete against large firms using water- and steam-driven engines and more efficient processes of production.

As you read "Technology and Republican Values," ask yourself the following questions:

1. Why did industrial technology tend to impoverish workers?

2. Jefferson wanted to achieve industrial production by means of farm labor. To what extent was this feasible? In what ways was it not feasible?

3. Were there any other ways to develop industry without causing the same results as in England?

SELF-TEST

Multiple Choice

1. In deciding who should rule, the answer that most state constitutions gave was:
   a. the same people who had ruled before the war.
   b. the same people, with more yeomen farmers, middling farmers, and artisans.
   c. fewer people than before the war.
   d. the same people who had ruled before the war minus the Loyalists.

2. Since the new governments would be republican, the consensus was that there should be:
   a. as much direct democracy as possible, with a unicameral house and no governor or council.
   b. very little democracy, with a strong governor and an elite council.
   c. a moderate amount of democracy, with separation of powers and checks and balances.
   d. a minimum of democracy in a mixed system limited by strict property requirements for voting.

3. The most significant achievement of the Articles of Confederation was:
   a. resolving the government's fiscal problems by raising a national tariff to raise revenues.
   b. establishing a western land policy through the land ordinances of the 1780s.
   c. maintaining democracy by carrying out the functions of government through a central legislature.
   d. initiating and carrying out the diplomacy that resulted in the Treaty of Paris in 1783.

4. The land policy of the Confederation Congress failed only in:
   a. establishing friendly relations with native Americans.
   b. persuading the states to give up their claims and place western lands in the public domain.
   c. organizing the surveying of public lands by means of a grid system.
   d. establishing procedures by which new territories in the West could become states.

5. The postwar crisis developed for *all* of the following reasons *except*:
   a. state governments were burdened by war debts and were forced to raise taxes.
   b. American trade, no longer protected by the Navigation Acts, slumped.
   c. political struggles developed between creditors and debtors.
   d. the British threatened to invade America from Canada.

6. The nationalists took *all* of the following assertive

actions to ensure the drafting of a new constitution *except*:
   a. calling for a convention in Philadelphia to consider revision of the Articles of Confederation.
   b. accepting the work of the convention and sending the Constitution to the states for ratification.
   c. specifying that the Constitution would go into effect if nine states ratified it.
   d. offering to the convention a completely different constitutional framework.

7. Who of the following was not at the Philadelphia convention?
   a. Benjamin Franklin   c. James Madison
   b. George Washington   d. John Adams

8. The Constitution offered to the states for ratification in 1787 represented a compromise on *all* of the following issues *except*:
   a. representation of the states in the two houses of Congress.
   b. representation of African-American slaves in the South.
   c. the extension of the judiciary into the states.
   d. the creation of a national government whose authority would be the supreme law of the land.

9. Who of the following former patriots was *not* an anti-Federalist?
   a. Robert Morris   c. George Mason
   b. Samuel Adams   d. Patrick Henry

10. The Federalists won ratification for *all* of the following reasons *except*:
    a. they included men who had fought in the Revolution and achieved fame and respect.
    b. they stood confidently for the future of the nation.
    c. they included many shrewd politicians who promised special favors in return for votes in state ratification fights.
    d. they were able to organize effectively, pay for campaign events, and buy newspaper space.

11. The immediate impact of the passage of the Bill of Rights was to:
    a. begin an era in which individuals could seek redress against the federal government through the Supreme Court.
    b. enhance the legitimacy of the Constitution by allaying the concerns of the anti-Federalists.
    c. lead to a broadening of suffrage to include women and free African-Americans.
    d. trigger a fierce debate about the powers of the Constitution.

12. In his financial program, Hamilton wanted to:
    a. empower the central government by connecting its interests to those of the elite.

b. outperform Thomas Jefferson in the cabinet and succeed Washington in 1796.

c. subvert the Constitution and revert to a government much like the British system.

d. broaden the powers of the federal government as stated in the Constitution.

13. Among the following ideas, the only one Thomas Jefferson did *not* believe in was:
   a. a strict reading of the Constitution.
   b. a democratic republic rooted in an agrarian yeomen farming population.
   c. rapid settlement of the West by farmers and the entrance of new territories into the Union.
   d. the abolition of slavery in the South.

14. Jay's Treaty included *all* of the following terms *except*:
   a. a return of property confiscated from Loyalists during the Revolution.
   b. acknowledgment of the British right to remove French property from American ships.
   c. repayment of prewar debts to British merchants.
   d. removal of British forts in the West.

15. The Republicans won the election in 1800 because:
   a. John Adams's administration had enacted the Alien and Sedition Acts.
   b. the Federalists were divided by internal disputes.
   c. the Republicans nominated Thomas Jefferson, a very popular candidate.
   d. Alexander Hamilton supported Thomas Jefferson.

16. The instability of government during the 1780s was reflected in the frequency of extralegal procedures and meetings occurring both within and outside of government. Which among the following actions was *not* extralegal?
   a. the call by nationalists at the Annapolis Convention for a convention to revise the Articles of Confederation
   b. meetings among farmers in western Massachusetts in 1786 to protest high taxes and aggressive creditors
   c. the decision among the members of the Constitutional convention to require only nine of the thirteen states to ratify the constitution for it to go into effect
   d. a 1792 Assembly in Pittsburgh to protest Hamilton's excise tax on whiskey.

Short Essays

Answer the following in a brief paragraph.

1. How did the colonial experience affect the structure of the state governments that were organized during and after the Revolutionary War? In general, were they more republican or more democratic? (pp. 198–200)

2. Why were the rights of women ignored during a revolution that was fought for the liberty, freedom, and equality of all? (pp. 200–201)

3. Why did the Articles of Confederation fail? (pp. 202–207)

4. What did the nationalists, who later called themselves Federalists, really want in trying to revise the Articles of Confederation and establish a new central government based on the Constitution of 1787? (pp. 207–214)

5. How and why did the anti-Federalists lose the ratification debates in 1787 and 1788? (pp. 210–213)

6. Why did both Washington and Adams, as well as the Republicans for that matter, consider it imperative to remain neutral and avoid war with either France or Britain in the 1790s? Given this general agreement how do you account for the acrimony of the political debates of the 1790s? (pp. 220–225)

7. Was the "Revolution of 1800" really a revolution? In what ways was it not a revolution? (p. 225)

ANSWERS

Chapter Précis

1. mixed
2. Judith Sargent Murray
3. Northwest Ordinance
4. prodebtor
5. Annapolis, Maryland
6. William Paterson
7. *The Federalist*
8. Thomas Jefferson
9. assumption
10. XYZ affair
11. Alien and Sedition Acts

Identification

1. John Adams
2. New Jersey
3. Mary Wollstonecraft

4. Robert Morris

5. Thomas Jefferson

6. Daniel Shays

7. France

8. anti-Federalists

9. twenty

10. Samuel Adams

11. Alexander Hamilton

12. Adam Smith

13. loose

14. French

15. Aaron Burr

Skill-Building Exercise

The precise motives of backcountry opposition to central power and a commercial Anglo-American elite varied from state to state. In New York, tenant farmers had long resisted the power of landlords who owned huge estates and dominated colonial government. In Massachusetts, the recent Shays's Rebellion reflected widespread western resistance to financial policies and laws that favored creditors and failed to protect debtors. In these colonies, as well as in Pennsylvania and Virginia, people living in the backcountry also sought more protection from colonial governments against the Indians. Further south, procreditor policies caused widespread opposition to colonial governments among frontier settlers. In the Mid-Atlantic states and the South, the recent influence of Scots-Irish and German immigrants intensified opposition to central power.

Self-Test

Multiple Choice

1. b	7. d	12. a
2. c	8. d	13. d
3. b	9. d	14. a
4. a	10. d	15. a
5. d	11. b	16. a
6. d		

Short Essays

1. Colonial governments were modeled on the government in Great Britain; each had an assembly, a council, and a governor representing the sovereignty of the people, the nobility, and the king, respectively. The structure was familiar, as were the checks and balances that limited the power of each branch and maintained liberty for all. Therefore, having just thrown off a central power, the republican influence led many new states to further empower the legislatures, at the expense of the power of the governor or judiciary.

2. Gender relations in the eighteenth century were based on the notions that men were intellectually superior and that only men could be economically independent. Women, it was argued, lacked the intelligence and independence of men and could not be proper citizens. Thus, they could not be given the right to vote, and their complaints could not be taken seriously.

3. Because the Articles of Confederation were unable to establish coercive power over the states they could not create a coherent public policy. They also did not include the power to tax and thus to fund programs without going to the states by requisitions or by borrowing. As a result, the government was chronically short of revenue, though the sale of public lands eventually eased this problem. Lacking funding, Congress was unable to launch national programs or finance the military and diplomatic corps. In consequence, the central government was weak and inefficient.

4. The nationalists wanted a stronger central government that could have power over the states and prevent the interstate squabbles and disputes that threatened the Confederation. Such a stronger government would, thus, create a new national realm, a nation, which could take its rightful place among other nations of the world. That many nationalists had served in the Revolution or had been diplomats and seen how important it was for a nation to have a strong central structure, only deepened their interest in establishing a new national framework.

5. The anti-Federalists were a diverse group reacting to actions already taken by the assertive nationalists. As a result, they were less organized and slower to bring their forces together. Moreover, they argued against rather than for something and provided no alternative except staying with the weak government under the Articles. Driven by fear and concern for the future rather than by expectation and hope, they viewed the plans of the Federalists with suspicion. Thus, they argued defensively and negatively. In the final debates they had less to bargain with because they had little to offer. The Federalists, in contrast, offered a new Constitution, a new nation, and a more secure government.

6. The United States benefited enormously by maintaining their neutrality and trading with both the British

and the French. After years of economic uncertainty, the prosperity of the 1790s established the nation on a firmer footing. In addition, for a new, uncertain country to ally itself with great powers would have endangered its independence, no matter which side it chose to ally itself with. It was important, as George Washington argued, to stay clear of another country's disputes and act in its own self-interest. The passion at the center of the debate in the United States derived from uncertainty over the meaning of factions or parties and fear that, given the fragility of the new republic, any dispute or disagreement that caused people to choose sides threatened national independence and unity with the threat of civil war. Many felt the fate of the republic was at issue.

7. The transfer of power from the elite, aristocratic Federalist party to the agrarian Democratic-Republican party was as much of a change in terms of who ruled as the Revolution had been. For Jefferson, the election of 1800 meant the Republicans could eliminate some of the centralist policies of the Federalist era, reducing the size and power of the federal government, strengthening the states, and broadening democracy. This transfer of power was revolutionary because it marked a rare moment in history when a total change in government could be effected in a peaceful and orderly fashion. Yet, because his election occurred according to procedures roughly spelled out in the Constitution, Jefferson's election simply confirmed and validated the political system established by the Constitution in 1787. Much of how that system operated had been established by Washington and Adams, and Jefferson simply continued the same government under the same constitution.

CHAPTER 8

Toward a Continental Nation 1790–1820

★ ★ ★

CHAPTER PRÉCIS

Westward Expansion   pp. 230–235

Native American Resistance

In 1783, Britain gave up its claim to lands west of the Appalachians and left isolated the native Americans who had allied with them during the Revolutionary War. native Americans were left to face an American nation determined to secure its claims on the new territory. To secure this land, the federal and state governments used military force, bribery, and fraud to coerce the native Americans to cede their claims to the vast lands of the Northwest Territory.

Settlers and Speculators

Right behind the military and government officials were waves of speculators and settlers seeking opportunity, land, and profit in the West. This mass migration to the West left many parts of the East drained of capital and labor, compelling eastern farmers to compensate for their losses by improving productivity through technological innovation and soil conservation and enhancement. Meanwhile, as new settlers opened farms and initiated the conquest of the vast interior of North America, overcoming the transportation bottleneck. transporting the agricultural wealth of the rich soil of the West to eastern markets became a high priority in the new states.

1. In 1794, General "Mad Anthony" Wayne defeated the Western Confederacy at the Battle of

   _____ . (p. 231)

2. By 1796, southerners moving West had formed two new states:

   _____ and

   _____ . (p. 232)

111

The Transportation Bottleneck

Even on improved roads or turnpikes, travel by land was slow and expensive. The comparative speed and ease of water transport increased the value of sites along rivers or navigable streams over which westerners could move their produce to markets. Spain controlled the major outlet of western trade, the port of New Orleans, at the southern end of the Mississippi River.

Republican Policy and Diplomacy pp. 235–246

The Jeffersonian Presidency

The "revolution of 1800," Thomas Jefferson's defeat of John Adams for the presidency, marked more than the first transfer of executive authority from one political party to another. Jefferson's attitude toward the Federalists was conciliatory, but he hoped to diminish the size and scope of national government and lessen the influence of northeastern merchants and creditors. Supported by a Republican Congress, Jefferson promoted both his political philosophy and his party by modifying or reversing Federalist policies. His administration reduced the national debt, the size of the army, and the length of U.S. residence required for naturalization; allowed the Alien and Sedition Acts to expire; and limited the power of the federal judiciary. On the other hand, Jefferson dropped his original opposition to the Bank of the United States, which he now considered critical to a healthy national economy.

3. Republicans sought to remove many of the last minute "_____" that John Adams had made in 1801 to pack the courts with Federalists to thwart Republican policy. (p. 235)

4. Jefferson's secretary of the treasury, _____ , believed that the national debt was "an evil of the first magnitude." (p. 236)

Jefferson and the West

Jefferson's belief that Republicanism could be strengthened through the settlement of the West by yeomen farmers prompted new initiatives and altered old beliefs. Although he had argued for a strict construction of the Constitution during the political debates of the 1790s, Jefferson shifted to a loose construction when given an opportunity to double the size of the nation by concluding a treaty with Napoleon's France for the purchase of Louisiana. Exploration of the area by Meriwether Lewis and William Clark soon followed.

Fearing that western expansion would ultimately weaken northeastern power, some New England Federalists talked of secession. Aaron Burr, the former Republican vice-president, who conspired to seize power in the West, was tried for treason. Hoping to get Burr convicted, Jefferson supported a loose construction of the Constitution's definition of treason. However, Chief Justice John Marshall acquitted Burr, insisting on a strict reading of the Constitution.

5. Jefferson feared that the secret transfer of Louisiana from _____ to _____ would jeopardize western expansion. (p. 238)

Crisis at Sea

During the Napoleonic Wars, the United States struggled to maintain neutrality. American merchants sought to profit from carrying goods previously shipped on vessels of the belligerent nations. Both Britain and France established policies restricting neutral trade, but British actions were especially galling. Nearly 8,000 sailors were impressed into the British navy from American ships. When the British warship *Leopard* forcibly boarded and searched the U.S. frigate *Chesapeake* for alleged British deserters, a crisis ensued. Rather than retaliate, Jefferson demanded that the British pay monetary reparations and end impressment. He emphasized his resolve by barring British warships from American ports. The British apologized for the incident but refused to change their impressment and blockade policies.

The Road to War

In an attempt to avoid additional confrontations that would lead to war, Jefferson implemented a policy of peaceful coercion. The Embargo Act of 1807 prohibited U.S. vessels from engaging in overseas trade until restrictions against American shipping were lifted. Federalist merchants violated the act whenever they could. The Force Act gave customs officials extraordinary powers, arousing fears of tyranny. The embargo was a failure: American trade languished and neither Britain nor France changed its policies.

Elected president in 1808, James Madison faced the same problems. Recognizing that the embargo had failed, he secured its repeal, but his own diplomatic efforts to protect America's neutral rights also floundered. To the west in the Ohio River valley, native Americans revived the Western Confederacy to prevent further American expansion into their territory. Republican congressmen, some of whom became War Hawks in 1812, were committed to western expansion, particularly to winning Canada from Britain and Florida from Spain. Charging Britain with assisting the Indian resistance, the western Republicans used this accusation as an effective rationale for war against Britain. Ultimately, their expansionist goals, translated into a defense of national honor, were more important in bringing on the War of 1812 than were issues concerning neutral rights.

The War of 1812

Militarily and politically unprepared, the War of 1812 was almost a disaster for the United States. Short of funds the Americans struggled and failed to launch an invasion of Canada, and suffered the embarrassment of Washington being invaded and burned. Though the Americans did gain control of the Great Lakes, the British remained in control of the Atlantic and interfered with shipping, thus strengthening seaport opposition to the war. In the interior, American forces eventually defeated the Western Confederacy, and killed Tecumseh. Convinced there was nothing to be gained from continuing the war, American diplomats negotiated a peace that restored prewar conditions and left unresolved issues open to future discussion. In the South, Andrew Jackson crushed the British at New Orleans after the treaty had been signed. This victory provided the nation with a boost of morale, which transformed a failed effort into a defining event that, if only on the surface, threw off British dependency, increased national confidence, and unified the nation. This caused the Federalist party, which had called for constitutional amend-

6. Although the American ship _____ had stopped in a U.S. port, Britain seized the ship for carrying sugar and molasses from the West Indies to France. (p. 240)

7. The Shawnee chief _____ and his brother, the Prophet Tenskwatawa, appealed to the pride in Indian ways to encourage military alliances among the western tribes. (p. 242)

8. One of the most ardent western War Hawks was _____ of Kentucky. Ironically, two years later he would help negotiate the Treaty of Ghent, which inconclusively ended the war. (pp. 242, 244)

9. The Western Confederacy formed by Tecumseh was defeated by American troops at the Battle of the _____ in southern Canada. (p. 244)

ments or even secession, to weaken, break into factions, and eventually evaporate.

The Treaty of Ghent, which ended the war through diplomacy, and Andrew Jackson's stunning victory over the British at the Battle of New Orleans rescued the Republican administration, discredited the Federalists, and introduced Jackson as a new national hero.

Regional Diversity and National Identity

pp. 246–261

Northern Seaboard Societies

Distinctive regional identities characterized the societies along the Atlantic coast. Most New Englanders shared the religion and culture of their Puritan ancestors and valued industry and education. The Middle Atlantic, Chesapeake, and Carolina regions, which had been settled by several Western European groups as well as by enslaved Africans, exhibited more ethnic, racial, religious, and cultural diversity. Although national elections, wars, and newspapers nurtured a national identity and common cultural values, most Americans identified more closely with their own regional culture.

10. The name _____ was given to New England residents because of their shrewd bargaining habits. (p. 246)

The Old Northwest

In 1893, the historian Frederick Jackson Turner suggested that migrants to the West had created a new American identity characterized by individualism and democracy. However, later historians agree instead that migrants settling north of the Ohio River and west of the Appalachian Mountains simply transplanted the ethnic and cultural diversity and the political conflicts of their New England and Middle Atlantic seaboard communities to the western frontier. In the absence of effective transportation and access to markets, frontier living remained primitive.

Slavery Moves into the Old Southwest

The transplanting of slavery distinguished frontier settlement in the Old Southwest from that in the Old Northwest. Through both natural increase and the importation of 250,000 new Africans prior to the banning of the transatlantic slave trade in 1808, the black population in the United States grew from 0.5 million to 1.8 million between 1775 and 1820. This expanded labor force was needed for growing tobacco, rice, sugar, and in that part of the West that would become Alabama and Mississippi, cotton. The expansion of cotton cultivation was stimulated by the English textile industry's demand for fiber and by the American invention of the cotton gin, which made growing short-staple cotton feasible.

The expansion of slavery dashed the belief that the institution would "die a natural death." Antislavery attempts to control its spread quickly spilled into the political arena over the admission of Missouri to the Union as a slave state. The Missouri Compromise of 1820, forged by Representative Henry Clay of Kentucky, balanced Missouri's entry as a slave state with Maine's admission as a free state. Despite the increasing power of the North in the House of Representatives, the Compromise

11. The Missouri Compromise prohibited slavery in that part of the Louisiana Territory north of latitude

_____ . (p. 251)

also established a principle capable of preserving the sectional balance in the Senate by maintaining an equal number of slave and free states.

African-American Society and Culture

In the South, a distinctive and more unified African-American society and culture began to emerge. The development of a more self-conscious free black society in northern cities, combined with the increase in native-born black society as a result of the end of the slave trade in 1808, and the fusing together of different black subcultures in the course of westward movement, converged to stimulate the development of a distinctive culture. Despite slavery, blacks were able to improve the quality of their lives by cultivating family life, establishing kin groups, creating distinctive forms of Christianity, and sustaining both a traditional and new African-American language and culture. These developments continued even as the expansion of the internal slave trade to the southwest exposed African-American society and its institutions to more disruptions and misery.

12. In 1822 in Charleston, South Carolina, _____ , a free black married to a slave woman, planned a slave revolt. (p. 253)

The Fate of Native Americans

Intent on westward expansion, the American government aimed at either the assimilation of native Americans through the destruction of their culture or their removal from land needed immediately for white settlement. White Americans defined native Americans as savage and demanded their rejection of traditional religious beliefs, tribal and clan allegiances, and attitudes toward the land. Confronted by cultural and military pressures, some Indians clung to traditional ways, while others blended elements of both cultures. Mixed-blood Cherokee sought to deflect white encroachments by adopting Christianity, English, and a government based on the Constitution; but they lost their power to full-bloods who resisted both assimilation and removal.

13. The Iroquois prophet _____ sought to counteract social disarray and cultural disorganization among the Indians by reviving traditional customs and practices. (p. 257)

14. Because of their ancestral values, most native American _____ refused to do field work. (p. 257)

Continental Empire: Spain and the United States

The American Republic pursued its policy of westward expansion against the Spanish Borderlands Empire, which Spain had established in the eighteenth century. Though Spain, like Britain, resisted through Indian alliances and prohibitions of trade, the Americans acquired through treaties rights to the southwest, free navigation on the Mississippi, the cession of east Florida to the United States, and a clarification of the boundary line between Louisiana and New Spain. These last actions were undertaken by Secretary of State John Quincy Adams who pursued an overtly expansionist American policy. He also worked to clarify the American-Canadian border, to keep the Russians out of Alaska, and articulated a policy that prohibited European powers from interfering in the affairs of new American Republics (this would later become known as the Monroe Doctrine). All of these developments envisioned a Continental Republic that would eventually extend to the Pacific.

EXPANDED TIMELINE

1784   Treaty of Fort Stanwix
Under the terms of this treaty, the Iroquois lost their land in Pennsylvania, western New York, and Ohio. The loss of native American land by treaty with the United States would be repeated again and again.

1787   Northwest Ordinance

1790s   Western (Indian) Confederacy
Indian tribes in the Northwest Territory—the Miami, Shawnee, Potawatomi, and Chipewyan—formed a Western Confederacy to defend their land against American expansion.

White settlers move into Northwest Territory
Seeking land and profit, settlers and speculators poured into land still occupied by native Americans.

Cotton production expands
With the invention of the cotton gin and the growth of a market for American cotton in Britain, planters expanded cotton cultivation in the Old Southwest and enlarged their labor force by increased importation of slaves from Africa.

Agricultural "improvement" in East
Turnpike and short canals built

1790–
1791   Little Turtle defeats American armies

1792   Kentucky joins Union; Tennessee follows (1796)

1794   General Wayne wins Battle of Fallen Timbers
Although the Western Confederacy fought successfully against American forces in 1790 and 1791, it was defeated by American troops led by General "Mad Anthony" Wayne at the Battle of Fallen Timbers.

1795   Treaty of Greenville
Following the Battle of Fallen Timbers, the Western Confederacy and the United States government signed the Treaty of Greenville. The United States renounced a general claim to ownership of Indian land by right of conquest, while the native Americans relinquished certain regions for annuities and acknowledged themselves to be under the protection of the United States government.

Jay's Treaty
Pinckney's Treaty
Fearing possible Anglo-American cooperation after the signing of Jay's Treaty, Spain signed Pinckney's Treaty with the United States. The treaty gave western settlers the right to ship exports through the Spanish-controlled port of New Orleans at the mouth of the Mississippi River.

1800s   Chesapeake blacks adopt Protestant beliefs
When African-Americans adopted Christianity, they modified its message to suit their needs, stressing Handsome Lake revival among Iroquois.

1800   Gabriel Prosser's rebellion in Virginia
In response to the tyranny of slavery, some blacks across the South resisted in organized ways. Gabriel Prosser organized a mass uprising. When his plan was discovered at the last moment, however, the rebellion was crushed and the leaders executed.

Political "Revolution of 1800"

1801–
1807   The presidency of Thomas Jefferson
Jefferson believed that his election to the presidency constituted a "revolution" because it would shift Federalist policy that sought to create a strong central government for the interests of northeastern creditors and merchants toward a limited government, which would benefit the yeoman farmers across the country. As president, Jefferson fulfilled his "revolutionary" agenda by challenging federalist control of the judiciary, limiting the size of government, reducing the national debt, abolishing internal taxes, reducing the cost of western lands, and adding vast territory to the nation.

Gallatin reduces national debt
During Jefferson's presidency, Secretary of the Treasury Albert Gallatin reduced the national debt from $83 million to $45 million.

Naval war with Barbary States
Price of federal land reduced

1802–
1815   Napoleonic Wars in Europe
Seizures of American ships and sailors

1803   Louisiana Purchase
The purchase of Louisiana from Napoleon's France doubled the size of the United States and, in Jefferson's view, ensured the future of republicanism by providing sufficient land for future generations of politically independent yeomen farmers.

1804–
1805   Lewis and Clark expedition
Following the Louisiana Purchase, Jefferson sent Meriwether Lewis and William Clark on an expedition to explore the area.

Aaron Burr and western secession
Aaron Burr, a former Republican vice-president, failed in his plot to seize power in the West and was charged with treason. Chief Justice John Marshall's insistence on a strict definition of treason resulted in Burr's acquittal.

1807   Embargo
Seeking to avoid further confrontation with Britain and hoping to coerce Britain and France into accepting peacefully the American definition of neutral rights, the Jefferson administration secured passage of the Embargo of 1807, which prohibited American ships from engaging in foreign commerce.

1808   Tecumseh and Tenskwatawa mobilize Indians
In an attempt to prevent additional losses of Indian lands to Americans in the West, the Shawnee chief

Tecumseh and his brother, the Prophet Tenskwatawa, revived the Western Confederacy.

Congress bans importation of slaves
Under the terms of Article 1, Section 9, of the
Constitution, the importation of slaves could not be
prohibited prior to 1808.

1810s   Expansion of slavery into Old Southwest
Slavery expanded into the Old Southwest with the
spread of cotton cultivation.

Cherokee resist white advance
Mixed-blood Cherokee sought to prevent a white
takeover of their lands by adopting the English
language and American political ways. In contrast,
most full-blooded Cherokee continued their
traditional oral culture.

Decline of Federalist party
In the presidential election of 1816, the Republican
James Monroe defeated the Federalist Rufus King
and carried every state except Massachusetts,
Connecticut, and Delaware. King was the last
Federalist to seek the presidency.

1811   War Hawks call for expansion
Battle of Tippecanoe
Politicians favoring the expansion of American
territory both further west and into Florida were
convinced that the British supported the Western
Confederacy with designs to encroach on American
territorial sovereignty. When war broke out with the
Shawnees, who were part of the Confederacy, the
matter seemed settled. Though the Americans led by
General William Henry Harrison defeated the
Shawnees at the Battle of Tippecanoe and dealt the
Confederacy a crushing blow, expansionists
increased their calls for war against Great Britain.

1812   War of 1812
The United States' declaration of war against Britain
in 1812 followed a lengthy period of tension over
Britain's practice of impressment, its rejection of
American neutral rights, and its attacks on Ameri-
can shipping. However, the expansionist goals of the
West's congressional War Hawks regarding British
Canada, Spanish Florida, and western Indian lands
were more important in bringing on war.

1814   Hartford Convention

1815   Andrew Jackson wins Battle of New Orleans
Treaty of Ghent ratified
The Treaty of Ghent ended the War of 1812,
restored prewar boundaries, and left unresolved
issues to future negotiation. The United States failed
to win Canada, acceptance of the American
definition of neutral rights, or British agreement to
end the practice of impressment. However, Andrew
Jackson's stunning victory over the British at the
Battle of New Orleans, which occurred after the
treaty was signed, confirmed the nation's successful
defense of its national honor and established
Jackson as a military hero.

1817   Rush-Bagot Treaty
The United States and Great Britain agreed to limit
their naval forces on the Great Lakes, thereby
establishing an unfortified boundary between the
United States and Canada.

Alabama joins Union, Mississippi follows (1819)

1817–
1825   Era of Good Feeling
The absence of a Federalist opposition led observers
to refer to the administration of James Monroe as
the Era of Good Feeling, but apparent political
harmony masked factionalism developing within the
Republican party.

1819   Adams-Onis Treaty: Florida annexed, and Texas
boundary defined
Andrew Jackson's military expedition into Spanish-
controlled East Florida frightened Spain into
relinquishing the area to the United States in the
Adams-Onis Treaty signed in 1819.

1820   Missouri Compromise
When controversy arose in Congress over the
admission of Missouri into the Union as a slave
state, Henry Clay of Kentucky forged a compromise
that balanced admission of Missouri as a slave state
with admission of Maine as a free state, set a
precedent for the future admission of states in pairs,
and attempted to prevent further problems by
setting latitude 36°30' as the dividing line between
slave and free territory in the Louisiana Purchase
area.

1823   Monroe Doctrine
Envisioning a continental empire for the United
States, President Monroe's Secretary of State John
Quincy Adams formulated a statement in 1823
warning Spain and other European countries not to
intervene in the newly independent nations of Latin
America. The statement also declared the Western
Hemisphere closed to further European
colonization. The policy became known as the
Monroe Doctrine thirty years later.

GLOSSARY

speculator A speculator is someone who enters a market
to buy and then resell at a higher price only to make
money. The early western land market was dominated by
speculators who acquired land at a low price through political influence then sold to settlers. (p. 232)

squatter Someone who settles on land they do not own.
Many settlers located on land before it was surveyed and
entered for sale. They would request the first right to purchase the land when sales began. In Kentucky, this right
was called a Preoccupancy title. (p. 232)

freehold A farmer who has freehold ownership of a plot of land possesses the title or deed and, therefore, completely owns it and can improve it, transfer, or sell it as he wishes. To gain a freehold title to a farm was the goal of most yeoman farmers in the United States. (p. 233)

crop rotation Farmers could increase the fertility of their soil by planting different crops, which maintained different nutrients in the soil, from year to year. This method was introduced in the East in the early nineteenth century to increase agricultural productivity. (p. 234)

turnpike A turnpike is a privately built road that the owner charges a fee or toll for someone to travel on. (p. 234)

townships A township was a geographical subdivision 6 miles square that was made up of thirty-six sections, each 1 square mile. (p. 236)

impressment When they engaged in impressment, the British forced, or pressed, American merchant sailors into service in the British navy. (p. 240)

peaceful coercion Thomas Jefferson developed a strategy to force the British and the French to accept the American definition of neutral rights by means short of war. The centerpiece of this policy of peaceful coercion was the Embargo Act of 1807. (p. 241)

John Bull The nickname for Great Britain, similar to "Uncle Sam" for the United States, that originated during the War of 1812. (p. 247)

personal liberty laws Personal liberty laws were passed to protect free blacks from being unlawfully enslaved. Northern states passed these laws in an effort to circumvent the federal Fugitive Slave Law of 1793. (p. 250)

task When they labored by the task, slaves were assigned a specific piece of work to accomplish in a day, instead of working for a specific number of hours. Once the slaves had finished their tasks, they could do what they wished. (p. 253)

assimilation A social policy that advocates that people who are different from the people of the dominant culture be made to become like the people of the dominant culture. Americans in the early nineteenth century advocated the assimilation of native Americans by destroying their culture, redefining their identities, and intermarriage. (p. 257)

IDENTIFICATION

Identify by filling in the blanks.

1. In 1790 and 1791 in Ohio, the Western Confederacy, led by _____ , defeated U.S. forces under General Josiah Harmar and General Arthur St. Clair. (p. 231)

2. In the Treaty of Greenville of 1795, native American chiefs ceded the future sites of two major cities: _____ and _____ . (p. 232)

3. In the opening decades of the nineteenth century, moving goods by _____ was the cheapest, most convenient form of transportation. (p. 234)

4. Before leaving office in 1801, President _____ assured that the Federalists would have some influence in government by appointing John Marshall to the Supreme Court. (p. 235)

5. The Land Act of 1820 enabled a farmer with $100 in cash to buy a minimum of _____ acres for _____ per acre. (p. 238)

6. Seeking information about the region acquired from France in 1803, Thomas Jefferson sent _____ and _____ to explore the Louisiana Territory. (p. 240)

7. _____ , who was Thomas Jefferson's vice-president, ran for governor of New York, killed Alexander Hamilton in a duel in 1804, and was tried and acquitted for treason concerning his role in an alleged conspiracy that sought to establish the Louisiana Purchase as a separate nation in 1807. (p. 240)

8. Although it was fought after the Treaty of Ghent was signed, the Battle of _____ made _____ a national hero and a symbol of the emerging West. (p. 244)

9. Before 1850, rather than observing Christmas as a festive occasion, most New England churches celebrated _____ to commemorate the first settlers in Massachusetts. (p. 247)

10. On the frontier, settlers lived in a _____ economy, exchanging goods and labor among themselves. (p. 248)

11. The spread of _____ production

into Georgia, Alabama, and Mississippi resulted in the forced migration of more than 835,000 slaves from the Chesapeake and Carolina regions. (p. 249)

12. In the 1790s Connecticut-born _____ developed a machine that separated the seeds from the fiber of short-staple cotton, thus dramatically increasing the productivity of cotton agriculture. (p. 249)

13. Native Americans viewed themselves not as individuals, but as members of a _____ , all descendants of the same person. (p. 258)

14. _____ , a mixed-blood Cherokee Indian, developed a written script for the Cherokee language in 1821. (p. 258)

SKILL-BUILDING EXERCISE

1. Locate and identify _____ , the city in which Richard Allen founded the African Methodist Episcopal Church.

2. Locate and identify the five states formed from the Northwest Territory. Their names are:

    (a) _____ , (b) _____

    (c) _____ , (d) _____ ,

    and (e) _____ .

3. Locate and identify _____ , the state in which Andrew Jackson won his celebrated victory over the British in 1815.

4. The Compromise of 1820 over the issue of slavery permitted the entrance of two states, one slave, _____ , and one free, _____ , into the Union. The southern boundary of _____ was determined as the line limiting the extension of slavery.

DOCUMENT EXERCISES

American Voices

The Battle of Tippecanoe—Chief Shabonee

To achieve the unity needed to resist white settlement in the Ohio River valley, the Shawnee chief Tecumseh and his brother, the Prophet Tenskwatawa, called for a political confederation and the revival of traditional spiritual beliefs among native American tribes in the trans-Appalachian West. Fighting broke out in the Indiana Territory. In 1811 in the Battle of Tippecanoe, Governor William Henry Harrison defeated the Shawnee and their Indian allies, among them the Potawatomi chief Shabonee.

As you read "The Battle of Tippecanoe," ask yourself the following questions:

1. Why was the Wabash River an important line for the Indians to hold?

2. Why did the "young men" think they would be able to defeat the Americans?

3. What does Shabonee think caused the failure of the Indian attack on Harrison's forces?

4. What was Shabonee's opinion of Harrison?

5. Why was it that Shabonee "lost all hope" after the Battle of Tippecanoe, whereas Potawatomi once again fought against the Americans in 1812?

A Seneca Chief's Understanding of Religion—Red Jacket

Unlike Handsome Lake, who combined elements of Christian belief and morality with traditional Indian ways in a movement that sought to revitalize the Seneca, Red Jacket stood firm against change and against conversion to Christianity. Red Jacket's beliefs can be seen as part of a native American "world view" that differed from that of the whites, emphasizing community rather than individualism; use rather than possession of the land; and the sacred as part of, rather than separate from, the natural world.

As you read "A Seneca Chief's Understanding of Religion," ask yourself the following questions:

1. What arguments did the Christian missionaries use in trying to convert Red Jacket to Christianity?

2. What evidence does Red Jacket provide to bolster his argument that Christianity was not meant for Indians?

3. Red Jacket says: "To you He has given the arts. To these He has not opened our eyes." What do you think he meant?

4. How did division among Indian leaders, such as that between Red Jacket and Handsome Lake, affect the native Americans' ability to maintain their culture and resist the whites' drive into Indian lands?

American Lives

Richard Allen and African-American Identity

After the American Revolution and the end of slavery in states north of Delaware, the free black community in Philadelphia, where Richard Allen settled, grew larger and forged an identity distinct from whites. Blacks took control of their religious lives by becoming members of a denomination of their own choice and by opposing segregation and racism in white churches. They joined the independent black denomination that Richard Allen founded—the African Methodist Episcopal Church. But more than religion defined the identity of their community. Led by Bishop Allen, Philadelphia's African-Americans also worked for black education, established the nation's first black newspaper, petitioned for the end of slavery and the slave trade, opposed the capture of fugitive slaves, and rejected colonization in Africa for free blacks.

As you read "Richard Allen and African-American Identity," ask yourself the following questions:

1. Why was religion so important to Richard Allen?

2. Why was Methodism more appealing to many blacks than either the Episcopal or the Quaker religions?

3. What factors led Allen to found the first independent black denomination in America, the African Methodist Episcopal Church?

4. Why did Allen initially support the American Colonization Society?

5. Could Richard Allen's success story have taken place in Charleston, South Carolina? Why or why not?

SELF-TEST

Multiple Choice

1. Jay's Treaty was important to United States control in the Old Northwest because according to its terms:

   a. the tribes of the Western Confederacy agreed to cede most of the future state of Ohio to the United States.
   b. Great Britain agreed to withdraw its military garrisons from the territory.
   c. Great Britain agreed to withdraw its naval vessels from the Great Lakes.
   d. Great Britain agreed to force Anglo-Canadian and French-Canadian traders to return to Canada.

2. As migration to the West drained agricultural areas in the East of labor, eastern farmers tried to compensate by doing *all* of the following *except*:

   a. growing potatoes, a high-yield, nutritious crop.
   b. rotating their crops with nitrogen-rich clover.
   c. utilizing cast-iron plows, which were more efficient than metal-tipped plows.
   d. buying reapers and cultivators to lessen the need for labor.

3. During his eight years as president, Thomas Jefferson changed the character of the national government by doing *all* of the following *except*:

   a. controlling government expenditures and using customs revenues to redeem government bonds.
   b. abolishing the Bank of the United States.
   c. reducing the size of the permanent army.
   d. abolishing all internal taxes.

4. Aaron Burr is regarded as one of the most notorious figures in early United States political history because:

   a. he always considered himself a Federalist but served as Thomas Jefferson's first vice-president.
   b. he shot and killed Alexander Hamilton, former secretary of the treasury, in a duel.
   c. he was tried and convicted of treason for leading a conspiracy in the West.
   d. he conspired to assassinate Supreme Court Chief Justice John Marshall because of Marshall's Federalist views.

5. Jefferson's policy of peaceful coercion can be characterized as *all* of the following *except* a(n):

   a. economic weapon designed to protect American interests while avoiding war.
   b. naive tactic that failed to force Britain and France to repeal their restrictions on United States trade.
   c. popular policy that won support from Republicans and Federalists alike.
   d. economic policy that caused American exports to decline significantly.

6. The attack on the *Chesapeake* by the *Leopard* raised the level of American antagonism against Britain because:

   a. the British government had previously promised to end the practice of impressment.

b. the *Chesapeake* was a ship of the U.S. Navy.

c. the British government offered compensation but refused to apologize for the incident.

d. President Jefferson authorized the U.S. Navy to retaliate.

7. The primary reason America declared war on the British and initiated the War of 1812 was:

a. British infringements on American neutrality rights.

b. British failure to recognize American sovereignty over western lands.

c. British support of the western Indian Confederacy under Tecumseh.

d. Republicans saw a political benefit in the war for it would discredit Federalists and establish for good the independence of the United States from Great Britain's interference in its affairs.

8. *All* of the following supported the War of 1812 *except*:

a. John C. Calhoun.   c. William Henry Harrison.

b. De Witt Clinton.   d. Henry Clay.

9. At the Hartford Convention, disgruntled Federalists hoping to reverse their party's decline proposed constitutional amendments that included *all* of the following *except*:

a. restriction of commercial embargoes to sixty days.

b. requiring a two-thirds majority in Congress to declare war.

c. rotation of the presidency among citizens from different states.

d. limiting the presidency to two four-year terms.

10. In the early nineteenth century, the highest level of female literacy was found in:

a. Massachusetts.   c. South Carolina.

b. Virginia.   d. Kentucky.

11. The new market for cotton in England impacted the South through the 1820s in *all* of the following ways *except*:

a. a search for a more efficient way to clean cotton, which would increase profits. The result was the cotton gin.

b. increases in profits made slavery profitable and reinvigorated the foreign slave trade.

c. a mass migration of cotton growers flooded the southwest looking for richer land upon which to plant cotton.

d. many slaves experienced the misery of broken families by the migration or sale of family members to the Southwest.

12. Many male slaves who worked on the sugar plantations of Louisiana:

a. lived longer than white workers in the North.

b. established stable families because of the Catholicism of the planters.

c. died quickly from disease and overwork.

d. were imported from Africa after the War of 1812.

13. *All* of the following were part of traditional native American culture *except*:

a. tribal identity.

b. private property.

c. clan totems or spirits.

d. female agricultural labor.

14. African-Americans in the lowland, rice-growing areas of South Carolina gained control over their work lives by:

a. winning the right to hire out their own time, so long as they returned their wages to their masters.

b. winning the right to labor by the task.

c. convincing their masters to include emancipation provisions in their wills.

d. threatening to slow down the pace of work if their demands were not met.

15. Blacks and whites shared *all* of the following elements of early nineteenth-century southern culture *except*:

a. names of British origin.

b. marriage between cousins.

c. the desire to create solid family bonds.

d. evangelical Christianity.

16. When the mixed-blood Cherokee adopted white customs as part of their resistance to being ousted from their lands in Georgia and the Carolinas, they tried *all* of the following *except*:

a. establishing a limited patrilineal inheritance system.

b. introducing a governmental charter modeled on the U.S. Constitution.

c. marrying white women.

d. dressing and behaving like white planters.

17. By the year 1820, *all* of the following states had been admitted to the Union *except*:

a. Maine.   c. Texas.

b. Florida.   d. Missouri.

Short Essays

Answer the following in a brief paragraph.

1. Why did many New England farm families choose to move west after 1790? (p. 232)

2. Why were transportation improvements important to the development of the West? (pp. 234–235)

3. Why did Thomas Jefferson believe that acquiring territory in the West was vital to the future of republicanism in the United States? (pp. 236–238)

4. Was not Jefferson's purchase of Louisiana a contradiction of his beliefs in strict construction of the Constitution and limited government? Reconcile this apparent contradiction. (p. 238)

5. What factors caused the decline of the Federalist party? (pp. 240–244)

6. Explain why the literacy rate was higher in New England than in Virginia. (p. 247)

7. How did the development of the Old Southwest as a center for cotton cultivation affect the lives of African-American slaves? (pp. 249–250)

8. How did African-Americans modify Christianity to suit their own needs as slaves? (pp. 253–254)

9. How did white political leaders justify the policies that demanded that native Americans assimilate or face expulsion from the nation? (pp. 256–258)

10. During the period 1800–1820 had American society become more unified or more diverse? (pp. 246–258)

ANSWERS

Chapter Précis

1. Fallen Timbers
2. Kentucky; Tennessee
3. midnight appointments
4. Albert Gallatin
5. Spain; France
6. *Essex*
7. Tecumseh
8. Henry Clay
9. Thames
10. Yankee
11. 36° 30'
12. Denmark Ves
13. Handsome La
14. men

Identification

1. Little Turtle
2. Detroit; Chicago
3. water
4. John Adams
5. 80; $1.25
6. Meriwether Lewis; William Clark
7. Aaron Burr
8. New Orleans, Andrew Jackson

9. Thanksgiving Day
10. barter
11. cotton
12. Eli Whitney
13. clan
14. Sequoyah

Skill-Building Exercise

1. Philadelphia
2. a. Ohio; b. Indiana; c. Michigan; d. Illinois; e. Wisconsin
3. Louisiana
4. Missouri; Maine; Missouri

Self-Test

Multiple Choice

1. b	7. b	13. b
2. d	8. b	14. b
3. b	9. d	15. b
4. b	10. a	16. c
5. c	11. b	17. c
6. b	12. c	

Short Essays

1. Many New England farm families moved west after 1790 because their home communities were overcrowded, their farmland was suffering from soil exhaustion, and their land holdings were insufficient to provide an adequate inheritance for all of their children.

2. Without efficient transportation, farmers in remote western lands would not have been able to afford to send their crops to distant markets and would have had to remain at subsistence levels of production.

3. Thomas Jefferson believed that acquiring land in the West was vital to the future of republicanism in the United States because he felt that the economic independence of yeomen farmers who owned their own land would guarantee their ability to act as independent citizens and not be politically controlled by the wealthy and the powerful.

4. Jefferson was aware of the contradictions of a president who argued a strict construction of the Constitution taking it upon himself to negotiate a land pur-

chase that was not expressly delegated to the president in the Constitution. He fudged it by arguing it was part of the treaty-making powers given to the president in the Constitution. Nevertheless, the scale of the prize and the potential for such a land purchase to fulfill his wildest dreams about western expansion and settlement overcame any such reservations.

5. Going back to the actions of John Adams and the internal disputes between party leaders, the Federalist party had been in decline. In many ways, the Republicans coopted the Federalists by moving somewhat toward the center during Jefferson's administration. But their opposition to the War of 1812 discredited the party when the United States achieved victory. This culminated at the Hartford Convention of 1814, at which the Federalists, on the basis of narrow New England interests, called for major reforms to the Constitution, and some even threatened secession.

6. Literacy was higher in New England than in Virginia because the Puritan legacy in New England emphasized primary schooling and Bible reading and because the slaveholding, political elite in Virginia refused to provide schooling for ordinary whites.

7. As cotton cultivation was established in newly settled areas of the Old Southwest, African-Americans experienced a disruption of their family bonds and kinship networks as a result of their forced relocation. But as slaves from different seaboard societies mingled in the Old Southwest, they created a more unified African-American culture.

8. Black Christians identified their plight as slaves with the persecution of Christ and emphasized God's liberation of his people. They stressed the equality of all before God and focused on heaven as a place of peace and justice.

9. White political leaders believed that replacing the primitive life of the Indians with civilization as represented by the American nation was part of the historical progress of mankind.

10. During this period the United States, paradoxically, became both more unified and more diverse at the same time. Republicanism, westward migration, and the national feelings that emerged from the War of 1812 all worked toward unifying the American culture. Regional identities among the various seacoast societies persisted, however. In addition, continued westward expansion and the reinvigoration and expansion of slavery, and with it the rapid increase of the African-American population, created new cultures in the northwest and southwest, as well as a distinctive African-American culture in the South. These regional divisions would result in new factional and sectional disputes, which politicians would try to mollify by defining a new national goal of an American continental Empire.

CHAPTER 9

Toward a Capitalist Protestant Republic 1790–1820

★   ★   ★

CHAPTER PRÉCIS

Political Economy: The Capitalist Commonwealth pp. 266–273

A Capitalist Society

During the early 1800s the American economy underwent a virtual revolution, shifting from traditional agriculture to a mixed economy based on farming, commerce, banking, and rural manufacturing. American merchants continued to trade actively with Great Britain and the West Indies while encouraging the development of expanded domestic markets. This thriving economy, which was based on capitalist concepts and promoted by the Bank of the United States, provided a wider range of occupations in cities and rural areas, created new jobs for men and women—for example, in shoe manufacturing—and increased per capita income. In return, however, many people gave up their economic independence as yeomen farmers to work as wage laborers. For the nation as a whole, the most important consequence of this economic revolution was the breaking of American dependence on Great Britain in both banking and manufacturing.

State Mercantilism: The "Commonwealth" System

State governments, rather than the federal government, took the lead in stimulating the economy and encouraging large-scale manufacturing and capital investment. The chief weapon of what came to be called the "commonwealth" system were charters of incorporation that granted companies monopolies, protected investors through limited liability, and

1. During the early nineteenth century American merchants encouraged rural families to produce goods for sale in what was known as the

   _____ system.

   (p. 268)

allowed companies to claim eminent domain to carry out their projects. By encouraging companies to undertake projects for "the public good," the commonwealth system privileged private activity that had a public purpose and, thus, stimulated economic growth.

The Law and the "Commonwealth": Republicans and Federalists

American economic growth under state mercantilism generated economic and legal controversy in the early 1800s, bringing to the fore conflict between the proponents of Federalist and Republican philosophies. Advocates of economic expansion espoused a "commonwealth" system that countered traditional thinking. They supported changes in statute law that gave priority to public needs over private interests, rejecting common-law principles that discouraged economic development and challenged the concepts of state mercantilism. Increasingly, the government became involved in matters that previously had been overseen by individuals.

The Federalist Law: John Marshall

During his thirty-four-year tenure as chief justice of the United States, John Marshall brought traditional Federalist principles to bear on the Supreme Court's rulings. The Marshall Court delivered opinions with far-reaching consequences for the country. By emphasizing national supremacy over states' rights and favoring static rather than dynamic property rights, the Court strengthened the power of the federal government and slowed the pace of economic growth. In a series of important cases, Marshall's defense of contracts and property struck down the right of states to tax all institutions within its borders, upheld contracts against state efforts to rescind them through new legislation, and defended the right of private corporations to govern themselves and avoid government regulation. In doing so, Marshall, perhaps unwittingly, unleashed the power of corporations to operate independently across state lines, thus laying the legal and political economic foundations of the Industrial Revolution. After 1821 Marshall's power was diminished by increasing numbers of Republican appointments to the Court, opening the way for more aggressive economic development in the years to follow.

Visions of a Republican Social Order pp. 273–282

Democracy Extended

In the early nineteenth century republicanism replaced Federalism as the national standard in both politics and society. The pursuit of republican ideals during the generation after Independence transformed American society by increasing social and geographical mobility, broadening the franchise, and democratizing access to education, institutions, and professions. Republicanism also transformed social behavior and attitudes.

2. In 1817 Representative John C. Calhoun sponsored passage of the _____ , which would have allowed the use of federal funds to build roads. (p. 270)

3. When judges consider their decisions in court cases, they often rely on _____ to shape their rulings—that is, decisions made previously in similar cases. (p. 271)

4. In the case of _____ (1803), the Supreme Court for the first time overturned a national law, thus implementing the power of judicial review. (p. 272)

5. John Marshall's defense of property rights was based on his interpretation of the _____ in the Constitution. (p. 272)

6. The most famous law school of the republican era was founded in _____ , Connecticut, in 1824 by Judge Tapping Reeve. (p. 277)

Everywhere, deferential behavior rooted in elitism, hierarchy, and tradition were in retreat. An increasing emphasis on democracy and egalitarianism revolutionized American attitudes and actions as states abolished property qualifications as a requirement for voting and officeholding. These moves toward greater democracy also affected the legal profession; relaxed standards for admission to the bar allowed increasing numbers of people to practice law.

Republican Families

Traditional family patterns underwent a profound change in the early nineteenth century. Parents' control of their children diminished, including their ability to arrange marriages for their sons and daughters. The change stemmed in part from the shrinking size of land holdings, which meant that parents had less property to share with their children. Another cause was the rising tide of sentimentalism, which encouraged marriage for love rather than for convenience or financial stability. Some marriage partners even tried to share responsibilities equally rather than always following the husband's lead. However, law and tradition determined that husbands would maintain their control over wives.

7. The noble republican ideal that encouraged individuals to make their spouse a best friend was known as "_____"marriage. (p. 278)

Raising and Educating Republican Children

Over the last half of the eighteenth century the birth rate in America declined appreciably; in some urban areas the drop had exceeded 50 percent by the early 1800s. Many people delayed marriage and consciously decided to limit the number of children they had. Methods of child rearing changed significantly. Some families continued to rely on strict discipline, but others chose affection and indulgence over authoritarianism. Republican ideology promoted education and responsible independence, and these ideas affected family relations.

8. At the turn of the nineteenth century, the United States faced a sharp decline in the birth rate, which is known as a _____ . (p. 279)

During the colonial and Federalist eras, education in America was limited to a select few who attended private schools or studied with tutors. By the 1820s more educational opportunities were available, although most students left school after the primary grades, where the emphasis was on basic skills and patriotic instruction. During this period a distinct American literature began to develop, focusing on American characters and themes. The United States still depended on Europe for the bulk of its culture, but the country was moving toward cultural autonomy.

9. The "blue-backed speller" that attempted to standardize vocabulary and grammar for the American people was written by _____ . (p. 281)

Protestant Christianity and Women's Lives

pp. 282–289

The Second Great Awakening

The growth of republicanism had a profound impact on religious expansion in the early 1800s. Significant gains in membership were recorded in denominations such as the Quakers, Baptists, and Congregationalists, which encouraged democratic practices. An upsurge of Protestantism, spurred by a new spirit of revivalism, swept across the country, especially the frontier regions of the South and West. The Second Great Awakening witnessed a shift from old-line denominations to evangelical churches and from competition to cooperation among ministers and local congregations.

Emphasizing faith and the power of free will to effect one's salvation, this Great Awakening suffused republican society with deepening humanistic impulses, free-will individualism, and a growing optimism in the power of human action. Gradually, evangelical Protestants would apply their missionary zeal and spiritual and moral intensity to American politics and the development of national identity.

Women and Religion

Increasingly Evangelical Protestant thought, responding to the prevalence of women in church affairs, regarded women, not men, as being primarily responsible for establishing a moral and virtuous society. As "republican mothers" women were urged to raise moral children, maintain a moral household, and exert a moral influence on their husbands, and thus contribute to public life by elevating its moral character. Expectations that women should play a higher moral role in society, though still circumscribed by gender attitudes, stimulated a movement to provide better women's education, increased women's role as teachers, and even encouraged some women to advocate moral and social reform by preaching or speaking in public.

10. During the Second Great Awakening a new sect known as _____ flourished in New England. It rejected the Calvinist concept of predestination and advocated salvation for all people. (p. 283)

11. One of the most articulate ministers of the Second Great Awakening who emphasized the power of each free will individual to shape their own salvation was _____ . (p. 284)

12. In *Thoughts on Female Education* (1787), _____ argued that American women should be afforded greater educational opportunities. (p. 286)

13. Founded in Great Britain, the _____ sect migrated to America with Mother Ann Lee in the 1770s, leading to the establishment of communities in several states. (p. 286)

EXPANDED TIMELINE

1780s   Rural outwork system, especially shoes and textiles
The introduction of rural manufacturing and production through outwork marked an early stage in the transformation of the American economy. Farmers mixed the raising of grain crops and livestock for food with the production of raw materials for manufacturing, such as milk for cheese and hides for leather goods. Rural manufacturing helped encourage the development of a market economy in the United States.

1781   Philadelphia merchants found Bank of North America
Needing new sources of credit to underwrite their commercial enterprises and allow expansion into new economic activities such as rural manufacturing, urban merchants encouraged the government to charter banks to lend money and extend credit. The Bank of North America set the standard and provided a model for the Bank of the United States, which was chartered in Philadelphia in 1791 under the new Constitution.

1782   St. Jean de Crèvecoeur, *Letters from an American Farmer*
In the half-century after America won its independence, many aristocratic Europeans traveled to the United States to study the new republic and compare the new nation with Europe and European institutions. One of the first, St. Jean de Crèvecoeur, praised the United States for establishing a democratic social order that allowed people to succeed on the strength of their own abilities rather than be locked into a tight structure by birth and family status.

1783   Noah Webster's *American Spelling Book* ("the blue-backed speller")
Noah Webster was one of the major contributors to the expansion and democratization of education in the young United States. His promotion of a common vocabulary and grammar and his standardization of spelling helped the American people break from their British heritage in teaching and learning. Webster's "blue-backed speller," based on common word usage among the people, had sold more than 60 million copies by the mid-nineteenth century.

1787   Benjamin Rush, *Thoughts on Female Education*

1790s State mercantilism encourages economic development

In their efforts to attract new enterprises and expand their economic bases, many states devised plans to make the incorporation of businesses easier. Corporate charters provided businesses with greater legal protection (limited liability) and with advantages not allowed to individuals (the right to take property under eminent domain). This push for state mercantilism facilitated the expansion of state and national economies and the development of a market economy.

Parents limit family size

At the turn of the nineteenth century the United States experienced a sharp decline in the birth rate. Many people chose to marry later in life and to have smaller families. This change grew out of economic reality: With less good land becoming available, parents were less likely to have large holdings to pass on to their children. Accordingly, they limited family size to ensure an adequate inheritance to all their children.

Second Great Awakening

For almost half a century—into the 1830s—the Second Great Awakening inspired an upsurge of revivalism and church growth. Old-line denominations fell out of favor, as evangelical churches—led by the Baptists and Methodists—spread Protestantism from New England to the South and into the frontier regions. In the climate of republicanism, the Second Great Awakening promoted democracy and cooperation among the churches and helped create a truly American form of Protestantism.

Republican motherhood defined

1791 First Bank of the United States founded; dissolved in 1811

Alexander Hamilton, as secretary of the treasury under George Washington, advocated the creation of a national bank (the Bank of the United States) to serve as the fiscal agent for the new nation under the Constitution. After successfully countering critics who believed the Bank to be unconstitutional, Hamilton won the president's support and congressional approval for the Bank. The Bank's twenty-year charter expired in 1811, but during its lifetime the national bank provided economic support for a growing economy.

1794 Lancaster Turnpike Company

During the nineteenth century the United States went through a transportation revolution that encouraged the movement of people into developing regions and the growth of the economy. The building of hard-surfaced roads was an important part of this revolution; the Lancaster Turnpike in Pennsylvania was a model for other states and regions to follow. The Lancaster Turnpike Company provided a good example of the growing relationship between state governments and private enterprise that allowed businesses to expand.

1795 Massachusetts Mill Dam Act

Under the commonwealth economic system, states gave priority to public good rather than private interests. The Mill Dam Act grew out of this new attitude. This law allowed mill owners to flood farmlands contiguous to their mills in return for "fair compensation" to the landowners whose farms were flooded. Massachusetts judged that more people would be served by the output of the miller than by that of the farmers whose land was lost.

1800s State-chartered banks proliferate

Following the examples of the Bank of North America and the Bank of the United States, in the early 1800s many states chartered banks to support economic development and expansion. These banks extended credit and loans to merchants and manufacturers. Despite some problems—some banks issued notes without adequate reserves of gold and silver—the development of a domestic banking system helped free the United States from its long-time dependence on British financial institutions.

Legal profession democratized

The rise of democracy had a broad impact on the American people and American institutions. The legal profession, for example, opened its doors by relaxing standards for admission to the bar. In addition, the creation of small-claims courts gave people an opportunity to seek redress of grievances without professional legal representation.

Rise of sentimentalism and republican marriage system

The predominance of republican values (especially support for greater democracy), increasing economic pressures on families, and the rise of sentimentalism dramatically altered attitudes toward marriage in the United States. Reason gave way to emotion, and concern for stability gave way to love. Instead of parents arranging marriages for their children, young men and women selected their own partners. Republican marriages lessened parental control over children but actually increased the power of husbands over wives, who no longer could turn easily to their parents for support.

1800s Women's religious activism

In the early 1800s many opportunities opened for women in church work. Outnumbering men in many denominations, women assumed a greater share of the responsibility for leadership and won the right to have mixed prayer in some churches. A few women, such as Jemima Wilkinson, achieved fame as revivalists. Women also practiced religious activism in their homes. As "republican mothers," American women shouldered the burden of guiding their children both morally and spiritually.

Spread of evangelical Baptists and Methodists

The growth of republicanism had a profound effect

on denominations, such as the Baptists and Methodists, that promoted democracy in church matters. Revivalism swept across the frontier regions of the country, stirring up audiences "as if by a storm," and brought huge gains in membership among whites and African-Americans. The religious look of the country changed dramatically, with evangelical churches becoming dominant in numbers and influence.

1801   Beginnings of Benevolent Empire
By linking salvation with social reform through the concept of benevolence, followers of the Second Great Awakening organized churches, charitable organizations, schools, and interdenominational societies and organizations to teach and spread their vision and reform society. This large religious movement added an intense religious aspect to politics and national identity that would change the course of history.

John Marshall becomes chief justice
Shortly before he left office, President John Adams appointed John Marshall as chief justice. For the next three decades, Marshall used the Supreme Court as a forum to proclaim the power of the federal government and ensure the federal government's supremacy over the states. Long after the Federalist party was dead in national politics, Marshall continued to voice Federalist doctrine and graft Federalism firmly onto the laws of the United States.

1803   *Marbury v. Madison* states theory of judicial review
Marbury is one of the landmark decisions of the Supreme Court, marking the first time the Court overturned a federal law—or, in this instance, a section of a federal law—as unconstitutional. This power of judicial review allows the Court to restrict the power of the executive and legislative branches and serves as a critical check within the system of checks and balances in the American government.

1805   Mercy Otis Warren, History of the American Revolution

1807   New Jersey excludes propertied women from suffrage
Through a loophole in the 1776 state law that granted suffrage to all property holders in New Jersey, women became active participants in electoral politics in the state. The Republican members of the state legislature, acting on Republican impulses, eliminated the property-holding requirements to vote and expanded the franchise to all adults. Soon after, arguing traditional biological ideas, women were excluded from citizenship and the vote. Republican theory, ironically in this case, worked against the rights of women.

1809   Washington Irving, *Diedrich Knickerbocker's History of New York*
Though a Federalist, aristocratic in taste, and a long-time resident of Europe, Washington Irving was one of the first American writers to make his living with the pen and established the beginnings of American literature.

**1810s   Expansion of suffrage for men
Lawyers important in politics**

1810   Albert Gallatin's *Report on Manufactures*
During the years preceding the War of 1812, with the United States cut off from British goods by Jefferson's policy of peaceful coercion, the country began to produce more goods for itself. Gallatin's *Report* gave the government an estimate of how well the United States was meeting its manufacturing needs.

***Fletcher v. Peck* expands contract clause**
The *Fletcher* decision prohibited the state of Georgia from reclaiming land granted to the Yazoo Land Company by the state legislature. The Court granted the right of a new legislature to rescind a law passed by a previous legislature but denied the right to rescind a contract executed under law. This ruling endorsed traditional concepts of property rights and contracts.

1816   Second Bank of the United States chartered
The creation of the Bank of the United States in 1791 had stirred political passions and engendered intense debate between the followers of Alexander Hamilton and those of Thomas Jefferson. The Second Bank, in contrast, won widespread approval in the climate of economic growth of the republican era. The Bank became a symbol of economic nationalism, reflecting the pride in their country that many Americans felt after the War of 1812.

1817   Bonus Bill vetoed by Madison

1819   *McCulloch v. Maryland* enhances power of national government
In *McCulloch*, the Marshall Court affirmed the power of Congress to take any actions deemed "necessary and proper" to carry out its responsibilities. This "elastic clause" in the Constitution provides for an expansion of national power. Looking at the specific situation in this case, the Court also ruled that states did not have the authority to tax the national government or federal institutions, in this case the Bank of the United States, noting in a key phrase that "the power to tax involves the power to destroy."

***Dartmouth College v. Woodward* protects corporate property rights**
Building on the decision in *Fletcher v. Peck*, in the *Dartmouth* case the Supreme Court ruled that "a contract within the letter of the Constitution, and within its spirit also," referring to the original colonial-era contract to found Dartmouth College, could not be impaired or overturned by a state law. Where *Fletcher* gave protection to individual property rights, *Dartmouth* guaranteed the protection of corporate property rights. At a time when states

were becoming more involved in economic expansion under the commonwealth system, *Dartmouth* slowed this process.

1818–
1821 **Democratic revision of state constitutions**
The close of the Federalist era in 1800 and a turn to republican ideology and popular sovereignty raised the "commonwealth" above private interests. In most states pressure was placed on legislators to democratize their political and economic systems and bring their state constitutions into line with these new attitudes and ideas. States became more active in promoting and funding internal improvements and public education, and removed property qualifications for voting. With these sorts of changes written into state constitutions, the country moved from traditional reliance on the elite to support for a broader base in the population.

1820s **Expansion of public primary school system**
Women became school teachers
Growth of cash-based market economy
In the early 1800s prominent Americans began to promote a wider distribution of knowledge to create a "republic of letters." In the 1820s these calls for change led to increased public funding for the primary grades. The curriculum was expanded and standards for teachers, most of whom were women, were raised, reflecting the belief that people needed to be educated to ensure success for the growing republic.

1821 *Cohens v. Virginia* **declares supremacy of national courts**
In *Cohens v. Virginia*, a case involving the sale of lottery tickets in Virginia, John Marshall and his colleagues on the Supreme Court ruled that federal courts had the authority to overturn decisions by state courts if a federal question was involved. This ruling fitted the patterns established by Marshall in his first two decades as chief justice, ensuring the supremacy of the federal government in its relationship with the states.

GLOSSARY

political economy   The political economy involves the interaction of political and economic processes through the formulation of governmental policies that support and encourage economic growth and development. Individuals who operate in the economy and, at the same time, enter politics or try to influence politicians to develop governmental policies favorable to their economic activities are acting within the political economy. (p. 266)

outwork or **putting-out system**   During the sixteenth century, English merchants supported the production of goods through an outwork system, using people in the countryside to produce textiles that the merchants in turn could sell in the market (see Chapter 1, text p. 28). The outwork system developed in the United States after the War of Independence. Farm families and rural artisans produced various goods, including tinware, cheese, cloth, and shoes the merchants sold in both domestic and overseas markets. This system created new job opportunities in rural America but cost some farmers their economic freedom because of their growing dependence on the merchants who sold their outwork and their transformation into consumers. (p. 268)

preindustrial   Full-blown industrial revolutions depended on technological innovations, such as the use of power-driven machinery, to do work that men and women traditionally did by hand. Reliance on hand crafting rather than on machinery for production is a prime characteristic of preindustrial (before machine-based) economies. This was the state of the American economy early in the nineteenth century. (p. 268)

corporate charters   During the colonial era, private investors in England often promoted the establishment of colonies through trading companies or joint-stock companies that were chartered by the Crown. Support from the government translated into a greater likelihood of success. The same system was used by state governments in the United States to encourage economic development. States awarded corporate charters to private businesses, assuring them of legal protection and an economic advantage over other businesses. In turn, these state-chartered corporations provided help to the states—for example, by building roads, bridges, and canals that encouraged expansion of the market economy. (p. 269)

commonwealth   In modern-day usage, *commonwealth* generally refers to a gathering of countries for political purposes, such as the British Commonwealth of Nations, which includes Great Britain and countries or colonies historically connected to Great Britain. In the United States in the early nineteenth century, the word had a more literal meaning: The "commonwealth" meant the public welfare, or the good of the people. State governments advocated a commonwealth system to achieve economic growth, giving emphasis and preference to public projects rather than private enterprise, and approved legislation that favored greater gains for the public. (p. 269)

limited liability   The establishment of joint-stock companies in England in the early 1600s facilitated the founding of colonies in America. A joint-stock company brought together several investors who shared risk and gained profit in proportion to their shares of the total investment (see Chapter 1, text p. 29). The idea of limited liability evolved in the nineteenth century to mean that the personal assets of shareholders could not be encumbered (that is, sold) to cover the debts of a corporation. Each individual could be held accountable for debts only to the extent of his or her investment in the corporation. (p. 270)

eminent domain   Under the law, this principle grants a government control of all property within its sovereign jurisdiction, with the power to take and use property for public purposes, provided that compensation is given for the property that is taken. Land can be taken and used even if the owner does not want to surrender title to the property. Under the early nineteenth-century system of state mercantilism, states granted this power to private corporations, which, like the states themselves, could seize property for public use—for example, for roads, bridges, and canals. (p. 270)

precedents   In jurisprudence (law) this term describes a previous instance or case that can serve as a model for judgment in a current case. By using previous rulings to provide a justification or a rationale for a decision, judges can maintain consistency and continuity over a long span of time. (p. 270)

common law   This law was based on nature, reason, and tradition and built up, case by case, precedent by precedent, over time. It was considered by conservatives to be unchanging and venerable. (pp. 270–271)

social utility   Under the commonwealth economic system that developed in the United States in the nineteenth century, state governments intruded into the economy in extraordinary fashion for that time. They emphasized public good over private interest, judging the value of their actions (legislation, court rulings, and so on) according to the number of people affected. In other words, the states favored changes that provided the greatest good for the greatest number of people. This approach flew in the face of traditional attitudes, which had favored the good of individuals, but it served the needs of the growing young nation. (p. 271)

judicial review   In the American system of government, the concept of checks and balances is paramount, ensuring that none of the three branches of government can dominate or control the others. For the judicial branch—that is, the federal courts—the key check is the power of judicial review, or the power to judge the constitutionality of laws passed by Congress and executive orders issued by the president. This power is implicit within the Constitution but came into practice in 1803 with the Supreme Court's ruling in *Marbury v. Madison*. (p. 272)

contract clause   Under the Constitution, Article I, Section 10, states are prohibited from passing laws "impairing the

Obligation of Contracts." The founders endorsed this contract clause in order to void state laws that protected debtors at the expense of their creditors. During John Marshall's tenure as chief justice, the Supreme Court expanded the scope of this clause. This prohibition of congressional impairment of contracts became the means the justices used to protect property owners and corporations against intrusion by state legislatures. The result—in *Fletcher v. Peck* (1810) and *Dartmouth College v. Woodward* (1819)—was a slowing of state mercantilism. (p. 272)

deferential   The politics of the eighteenth century assumed that elite men, having status, experience, wealth, and time, could best represent the people and should, therefore, be allowed to hold office. This idea was rejected by republicans. (p. 274)

sentimentalism   From the colonial era into the early republic, the United States tended to import ideas from Europe rather than develop uniquely American ideas. For example, the Enlightenment (emphasizing reason) and Pietism (emphasizing emotion) shaped American society and thought in the mid-1700s. Later in the century, the Romantic movement in Europe spawned sentimentalism, which had a similar influence on American attitudes and actions. The emphasis in sentimentalism was on feelings and emotions rather than reason and logic, and the impact on the American people was profound. Love became as important in marriage as financial considerations; religion took on a more emotional feel, to the point of encouraging a new awakening among the people. (p. 278)

demographic transition   A significant shift in the size of the population owing to a sharp change—a rise or a fall—in either the birthrate or the death rate, is referred to as a demographic transition. Around the turn of the nineteenth century, the United States experienced this sort of transition when the birthrate declined dramatically. In some urban areas the decline over a half-century was 50 percent among white women. Smaller families meant reduced population pressure in settled areas and a greater opportunity for social and economic stability. (p. 279)

benevolence   Broadly conceived as the desire to do good for others, *benevolence* became a seminal concept in American religious thinking during the Second Great Awakening. Rejecting the Calvinist notion of predestination in favor of universal salvation, promoters of benevolence suggested that people who had experienced saving grace could inspire other people to find salvation. Some acted individually, others worked through benevolent organizations that aspired to reform society. (p. 285)

IDENTIFICATION

Identify by filling in the blanks.

1. In the late 1700s and early 1800s the greatest success for the rural outwork system occurred in the making of _____ . (p. 268)

2. As capitalism developed and people began to specialize and improve productivity and efficiency a cash economy began to replace the traditional _____ system. (p. 269)

3. The power of a government to take control of private lands for state or national use, such as acquiring rights-of-way for roads, is known as _____ . (p. 270)

4. The power of the federal courts to determine whether laws are constitutional is known as _____ . (p. 272)

5. During the Revolutionary Era, attorneys promoted laws designed to prevent untrained lawyers known as "_____" from entering the legal profession. (p. 277)

6. Among the most famous graduates of the Litchfield law school were two future vice-presidents, _____ and _____ . (p. 277)

7. Born out of the Romantic movement in Europe in the late 1700s, _____ celebrated the role of "feeling" rather than reason as the best way to understand the experiences of life. (p. 278)

8. Among republican families the traditional authoritarian Calvinist approach to child rearing was being replaced by a more _____ approach. (p. 280)

9. The American writer of the early 1800s who enthralled readers with tales of Dutch-American life in works such as *The Sketch Book* was _____ . (p. 282)

10. During the Second Great Awakening the most spectacular growth in membership was experienced by the _____ and _____

churches, making them the largest religious denominations in the United States. (p. 283)

11. Across the West the Second Great Awakening was spread by ministers who traveled from place to place and held revivals. These ministers were called _____ . (p. 283)

12. Protestants who believed in a single "united" God were called _____ . (p. 284)

13. The first institutions of higher education for women were called _____ . (p. 287)

SKILL-BUILDING EXERCISE

1. At the turn of the nineteenth century, American territory east of the Mississippi River had been carved into territories or states. On the map above locate and identify the three regions that were territories rather than states.

2. By 1830 all but six states had eliminated property ownership as a qualification for voting for white men. On the map above locate and identify those six states:
   a. two states of the Old South
   b. one state in the new West
   c. one state that had been one of the middle colonies
   d. two states in New England

DOCUMENT EXERCISES

American Voices

Manners in the New Republic— Charles W. Janson

During the early 1800s, hundreds of upper-class Europeans traveled to the United States, some for pleasure and others to assess the state of the new nation. The most famous visitor was Alexis de Tocqueville, a French aristocrat, who gave fairly high marks to the United States. The largest number of visitors probably came from Great Britain. Charles Dickens, Harriet Martineau, and Frances Trollope led the British contingent, giving the American experiment in democracy and individualism mixed reviews. The more derisive comments about American society—focusing negatively on equalitarianism, republicanism, and slavery—fueled an Anglophobia that had begun to build in Anglo-American relations.

As you read "Manners in the New Republic," ask yourself the following questions:

1. What words in the first part of this selection indicate Charles Janson's displeasure about his treatment?

2. What is Janson's view of mealtime manners in America?

3. What does Janson say about the attitudes of servants? How does his meeting with the "servant-maid" reinforce these views?

4. What implications can you draw about relations between whites and African-Americans in the United States from reading this selection?

The Dilemmas of Womanhood— Eliza Southgate

In the early nineteenth century the United States experienced profound changes in attitudes and values. Republican ideology encouraged greater democratization of society; popular sovereignty, a staple of republican thought, encouraged people to make their own decisions. Educational opportunities also expanded, and the doors to schools began to open for girls as well as boys. Young women learned about equality, although they frequently continued to play subordinate roles. In this selection, Eliza Southgate writes of this dichotomy between equality and subordination.

As you read "The Dilemmas of Womanhood," ask yourself the following questions:

1. In what aspect of a woman's life was "inequality of privilege" between men and women the most telling?

2. Why did this inequality between men and women not seem to bother Eliza?

3. In what ways did she see men and women as equal? Could men and women be equal and still find "harmony" in their lives? Or was inequality actually preferable?

American Lives

Unruly Women: Jemima Wilkinson and Deborah Sampson Gannett

Jemima Wilkinson and Deborah Sampson Gannett, emboldened by the converging currents of the Second Great Awakening and republican ideology that called upon women to play a more public role in shaping public morality, were not content to stay within the limitations prescribed by this ideology. Both Wilkinson's and Gannett's conversion experiences resolved them to seek truth and avenge wrong. Both broke through the strictures placed on female behavior and participation in religion and politics and participated in public—at the risk of being considered "disorderly (or unruly) women." While Wilkinson, a striking woman with a magnetic personality, preached and established a utopian community in western New York, Gannett disguised herself as a man and served in the Continental army for seventeen months. Though neither woman won a major battle or devised any new system of doctrine or social values, they did challenge contemporary social ideology and articulated a more active and public role for women.

As you read "Unruly Women," ask yourself the following questions:

1. How were both women affected by the radical implications of the Second Great Awakening and republicanism?

2. Compare and contrast the ways Wilkinson and Sampson went about achieving their goals.

3. How did each woman carry through on her initial challenges to the social ideology of gender and class?

4. What was the impact of these women on history?

SELF-TEST

Multiple Choice

1. During the colonial period the economic life of seacoast cities was dominated by:
   a. farmers.   c. merchants.
   b. artisans.   d. ministers.

2. John Jacob Astor's fortune was based largely on real estate investments that he financed with profits from:
a. farming in Pennsylvania.
b. the fur trade.
c. rural manufacturing of tinware.
d. the sugar trade with the West Indies.

3. The *Letter on Manufactures* (1810), which described dramatic growth in the American economy, was written by Secretary of the Treasury:
a. Robert Oliver.
b. Robert Morris.
c. Alexander Hamilton.
d. Albert Gallatin.

4. The "Commonwealth System" involved *all* of the following policies *except*:
a. corporate charters with limited liability.
b. monopoly charters with eminent domain for transportation projects.
c. high tariffs against imports.
d. judicial support of corporate activity on the basis of "social utility."

5. One of the early successes in solving transportation problems in the United States was the construction of the Lancaster Turnpike in 1794 in:
a. Pennsylvania.   c. Virginia.
b. New York.   d. North Carolina.

6. Under the terms of the Massachusetts Mill Dam Act of 1795:
a. the state set a fair market price for mill goods.
b. mill owners could flood farmlands adjacent to their mills if they paid "fair compensation" to the farmers.
c. farmers could sue mill owners for triple damages if they overcharged for mill products.
d. Massachusetts and Connecticut agreed not to place dams anywhere along the Connecticut River.

7. *All* of the following describe the ideas and principles of Chief Justice John Marshall *except* he:
a. was a loose constructionist.
b. used contract clause to defend property rights.
c. believed in the "Commonwealth System" notion of government.
d. claimed the right of judicial supremacy.

8. The Supreme Court upheld the constitutionality of the Bank of the United States in the case of:
a. *Marbury v. Madison.*
b. *Fletcher v. Peck.*
c. *McCulloch v. Maryland.*
d. *Cohens v. Virginia.*

9. By the end of the 1820s property qualifications for voting remained in place in *all* of the following states *except*:

a. Rhode Island.   c. Louisiana.
b. Virginia.   d. New Jersey.

10. In the early nineteenth century, the pursuit of Republican ideals gradually transformed American politics and society in *all* of the following ways *except*:
a. increasing social mobility.
b. expanding suffrage to include all men and women.
c. compelling professions to open entrance standards and limit elitist practices.
d. cultivating the development of more egalitarian "companionate marriages" at the core of more affectionate, egalitarian families.

11. During the early 1800s traditionally strict child-rearing practices such as punishment rather than affection were the norm for *all* of the following religious groups *except*:
a. Anglicans.   c. Congregationalists.
b. Baptists.   d. Methodists.

12. The most outspoken and active feminist in the United States in the early nineteenth century was:
a. Eliza Southgate.   c. Mary Wollstonecraft.
b. Jemima Wilkinson.   d. Ann Lee.

13. Emma Willard became prominent in the United States in the early 1800s when she:
a. established a large Shaker community in Indiana.
b. publicly advocated higher education for women.
c. founded *Mother's Magazine*.
d. became the first woman lay preacher in the Methodist church.

14. During the early 1800s democratic forms of church government were typical in *all* of the following denominations *except*:
a. Baptists.   c. Quakers.
b. Congregationalists. d. Episcopalians.

15. The most famous Unitarian minister of the early nineteenth century was:
a. Jonathan Edwards.
b. Lyman Beecher.
c. William Ellery Channing.
d. Samuel Hopkins.

16. In *Letters from an American Farmer* (1782), St. Jean de Crèvecoeur praised the American people for their:
a. development of a mixed economy that emphasized manufacturing as well as agriculture.
b. willingness to experiment with new grain crops, such as wheat, for sale on the world market.
c. creation of a new social order that rejected elitism and aristocracy.
d. ability to change administrations from one political party to another without resorting to violence.

17. In the early nineteenth century the American people created a new national culture and social order based on *all* of the following *except*:
    a. the principles of republicanism.
    b. social equality among racial and ethnic groups.
    c. commercial capitalism.
    d. evangelical Protestantism.

Short Essays

Answer the following in a brief paragraph.

1. How did the emergence of capitalism out of a market economy restructure economic and social relationships? Were the effects of specialization, monetary exchange, and market competition positive or negative? (pp. 266–269)

2. How did John Marshall use his position as chief justice of the United States to strengthen the power of the national government? (pp. 269–273)

3. Was "demographic transition" caused more by economic or cultural factors? (pp. 279–280)

4. In what ways did American education reflect the ideals of the growing republic in the early 1800s? (pp. 279–287)

5. How did the role of women change in the United States in the early 1800s? (pp. 279–287)

6. What historical developments of the republican era helped create a distinctly national character in the United States by the 1820s? (p. 285 and throughout Chapter 9)

ANSWERS

Chapter Précis

1. outwork or putting-out
2. Bonus Bill
3. precedents
4. *Marbury v. Madison*
5. contract clause
6. Litchfield
7. companionate
8. demographic transition
9. Noah Webster
10. Universalists
11. Lyman Beecher

12. Benjamin Rush
13. Shaker

Identification

1. shoes and/or boots
2. barter-exchange
3. eminent domain
4. judicial review
5. pettifoggers
6. Aaron Burr, John C. Calhoun
7. sentimentalism
8. affectionate rationalist
9. Washington Irving
10. Baptist; Methodist
11. circuit-riders
12. Unitarians
13. female seminaries

Skill-Building Exercise

For locations, see Map 9.1, text p. 276.
1. Indiana Territory, Ohio Territory, and Mississippi Territory.

2. a. Virginia and South Carolina
   b. Tennessee
   c. New Jersey
   d. Connecticut and Rhode Island

Self-Test

Multiple Choice

1. c	7. c	13. b
2. b	8. c	14. d
3. d	9. d	15. c
4. c	10. b	16. c
5. a	11. a	17. b
6. b	12. c	

Short Essays

1. Farmers moved from self-sufficiency to producing crops or manufactured products for a cash market. They became more productive and worked harder,

but now, instead of being self-sufficient and supplying all their own needs, they specialized in producing one thing and acquired the rest of their needs for barter or cash from others in the town, and increasingly for cash or credit from a merchant. Though individuals began to work for their own self-interest, this meant they also worked increasingly for others, and were more dependent on other people's actions and decisions as well as on the workings of the market. Hence, farmers lost some of their autonomy even as they became more productive and better off.

2. As an old-line Federalist, John Marshall believed that the national government was supreme in its relationship to the states. As chief justice of the Supreme Court, Marshall was in a good position to champion this belief. In *Marbury v. Madison,* the Marshall Court proclaimed the right of judicial review by declaring a national law unconstitutional. In *McCulloch v. Maryland,* the Court prohibited states from taxing the federal government and reaffirmed the power of Congress to do whatever was "necessary and proper" to fulfill its responsibilities. In *Cohens v. Virginia,* Marshall proclaimed the supremacy of federal courts over state courts. These decisions incorporated Federalist principles into the law of the land and enhanced the power of the national government.

3. Shrinking farm sizes and declining real income in the East encouraged people to reduce the size of their families. In addition, as many people responded economically to the declining size of farms by migrating West in search of better, cheaper land, they decreased the availability of marriage partners, delaying marriages and, thus, reducing the number of children being born. Nevertheless, because republicanism valued children more, and advocated a more intensive affectionate rational approach to parenting, couples began to reduce the number of children they had so as to concentrate their efforts on raising fewer, better, republican citizens. Likewise, the increasing demands to educate children increased the cost of raising children. Finally, the enhanced role and status of women as equal partners in marriage probably affected how couples made reproductive decisions.

4. In America's early history, educational opportunities were limited to a select few who attended private schools or studied with personal tutors. In the early 1800s increasing numbers of people, including Thomas Jefferson, proposed an expansion of educa-

tion to create a "republic of letters." By the 1820s the call for change had been answered, with state funds being used to support a broad system of public education for the children of ordinary citizens. The core of instruction continued to be the "three R's," with American history also becoming a staple of the curriculum in an effort to instill patriotism in young Americans. The "blue-backed speller" helped give Americans a common vocabulary and grammar. The result was more children going to school, at least in the primary grades, to become part of a better-educated citizenry.

5. During the colonial era women were subservient to men in law and in custom. In the early nineteenth century the role of women changed dramatically. They were still kept out of the political arena, and under law women continued to suffer male domination. However, in many ways the sphere of women in society was enlarged, to the advantage of women and the country as a whole. As "republican mothers," women were given greater responsibility for the moral upbringing of their children and for the political instruction of their sons. Women took on leadership roles in churches and encouraged changes in religious practices. Women's educational opportunities also expanded. Seminaries and schools for girls provided greater access to knowledge, and women began to displace men as teachers in public schools. The role of women in American life was much greater than it had ever been.

6. Three major developments came together by the 1820s to create a distinct national character for the American people. The rise of a market economy, including the growth of rural manufacturing, initiated a shift from agriculture to a mixed economy that blended agriculture and manufacturing. The growth of republicanism, including the promotion of democracy and popular sovereignty, encouraged people to think for themselves and to value individuality rather than defer to an aristocratic elite. Finally, the Second Great Awakening inspired the emergence of a distinctly American version of Protestantism, characterized by democratic practices and stirring emotionalism. These economic, political, social, and religious changes pushed the American people to break away from their European cultural heritage and celebrate their American identity.

PART 3

Early Industrialization and the Sectional Crisis *1820–1877*

Part 3 covers American history from the early Industrial Revolution to the end of Reconstruction. The Thematic Timeline (p. 292) lists the main developments under five topical headings: the economy, society, culture, politics and government, and sectionalism. Read the Timeline and the Part introduction together, beginning with the left-hand Timeline column.

The first column traces the main stages of the most transforming development of this period, the Industrial Revolution. The significance of industrialization is explained in the first two paragraphs of the Part introduction.

Another consequence of industrialization, as documented in the second column of the Timeline, was the emergence of a new class structure. Social structure was altered even more dramatically by the end of slavery. Paragraphs three and four of the Part introduction discuss these developments.

Third, social and economic change produced a wide variety of reform movements, from tranquil utopian communities to abolitionism's fervent challenges to the established order. The fifth paragraph of the Part introduction explains the significance of reform in the antebellum and Reconstruction eras.

Fourth, as the nation expanded westward, political life became more democratic. Paragraph four examines the impact of democratization on the American party system.

The final column, Sectionalism, traces the struggle between North and South throughout this period, from the compromises and crises of the prewar period, through the establishment of the Confederacy, to the readmission of the southern states to the Union. The last three paragraphs of the Part introduction outline the causes of the Civil War and assess the accomplishments and legacy of Reconstruction.

Now read across the Timeline, looking for relationships among events taking place in the same period. The entries for 1850–1860, for example, suggest a connection between the publication in 1852 of the powerful antislavery novel *Uncle Tom's Cabin* and the events later in the decade—the Kansas-Nebraska Act, the *Dred Scott* decision, and John Brown's raid—all of which heightened the sense of crisis prior to the Civil War.

Part Questions

After you have completed studying the chapters in Part 3, you should be able to answer the following questions:

1. What circumstances explain the rapid spread of the Industrial Revolution in the northern United States? Why did the same thing *not* happen in the South?

2. Explain how the introduction of the factory system influenced the structure of American society.

3. Compare and contrast the reform objectives of the Benevolent Empire and the calls by transcendentalists and other utopians, woman suffrage advocates, and abolitionists for radical change in American society. What did each of these reform movements accomplish?

4. What explains the democratic movement in American politics and the rise of Andrew Jackson?

5. Describe American expansionism from the acquisition of Florida (1819) to the Mexican War and the adventurism of Franklin Pierce. Why did the United States pursue an expansionist foreign policy during these years? What were the consequences?

6. Why did slavery become an increasingly divisive issue after 1820? In framing your answer, consider social and economic realities, the power of abolitionist and proslavery arguments, and the cohesiveness of the national parties.

7. How do you explain the Union victory in the Civil War?

8. Why did the North not take full advantage of its victory during Reconstruction?

CHAPTER 10

The Industrial Revolution 1820–1840

★ ★ ★

CHAPTER PRÉCIS

The Rise of Northeastern Manufacturing

pp. 296–303

New Organization and New Technology

The Industrial Revolution in America concentrated in the Northeast, where the first factories brought workers together in one place and applied the principle of division of labor. This increased productivity, which also benefited from many technological innovations. The combination of the factory and technological creativity dramatically improved output.

1. The dramatic gain in productivity that occurred in American industry during the Industrial Revolution was due to the combination of _____ and _____ . (p. 297)

The Textile Industry

The American textile industry owed its beginning to British mechanics who brought their knowledge of British machinery with them to the United States. Although the newborn American textile industry had available abundant raw materials and water power, manufacturers found it difficult to compete against established British mills, which, due to a cheap labor force, were able to pay workers far less.

2. Factors that made American industry noncompetitive with regard to British manufacturing included _____ , _____ , and _____ . (p. 299)

The Boston Manufacturing Company

In 1814 the Boston Manufacturing Company opened a textile plant in Waltham, Massachusetts, which was the first in the United States to perform under one roof all the operations of making cloth. This mill recruited its work force among the girls and young women of New England farm families, and they made up the bulk of the labor force in the early textile industry. Other textile manufacturers employed entire families. The availability of this cheap work force enabled American textile mills to overtake British manufacturers. It also made it possible for New England manufacturers to best other American textile producers.

American Mechanical Genius

Mechanics and merchants most often provided the capital for new industrial enterprises. Craftsmen also contributed to the Industrial Revolution inventions that improved American manufacturing. Development of the machine-tool industry made it possible for the Industrial Revolution to spread throughout American manufacturing.

The Expansion of Markets   pp. 303–314

Regional Trade Patterns

A national system of markets developed as an accompaniment to the Industrial Revolution. Exports declined and domestic trade increased as more and more goods were exchanged between regions and within regions. The cotton-producing South was the exception, its economy being more closely tied to Britain's.

The Growth of Cities and Towns

Economic expansion and the growth of trade stimulated the pace of urban growth in the United States. Cities that were manufacturing centers and those located at transportation junctions flourished. During the 1820s and 1830s, New York City became the nation's most important economic center—thanks in large part to the construction of the Erie Canal, which connected the city to the interior of the continent.

The West: Farming New Land

Even as American cities grew in size and number, farm families were settling new lands. They were drawn westward primarily by the availability of low-priced land and virgin soil. Farm work was made easier and more productive by new farming implements. This agricultural expansion encouraged industrial and urban growth by providing raw materials for factories, food supplies for urban populations, and markets for manufactured goods.

The Transportation Revolution

Economic expansion, both industrial and agricultural, was made possible in part by transportation improvements that included better roads and new waterways, the most important of which was the Erie Canal between Albany and Buffalo, New York. This publicly funded project stim-

3. The mid-Atlantic and Southern states were not able to compete with New England textile manufacturing because _____ . (p. 301)

4. One of the most important keys to success for small entrepreneurial manufacturers was the ability to rely on _____ . (p. 302)

5. Unlike the North, which focused on regional trade, the South became a major exporter, primarily to _____ . (p. 306)

6. The fastest-growing industrial towns in the 1820s and 1830s were those located along the fall line due to their access to _____ . (p. 306)

7. Congress significantly encouraged western expansion by reducing the price of _____ in 1820. (p. 309)

8. Much of the funding for the boom in canal construction was provided by _____ , which often borrowed the necessary funds. (p. 311)

ulated the economic development of the entire region it traversed. The steamboat increased the speed of water transportation and reduced its cost. The initial construction of railroads also began during these years, but the main railroad boom lay in the future.

Government and the Business Corporation

State governments assisted economic growth by gradually making it easier for business enterprises to use the corporate form of organization. The Supreme Court under Chief Justices Marshall and Taney encouraged business enterprise in a number of important decisions.

9. In *Charles River Bridge v. Warren Bridge*, Chief Justice Roger B. Taney stimulated economic competition by striking down _____ . (p. 314)

Social Structure in Industrializing Society

pp. 314–323

The Industrial Revolution raised the standard of living of most Americans, but it also increased the distance between social classes and encouraged class antagonisms. By so doing it challenged the nation's republican and democratic ideals.

The Concentration of Wealth

The share of the national wealth held by the richest American families increased substantially between 1800 and 1860. The concentration of wealth in the hands of a few was especially marked in the major port cities. This happened because wealthy families were better able to take advantage of the new economic opportunities. The middle class also grew rapidly.

10. Those individuals who designed and/or put into operation _____ enjoyed the highest growing profits and incomes. (p. 314)

The New Urban Poor

At the same time a substantial portion of the nation's population—as many as half of its free workers—labored for wages and had little social mobility. Their incomes remained very low when measured in terms of the cost of living. Of all free workers, day laborers faced the greatest economic hardships and the worst insecurity. One result of these deteriorating conditions was increased alcohol abuse.

11. The lack of _____ ownership by wage laborers led to the development of an increasingly permanent class of transient casual laborers. (p. 316)

The Rise of the Business Class

As the business class expanded during the 1820s and 1830s, its members became increasingly conscious of the differences between themselves and the working class. The business class included wealthy factory owners, merchants, and financiers, and a new "middle class" of clerks, foremen, mechanics, shopkeepers, and prosperous farmers who shared their values. The business class believed in the virtue of hard work and the ideal of the "self-made man." Some recognized that although their values were democratic, the economic system was not.

12. Benjamin Franklin's widely read *Autobiography*, published in 1818, extolled the business-class values of _____ , and _____ . (p. 319)

The Benevolent Empire

Physical proximity in the cities ensured that the well-to-do would be aware of working-class poverty and disorder. So members of the business class supported a variety of reform associations to encourage greater social discipline. Women were particularly active in these reform organizations, which had among their objectives ensuring a more solemn observance of the Sabbath.

Business-Class Revivalism and Reform

Charles Grandison Finney, the most important Protestant revivalist of this period, preached a religious message that aided these reform efforts. Finney taught that each person possesses a free will, which he or she should use to accept God's saving grace. At his dramatic revivals, members of the business class and some of the poor found moral strength and social respectability. Converts pledged to reform their own lives and those of their workers, especially by curtailing alcohol abuse. They hoped to create a society based on Protestant evangelical principles. This form of revivalism swept through communities from New England to the Ohio River Valley. As it did so, it strengthened the campaign of the American Temperance Society and encouraged adherence to the work ethic. These were the values that shaped the identity of the American business class.

13. Lyman Beecher, a leading Presbyterian minister, captured the essence of the Benevolent Empire when he called for the restoration of the

_____ of God. (p. 319)

14. Evangelical reform appealed particularly to the new middle class because it reinforced _____ within the business class and encouraged

_____ . (p. 323)

EXPANDED TIMELINE

1765	**James Hargreaves invents spinning jenny**
1782	**Oliver Evans develops automated flour mill**
1790	**Samuel Slater's cotton mill opens in Providence, R.I.** Slater, a British mechanic, introduced advanced British spinning technology to America. The opening of his cotton mill marked the beginning of the Industrial Revolution in the United States.
1793	**Eli Whitney manufactures cotton gins** Whitney's cotton gin revolutionized cotton production. Later he pioneered the construction of machine tools, which made it possible to manufacture products with interchangeable parts, the crucial first step toward mass production. In 1798 Whitney secured a federal contract to manufacture 10,000 muskets.
1807	**Robert Fulton launches the *Clermont*** Much faster and more reliable than sailing vessels, the steamboat dramatically reduced transportation costs on inland rivers.
1814	**Boston Manufacturing Company builds Waltham cotton mill** The Waltham mill combined innovations in technology—Paul Moody's high-speed power

loom—with innovations in organization. It was the first plant in America to combine all the operations of cloth making under one roof, while the Waltham plan provided a reliable supply of young women workers.

1817	**New York Stock Exchange founded** **Erie Canal begun**
1819	**Cast-iron plow invented** The cast-iron plow and other improvements in the tools used by farmers increased productivity by making farm labor easier.
1820	**Price of federal land reduced to $1.25 per acre** Public land had been relatively inexpensive at $2.00 per acre. The new, lower price meant that a still greater number of farmers could acquire western lands. This fact, combined with a rapidly growing population, spurred the westward migration.
1824	**Franklin Institute founded** Established by Philadelphia mechanics, the Franklin Institute actively encouraged technological innovation and professionalism. Mechanics founded similar institutions in other cities.
	Passage of a major protective tariff This was the first significant tax on imported goods (iron, woolens, cotton, and hemp) to protect American industries from cheaper imported goods.

Supreme Court strikes down a monopoly in *Gibbons v. Ogden*
The Supreme Court struck down a state-granted, steamboat passenger service monopoly, opening up business competition.

1825   **Erie Canal completed**

Jefferson proclaims U.S. technological independence.

1828   **Baltimore and Ohio Railroad chartered**
Chartering of the Baltimore and Ohio marks the beginning of the construction of a railroad system that would be indispensable to the future industrial expansion of the United States.

1831   **Charles Grandison Finney begins Rochester revival**
Finney had already achieved impressive successes in the smaller towns and villages of New York State. His Rochester revival lasted six months, continuing into 1831.

1832   **First die-forging machine built**
Devised by David Hinman and Elisha K. Root, the die-forging machine forced hot metal into dies, or cutting forms. This development was essential for the perfection of machine tools.

1833   **National Road crosses Ohio River**
Construction of the interstate National Road from Cumberland, Maryland, to Vandalia, Illinois, took from 1818 to 1850.

1837   **Supreme Court decides *Charles River Bridge v. Warren Bridge***
Led by Chief Justice Roger B. Taney, the Court ruled against the monopolistic privilege granted to the older Charles River Bridge Company by the Massachusetts legislature. Thus, the Court favored economic competition at the expense of vested economic interests.

GLOSSARY

mechanics   In preindustrial society, goods necessary to daily life such as boots, shoes, barrels, glass bottles, soap, candles, pots and pans, furniture, and clothing were made by hand by skilled craftsmen and artisans. During the early Industrial Revolution, these skilled workers came to be called mechanics. (p. 297)

fall line   The fall line refers to the boundary between two geological zones lying east of the Appalachian Mountains. It runs at an angle from the northeast to the southwest and is closer to the coast in the northeastern sector. The rivers flowing from the Appalachians to the Atlantic drop in waterfalls and rapids, where they cross from one geological zone to the other, thus providing ideal sites to harness the power of flowing water. (p. 299)

tariff   A tariff is a tax placed on imports. Such taxes can be used by a government to discourage the importation of certain types of goods or goods from a specific country, usually to protect the home nation's own producers from foreign competition. The tariff is one of the most important devices by which governments control their foreign trade and encourage economic activities. (p. 299)

machine tools   The most important contribution of American mechanics to the Industrial Revolution was the invention of machine tools—machines that could be used to produce other machines. Machine tools produced interchangeable parts that required very little filing or fitting, greatly lowering the costs of machine production. (p. 302)

packet service   Packet boats, originally so named because they carried packets of mail, followed regular routes, carrying passengers, freight, and mail. Packet service, by extension, designated sailing vessels that operated on regular schedules rather than waiting for wind, weather, and tide. The regularity of packets made them especially useful to businessmen, who could rely on reasonably consistent communications and transportation. (p. 307)

camp meeting   The first camp meeting gathered at Cane Ridge on the Kentucky frontier in 1800, and this revival technique quickly spread in frontier areas. Camp meetings brought people together in areas where population was dispersed. Whole families would come from miles around to the meeting where they would camp out in huts or tents for perhaps a week. This intensified the emotional impact of the preaching, which went on almost continuously. It was also a lot of fun. (p. 322)

IDENTIFICATION

Identify by filling in the blanks.

1. The _____ brought the elements of production together in one place and facilitated the specialization of tasks. (p. 296)

2. The most important of the mechanics who brought British technology to New England was _____ . (p. 297)

3. The paternalistic system that provided boarding houses and supervision of young women textile workers is known as _____ . (p. 300)

4. The _____ in Philadelphia supported the development of mechanical skills and knowledge. (p. 302)

5. American cities grew rapidly in number and size from 1820 to 1840, but _____ outpaced every other city and the nation as a whole in its spectacular growth. (p. 307)

6. By 1840 approximately _____ of the American population lived west of the Appalachian Mountains. (p. 309)

7. The federal government's most important contribution to the transportation revolution was _____ . (p. 310)

8. The Supreme Court justices who most strongly influenced federal laws affecting business and economic enterprise were _____ and _____ . (p. 314)

9. The widely read work, published in 1818, extolling the values of the business class was _____ .(p. 319)

10. To promote proper observance of the Sabbath, _____ and other Protestant ministers founded _____ in 1828. (p. 320)

11. The most influential Protestant revivalist in the 1830s was _____ . (p. 321)

12. Organized in 1828, _____ was the most successful evangelical reform group. (p. 322)

SKILL-BUILDING EXERCISE

1. Locate the following on the outline map on the right:
   a. The four largest American cities in 1840
   b. Six of the most important manufacturing sites in 1840

2. Trace the three streams of westward migration (by using arrows).

3. Trace the route of the Erie Canal.

DOCUMENT EXERCISES

American Voices

Early Days at Lowell—Lucy Larcom

The experience of the workers in the first American factories is a subject of special interest, partly because so many

Americans associated industrial activity with vice. The beginning of the factory system, however, did not provoke the opposition and resistance that one might have expected after reading the Jeffersonians' condemnations of cities and industry. This American Voice helps us understand why Americans accepted the Industrial Revolution with such ease.

As you read "Early Days at Lowell," ask yourself the following questions:

1. What does this account suggest about the work atmosphere in the mill?

2. How would you describe Lucy Larcom's attitude toward the machinery?

3. What qualities does she admire in the young women with whom she works?

4. What career choices did these young women have? In what sense did mill work offer the women opportunity?

5. In light of this account, why did the coming of industry *not* seem to violate the Jeffersonian vision of America?

A Food Riot in New York—Philip Hone

Crowd actions were well established as a social activity long before the incidents described in this piece. The Stamp Act riots and the Boston Tea Party are only the best remembered of the numerous outbursts of group violence in early American history. Philip Hone's account is of special interest because it reveals some of the dynamics of group violence in the growing cities during the Industrial Revolution.

As you read "A Food Riot in New York," ask yourself the following questions:

1. What seems to have happened?

2. What is Philip Hone's attitude toward the rioters and the events he describes? What is the point of his ironic use of the word "notable" in the first sentence?

3. Why are the weather conditions significant?

4. What seems to have caused the riot?

5. Who stopped the first attack?

6. In light of this account, what conclusions can you draw about living conditions and class antagonisms in New York City during the Industrial Revolution?

American Lives

Eli Whitney: Machine Builder and Promoter

Eli Whitney, one of America's most famous inventors, transformed both southern agriculture and the manufacturing process, yet he profited very little from his ideas.

As you read "Eli Whitney," ask yourself the following questions:

1. What problems was Whitney attempting to solve when he devised the cotton gin and machine tools?

2. What obstacles or situations prevented Whitney from profiting by his inventions?

3. What does Whitney's life tell you about the changes that were taking place in the American economy?

New Technology

Cotton-Spinning Machines

The text points out that a combination of two factors drove the Industrial Revolution. One factor involved new ways of organizing workers engaged in a manufacturing enterprise. The other was the development and application of technological innovations. The textile industry in both Britain and the United States was important economically for reducing the cost and increasing the availability of thread, cloth, and clothing. This was one part of the Industrial Revolution. Textile manufacturing also provides a concrete and specific example of how a combination of new work arrangements and the application of powered machines transformed one industry.

As you read "Cotton-Spinning Machines," ask yourself the following questions:

1. How did the spinning jenny differ from the spinning wheel? How did a worker operate a spinning jenny?

2. What advantages did the water frame possess over the spinning jenny?

3. What steps were involved in operating a water frame?

4. Why was the thread produced by the water frame so useful in American textile manufacturing?

5. What effect did the mechanization of the textile industry have on other industries?

SELF-TEST

Multiple Choice

1. One consequence of the Industrial Revolution in America during the 1830s and 1840s was that it:
   a. raised the standard of living of all Americans.
   b. increased the standard of living of most Americans.
   c. eased tensions between rich and poor.
   d. encouraged a more equitable distribution of wealth.

2. British textile manufacturers possessed *all* of the following advantages in competing with Americans *except*:
   a. low shipping rates.   c. low wage rates.
   b. low interest rates.   d. a protective tariff.

3. Oliver Evans's flour mill did *all* of the following *except*:
   a. highlight the efficiency of new organizational techniques.
   b. require fewer workers to run it.
   c. use water power to run.
   d. become a model for flour milling in the United States.

4. The Waltham and Fall River Plans were devised to find employees for the first textile factories because:
   a. young men had better opportunities in farm or construction work.
   b. young women were eager to leave their families to work.
   c. laws prohibited the use of children as workers.
   d. women and children were not capable of using the heavy machines in the earliest factories.

5. The development of machine tools is significant because they:
   a. facilitated the repair of complicated equipment.
   b. produced machines that made standardized parts rapidly and cheaply.
   c. produced machines that could be run by women and children factory workers.
   d. were of higher quality than similar British equipment.

6. The primary industrial activity that occupied the energies of inventor Eli Whitney was the manufacture of:
   a. cotton gins.
   b. cotton and woolen cloth.
   c. farm machinery.
   d. firearms.

7. Cities such as Buffalo, Chicago, and Detroit grew rapidly in the 1830s because:
   a. their location facilitated the use of water power in factories.
   b. their mayors and other city officials used public funds to build new ports and harbors to increase trade.
   c. they were located where goods had to be transferred from one mode of transportation to another.
   d. they facilitated the transfer of goods within regions.

8. New York City's economic advantages included *all* of the following *except*:
   a. many enterprising merchants.
   b. a fine harbor.
   c. the fact that it was the state capital.
   d. the Hudson River–Erie Canal network.

9. When southern cotton producers moved West, they moved primarily to:
   a. southern parts of Ohio, Indiana, and Illinois.
   b. Mississippi, Alabama, Arkansas, and Louisiana.
   c. northern parts of Ohio, Indiana, and Illinois.
   d. Missouri, Nebraska, Michigan, and Wisconsin.

10. The growth of farming in the West was significant to the country's industrialization for all of the following reasons except:
    a. farmers grew or raised cheap raw materials for industrial production.
    b. western farms increased opportunities for young men in farm work.
    c. farmers provided inexpensive food for factory workers and other urban residents.
    d. farmers bought equipment produced in eastern factories.

11. The free workers who faced the worst working and living conditions were:
    a. mill hands.
    b. mechanics.
    c. day laborers.
    d. canal-boat crews.

12. The rise of the business class shattered the social order by:
    a. creating greater differences between agricultural and industrial workers.
    b. stimulating religious reform groups that tried to stop factory workers from drinking alcohol.

c. increasing the differences between manufacturers and their employees.
d. providing the middle class with new manufactured products.

13. The Benevolent Empire tried to accomplish *all* of the following *except*:
    a. end alcohol abuse.
    b. rescue prostitutes from degradation.
    c. ensure that convicts were more harshly punished.
    d. improve care of the mentally ill.

14. One key to Charles Grandison Finney's revival success was that he rejected:
    a. an emphasis on original sin.
    b. free will.
    c. the need for God's grace.
    d. the importance of preaching.

15. A major result of the growth of revivalism and reform was:
    a. a decrease in prostitution in the new urban centers.
    b. greater religious tolerance for all Christian denominations.
    c. an increased emphasis on nonmaterial values among the business class.
    d. a belief among the business class in their own moral superiority.

Short Essays

Answer the following in a brief paragraph.

1. What explains the success of the textile industry once it became established in the United States? (pp. 296–300)

2. Why were the promoters of the textile industry able to ease anxieties about the moral dangers so many Americans associated with industrialization? (p. 300)

3. What explains the simultaneous growth of cities and expansion of agriculture during these years? (pp. 303–308)

4. What did state and federal governments contribute to the transportation revolution? (pp. 310–312)

5. How did the Industrial Revolution change the structure of free society in the United States? (p. 318)

6. Why did Charles Grandison Finney's revivals appeal much more strongly to members of the business class than to other social groups? (pp. 321–322)

7. If you think of the Industrial Revolution during these years as a phase in the modernization of American society, what would you conclude are the distinctive features of a "modern" society?

ANSWERS

Chapter Précis

1. new organizational techniques; technological innovations
2. low trans-Atlantic shipping rates; a large, inexpensive British labor force; lack of tariff protection for American indutries
3. labor costs were higher
4. family financial resources
5. Great Britain
6. water power
7. federal land
8. state governments
9. monopoly privilege
10. new machinery
11. property
12. hard work; saving; moderate habits
13. moral government
14. common identity; moral values and discipline

Identification

1. factory system
2. Samuel Slater
3. the Waltham Plan
4. Franklin Institute
5. New York City
6. one-third
7. the National Road from Cumberland, Maryland, to Vandalia, Illinois
8. John Marshall; Roger B. Taney
9. Benjamin Franklin's *Autobiography*
10. Lyman Beecher; the General Union for Promoting Christian Observance
11. Charles Grandison Finney
12. the American Temperance Society

Skill-Building Exercise

1. a. Boston, New York City, Philadelphia, and Baltimore

    b. All of the following were important manufacturing sites: Lowell, Massachusetts; Hartford, Connecticut; Troy, Albany, Rochester, and Buffalo, New York; Trenton, New Jersey; Wilmington, Delaware; Pittsburgh, Pennsylvania; and Cincinnati, Ohio.

2. One arrow should go from the lower South westward through Alabama to Mississippi. A second arrow should go from the upper South westward across the southern portions of Ohio, Indiana, and Illinois. The third should originate in New England, cut across upper New York State along the line of the Erie Canal, and continue into the northern sectors of Ohio, Indiana, Illinois, and into southern Michigan.

3. The Erie Canal linked Albany and Buffalo via Rochester.

Self-Test

Multiple Choice

1. b	6. d	11. c
2. d	7. c	12. c
3. a	8. c	13. c
4. a	9. b	14. a
5. b	10. b	15. d

Short Essays

1. The favorable circumstances included the availability of raw materials, especially cotton, abundant and inexpensive water power, an energetic work force, clever inventions, and modest amounts of capital.

2. The location of so many mills in villages and small towns, rather than in the largest American cities, helped to discourage the view that factories and urban vice went together. In addition, the moral protection and supervision provided for the young women workers allayed fears that industry bred corruption.

3. Two important factors were the rapidly growing American population, which meant that there were people enough to populate cities and new farms, and the availability of so much sparsely inhabited land. Public policy, which was to sell land cheaply, also encouraged this double process.

4. Federal and state governments helped construct interstate roads, especially the National Road. State gov-

ernments also helped finance the construction of canals, most notably the famous Erie Canal.

5. Among other consequences, the Industrial Revolution brought the business class into existence. It also created a new class of factory workers who tended machines, a social group quite distinct from the highly trained craftsmen and artisans of preindustrial manufacturing. The establishment of the factory system sharpened the social differences between the wealthy and middle-class members of the business class on the one hand and the working class on the other.

6. Finney's central religious message was that each person is a free moral agent whose salvation depends on his or her own choices. One should use that freedom to accept Christ immediately as one's savior and receive God's saving grace. Hence, each individual's salvation was his or her own responsibility. The implication was that each person was also responsible for his

or her social status and economic well-being. Thus, members of the business class were not responsible for the disorderly lives of their workers, although they did need to make certain that workers were exposed to evangelical principles.

7. During these years the Industrial Revolution was transforming America from a preindustrial society into an industrializing one. One feature of a modern society, then, is the possession of an industrial economic sector. This implies another feature of modern society, the willingness (indeed eagerness) to use technology to manipulate resources and the environment. And threaded through the views of Americans who benefited most directly from the Industrial Revolution was a strong faith in progress, in the idea that technological innovation will raise people's standard of living and make life more secure and comfortable.

CHAPTER *11*

A Democratic Revolution
1820–1844

★ ★ ★

CHAPTER PRÉCIS

Democratizing Politics, 1820–1829   pp. 328–331

Democratic Institutions

As the Industrial Revolution accelerated the pace of democratization, most Americans supported expansion of the franchise to include all adult white males and direct popular election of most officials. By 1840, 90 percent of adult white men could vote, although blacks and women continued to be excluded from the franchise. Responding to an expanded electorate, political parties increased their organization and discipline to forge their diverse membership into workable coalitions.

1. In order to keep party members in line, political parties focused on
_____ and
_____ . (p. 328)

The Election of 1824 and the "Corrupt Bargain"

As the Republican party fragmented in 1824, Andrew Jackson won the most popular votes through his image as a war hero, his appeal to nationalistic pride, and his supporters' promises to eliminate governmental corruption. No candidate had a majority in the electoral college; therefore, the winner was chosen by the House of Representatives, where Henry Clay swung votes behind John Quincy Adams. Adams's subsequent choice of Clay as secretary of state led Jackson supporters to accuse the two of a "corrupt bargain."

2. In the presidential election of 1824, the candidates were nominated by an informal meeting of congressional leaders called the _____ .
(p. 329)

The Presidency of John Quincy Adams, 1825–1829

Adams believed in vigorous government action to promote national economic and social development. He supported the basic features of Henry Clay's American System: a protective tariff, internal improvements, and a national bank. Politicians saw his plans as favoritism to the business class; others believed the Constitution did not permit such government action. Adams's successes while in office were minimal. Jackson men won control of Congress and put through a new, higher tariff to increase northern support for Jackson in the next presidential election. Adams also alienated southerners and westerners by his defense of rights for the Creek nation.

The Election of 1828: The Birth of the Democratic Party

Jackson's followers created a broad, diverse coalition including northern urban workers, southern planters, western farmers, and former Federalists. Jackson won in 1828 by vowing to use the executive office to root out special privilege and by appealing to opponents of the American System. He represented virtue and democracy against corruption, an appeal that united his varied followers. Southerners also expected him to remove native Americans from their states. Jackson's victory unsettled the northern business class, which feared that his administration would lead to mob rule.

The Jacksonian Presidency, 1829–1837

pp. 332–342

Jackson transformed the presidency into an agent of popular will by decreasing Congress's power over national politics and giving that power to the Democratic party. He also eliminated governmental obstacles to individual economic activity.

Party Government

Jackson awarded public offices to his supporters, while at the same time correcting some abuses and supporting talented officeholders. This increased the power and popular appeal of the Democrats. He thus transformed public service, opening it to common men, not only the social elite, and making it an instrument of political patronage. He relied on friends, his Kitchen Cabinet, for most political advice.

Jackson versus the Bank

The Second Bank of the United States stabilized the nation's money supply. Jackson vetoed the Bank's recharter, denouncing the Bank as an agent of special privilege and monopoly power that was a burden on wage earners and state bankers. With broad public support for his Bank veto, Jackson won reelection in 1832. He then moved to destroy the Bank by removing government funds to favored state banks.

The Tariff and the Nullification Crisis

South Carolinians, fearful that the United States would abolish slavery and resenting tariffs that cost them dearly and benefited the North, declared the tariffs of 1828 and 1832 null and void. Because of Calhoun's defense of South Carolina's position, Jackson dropped him from the

3. As president, Adams's program appeared to support the interests of the _____ . (p. 329)

4. Jackson's supporters emphasized that he was a "natural aristocrat," meaning that he had _____ . (p. 331)

5. Rotation in office enabled President Jackson to reward _____ by appointing them to office. (p. 332)

6. The Second Bank of the United States stabilized the nation's money by demanding that state banks redeem their notes in _____ . (p. 333)

7. To protect an individual state from Congressional laws passed by a majority, John C. Calhoun declared that a state had the right to declare a federal law _____ . (p. 333)

Democratic ticket in May 1832. Calhoun resigned in December of the same year. Jackson defended federal law, promising that he would use the military to compel state obedience. South Carolina submitted only after Congress lowered tariff rates.

Andrew Jackson's Legacy for American Government

Jackson increased the power of the presidency and strengthened the federal government against the states. He opposed increasing governmental powers only when legislatures granted special privileges or became corrupt. He believed that as president he was the direct representative of the people.

Westward Expansion and Conflict

By the 1820s, Americans had come to believe that economic opportunities in the form of fresh western land were necessary to preserve democracy. Native Americans, who occupied much of that land, appeared to stand in the way. Andrew Jackson, who came to the presidency on the basis of support from common men, championed their cause. On Jackson's orders, the army chased the Sauk and Fox tribes out of land white settlers wanted in western Illinois, breaking their resistance at the Bad Axe Massacre. He removed the "Five Civilized Tribes" from land in the Southeast, despite rulings from the Supreme Court in favor of the native Americans. Martin Van Buren continued this policy, culminating in the Trail of Tears in 1838.

When Mexico attempted to restrict American immigration to Texas and to end slavery there, Americans who had moved into Texas during the 1820s and 1830s to plant cotton using slave labor declared Texas independent. Mexico was unable to reconquer Texas; thus, American Texans were free to seek U.S. statehood. Presidents Jackson and Van Buren, however, feared political disruption if another slave state came into the Union, so they did nothing.

8. The Cherokee were termed "civilized" by white Americans because they had a _____ . (p. 338)

9. As Americans in large numbers moved into Texas, the Mexican government attempted to limit this immigration and to prohibit the _____ . (p. 340)

The Early Labor Movement, 1794–1836

pp. 342–347

The response of mechanics to the Industrial Revolution depended on whether they were hurt by or benefited from changed methods of production.

Artisan Self-Consciousness

Traditional artisan organizations, the earliest labor unions, resisted wage cuts, but courts declared their actions illegal. Mechanics developed broader group consciousness as the Industrial Revolution progressed. Though they still excluded blacks, women, and unskilled workers, they expanded their group identity to include workers in other crafts, and began to think of themselves as a class.

10. Many artisans with traditional skills believed that there was an inevitable _____ between laborers and their employers. (p. 342)

Workers in the Building Trades

Economic prosperity led to an increased demand for construction skills; construction workers used that demand to acquire better pay and a ten-hour day. They then formed the Working Men's party, calling for equal taxation, the abolition of banks, and public education.

The Threatened Artisans

Many mechanics, whose jobs had become obsolete due to technological innovations, proposed that the price of a product should reflect laborers' efforts, and that profits should go to the people who made the products. These mechanics created craft unions and united across trades to achieve goals such as a ten-hour day, higher wages, universal white male suffrage, the abolition of imprisonment for debt, and personal property taxes. Jackson eventually granted a ten-hour day to some federal employees.

Factory Workers

Young women, the first factory workers, poorer and with fewer skills than mechanics, organized to resist pay cuts and onerous work rules. Unable to overcome the power of employers, these workers achieved few victories. Their organizations remained weak and short-lived.

Employers on the Counterattack

As laborers' organizing efforts increased, employers joined to resist unions by creating blacklists and by challenging the closed shop in the courts. Courts supported employers by ruling against the unions.

Democrats and Whigs: The Second Party System, 1836–1844   pp. 347–354

As Jackson and his party challenged the growing power of business interests, the northern business class and southern middle class created the Whig party to fight Jackson.

The Emergence of the Whigs

United by their opposition to Jackson, congressional leaders such as Daniel Webster, Henry Clay, and John Calhoun allied themselves in the new Whig party. They charged Jackson with abusing his executive powers. The Whigs supported democracy by championing equal opportunity for upward mobility, but they believed that those who did become wealthy were best suited to govern all citizens. The Whigs accused Jackson of creating dissension among social classes. Webster and Clay had common economic interests in the American System. John Calhoun, on the other hand, believed that northern capitalists and southern planters should be allies in opposition to workers, slave and free. The other Whig

11. The Mechanics' Union of Trade Associations wanted to establish a _____ between social classes. (p. 343)

12. The _____ stated that most of the profit from production should go to the person who made the goods. (p. 343)

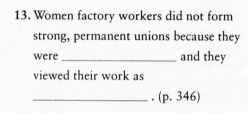

13. Women factory workers did not form strong, permanent unions because they were _____ and they viewed their work as _____. (p. 346)

14. Employers' ability to use the government, particularly in the form of the courts, was threatened by the growing _____. (p. 347)

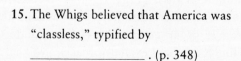

15. The Whigs believed that America was "classless," typified by _____. (p. 348)

leaders disagreed with him, and the Whig party gained its principal support from the northern middle class.

The Whig Coalition

Whigs encompassed many diverse groups that agreed with the goals of Henry Clay's American System as well as some of those interested in moral reforms. The Whig vote in 1836 was strong, but not enough to defeat Jackson's vice-president and hand-picked successor, Martin Van Buren, who ran on Jackson's record.

The Depression of 1837–1843

When England began to restrict investment in the United States and decreased its cotton purchases, the American economy slid into a severe depression. The labor movement disintegrated as unemployment rose. Workers then turned to politics as a way to achieve their goals.

The Election of 1840

The Whigs campaigned by associating the depression with the Democrats and by running their own version of a military hero and self-made man, William Henry Harrison. The Harrison campaign was the first in American history to be run as a popular spectacle, and it succeeded, winning both the presidency and control of Congress.

The Resurgence of the Democratic Party

Harrison's untimely death led to the presidency of John Tyler, who blocked the Whig program by opposing tariff increases and a national bank.

In the 1840s, Democrats forged a new coalition of small farmers, Southern planters, urban laborers, and immigrant workers. Thus, two national parties, each claiming to be the better democrats, organized to gain mass electoral support.

16. Whigs, in agreement with the business class, believed that _____, including such things as internal improvements, was necessary for business development. (p. 349)

17. American banks responded to the depression by holding larger amounts of _____ , thus deepening the severity of the crisis. (p. 351)

18. The Independent Treasury Act, which required the federal government to keep its cash in government vaults, confirmed the Democratic party as the _____ party. (p. 352)

19. Each of the two major parties had strong opinions regarding _____ : The Whigs favored it and the Democrats were suspicious of it. (p. 353)

EXPANDED TIMELINE

1821   Mexico encourages immigration to Texas
In response to growing numbers of Americans settling in Texas, the Mexican government began to welcome American settlers, hoping they would become loyal Mexicans.

1825   John Quincy Adams elected president by the House of Representatives
Clay's support won Adams the presidency even though Jackson had the most popular votes. Jackson and much of the public accused Clay and Adams of a "corrupt bargain" when Adams made Clay his secretary of state.

1827   Philadelphia Working Men's Party organized
This was the first political party formed by workers; the party's goals were equal taxation, the abolition of banks, and universal free public education.

1828   The Tariff of Abominations
This tax on imported goods protected domestic manufacturers in the North and West but hurt southerners, who had to pay higher prices for the goods they bought. Southern planters, especially South Carolinians, denounced it.

Andrew Jackson elected president
The Democratic party came to power and Jackson began his attack on congressional power and northern commercial interests.

The South Carolina Exposition and Protest

In response to the Tariff of Abominations, Calhoun asserted that states should have the right to nullify acts of Congress and to secede.

1830   **Jackson's Maysville Road veto**

Mexico restricts immigration and prohibits the importation of slaves
The Mexican government, worried by the large number of American immigrants into Texas, put restrictions on their settlement.

Journeymen cordwainers organize
The Massachusetts shoemakers formed one of the first organizations to defend their mutual interests and establish their independence from the shoe manufacturers.

Indian Removal Act
To satisfy white southern settlers, Jackson attempted to compel southern native Americans to give up their lands and move west of the Mississippi.

1831   *Cherokee Nation v. Georgia*
John Marshall, the chief justice of the Supreme Court, supported the independence of the Cherokee in their struggle with the state of Georgia to retain their lands. President Jackson defied Marshall and ignored the Court's decision.

1832   **Bad Axe Massacre**
The federal army chased Sauk and Fox followers of Black Hawk out of Illinois, resulting in the massacre of 850 warriors out of 1,000.

Jackson vetoes renewal of charter of Second Bank of the United States
Believing that the Bank represented special privilege and northern commercial interests, President Jackson vetoed an extension of the Bank's charter.

South Carolina nullifies the Tariff of Abominations
South Carolina declared the federal law null and void and refused to collect tariff duties, thus proclaiming states' rights to be superior to federal law.

1833   **Force bill and Compromise Tariff**
In response to South Carolina's nullification of tariff duties, President Jackson got Congress to give him the power to use the military to enforce the collection of tariff duties. Violence was avoided when Congress lowered the tariff.

1835   **Ten-hour day for skilled workers**
Philadelphia established the ten-hour day on public works, the first major victory for supporters of the ten-hour day. President Jackson would establish a ten-hour day for the Philadelphia navy yard in 1836.

1836   **Texans proclaim independence from Mexico**
When Mexico attempted to restrict American immigration to Texas and to prohibit the importation of slaves, American Texans declared Texas an independent country.

Martin Van Buren elected president
Running on Jackson's record of hostility to the Bank, Martin Van Buren followed Jackson as president.

1837   **Depression of 1837–1843 begins with the Panic of 1837**
When England reduced investment in the United States and cut its cotton purchases, America fell into a severe depression.

1838   **Trail of Tears**
The U.S. Army forcibly removed 15,000 Cherokee from Georgia to Oklahoma, marching them across 1,200 miles in winter. Over 4,000 Cherokee died.

1840   **William Henry Harrison elected president**
The Whigs successfully identified the Democrats with the depression. Using many of the campaign tactics of the Democrats, the Whigs also portrayed Harrison as a military hero and self-made man.

1841   **John Tyler succeeds to presidency**
Harrison's untimely death put Tyler into the presidency, where he blocked Whig programs.

Preemption Act
Under the Preemption Act, settlers could stake a claim to land, then buy it at a standard price after they had made improvements to the property. This pleased westerners, who often squatted on land before formally filing claim to it.

1842   *Commonwealth v. Hunt*
The state Supreme Court of Massachusetts ruled that union organization was not a criminal activity unless it had criminal objectives, and that unions could strike to achieve a closed shop.

GLOSSARY

congressional caucus   A caucus is an informal meeting of politicians. In 1824, congressional leaders met in a caucus to nominate candidates for the presidency. This was the last time this was done. The congressional caucus was later replaced by party nominating conventions. (p. 328)

"corrupt bargain"   Jackson's supporters accused Henry Clay of swinging votes in the House of Representatives to John Quincy Adams in exchange for obtaining the position of secretary of state. (p. 329)

spoils system   Andrew Jackson began the practice of awarding public jobs to political supporters to fulfill his campaign promise to introduce rotation. His supporters more bluntly referred to his practice as the spoils system, as in "to the victor belong the spoils." (p. 332)

"hard" money   Paper money could be redeemed for "hard" money—that is, specie (gold and silver coins)—on demand. (p. 333)

bank notes   Paper money issued by banks could be redeemed on demand for specie. (p. 333)

"pet banks"   To destroy the Second Bank of the United States, President Jackson removed the government's funds from the Bank and put these funds into state banks, called "pet banks" by his enemies. (p. 334)

states' rights   John C. Calhoun originated the concept, supported by many southerners, that a state could nullify any federal law and secede from the Union if the federal government persisted in actions unfavorable to it. (p. 335)

labor theory of value   Leaders of the craft unions wanted to differentiate their status from that of the business class and unskilled workers. They argued that the price of a product should reflect the labor required to produce it and that most of the profit should go to those who made the product. (p. 343)

journeyman   In a tradition that goes back to the Middle Ages, a journeyman is an artisan who has completed an apprenticeship in a trade and works for another, whether a master or an employer. (p. 343)

blacklist   Employers would circulate the names of workers they considered troublemakers—those who participated in union activities—so that no other employer would hire them. (p. 346)

closed shop   Unions sought to establish closed shops—workplaces that would hire only union members. (p. 346)

IDENTIFICATION

Identify by filling in the blanks.

1. The New York politician who was a pioneer in the development of party organization, emphasizing party loyalty and discipline, was _____ . (p. 328)

2. In the election of 1824, _____ swung the determining votes in the House of Representatives for John Quincy Adams. (p. 329)

3. The 1827 law that taxed imported raw materials and manufactured goods was known as the _____ . (p. 330)

4. During the campaign of 1828, to emphasize their focus on the newly enfranchised common man and the will of the majority, Jackson and his supporters

called themselves the _____ . (p. 331)

5. Instead of consulting his appointed Cabinet officers, Jackson relied on his old political cronies, known as the _____ . (p. 332)

6. The primary congressional supporters of the Second Bank of the United States were _____ and _____ . (p. 333)

7. John C. Calhoun's idea of the supremacy of states over the federal government became the basis for the concept of _____ . (p. 335)

8. President Jackson ordered native Americans removed from Georgia despite the ruling of Chief Justice _____ . (p. 339)

9. When General _____ became president of Mexico, his attempts to increase Mexican control over Texas led to the rebellion of American Texans. (p. 340)

10. The _____ wanted to establish universal, free, tax-supported schools. (p. 343)

11. President Jackson responded to workers' grievances by establishing the _____ for federal employees in Philadelphia. (p.344)

12. Workers sought _____ agreements from their employers to hire only union workers. (p. 346)

13. Whigs asserted that the strongest, most active branch of the federal government rightfully should be the _____ branch. (p. 348)

14. The Whig economic plan embraced the _____ , which Henry Clay had long emphasized. (p. 349)

15. The early labor movement disintegrated in the late 1830s primarily due to the _____ . (p. 351)

16. _____ , the Whig who won the

presidency in 1840, adopted the campaigning tactics of the Democrats. (p. 352)

17. The _____ recognized that many people settled on land before buying it from the government. (p. 353)

SKILL-BUILDING EXERCISE

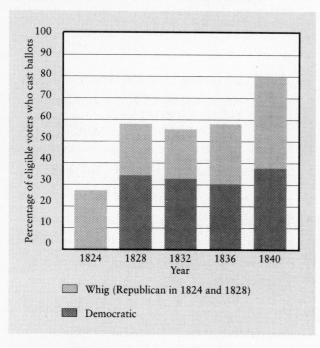

Whig (Republican in 1824 and 1828)

Democratic

1. Why did the percentage of eligible voters who cast ballots increase so much in 1828?

2. What caused the voter increase in 1840?

3. Why did Whig voter participation, in particular, increase so much in 1840?

DOCUMENT EXERCISES

American Voices

Prelude to the Black Hawk War—Black Hawk

President Andrew Jackson, as well as others, believed that Indian removal was actually a humane policy. As long as native Americans lived on land desired by white settlers, their lives were in danger, Jackson contended. Protestant missionaries, on the other hand, believed that if Indians were removed to more secure places, it would be easier to "civilize" them.

As you read "Prelude to the Black Hawk War," ask yourself the following questions:

1. From information in this passage, how would you describe life in Black Hawk's village?

2. Do you agree with Black Hawk's decision to try to stay in his village, or with Ke-o-kuk's decision to leave?

3. How effective was Black Hawk's nonviolent resistance?

4. What other steps might Black Hawk have taken?

A Tejano and the Texas Rebellion—Juan Seguin

Many Tejanos sided with Anglo-Americans in the Texas rebellion because they believed the Anglo-American immigrants would bring wealth and trade with them. His optimism and faith in harmonious relations with the Anglo-Americans declined, however, as new figures came from the United States into Texas.

As you read "A Tejano and the Texas Rebellion," ask yourself the following questions:

1. What contacts and experiences had Seguin had with the Anglo-Americans prior to the rebellion?

2. What role did Seguin play with regard to his fellow Tejanos during the rebellion?

3. On whom did Seguin blame his problems with the Anglo-Americans?

American Lives

Frances Wright: Radical Reformer

Dramatic changes in the United States caused by the Industrial Revolution led many idealistic individuals to criticize society by attempting to form their own utopian communities. Frances Wright abhorred slavery and reacted against strict limits on women's activities. Her radical views drew large, but hostile, crowds at her public appearances.

As you read "Frances Wright: Radical Reformer," ask yourself the following questions:

1. What were the major influences on Wright that shaped her radical views?

2. In what ways did Wright put her ideals into practice in her own life?

3. What were the major obstacles to her radical experiments?

4. Explain Wright's criticisms of evangelical religion.

Multiple Choice

1. Expansion of the franchise increased the development of political parties because:
   a. major issues were too complicated for voters to understand without explanations from politicians.
   b. voter apathy required politicians to try to increase the public's interest in issues.
   c. newly enfranchised women voters were eager to join social organizations.
   d. politicians had to organize their appeal to newly enfranchised voters.

2. The democratization of politics in the 1820s and 1830s was the result of *all* of the following *except*:
   a. extension of the franchise to women.
   b. removal of property requirements for voting.
   c. direct popular election of most offices.
   d. development of modern political parties.

3. Andrew Jackson and his supporters were upset in the election of 1824 for *all* of the following reasons *except*:
   a. use of the congressional caucus for nominations.
   b. expansion of the franchise.
   c. Henry Clay's decision to support Adams.
   d. the "corrupt bargain."

4. As president, John Quincy Adams supported *all* of the following *except*:
   a. Indian removal from lands desired by white settlers.
   b. internal improvements such as canals and roads.
   c. protective tariffs for manufacturing.
   d. a national bank to stabilize national currency.

5. In the election of 1828, Jackson's supporters included *all* of the following *except*:
   a. western settlers.
   b. northern manufacturers.
   c. urban workers.
   d. southern farmers.

6. Jackson's appointment of political allies to public office became known as:
   a. the congressional caucus.
   b. the spoils system.
   c. the Kitchen Cabinet.
   d. special privilege.

7. President Jackson wanted to destroy the Second Bank of the United States because he:
   a. believed it embodied special privilege and monopoly power that created financial instability.
   b. preferred to deposit the government's funds in a state bank where he had investments.
   c. believed it extended credit too easily and would cause a financial panic.
   d. distrusted the states' "pet banks."

8. The nullification controversy developed over southern resistance to:
   a. a protective tariff.
   b. the Second Bank of the United States.
   c. northern antislavery activity.
   d. congressional laws regarding the Cherokee.

9. President Jackson strengthened the presidency when he did *all* of the following *except*:
   a. defied the Supreme Court regarding the Cherokee.
   b. replaced public officeholders with his supporters.
   c. used the power of the federal government to construct roads, increase a protective tariff, and establish a national bank.
   d. threatened to use the federal army against South Carolina.

10. In his decisions regarding the state of Georgia and native Americans, Chief Justice John Marshall stated that the:
    a. Indians were blocking the advance of citizen farmers and should give up their land.
    b. Cherokee were such successful farmers that they should be able to keep their land.
    c. Indians should be removed to protect them from greedy white settlers.
    d. Indians were domestic dependent nations with rights to their own land.

11. President Jackson did not annex Texas because he did not:
    a. want to offend the Mexican government.
    b. believe Texas should become part of the United States.
    c. want to annex an area whose citizens were mostly Catholic.
    d. want to disrupt the balance of slave and free states.

12. In 1806, a Philadelphia court determined that workers' organizations were:
    a. in violation of the constitutional requirement for due process when they went on strike.
    b. prohibited from organizing closed shops.
    c. illegal, "a government unto themselves."
    d. prohibited from recruiting for members during working hours.

13. Workers who often led the unionization movement because their skills had become more valuable due to the Industrial Revolution were employed in

    _____ .
    a. the building trades.
    b. railroad and canal construction.
    c. textiles.
    d. farming.

14. Women factory laborers protested against *all* of the following *except*:
    a. fines for lateness.

    b. increased boardinghouse charges.

    c. employers' requirements that they remain unmarried.

    d. pay cuts.

15. Employers fought labor union demands through:
    a. closed shops.
    b. court decisions against union activity.
    c. use of slaves as replacement workers.
    d. use of the military to stop strikes.

16. John C. Calhoun believed that:
    a. the interests of all classes in America were actually harmonious.
    b. the ideal of equal opportunity was not practical.
    c. the common man's role in American government should increase.
    d. moral reform was necessary for business success.

17. In the election of 1836, evangelical Protestants tended to support:
    a. the Democrats.
    b. the Working Men's party.
    c. Martin Van Buren.
    d. the Whigs.

18. The Independent Treasury Act required the federal government to:
    a. keep government funds in "pet banks."
    b. charter a national bank.
    c. keep federal funds in government vaults.
    d. stabilize the currency.

19. The "log-cabin" campaign was most noteworthy for:
    a. the vicious mud slinging among the candidates.
    b. its modern campaign style.
    c. the death of the Whig candidate before the election.
    d. the resurgence of the Democratic party.

20. The new Democratic coalition included *all* of the following *except*:
    a. Protestant reformers.
    b. poor northern farmers.
    c. small southern farmers.
    d. Catholic immigrants.

Short Essays

Answer the following in a brief paragraph.

1. How did politics become more democratic in the years 1820 to 1844? (pp. 328, 331–332, 343–344, 353–354)

2. Explain John Quincy Adams's program for national development. (pp. 329–330)

3. What were the major factors behind Andrew Jackson's popular appeal? (pp. 331, 337)

4. What were the primary functions of the Second Bank of the United States, and why was it criticized? (pp. 333–334)

5. What were the primary issues that brought workers together in the 1820s and 1830s? (pp. 343–346)

6. How did the Whigs and the Democrats differ regarding the benefits or disadvantages of industrial development? (pp. 348–349)

7. How did presidential political campaigns change with the election of 1840? (pp. 352–353)

ANSWERS

Chapter Précis

1. organization; discipline

2. congressional caucus

3. Northeast business class

4. achieved success through his own efforts and was not born to privilege

5. loyal Democrats

6. gold and silver

7. null and void

8. centralized political system, formed successfully, and they adopted the mannerisms of a plantation society

9. importation of slaves

10. conflict of interest

11. just balance of power

12. labor theory of value

13. overpowered by their employers; temporary and unimportant to their lives

14. democratization of national politics

15. social harmony

16. positive government action

17. specie

18. antibanking

19. industrialization

Identification

1. Martin Van Buren

2. Henry Clay

3. Tariff of Abominations

4. Democrats

5. Kitchen Cabinet

6. Daniel Webster; Henry Clay

7. States' rights

8. John Marshall

9. Antonio López de Santa Anna

10. Working Men's party

11. ten-hour day

12. closed shop

13. legislative

14. American System

15. depression of 1837–1843

16. William Henry Harrison

17. Preemption Act of 1841

Skill-Building Exercise

1. Jackson's campaign against special privilege worked; he stood as an example of someone who had been tricked out of the presidency by Adams and Clay, in defiance of the popular will. Voters cast their ballots in favor of Jackson, both to right the wrong of 1824 and to increase democratic control over public office.

2. As the Whigs turned to popular campaigning in 1840, they increased the sense of democratic participation and competition between the two parties, bringing out more voters. Second, the depression that had begun in 1837 brought out voters who wanted to turn the Democrats out of the presidency.

3. Whigs adopted the campaign tactics of the Democrats and portrayed William Henry Harrison as a western hero and a man of the people. The Whig campaign was run as a celebration of democracy, which made political participation both patriotic and fun.

Self-Test

Multiple Choice

1. d	6. b	11. d	16. b
2. a	7. a	12. c	17. d
3. b	8. a	13. a	18. c
4. a	9. c	14. c	19. b
5. b	10. d	15. b	20. a

Short Essays

1. As the franchise expanded to include most adult white males and as popular elections became standard for most public offices, politicians had to win over a broader base of voters. Men such as Martin Van Buren began to develop organized, disciplined political parties that could appeal to a wide electorate. These parties ran exciting, celebratory political campaigns designed to marshal popular support for their candidates.

2. Adams believed that government should actively promote the economic and social development of the country. He supported Clay's American System of tariffs, internal improvements, and a national bank to encourage manufacturing, better transportation for commercial development, and a stable business currency. He also believed in the country's scientific development, again with government assistance, and called for an observatory and a national university, among other such schemes.

3. Jackson was a military hero who embodied nationalistic pride. He was also the popular underdog who, it appeared, had been cheated out of the presidency in 1824. Jackson's attacks on special privilege and monopoly power were assaults on the new business class and brought him much support from southern and western farmers who were suspicious of the vast wealth and political power that northern capitalists were amassing from the Industrial Revolution. Jackson appeared to be the champion of the common people against the wealthy.

4. The Second Bank of the United States stabilized the nation's currency by requiring smaller local banks to keep enough "hard" money—gold or silver—on hand so that they could redeem their notes in coin. This kept the smaller banks from issuing excessive amounts of credit. The Bank also held the funds of the U.S. government. It was criticized by those who wanted looser credit standards, as well as by those state bankers who wanted to be less restricted. Many wage earners resented banks whose shaky notes they often received as wages. Many Americans simply distrusted all banks, believing them to be seats of special privilege.

5. Workers came together to protest wage cuts and onerous work rules. They particularly supported the ten-hour day. The Working Men's party sought social changes such as universal public education, equal taxation, and the abolition of banks. Their emphasis on universal education was an attempt to ensure that their children would have access to social mobility in the future.

6. Whigs were optimists regarding industrial development. They believed that all Americans had equal opportunities for upward social mobility and that manufacturing growth would elevate everyone. Through

the American System, they sought government stimulation of industry and transportation growth, as well as banking. The Democrats, on the other hand, appealed to those who were suspicious of industrial development, including southern small farmers and northern artisans. They were convinced that government planning and programs such as the tariff and internal improvements benefited only northern capitalists.

7. The presidential campaign of 1840 was the first where both parties made an all-out appeal to the popular vote. The Whigs, who had earlier been much more restrained, in 1840 created an exciting celebration, focusing on images of their candidate, Harrison, as a democratic man of the people and war hero, precisely the way the Democrats had portrayed Jackson in earlier elections. Each party used a network of national newspapers to get their messages to the public.

CHAPTER 12

Freedom's Crusaders 1820–1860

★   ★   ★

CHAPTER PRÉCIS

While the Industrial Revolution and territorial expansion opened new opportunities for many Americans, they also led to more standardization in individuals' lives. Reform movements grew out of this tension between individualism and the demands of the new industrial order.

Transcendentalists and Utopians   pp. 358–367

The transcendentalists were a group of intellectual reformers in New England.

Ralph Waldo Emerson

In 1832 the Unitarian minister Emerson left his pulpit to celebrate the individual free of tradition and custom, self-reliant and nonconformist. Emerson believed in the ability of people to attain, through solitude and the contemplation of nature, a mystical union with "currents of Universal Being." Emerson's challenge of traditional religion and emphasis on the individual became popular as he toured the North, speaking to thousands. Emerson was more radical than many people understood; his pantheism was outside Christian doctrine, and he criticized the new industrial society for its shallow exaltation of material consumption. Emerson became the leader of the new intellectual movement known as transcendentalism.

1. By celebrating the liberated individual free of traditional restraints and social pressures, transcendentalists attacked _____ and _____ . (p. 358)

2. Emerson believed that _____ was a route to finding God. (p. 359)

Emerson's Disciples

A generation of young intellectuals responded to Emerson's call to create a genuinely American literature characterized by an emphasis on democracy and individual freedom. Henry David Thoreau, who tried to live a life of absolute simplicity during his stay at Walden Pond, told a story of radical nonconformity and a search for spiritual meaning in nature, distant from society's demands. Walt Whitman's exuberant poetry elevated the individual and the common person, almost to divinity. Whitman's exultant democracy challenged society and traditional religion. In contrast, the novels of Nathaniel Hawthorne and Herman Melville criticized excessive individualism as having a destructive impact on society. Their gloomy visions did not find popular audiences until years later.

Brook Farm

Some transcendentalists tried to create ideal communities that would encourage individualism and personal freedom and set an example for the larger society. Brook Farm, founded in Massachusetts in 1841, was the most famous; its intellectual community included Emerson, Hawthorne, the editor Margaret Fuller, and other noted transcendentalists. Young Bostonians found the environment stimulating, but Brook Farm never established an economic base and declined by 1846. In the 1850s transcendentalists became less radical and joined mainstream New England culture.

The Decline of Transcendentalism

With Brook Farm's decline, many transcendentalists gave up their attempts at comprehensive reform; however, some remained radically committed to the cause of abolitionism.

The Phalanxes

Inspired by the communal ideas of the Frenchman Charles Fourier, phalanxes were cooperative work and living units in which all residents held shares, thus holding all property in common. Laborers received the bulk of profits from the production of the community. Arthur Brisbane brought this idea to the United States, helping to create about one hundred such communities in the North and Midwest. They, too, had problems supporting themselves.

The Shakers

The Shakers came from England in 1774, led by their founder, Mother Ann Lee. They believed that God was both male and female, and the leadership in their communities thus included men and women. Shakers believed in celibacy, and practiced strict separation of the sexes. They welcomed African-Americans into their fold. Their rigid communities also embraced abstinence from alcohol, tobacco, politics, and war. Flourishing during the 1820s and 1830s, these communities attracted people who agreed with the Shaker belief that sin is a product of society.

3. Two major works of the 1850s that lauded social restraint and criticized individualism were _____ and _____ . (pp. 360–361)

4. Residents of Brook Farm farmed in order to remain independent from the _____ . (p. 362)

5. As were transcendentalist communities, phalanxes were designed as alternatives to _____ . (p. 364)

6. To Shakers, Mother Ann was _____ . (p. 364)

The Oneida Community

John Humphrey Noyes was the leading "perfectionist" of his day, believing that the Second Coming of Christ had already occurred and that people could, therefore, aspire to freedom from sin. The major obstacle to this was marriage, which promoted exclusiveness and jealousy. Noyes created a community in Oneida, New York, which practiced "complex marriage," the belief that every person was married to every other person. Oneida residents also practiced community ownership of property. The Oneidans' sexual practices scandalized society, forcing Noyes to flee prosecution. Shakers and Oneidans tried to free individuals from the sinful effects of society, in which traditional gender relations were, both communities felt, integral.

7. Oneidans believed that traditional family arrangements made women and children the _____ of their husbands and parents. (p. 365)

The Mormon Experience

Joseph Smith, inspired by religious revelations, founded the Mormon Church in New York. Deeply critical of society's growing emphasis on individualism, Smith, who led his followers west to find a haven in the wilderness, met his death at the hands of a mob in Illinois in 1844. Brigham Young took over the Mormon leadership as he led over 10,000 people to establish disciplined communities in Utah where they made innovations in the areas of irrigation, communal labor, and water rights. Appointing Young as governor of Utah Territory, Congress rejected a Mormon petition to create a Mormon state extending from Utah to the Pacific. President James Buchanan precipitated the bloodless Mormon War in 1857–1858 when he sent federal forces to Utah, but chose negotiation over attack.

8. Smith's theology addressed the growing tension between the _____ and the _____ . (p. 366)

The Women's Movement   pp. 367–373

Women's activities in reform movements, particularly abolitionism, led many women to insist on women's political and social equality with men.

Origins of the Women's Movement

While the Industrial Revolution created a new industrial society that seemed to exclude women from paid employment, middle-class women restricted to the home became guardians of family and religious morality precisely because they were outside the commercial world. From this elevated position, many women became ardent reformers who sought to rid society of the evils of industrialism. At the same time, evangelical religion emphasized that women's salvation and social responsibilities were as important as those of men. Women formed societies to attack prostitution and to improve the care in hospitals, jails, and other social institutions.

9. Evangelical revivals propelled women into reform movements by involving them in _____ and enhancing their _____ . (p.368)

10. In 1840, the American Anti-Slavery Society split when _____ was elected to the business committee. (p. 369)

Abolitionism and Women

A few women abolitionists, such as the Grimké sisters, came to equate traditional female roles with slavery. Among the male abolitionists who did not resist this equation was William Lloyd Garrison, who insisted on "universal emancipation." Women's experiences within the abolitionist movement taught them organizational and political skills that they carried over to the women's rights movement.

The Program of Seneca Falls

Most women were not so radical as to equate marriage with slavery but chose instead to focus on women's legal position. In 1848 Elizabeth Cady Stanton and Lucretia Mott, leading female abolitionists, called the first United States convention to address women's rights, in Seneca Falls, New York. Basing their program on the republican principles of the Declaration of Independence, these women asserted women's full equality with men. After Seneca Falls, national women's rights meetings were annual events. Susan B. Anthony joined Stanton in the 1850s, creating effective political lobbying campaigns for women's rights. Their only legislative accomplishment was the revision of states' property laws, allowing married women to keep their own property and working women to keep their own wages. Other women, such as Harriet Beecher Stowe and Sojourner Truth, criticized slavery for its destruction of families, black and white.

11. Most women critics of domestic life did not challenge traditional domestic institutions, but instead wanted to enter the _____ . (p. 369)

The Antislavery Movement, to 1844 pp. 373–379

African-Americans and white evangelists joined their efforts in the 1830s to create the abolitionist movement. Four approaches to ending slavery competed between 1820 and the 1850s: colonization, escape or rebellion, an appeal to the Christian conscience of slaveowners, and free soil.

African Colonization

The American Colonization Society, founded in 1817, hoped to emancipate slaves gradually by compensating their owners and then sending the former slaves, as well as free northern African-Americans, to a colony in Africa. Northerners, with a racist opinion of blacks as degenerate, found colonization attractive because it promised to remove African-Americans from society. Southerners felt colonization was necessary to prevent a race war. Popular among many people who disliked African-Americans but opposed slavery, the American Colonization Society established the colony of Liberia on the western coast of Africa but sent only 1,400 African-Americans there.

12. The American Colonization Society was more interested in shoring up slavery by removing _____ than in a program of emancipation. (p. 374)

A Radical Solution

Most African-Americans considered the United States their home and denounced colonization as well as slavery. Free African-Americans in the North began newspapers and published pamphlets supporting immediate abolition. David Walker's pamphlet supporting slave rebellions to end slavery began to reach the free black community in the South.

13. The rebellion of _____ appeared to be a fulfillment of David Walker's prophecies in *Appeal . . . to the Colored Citizens.* (p. 375)

Evangelical Abolitionism, to 1840

Evangelical religion inspired many young men to call for the end of slavery as a Christian duty. William Lloyd Garrison founded the antislavery paper *The Liberator* in 1831 and the New England Anti-Slavery Society in 1832, both of which demanded immediate abolition. He attacked colonization as racist and even criticized the Constitution for recognizing slavery. Garrison's radicalism attracted a loyal few but repelled most. In contrast, Theodore Dwight Weld was a more moderate abolitionist. Weld preached antislavery in churches throughout the North and the Old Northwest. He believed opposition to slavery was a Christian's moral duty. His sermons and writings gave wide publicity to the cruelty of slavery.

Weld, Garrison, and the wealthy Tappan brothers helped found the American Anti-Slavery Society in 1833, planning to use religious revivals and mass communications to create a public climate hostile to slavery. They also planned to have local antislavery groups pressure Congress through petitions against slavery. The middle class responded with passion to these strategies. Thoreau's works supporting nonconformism and radical responsibility aided their efforts. Women abolitionists contributed their efforts and founded their own antislavery societies.

14. The newly invented _____ enabled abolitionists to distribute thousands of pieces of literature in the 1830s. (p. 376)

15. By the late 1830s, abolitionism had mobilized the energies of both _____ and _____ . (p. 377)

Hostility to Abolition

Southern fears of slave rebellion increased after Nat Turner's rebellion and led southerners to pass harsher laws limiting slaves' activities. Southerners worked to keep any news of abolitionism out of the South, where it might influence slaves to revolt. Southern leaders moved from admitting that slavery was a necessary evil to defending it as a "positive good," arguing that slavery benefited slaves by protecting them from the harshness of industrial society. Southern ministers also cited the biblical command that servants should obey their masters.

Some northerners sympathized with the southern argument, fearing that an attack on slavery might become a more general attack on private property. The economic self-interest of northern textile manufacturers who depended on southern cotton led them to fear abolition activities. Wage earners, too, feared competition for their jobs. The result was that northern mobs attacked abolitionist speakers. Southerners succeeded in passing a "gag rule" in the House of Representatives that prohibited the acknowledgment of antislavery petitions. This violence against abolitionism and suppression of free speech shocked many northerners, who became more sympathetic to the antislavery cause.

16. Planters began to see themselves as the only people who deserved _____ . (p. 378)

The Rise of Political Abolitionism

In the 1840s evangelical abolitionists turned to practical politics, seeking the support of moderate voters. Garrison, who had become more committed to broad-based social transformation, split the antislavery movement. Many of those who differed with Garrison turned their attention to electoral politics through the newly organized Liberty party.

17. Liberty party supporters believed that slaves were automatically free when they entered areas of _____ . (p. 379)

EXPANDED TIMELINE

1817 **American Colonization Society founded**
Northerners who wanted to remove free African-Americans from northern society and southerners who felt that blacks could not cope in a free society joined to create the American Colonization Society, whose goal was to send African-Americans to Africa. Its supporters eventually founded the colony of Liberia.

1818 **Publication of Benjamin Franklin's autobiography**
Franklin encouraged individuals to attempt to reach moral perfection through self-improvement, a precursor to transcendentalist attitudes.

1826 **American Lyceum founded**
The Lyceum organized lecture tours throughout the country, acquainting thousands of Americans with transcendentalist speakers.

1829 **David Walker's** *Appeal*
This pamphlet by a free African-American living in Boston advocated and threatened a slave rebellion. When it began to reach southern free African-Americans, the white South's fear of slave violence increased. Walker and other African-American abolitionists called a national convention where free blacks condemned northern discrimination as well as slavery. They advocated legal means to improve their situation.

1830 **Joseph Smith publishes** *The Book of Mormon*
Responding to angelic revelation, Smith told of Christ's visit to the western hemisphere. His book became doctrine for Mormonism.

1831 **William Lloyd Garrison begins publishing** *The Liberator*
Garrison's paper gave him a national forum to demand an immediate end to slavery and condemn colonization. Garrison's passionate abolitionism led him to condemn the Constitution because it recognized slavery. *The Liberator* made him a leader among radical abolitionists and helped convince southerners that the North was hostile to them.

Nat Turner's rebellion
Turner, an educated, favored slave with deep Christian beliefs, felt himself to be entrusted with a divine mission; he killed almost sixty white southerners. The white South reacted by using terror as a deterrent to other would-be rebels.

Alexis de Tocqueville begins his tour of America
After visiting the United States, de Tocqueville wrote a famous book describing the effects of democracy on American character.

1832 **Ralph Waldo Emerson resigns his pulpit**
Emerson's resignation marked the beginnings of the transcendentalist movement as Emerson left organized religion, choosing to emphasize individuality, self-reliance, dissent, and nonconformity in his popular public lectures and writings.

New England Anti-Slavery Society founded
William Lloyd Garrison founded this organization to press politically for the immediate abolition of slavery. It embraced his radical approach to reform.

1834 **New York Female Moral Reform Society established**
From their position as society's moral guardians, women reformers attempted to protect the home through public action. The New York Female Moral Reform Society was the first major women's organization that tried to end prostitution. Women reformers also tried to improve the conditions in mental asylums and jails.

1836 **House of Representatives adopts "gag rule"**
The "gag rule" allowed southern congressmen to table all antislavery petitions so that they could not be debated or even acknowledged. This suppression shocked northerners, who saw it as indicative of a "Slave Power" conspiracy against basic American values such as freedom of speech.

1837 **Emerson's lecture "The American Scholar"**
Emerson declared the independence of American literature from European tradition. In this Harvard speech, he called for American writers to celebrate American democracy and individual freedom in their works.

Mob kills Elijah P. Lovejoy
Lovejoy, an abolitionist editor in Illinois, was killed by a mob hostile to antislavery activity. His murder was indicative of the violence inherent in northern opposition to abolition.

1839 **Mormons found Nauvoo**
Seeking a haven in the west, Smith and his followers founded this utopian community in Illinois.

1840 **Liberty party launched with James G. Birney as its candidate**
Founded by moderate abolitionists who had split with Garrison, the Liberty party was the first political party to focus on abolition. It was relatively unsuccessful until it changed its emphasis to criticizing slavery as a threat to republican ideals.

1841 **Transcendentalists found Brook Farm**
Brook Farm was an attempt by transcendentalists to create a society based on individual self-realization and harmony, as opposed to conformism and commercialism. The enterprise failed for many reasons, especially its inability to become economically self-sufficient.

Dorothea Dix begins her investigations
Dix's work started with her investigation into the conditions in a Massachusetts jail for women. She went on to reform thousands of prisons and asylums for the mentally ill.

1844 **Margaret Fuller's** *Woman in the Nineteenth Century*

Fuller's work, which asserted the equality of women with men, was based on the transcendentalist faith in individualism.

Mob kills Joseph Smith
Led by Illinois militia members, a mob killed Smith while he was being held in jail on a charge of treason.

James G. Birney runs again for president

1845 **Thoreau withdraws to Walden Pond**
Thoreau's experiences become the basis for *Walden*, in which he celebrated simplicity and a nature mysticism that exalted self-discovery over the demands of civilized society.

1846 **Mormons begin trek to Salt Lake**
Seeking their religious independence and physical safety, Mormon leaders under Brigham Young led over 10,000 followers across the plains.

Brook Farm disbanded
Unable to achieve economic self-sufficiency, Brook Farmers disbanded after a serious fire.

1847 **Liberia declared an independent republic**
Founded by American Colonization Society members, Liberia was a colony settled by American blacks. Liberia's creation was a result of white Americans' desire to remove all blacks from their society.

1848 **John Humphrey Noyes founds Oneida Community**
Oneida was a utopian community based on cooperation and Christian ethics. Noyes believed that perfection—freedom from sin—was possible and attempted to achieve this goal through his advocacy of "complex marriage," which became a scandal to mainstream society.

Seneca Falls convention
This first meeting of women's rights supporters outlined a program for equality that was rooted in the republican ideology of the Declaration of Independence.

1850 **Publication of Nathaniel Hawthorne's *The Scarlet Letter***
This novel criticized excessive individualism and defended the needs of the social order.

1851 **Herman Melville's *Moby Dick***
This American classic attacked individualism and self-reliance, the transcendentalists' creed, as dangerously mad.

Susan B. Anthony joins movement for women's rights
With experience in antislavery and temperance reform movements, Anthony committed her organizational talents to the women's cause.

1852 **Harriet Beecher Stowe's *Uncle Tom's Cabin***
Stowe's emotional book criticized slavery for its destruction of the slave family. In the North, it became one of the most popular books of its day.

1854 **Presidential veto of Dorothea Dix's program for national asylums**
President Pierce refused to use federal resources to fund asylums for the insane.

1855 **First publication of Walt Whitman's *Leaves of Grass***
Whitman published his poetic celebration of individualism and American democracy.

1858 **The "Mormon War"**
President Buchanan sent federal troops into Utah after removing Brigham Young as territorial governor; however, Buchanan negotiated a peaceful resolution.

GLOSSARY

transcendentalism Followers of transcendentalism believed in an ideal world of mystic unity and harmony beyond the world of the senses. Famous transcendentalist intellectuals such as Emerson and Thoreau emphasized individuality, self-reliance, and nonconformism. (p. 358)

American Lyceum The American Lyceum was a speakers' bureau that sent ministers, transcendentalists, and scientists all across the North on speaking tours. It did much to spread transcendentalism and reform movements. (p. 358)

phalanx A phalanx was a cooperative community in which all members were shareholders in the community and laborers received the largest portion of the community's earnings. Phalanxes spread from Massachusetts to Michigan during the 1840s. (p. 364)

perfectionism Perfectionists held the religious belief that people could be perfect, or free from sin, because the Second Coming of Christ had already occurred. Perfectionism was an evangelical movement that impelled reformers to attempt to correct social wrongs. (p. 365)

complex marriage John Humphrey Noyes led his Oneida Community in the practice of complex marriage, based on the belief that all members of the community were married to one another. Noyes sought to control the sexuality of the entire community. (p. 365)

moral reform One of the first reform movements in which women publicly participated, moral reform attempted to end prostitution and to protect single women, among other goals. The first moral reform society was founded in New York City in 1834 and quickly became a national organization. (p. 368)

colonization The American Colonization Society, founded in 1817, supported the movement to end slavery by sending free African-Americans to Africa. Colonization supporters included those who wanted to end slavery as well as those who were concerned chiefly with removing blacks from white society. (p. 374) "gag rule"   Southerners achieved passage of a "gag rule"—a procedure that enabled congressmen to ignore antislavery petitions. The "gag rule" infuriated northerners, who saw in it a violation of freedom of speech. (p. 379)

IDENTIFICATION

Identify by filling in the blanks.

1. The _____ spread public awareness of transcendentalism by arranging speaking tours for men such as Emerson. (p. 358)

2. Henry David Thoreau named his most famous book after _____ , where he went to experiment with a life of simplicity. (p. 359)

3. The novelist _____ set his book *The Blithedale Romance* at Brook Farm. (p. 362)

4. _____ was the one cause that many former transcendentalists continued to embrace in the 1850s. (p. 363)

5. Phalanxes were based on the ideas of the French utopian _____ . (p. 363)

6. The founder of the Oneida community was _____ . (p. 365)

7. After the death of Joseph Smith, _____ led settlers to the Great Salt Lake. (p. 366)

8. Middle-class women built a common identity around the concept of _____ . (p. 367)

9. Through their experiences in the _____ movement, the Grimké sisters came to assert the equality of men and women. (p. 368)

10. Women at the Seneca Falls convention based their declaration of principles on the _____ . (p. 369)

11. The activities of American Colonization Society supporters led to the creation of the African nation of _____ . (p. 374)

12. In his *Appeal . . . to the Colored Citizens,* _____ justified and advocated slave rebellion, which terrified white southerners. (p. 374)

13. Thoreau claimed that citizens could transcend their complicity in slavery and redeem the state through _____ , also the title of his essay. (p. 377)

14. The _____ prevented antislavery petitions from being debated in Congress. (p. 368)

15. The major financial backer for the American and Foreign Anti-Slavery Society was _____ . (p. 379)

SKILL-BUILDING EXERCISE

On this map locate:
1. Sites of the major utopian communities: (a) Brook Farm; (b) areas of phalanx establishment; (c) areas of Shaker settlement; (d) Oneida Community; and (e) New Harmony.

2. Seneca Falls.

3. sites of northern antiabolitionist violence.

DOCUMENT EXERCISES

American Voices

Woman in the Nineteenth Century— Margaret Fuller

Transcendentalists emphasized the potentiality of the individual. Here, Margaret Fuller, the editor of the foremost transcendentalist journal, *The Dial*, applied that sense of individual grandeur to women and used that argument to claim greater social freedom for women.

As you read "Woman in the Nineteenth Century," ask yourself the following questions:

1. In what ways did Fuller use religion to support her argument?

2. How did Fuller challenge the concept of "woman's separate sphere"?

3. How did Fuller claim that her ideas would improve traditional family life?

The Question of Women's Rights— Lucy Stone

Women's rights leaders struggled to formulate a criticism of traditional roles at a time when American society was becoming more democratic for white males. Stone was a committed abolitionist who, when she married Henry Blackwell in 1857, publicly rejected the legal domination of husband over wife; Stone kept her maiden name after the wedding.

As you read "The Question of Women's Rights," ask yourself the following questions:

1. What disappointments in her life does Stone describe?

2. Nineteenth-century society regarded women as morally superior to men; in what ways does Stone find that society hypocritical?

3. How does Stone use religion to defend her position?

American Lives

Dorothea Dix: Innovative Moral Reformer

Dix was the foremost social reformer of the nineteenth century. Starting with a concern for people living in insane asylums, she broadened her emphasis to include a career as Union superintendent of nurses during the Civil War.

As you read "Innovative Moral Reformer," ask yourself the following questions:

1. In what ways did Dix's early experiences prepare her for her reform activities in the 1840s and on?

2. What tactics did Dix employ in her reform efforts?

3. What led Dix to believe that federal activism was necessary to improve care for mental patients?

4. What role did outside national issues have in shaping Dix's career as a reformer?

SELF-TEST

Multiple Choice

1. Emerson believed that an awareness of an ideal reality that transcended everyday existence:
   a. was possible only for educated individuals.
   b. was available through intense study of German philosophers.
   c. could be known through mystical knowledge.
   d. was possible only after death.

2. Critics of transcendentalism such as Nathaniel Hawthorne and Herman Melville focused on:
   a. the perils of excessive individualism.
   b. scandals in the private lives of prominent transcendentalists.
   c. the emphasis on social reform among the transcendentalists.
   d. the lack of financial stability within transcendentalist communities.

3. Brook Farm appealed primarily to:
   a. religious zealots.
   b. New England intellectuals.
   c. farmers and craftsmen.
   d. perfectionists.

4. Arthur Brisbane promoted the concept of the phalanx in:
   a. *Self-Reliance.*
   b. *Democracy in America.*
   c. *The Dial.*
   d. *The Social Destiny of Man.*

5. Ideas that the Shakers supported include *all* of the following *except*:
   a. celibacy.
   b. abstention from alcohol.
   c. complex marriage.
   d. abstention from politics and war.

6. Perfectionists believed that freedom from sin was possible:
   a. if people isolated themselves from society.
   b. if people practiced celibacy.
   c. because Christ's Second Coming had already occurred.
   d. for communities that practiced group ownership of property.

7. Congress rejected a Mormon petition to create a new state called _____ , which would have extended to the Pacific Ocean.
   a. Nauvoo
   b. Carthage
   c. Moroni
   d. Deseret

8. Moral reform was primarily a women's movement to:
   a. end prostitution.
   b. restrict the consumption of alcohol.
   c. enforce Sabbath rules.
   d. work for antislavery.

9. Famous women abolitionists who became active in the women's rights movement include *all* of the following *except*:
   a. Lucy Stone.
   b. Elizabeth Cady Stanton.
   c. Sarah Grimké.
   d. Harriet Beecher Stowe.

10. Before the Civil War, women achieved *all* of the following legislative victories in the state of New York *except* the right:
    a. of widows to keep their property after their husbands' deaths.
    b. to collect their own wages.
    c. to vote.
    d. to bring suit in court.

11. Reasons for supporting the American Colonization Society include *all* of the following *except* the:
    a. desire to remove free African-Americans from the North.
    b. belief that African-Americans were inferior.
    c. belief that blacks should live in equality with whites.
    d. desire to avoid race war in the South.

12. Southerners were frightened by *all* of the following *except*:
    a. Nat Turner's rebellion.
    b. David Walker's pamphlet.
    c. Frederick Douglass's speeches.
    d. John C. Calhoun's speeches.

13. The American Anti-Slavery Society used *all* of the following approaches against slavery *except*:
    a. donating substantially to the American Colonization Society.
    b. pressuring Congress through petitions.
    c. sending abolitionist pamphlets throughout the country.
    d. holding dramatic public meetings with passionate speakers.

14. Many northerners were troubled by abolitionist tactics for *all* of the following reasons *except*:
    a. freed slaves might take jobs of northern wage earners.
    b. Christian doctrine appeared to support slavery.
    c. abolitionists involved women actively in the movement.
    d. many northerners feared racial mixing.

15. The Liberty party found supporters primarily among:
    a. western settlers.
    b. prior Garrison allies.
    c. women.
    d. northern antiabolitionists.

Short Essays

Answer the following in a brief paragraph.

1. In what ways did Hawthorne, Melville, and Poe criticize individualism? (pp. 360–361)

2. Why was communal ownership of property a common feature in many different types of utopian communities? (pp. 361–365)

3. Compare and contrast the roles of women in Shaker communities and in John Humphrey Noyes's Oneida Community. (pp. 364–365)

4. What issues were the most important to women's rights reformers? (pp. 367–369, 372–373)

5. Which economic class of men supported the women's rights movement? What were their most common reasons for doing so? (p. 372)

6. Explain the "positive good" argument for slavery. (p. 378)

7. Name two groups of northerners whose economic self-interest led them to be hostile to abolitionism. Why were they against it? (p. 378)

8. What were the major differences between the Liberty party and the Free Soil party? (pp. 368–369)

ANSWERS

Chapter Précis

1. traditional religion; industrial society
2. nature
3. *The Scarlet Letter; Moby Dick*
4. marketplace
5. industrial society

6. God's female element

7. property

8. claims of the individual; need for social order

9. community life; self-esteem

10. Abby Kelley

11. mainstream of American life

12. free African-Americans from the South

13. Nat Turner

14. steam press

15. religious revivalism; transcendentalism

16. genuine freedom

17. federal authority

Identification

1. American Lyceum

2. Walden Pond

3. Nathaniel Hawthorne

4. Antislavery

5. Charles Fourier

6. John Humphrey Noyes

7. Brigham Young

8. womanhood

9. abolitionist

10. Declaration of Independence

11. Liberia

12. David Walker

13. civil disobedience

14. "gag rule"

15. Lewis Tappan

Skill-Building Exercise

1. a. West Roxbury, Massachusetts; b. Massachusetts to Michigan, along the Erie Canal (Buffalo, New York to Erie, Pennsylvania); c. New England, New York, Ohio; d. Oneida, New York; e. New Harmony, Indiana

2. Seneca Falls, New York

3. Boston, Massachusetts; Utica, New York; New York City; Ohio Valley; Alton, Illinois

Self-Test

Multiple Choice

1. c	6. c	11. c
2. a	7. d	12. d
3. b	8. a	13. d
4. c	9. d	14. b
5. c	10. c	15. b

Short Essays

1. Hawthorne and Melville stressed the negative aspects of individualism, criticizing its vanity, corruption, and destructive egoism. Individualism, if allowed to run rampant, would destroy both the individual and society. Hawthorne and Melville saw virtues in social order. Poe drew visions of individualism degenerating into insanity.

2. A common thread among all the utopian communities was their hostility to commercial, materialistic society and to the greed of industrial growth. The utopians created communities directly opposed to this grasping sense of individual gain. In utopias, workers were expected to contribute for the good of everyone, over and above personal self-interest.

3. The Shakers, founded by a woman who believed herself to be the Second Coming of Christ, believed God was both male and female; thus, they considered women to be as spiritually important as men. Shakers practiced a gender division of labor, fearing lust if men and women worked together, but they gave women religious and economic leadership roles in their communities. Oneidans rid women of the restraints of traditional marriage and made each person the spouse of every other. Noyes, however, remained the leader of the community.

4. While some women wanted the vote, legal reform seemed the most immediately important: the right of married women and widows to keep their own property, the right of working women to collect their own wages, and the right to bring suit in court.

5. Upper-class fathers wanted to pass their property on to their daughters without fear of dissolute, incompetent, or malicious sons-in-law. Upper-class husbands wanted to protect their property in case of bankruptcy by keeping their wives' property intact.

6. According to the "positive good" argument, slavery sheltered slaves from the evils of industrial society,

protecting and caring for them better than northern manufacturers cared for their workers. Slaveowners, naturally superior, were loving fathers to their slaves. These factors promoted "harmony" between the races. Both the Old and New Testaments provided instances of slavery, justifying the enslavement of Christian blacks.

7. Northern antiabolitionists included business people, particularly those who depended on southern cotton, such as merchants and textile producers. Northern wage earners feared competition for jobs if slaves were freed.

8. Liberty party supporters believed that the Constitution did not sanction slavery and that slaves became free as soon as they entered federal territory. When they failed to attract substantial support, Liberty party members reorganized as the Free Soil party, de-emphasizing even further the moral and political rights of slaves and focusing on slavery as a threat to republican ideals rather than an individual sin. The Free Soil party appealed to moderate northerners by allying antislavery to republican ideals such as free speech and democratic institutions. This movement portrayed slaveowners as a "Slave Power" seeking to destroy the republic. Free soil also emphasized keeping slavery out of the territories, but more for the sake of freedom of whites in the new territories than for freedom for slaves.

CHAPTER 13

Sections and Sectionalism 1840–1860

★ ★ ★

CHAPTER PRÉCIS

The Slave South: A Distinctive Society

pp. 383–393

The Slave Economy

Between 1840 and 1860, the South developed an agricultural plantation economy dependent on slave labor. Exports of cotton to Britain and tobacco, rice, and sugar to Europe gave the South the highest increases in per capita income in the country. This dependence on European markets made the South economically independent from the rest of the United States.

Southern agricultural prosperity relied also on fresh land and slave labor. Cotton's exhaustion of the soil necessitated the constant development of new plantations, impelling movement into western Georgia and Texas. Immigrants avoided the South, and free workers migrated out of the South; thus, planters depended on slave labor, which they could organize on the gang-labor system—an agricultural equivalent of the factory system—which free laborers refused to tolerate. Because southerners invested their money in cotton and slavery, the South had little manufacturing and few cities. Nor did planters put any of their resources into education for their workers, a decision that hampered long-term economic development in this region.

1. The South actually lost free workers as a significant proportion of its white population because they migrated to

_____ . (p. 385)

Realities and Ideals of the Planter Class

Planters, who constituted only a small minority of the population, dominated southern society. Their spectacular economic prosperity acted as an incentive to the majority of southern whites who hoped one day to have similar wealth. In the 1830s, planters began to justify both their dominance and the institution of slavery by creating an image of themselves as noble and deserving of social and political leadership because of their superior qualities. Planters' wives shared in this idealization, becoming symbols of moral virtue and sexual purity.

Planters used racist ideology to maintain the loyalty of non-slaveholding whites and their acquiescence to planter domination. Slavery, they said, had created a "mud-sill" class to perform society's most degrading chores, allowing whites to build a civilized society that promoted democracy and freedom. Because much of the southern population was either related to slaveowners or economically dependent on them, this doctrine of racial superiority met with little opposition. At the same time planters actively isolated southern culture from new ideas, especially those that might be critical of slavery.

2. New or threatening ideas were slow to penetrate the South because there were few _____ . (p. 388)

Slave Life

Slaves were legally considered personal property. However, with the prosperity of the plantation system they did experience some improvement in their material conditions because owners needed to protect their investments. Some slaves may have been better housed and better fed than the North's poorest whites, but the working conditions of slaves varied widely. Planters in the Old South, where the soil was exhausted, sold over 25,000 slaves a year to new plantations in the Old Southwest, which had the harshest working conditions because of rapid, exploitative growth.

These sales often broke up slave families, a valued source of protection and nurturance under the brutal institution of slavery. Slaves developed extended kinship networks that provided them with a "family" when parents and spouses were sold "down the river." The rich communal life of the slave quarters also emphasized devotion to Christianity. Christ, slaves knew, had a particular love for the oppressed.

3. Slave religion focused on the story of the _____ in Egypt to give slaves hope for eventual deliverance. (p. 391)

Resistance and Rebellion

The underground railroad, a secret network of abolitionists, helped thousands of escaped slaves find their way to the North and to Canada. Free African-Americans in southern cities were the most important source of help, risking their lives to aid escapees. Slave rebellion took many forms, but most slaves realized that violent rebellion—the thought of which terrified whites—stood little chance of success.

4. A major factor that discouraged slaves from rebelling was that the ratio of blacks to whites in the South was _____ than any other slave society in the _____ . (p. 392)

Free Blacks

Most free African-Americans lived either in the North or the Upper South; however, throughout the country, they were second-class citizens, generally deprived of the right to vote, testify in court, or hold government jobs and subject to severe discrimination. Yet shortages of skilled labor in southern cities led to opportunities for artisans who created vibrant free black communities where churches and benevolent societies met many social needs.

5. Southern states enacted vagrancy and apprenticeship laws designed to force _____ into slavery. (p. 392)

The Northeast and the Midwest: The Industrial Revolution Accelerates pp. 393–407

Factories Triumphant

By 1860 the United States was the third most industrialized country in the world. The stationary steam engine allowed factory owners to build away from rivers, in the nation's largest cities and in new cities in the Old Northwest. With cheap immigrant labor, sophisticated financial services, and growing urban markets, cities such as Chicago boomed. Increasing industrialization required more machine tools and new assembly-line techniques, including the division of labor. This acceleration of production led to periodic overproduction and layoffs in a boom-and-bust cycle.

Immigration

When young women, the first factory workers, protested increasingly onerous and speeded-up working conditions, employers hired Irish and German immigrants who made up most of the 4 million people entering the United States between 1820 and 1860. Taking unskilled factory jobs in northeastern cities, the Irish experienced difficult conditions and stressful lives that led to increased rates of disease and alcoholism. The strain on public health was significant, as death rates in these cities were more than double those in rural areas.

6. Irish immigration had more to do with _____ than with economic opportunity in the United States. (p. 395)

Irish Identity and Anti-Catholicism

To meet the spiritual and material needs of Irish immigrants, the Catholic Church in America grew along with immigration. The Church created new institutions, such as charitable groups and orphanages, which helped the Irish maintain their cultural identity. The Irish became dominant in the Catholic Church.

Many American Protestants, disturbed by this influx of Irish Catholics and fearing that loyalty to the pope would lead Catholics to subvert republican institutions, created Native American Clubs. Mechanics experiencing the uncertainties of the factory system as well as other workers fearing competition for their jobs from immigrants supported these organizations, slowing the development of a labor movement across ethnic lines. The anti-Catholic movement often turned violent.

Anti-Catholic groups created the American party, also known as the Know-Nothings, to make it harder for immigrants to become citizens with voting rights. They also tried to restrict public offices to native-born Americans and allow the use of only the Protestant version of the Bible in public schools. In 1854 they tried to ally northern and southern voters against immigrants, but the slavery issue dominated national politics.

7. Protestants were upset by proposals from Catholic clergy and Democratic politicians to use the taxes of Catholics for _____ . (p. 397)

Business-Class Consumption

Industrialization transformed the life of the middle class in the North, further emphasizing its differences with the South. New balloon frames for houses facilitated the rapid construction of cheaper housing for the middle class. Mass-produced household goods furnished homes with an array of conveniences, including clocks that brought a heightened awareness of time into people's lives. People individualized their living spaces with these furnishings and decorations, such as prints that brought news and culture into the home.

Middle-Class Literature

As technology made it possible to mass-produce cheap books and magazines, the middle class, particularly women, developed a voracious appetite for reading material, from Bibles to popular novels to newspapers. Women authored a new literature with American themes that supported the religious and family values of business-class evangelists. These works described women as occupying a "separate sphere" within the home, where they exerted a moral superiority that improved public life as well as family life.

Education

The northern business class invested heavily in the education of its children. As communities expanded and improved public education, young women staffed these schools. Towns preferred to hire women because they worked more cheaply than men, but it was the moral and missionary aspects of teaching that attracted the women.

Family Planning and Population Growth

Members of the northern business class began to limit the size of their families in order to have more money available for purchasing goods. They did not need large families to work the land. Those rural areas, however, where land was cheap continued to experience high birthrates. As a result of immigration and high rural birthrates, the North and the Great Lakes region accounted for two-thirds of the country's population growth between 1840 and 1860.

The Midwest

Industrial technology and railroads accelerated movement into the Old Northwest, strengthening ties between the Midwest and the Northeast. Railroads turned places such as St. Louis and Chicago into boom towns while undermining older river cities such as Cincinnati. Cultural and economic ties followed the paths of immigration, and the Northeast and the Midwest became tightly linked.

Conflict over the Trans-Mississippi West, 1844–1846 pp. 407–411

The South and the North both tried to dominate westward expansion—the South by establishing plantations and selling slaves in western terri-

8. Industrialization transformed the North as _____ became marks of economic success. (p. 397)

9. James Fenimore Cooper's heroes exemplified American virtues such as _____ and _____ . (p. 399)

10. The northern business class invested heavily in education for its children because education seemed to promise _____ and _____ . (p. 402)

11. The _____ indicated that most people felt confident about their ability to provide for a large number of children. (p. 403)

12. The growth of midwestern agriculture depended heavily on northeastern _____ and _____ . (p. 404)

tories, the North by extending the farming, urban, and industrial society of the Northeast.

Manifest Destiny

Southern imperialists, the northern business class, and even America's artists shared a belief that the United States had a "manifest destiny" to expand to the Pacific. This vision expressed a cultural arrogance that longed to carry American democracy and Protestantism to "inferior" peoples. Economic motives led many merchants and farmers to support this vision. When Perry landed in Japan, he secured a commercial treaty with the Japanese.

13. Manifest Destiny implied that Americans had a _____ to make the entire continent part of American democracy. (p. 407)

The Great American Desert and Oregon Fever

Before 1840, Americans considered the Great Plains unfit for cultivation and, thus, did not settle there. After 1840, settlers from the North and Old Northwest began to move into Wisconsin, Iowa, and Minnesota, while others looked toward Oregon, which was shared between Britain and the United States. The Oregon Trail carried over 350,000 people westward between 1842 and 1860. A few farmers on the Oregon Trail chose to settle in the Sacramento Valley with hopes of bringing California into the United States. The Mexican government, only recently independent of Spain, pursued economic development by welcoming American traders and by secularizing large cattle ranches owned by the Catholic missions.

14. New England merchants who had begun to develop _____ valued Oregon for its harbors. (p. 408)

Southern Imperialism

Planters, who were forced to move continually west to find new land for cultivation, sought to keep slavery legal in the territories and to extend it into areas such as Texas and California. Southerners feared the growing power of the North in Congress as new free states came into the Union; they also feared British abolitionists, who ended slavery in the West Indies in 1833. Free-soil areas in the Caribbean might become bases for abolitionist raids into the South, encouraging slaves to rebel. This fear led the United States into a war with Mexico to acquire new land for slavery; eventually it resulted in civil war.

15. Southerners feared that Britain was trying to erect an _____ from the West Indies through Texas and Mexico to California. (p. 410)

The Election of 1844

In 1843 most Americans wanted to seize all of Oregon and oust the British. President John Tyler, who had recently joined the Democratic party, attempted to win that party's nomination for the presidency by appealing to northern and southern expansionists. He supported the annexation of Texas and the seizure of Oregon, but Martin Van Buren and Henry Clay, the other contenders for the presidency, united Whigs and northern Democrats against this proposal.

The Democrats selected James K. Polk to run for the presidency in 1844, and the Whigs chose Henry Clay. Polk was popular because of his strong commitment to expansion. Clay emphasized the American System but was ambivalent on Texas; this waffling led both southern and north-

16. The war cry of the Democratic campaign in 1844 was "_____," expressing popular desire for the acquisition of Oregon. (p. 415)

ern Whigs to desert him in the general election. James G. Birney of the Liberty party took antislavery votes from Clay in the North. Polk won the election on an expansionist platform. Congressional Democrats, witnessing Polk's victory, annexed Texas before Polk was inaugurated, a move Mexico refused to acknowledge.

EXPANDED TIMELINE

1841   **Catharine Beecher's *Treatise on Domestic Economy***
A standard and popular text on housekeeping, Beecher's book instructed women on how to use their superior moral authority to create loving, nurturing homes.

James Fenimore Cooper's *The Deerslayer*
Cooper's works celebrated the frontier where Americans, under the influence of nature, would remain free and pure from urban decadence.

1842   **Charles Wilkes reports on Pacific Explorations**
Wilkes reported that Oregon country had excellent potential harbors, exciting the interests of Yankee merchants involved in the China trade.

Migration to Oregon begins
The first large party of settlers crossed the Oregon Trail in 1842. Reports from this group led thousands to follow, producing the division of the Oregon Territory between Britain and the United States in 1846.

1843   **Calhoun warns of a British conspiracy to block expansion**
Southerners feared that the British would encourage abolition in the South, undermining the southern economy and replacing its agricultural dominance with dependence on products from British colonies.

Thomas Oliver Larkin becomes U.S. consul in California
Unlike many New England merchants who assimilated into Californio society, Larkin surreptitiously worked toward the peaceful annexation of Upper California into the United States, all the while maintaining friendly relations with Mexican authorities.

Oregon conventions organized
Bipartisan national conventions urged President Tyler to terminate joint occupation, remove the British from Oregon, and seize Oregon all the way to 54'40. President Tyler agreed, supporting annexation of Texas as well.

1844   **Anti-Catholic rioting in Philadelphia**
When a Catholic bishop persuaded school officials to use both Catholic and Protestant versions of the Bible in public schools, rioting broke out, signifying the hostility of native-born laborers toward immigrants.

Tyler appoints John C. Calhoun as secretary of state
Calhoun, who had come to fear Whig abolitionism and British expansion, assisted Tyler in presenting a proposal to Congress supporting Texas annexation. Whigs led by Henry Clay and Democrats under Martin Van Buren defeated this proposal.

James K. Polk elected president
Campaigning to seize all of Oregon and annex Texas, the Democrat Polk defeated Whig Henry Clay, who was reluctant to support expansion. This victory was taken by Polk as a popular mandate in favor of territorial acquisition.

1845   **Lowell Female Labor Reform Association formed**
As manufacturers speeded up factory routines, workers formed organizations to resist this process. These were the earliest labor organizations in the United States.

Editor John L. O'Sullivan coins the term *Manifest Destiny*
O'Sullivan's naming of this American vision of expansion to the Pacific heightened the expansionist movement and contributed to the Mexican War. O'Sullivan's belief that Americans had a divine mission to bring American democracy to new lands appealed both to southern imperialists and to northerners who wanted to extend American industry and agriculture.

Texas admitted to the Union as a slave state
Presidents Jackson and Van Buren had been reluctant to admit Texas to the Union, fearing to stir up the slavery issue. After Polk's election to the presidency, however, Congress admitted Texas to the Union as a slave state.

1846   **Democratic Congress restores the Independent Treasury**
Walker Tariff passed
Mexican War begins
This war brought Texas into the Union; decisions about the role of slavery in the Mexican cession later precipitated the Civil War.

Cyrus McCormick opens Chicago factory
With war assembly-line techniques, McCormick used a power-driven conveyor belt to manufacture his reapers. This application of technology to the production of farm machinery revolutionized agriculture.

1847   **Refugees from Irish potato famine arrive in large numbers**
A devastating potato famine in Ireland drove

millions of Irish people to emigrate to the United States. Most of them settled in northeastern cities, where native-born American workers responded with hostility by forming Native American Clubs.

Hoe rotary press introduced
This invention made possible the mass production of cheap books, which were read avidly by the new middle class.

1849 **Cholera epidemics in cities**
Cholera struck major cities, killing more than 5,000 people in New York City alone. Poor sanitation systems in overcrowded immigrant neighborhoods worsened the epidemic.

1850 **A. J. Downing's *The Architecture of Country Houses***
Downing argued that his larger houses with their greater individual space would promote stronger families as well as truth, beauty, and order.

1851 **Crystal Palace Exhibition**
At this London exhibition, Americans displayed their superior machine-tooled products, to the wonderment of the British. This demonstrated American dominance in manufacturing.

1852 ***Uncle Tom's Cabin***
Harriet Beecher Stowe's book criticized slavery for its destructive impact on the home and idealized women as morally superior to men. Vastly popular, this book sensitized many northerners to the inhumanity of slavery.

1857 **Economic panic begins depression**
Rapidly accelerating manufacturing production led to periods of overproduction and layoffs, resulting in temporary depressions that kept unemployment high.

1858 **Mason jar introduced**
The Mason jar allowed families to preserve food safely, expanding dietary options.

1859 **Railroads carry more freight than do canals**
Railroads promoted midwestern development and tied that area to the Northeast by carrying agricultural products to the great manufacturing cities and finished goods back to rural areas.

GLOSSARY

gangs   Teams of slaves were driven to work at a frenetic pace by overseers and drivers. The gang-labor system created a kind of factory in the fields. (p. 385)

overseers   Overseers were generally whites hired by plantation owners to direct slave field workers. They often used terror and violent punishments to elicit cooperation. (p. 385)

drivers   Drivers were favored slaves put in charge of other slaves to direct their work. (p. 385)

task system   Under the task system slave labor was organized in such a way that each slave or group of slaves worked at an assigned task. It was somewhat less demanding than the gang-labor system, which replaced it. (p. 385)

cavaliers   Southern planters likened themselves to chivalrous English knights and gentlemen, creating a self-image of nobility and superiority to justify their dominance in southern society and their control over slaves. (p. 387)

"mud-sill" class   In 1858, James H. Hammond called slaves a "mud-sill" class that did all the South's dirtiest work, leaving whites free to cultivate a refined society. This lowest group in society guaranteed freedom and democracy to whites, according to Hammond. (p. 388)

chattel   Slaves were considered personal property according to law, and owners could do whatever they pleased with their chattel. This legal interpretation permitted slaveowners to sell their slaves at will and to use the harshest measures to keep their slaves from disobeying or rebelling. (p. 388)

underground railroad   Abolitionists set up a secret network, known as the underground railroad, to help escaped slaves get to the North and to Canada. Free African-Americans living in southern cities, though they risked death, were the most important source of help. (p. 391)

six-shooter   Samuel Colt's revolver was mass-produced in Connecticut; it became enormously popular in the Southwest. (p. 393)

balloon frame   These strong wooden frames allowed the rapid, inexpensive construction of homes, speeding up the development of cities such as Chicago. They also gave new middle-class families more space and privacy. (p. 397)

boosters   Many community leaders celebrated the benefits and advantages of their towns, bringing in new immigrants attracted by the boosters' promises of prosperity. (p. 407)

Manifest Destiny   A common American vision that the country was fated to stretch from the Atlantic to the Pacific, Manifest Destiny inspired expansionist actions such as the Mexican War, the movement into Oregon, and southern imperialistic designs on Central America. The term was used for the first time in a newspaper in 1845. (p. 407)

"Great American Desert"   Prior to the 1840s, the Great Plains were known as the "Great American Desert" because until then mapmakers had led easterners to believe that the area was a desert, unfit for cultivation. (p. 408)

mestizos   A common blend in areas of the Mexican cession, *mestizos* are people with mixed Spanish and Indian heritage. (p. 409)

Californios   The *Californios*, members of prominent Mexican families in California before that area became part of the United States, often lost their land to Americans through legal machinations and vigilante tactics after California became a state. (p. 409)

IDENTIFICATION

Identify by filling in the blanks.

1. By the 1830s, the South was producing more than _____ of the world's cotton. (p. 384)

2. The belief that planters were particularly noble, chivalrous, and superior is called the _____ . (p. 387)

3. Southerners described slaves as a _____ that performed society's most degrading jobs, allowing whites to develop a refined culture of freedom and democracy. (p. 388)

4. The group that gave the most assistance to escaped slaves was _____ . (p. 391)

5. Manufacturers were able to locate their factories in cities, and not on rivers, due to the development of the _____ . (p. 393)

6. The second-largest group of immigrants to the United States in the 1840s and 1850s came from _____ . (p. 394)

7. The organization that did the most to meet the needs of Irish immigrants was the _____ . (p. 396)

8. The _____ , lighter and stronger than traditional wood architecture, permitted the rapid construction of inexpensive housing. (p. 397)

9. Women novelists told their readers that women could achieve their highest potential only by focusing on _____ . (p. 402)

10. An antislavery novel made its author, _____ , the most successful novelist of the 1850s. (p. 402)

11. _____ founded academies where young women could train to become teachers. (p. 403)

12. John Deere's _____ made midwestern farming much easier and cheaper. (p. 404)

13. Two groups of artists who depicted the concept of Manifest Destiny were _____ and _____ . (p. 407)

14. Yankee traders in California found alliances with the elite Mexicans known as _____ profitable. (p. 409)

15. Southerners feared that Britain wanted Mexico to cede _____ to Britain as payment for back debts. (p. 410)

16. In 1844 the Whig Henry Clay lost to the Democrat _____ , who enthusiastically supported expansion. (p. 411)

SKILL-BUILDING EXERCISE

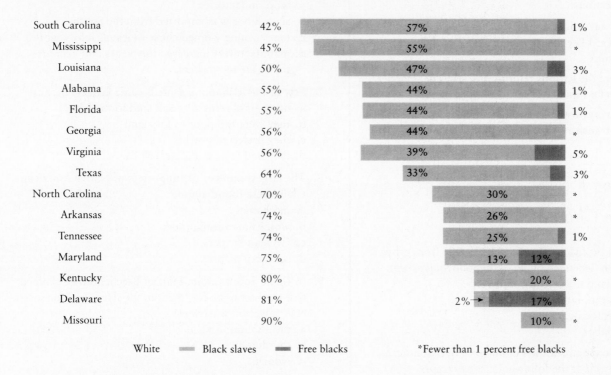

State	White	Black slaves	Free blacks
South Carolina	42%	57%	1%
Mississippi	45%	55%	*
Louisiana	50%	47%	3%
Alabama	55%	44%	1%
Florida	55%	44%	1%
Georgia	56%	44%	*
Virginia	56%	39%	5%
Texas	64%	33%	3%
North Carolina	70%	30%	*
Arkansas	74%	26%	*
Tennessee	74%	25%	1%
Maryland	75%	13%	12%
Kentucky	80%	20%	*
Delaware	81%	2%	17%
Missouri	90%	10%	*

White ▬ Black slaves ▬ Free blacks

*Fewer than 1 percent free blacks

Use the chart to answer the following questions.

1. Which three states had the highest percentage of free blacks and why?

2. Why did Delaware, Missouri, Maryland, and Kentucky have such a low percentage of slaves in their populations?

3. Where were slaves the majority of the population?

DOCUMENT EXERCISES

American Voices

A Slaveholder's Diary— Mary Boykin Chesnut

The wives of southern planters knew that their economic and social status depended on slavery. At the same time, these women were acute critics of slavery. Like Mary Boykin Chesnut, they condemned slavery for its corruption of white men and women.

As you read "A Slaveholder's Diary," ask yourself the following questions:

1. How does Chesnut describe the situation of slave women?

2. In what ways does Chesnut believe that slavery degrades white men?

3. How does Chesnut describe the life of southern white women?

4. According to Chesnut, how did slavery adversely affect white women?

Slave Songs—Frederick Douglass

Frederick Douglass was raised a slave but escaped to the North as a young man. He became a leader of the abolitionist movement and was one of those who persuaded Abraham Lincoln to issue the Emancipation Proclamation.

As you read "Slave Songs," ask yourself the following questions:

1. According to Douglass, what were some of the reasons that slaves sang?

2. What are the messages in the song he relates?

3. How does Douglass describe the slaveowners?

4. What misconceptions of slaves does Douglass believe northerners have?

American Lives

The Beecher Family: Cultural Innovators

The Beechers were one of the most remarkable families of the century. The activities of individual Beecher family members embraced evangelical reform, women's roles, and abolitionism.

As you read "The Beecher Family," ask yourself the following questions:

1. In what ways did the religious ideas of Lyman and Henry Ward Beecher represent the Second Great Awakening?

2. How were the various reforms of Catharine, Harriet, and Isabella similar? Where did they differ?

3. In what ways were the Beechers in the forefront of changes transforming the middle class?

SELF-TEST

Multiple Choice

1. The high profits southern planters made from growing cotton depended on *all* of the following *except*:
   a. fresh land in the Old Southwest.
   b. immigrant labor.
   c. British textile markets.
   d. gang labor.

2. Planters maintained their dominance over southern society by *all* of the following means *except*:
   a. most whites hoped to enter the planter class.
   b. the benevolence of slaveowners who protected their slaves from the harsh realities of wage labor.
   c. The propagation of the idea that slavery guaranteed equality, freedom, and democracy for whites.
   d. the belief that African-Americans were an inferior race.

3. The North Carolina Supreme Court declared in 1853 that:
   a. slave marriages were not valid in law.
   b. slaves could not own property.
   c. the domestic slave trade was legal.
   d. slaves were entitled to attend church if they wished.

4. Slave rebellions met with little success due to *all* of the following factors *except*:
   a. whites were well-armed.
   b. planters used the fear of rebellion to get the support of non-slaveholding whites.
   c. there were few isolated locations good for hiding out.
   d. rebellions rarely occurred because slaves passively accepted their state.

5. A southern free black who led a slave rebellion was:
   a. Denmark Vesey.   c. David Walker.
   b. Nat Turner.   d. Frederick Douglass.

6. One change in the factory work force by the 1840s was:
   a. greater numbers of free blacks came North to work in factories.
   b. slave labor was imported from the South.
   c. many young women chose to leave factory work.
   d. manufacturers increased the wages and benefits they gave to workers.

7. Few of the Irish immigrants became farmers because:
   a. most areas refused to sell land to the Irish.
   b. they were too poor to buy land.
   c. they preferred city life.
   d. they had few agricultural skills.

8. The largest number of supporters of Native American Clubs were found among:
   a. mechanics.
   b. women factory workers.
   c. German farmers.
   d. southern planters.

9. In *Uncle Tom's Cabin*, Harriet Beecher Stowe claimed that the best hope for freedom for slaves and for society's salvation was(were) _____ .
   a. the abolitionists.
   b. the churches.
   c. women.
   d. the American Colonization Society.

10. In the late 1830s, towns began to hire women as teachers rather than men because:
    a. they were cheaper.
    b. teaching small children was a natural calling for women.
    c. young men refused to work as teachers.
    d. young women were better educated than young men.

11. Birthrates decreased for *all* of the following reasons *except*:
    a. some farm families in the Northeast did not have enough land to leave to their children.
    b. business-class families emphasized education, not the use of their children as labor.
    c. frontier families could not depend on adequate medical care during childbirth.
    d. birth control practices were moderately effective.

12. The rapid settlement of the Midwest resulted from:
    a. inexpensive German immigrant labor.
    b. agricultural technology such as the steel plow.
    c. overcrowding in southern cities.
    d. a growing number of migrants from southern states.

13. The editor who coined the term "Manifest Destiny" was:
    a. Horace Greeley.   c. Thomas Cole.
    b. John Hammond.   d. John L. O'Sullivan.

14. In the 1820s and 1830s, Americans found *all* of the following California products desirable *except*:
    a. hides.   c. gold.
    b. sea otter pelts.   d. tallow.

15. Southern planters were most worried about the expansionist plans of:
    a. Mexico.   c. Spain.
    b. France.   d. Great Britain.

16. James Polk won the presidential election of 1844 because:
    a. the Free Soil party took votes away from the Republican candidate.
    b. Polk's commitment to expansion was broadly popular.
    c. Polk was a popular war hero.
    d. the Democrats won the support of northern Know-Nothings.

Short Essays

Answer the following in a brief paragraph.

1. In what ways were slaveowners similar to northern entrepreneurial capitalists? (pp. 384–385)

2. Compare the lives of (a) northern factory workers (primarily immigrants) and (b) southern slaves. (pp. 385–386, 390, 395)

3. Compare and contrast racist ideology with northern nativism. (pp. 388, 396–397)

4. How did white southerners reconcile their racist ideology with democratic tenets? (p. 388)

5. Compare the ways in which slaves attempted to maintain their identities with the ways Irish immigrants sought to keep their cultural identities. (pp. 391–392, 396)

6. How did the transportation revolution contribute to the development of a market economy in the Old Northwest? (pp. 393, 404–406)

7. How did the Industrial Revolution modernize the northern middle class? (pp. 397–398, 402–403)

8. Why were critics of Manifest Destiny so unsuccessful? (p. 407)

9. Describe the dreams and realities that lay behind expansion into Texas and California. (pp. 409–410)

ANSWERS

Chapter Précis

1. Ohio River Valley or to Oregon or California

2. schools, magazines, and newspapers

3. Israelites

4. lower; Western Hemisphere

5. free blacks

6. poverty in their homeland

7. parochial schools

8. consumer goods

9. self-reliance; nonconformity

10. higher status; greater income

11. high national birth rate

12. markets; industrial technology

13. divinely inspired mission

14. trade with China

15. antislavery barrier

16. Fifty-four forty or fight!

Identification

1. two-thirds

2. Cavalier myth

3. "mud-sill" class

4. free African-Americans in southern cities

5. steam engine

6. Germany

7. Catholic Church

8. balloon frame

9. marriage

10. Harriet Beecher Stowe

11. Catharine Beecher

12. steel plow

13. Hudson River School; Rocky Mountain painters

14. Californios

15. California

16. James K. Polk

Skill-Building Exercise

1. Delaware, Maryland, Virginia; soil in these states had been depleted by tobacco, then cotton agriculture, making slaveholding increasingly costly. In addition, during the Revolutionary Era many whites, inspired by the idea of independence, had freed their slaves. These African-Americans often sought employment in commercial centers and port cities such as Baltimore.

2. Plantation agriculture in Delaware and Maryland was no longer profitable due to soil depletion, so many slaves had been either freed or sold "down the river" to the newer areas of the Old Southwest. Kentucky and Missouri were border states and had been settled by non-slaveholding small farmers. Their soil was not amenable to plantation farming.

3. South Carolina and Mississippi

Self-Test

Multiple Choice

1. b	7. b	13. d
2. b	8. a	14. c
3. a	9. c	15. d
4. d	10. a	16. b
5. a	11. c	
6. c	12. b	

Short Essays

1. Planters sought to maximize their profits. They invested in cotton because British textile mills provided an enormous demand for that crop. Planters' profits averaged about 10 percent a year, higher than the profit margin for any other potential investment. Planters also exploited their labor force to maximize their gain. They forced slaves to work in the gang-labor system because that way they could push them hardest.

2. Slaves often worked in gangs, much as workers did in industrial factories. They were managed by drivers and overseers who had far more power over them than factory bosses had over industrial workers. Because slaves were their property, many slaveholders attempted to keep slaves in good working condition, whereas in the North, a worker who performed unsatisfactorily would be fired. In the North, urban living conditions produced periodic epidemics. Slaves had no control over their families and could lose a spouse or child to the domestic slave trade at any time. Finally, they had no protection from slaveholders' violence against them.

3. Southern racists described African-Americans as a permanently inferior class unsuited for freedom and incapable of caring for themselves. Slaveowners believed that rigid control was needed both to take care of the slaves and to restrain their supposedly violent nature. Northern nativism, directed against immigrants, focused partly on religion. Catholics, nativists said, intended to subvert the republican ideals of the United States and hand the country over to a monarchy, to the pope, or both. Immigrants were blamed for the crowded, disease-ridden conditions in the big cities. Northern laborers resented the job competition that the immigrants seemed to present. Nativists sought to restrict the political rights of immigrants.

4. Southerners described African-Americans as inferior beings who could not handle freedom or democracy. Slavery was therefore the best system to care for them. Slaves constituted a "mud-sill" class that did all the hard, dirty work, leaving whites free to develop an advanced democratic civilization. Slavery therefore facilitated development of democracy.

5. Slaves and the Irish both found solace in religion. Slave Christianity emphasized the endurance and ultimate deliverance of the Israelites from Egypt. Religious services allowed slaves to come together to express their love for one another and experience a sense of community. The Irish strengthened and came to dominate the Catholic Church in America, which also heightened their sense of community. The Church met many of the immigrants' needs with institutions such as schools, hospitals, and orphanages.

6. Roads, canals, steamboats, and railroads allowed farmers to move their crops quickly and cheaply to market for sale. Farmers saw profitable reasons for extending their activities to produce enough for the commercial market, whereas earlier, unable to reach large markets, they had had little incentive to go much beyond subsistence farming. The growth of large industrial cities in the Northeast, such as Boston and New York, provided these farmers in the Old Northwest with an enormous market that bought everything they could produce, and at good prices. The transportation revolution was a necessity if they were to reach this market.

7. The Industrial Revolution in the North created a middle class of consumers by giving more disposable income to that group and by producing inexpensive consumer items. Innovations in housing construction permitted more Americans to build comfortable homes; inexpensive consumer goods, both appliances and decorations, enabled middle-class families to individualize their homes. Finally, as the middle class adjusted to the new rules for the business success brought about by the Industrial Revolution, families saw the value of education for their children and made greater investments in their upbringing. This also led to smaller families as middle-class parents decided to have fewer children but educate them further.

8. Manifest Destiny expressed Americans' positive feelings about themselves in a romantic vision; it was the way Americans wanted to see themselves. It also ap-

pealed to the economic interests of a large number of people, including southern planters, small farmers, and merchants in the Northeast. Through publications and works of art, which gave the notion much publicity, Manifest Destiny became an expression of popular patriotism.

9. Americans envisioned their expansion into areas once held by Mexico as divinely inspired to bring democ- racy, Protestantism, and education to inferior peoples. In reality, Americans conquered both the Mexican Texans and the *Californios*. In California, they used legal technicalities to deprive *Californios* of the best land and mines as well as of their legal rights.

CHAPTER *14*

Disrupting the Union 1846–1860

★   ★   ★

CHAPTER PRÉCIS

The Mexican War and Its Aftermath, 1846–1850   pp. 416–429

The Mexican War, 1846–1848

Polk, hoping to take Alta California, sent secret orders to Thomas O. Larkin, his agent in Monterey, and to John Sloat, the United States Navy commander in the Pacific, to prepare to seize and annex California. He also sent an expedition under John C. Frémont to explore the area. Polk's emissary to Mexico, John Slidell, offered to buy New Mexico and California for $30 million, an offer Mexico rejected, refusing to see Slidell.

Polk responded by creating an incident designed to bring on war. He sent United States troops under Zachary Taylor into the disputed area between the Rio Grande and the Nueces River. When skirmishes broke out between the Mexican and American forces, Polk claimed that United States territory had been invaded and won a declaration of war from Congress. To avoid a simultaneous war with Great Britain, he and the Senate agreed to divide Oregon with the British at the 49th parallel.

Before war was declared, Polk ordered Frémont's forces back into California. These troops supported American settlers who had revolted from Mexican authority and formed an independent republic. Once these groups learned that war had been declared, they announced that California was part of the United States. American forces quickly captured New Mexico, but in southern California they faced stiff Mexican resistance, which was overcome by reinforcements.

1. Officials of the Mexican government refused to see John Slidell because they wanted to _____ and _____ . (p. 416)

United States forces, outnumbered but with advantages in weaponry, quickly seized northeastern Mexico. Patriotism prevented the Mexican government from agreeing to peace, so Polk sent Winfield Scott to attack the heart of Mexico. Scott invaded Mexico at Veracruz and marched west, seizing Mexico City on September 14, 1847, and forcing the Mexican government to accept a peace treaty.

Initially Americans supported the war enthusiastically, believing that it would spread American republican institutions and free Mexico from governmental corruption. "Conscience Whigs," however, denounced the war as part of the proslavery conspiracy. The possibility of additional slave states, the capture of Mexico City, and mounting casualties won more northern Whigs to their side. A northern Democratic congressman with free-soil beliefs, David Wilmot, proposed that slavery be prohibited in any territory acquired from Mexico. This proposal, although never approved by the Senate, rallied northerners to the free-soil movement. Conversely, Democratic expansionists sought the seizure of northern Mexico. To appease free-soil Democrats, Polk's administration compromised in the Treaty of Guadalupe Hidalgo, taking only Alta California and New Mexico for the United States.

The Free-Soil Movement

Abolitionists in the mid-1840s redefined their movement, deemphasizing the natural right of slaves and, instead, stressing that a Slave Power conspiracy was a threat to republican institutions. The Liberty party reorganized in 1848 under this program, calling itself the Free Soil party and insisting that slavery be kept out of the territories to protect the freedom of whites from slave competition. This approach attracted broad popular support.

The Election of 1848

The presidential election of 1848 pitted the Democratic expansionist Lewis Cass against the Mexican War hero General Zachary Taylor. Cass supported the concept of popular sovereignty to resolve the question of slavery in the territories. The Free Soil party, running Martin Van Buren, won support from many northern Democrats and Whigs. Taylor won primarily because of his popularity as a military hero.

Alternatives to the Wilmot Proviso

Southern politicians developed three strategies to protect slavery in the territories. John C. Calhoun, following the "common property" doctrine, insisted that Congress could not prevent a citizen from taking his property into another state or state-owned territory. Moderate southern leaders supported extension of the Missouri Compromise line across the Mexican cession. Popular sovereignty would allow territorial governments to decide the legality of slavery.

2. Once the _____ regained control of Congress in 1846, they became bolder about opposing the Mexican War. (p. 420)

3. Garrison and Douglass were bothered by the _____ of the Free Soil party. (p. 422)

4. The swift growth of the Free Soil party stunned southerners, who responded by becoming more aggressive in the _____ . (p. 423)

5. Popular sovereignty was ambiguous on at what point the people of a territory could _____ . (p. 426)

The Compromise of 1850

California, quickly populated as a result of the gold rush, applied for admission to the Union as a free state in 1849. Southern politicians would accept California's statehood only if the federal government agreed to protect the future of slavery. The Compromise of 1850 admitted California as a free state and passed the Fugitive Slave Act, as well as four lesser provisions.

Sectional Strife and the Third Party System, 1850–1858 pp. 429–439

The Fugitive Slave Act

The Fugitive Slave Act required federal officials in the North to participate in the capture of African-Americans accused of being runaway slaves. Effectively enforced, the act personalized the plight of slaves in the North and led abolitionists to defy the law. Northern state governments passed personal liberty laws to protect African-Americans, and the Wisconsin Supreme Court ruled that a state could declare an act of Congress unconstitutional. The United States Supreme Court, however, ruled that these state laws were unconstitutional.

Southerners organized conventions to respond to northern hostility toward the act. Moderates won out in those meetings, refusing to support secession.

The Election of 1852: A Shift in Party Balance

In 1852 the Whigs split along regional lines. Many southern Whigs deserted the Whig candidate and Mexican War hero Winfield Scott, some even voting for the Democratic ticket and for stronger support for the Compromise of 1850. Northern Whigs wanted firmer opposition to slavery and immigration. The Democrats won the election with New Hampshire's Franklin Pierce, who was sympathetic to the South and attracted the votes of southern Whigs and northern Democrats who had favored free soil in 1848. The Democratic party remained viable nationally with its commitment to popular sovereignty.

Pierce's Expansionist Foreign Policy

Pierce attempted to divert national attention from slavery and increase his support with an expansionist foreign policy. He achieved a full commercial treaty with Japan, its first such treaty with only industrial power. Pierce funded expeditions to Cuba, hoping to stimulate a revolution in which the United States could seize the island, but the opposition of northern politicians prevented this. After leading a failed rebellion in northern Mexico, William Walker invaded Nicaragua, where he set himself up as a dictator. Although the Pierce administration recognized Walker's government, he was driven out of power and executed by a firing squad. Pierce's plans to focus on expansion and thus overshadow slavery did not succeed.

6. During the debate over California's admission to the Union, John C. Calhoun stated that unless Congress protected slavery in all the territories, there would be _____ . (p. 427)

7. Harriet Beecher Stowe wrote _____ in direct response to the Fugitive Slave Act. (p. 429)

8. The Democratic party appealed to many voters who believed that it was more important to _____ than to protect or to destroy slavery. (p. 431)

9. The primary reason the United States desired the land known as the Gadsden Purchase was to _____ to the Pacific Ocean. (p. 432)

Kansas-Nebraska and the Republicans

To facilitate the construction of a transcontinental railroad, the Illinois Democrat Stephen A. Douglas proposed to create and organize the territories of Kansas and Nebraska according to popular sovereignty. In the North, abolitionists and free-soilers greeted the Kansas-Nebraska Act as a repudiation of the old Missouri Compromise line and rallied to form the Republican party, opposing the expansion of slavery in the territories. The Republicans received Know-Nothing and free-soil support, winning a majority in the House of Representatives in 1854.

10. Southerners believed they would have a better chance to dominate the new Kansas territory than the Nebraska territory because _____ . (p. 433)

Republican Ideology versus the Defense of Slavery

Republicans criticized slavery as producing a society of corrupt masters and subservient, ignorant slaves. Northern society, by contrast, had no permanent class divisions because of its freedom and mobility. Every man had the opportunity to work diligently and rise to the status of an employer. Southerners, conversely, began to defend slavery on the basis that masters were more benevolent and caring toward their slaves than northern capitalists were toward their employees.

11. Although in the industrial North class divisions were increasing, the Republicans asserted the values of _____ and _____ . (p. 434)

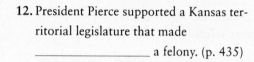

"Bleeding Kansas"

Kansas became an object of competition between proslavery and antislavery forces as supporters on both sides sent armed settlers into Kansas. The Pierce administration backed the proslavery settlers when they organized a territorial government favorable to slavery. In 1856 the sack of free-soil Lawrence by a proslavery gang led the militant abolitionist John Brown to retaliate with the massacre of five proslavery settlers at Pottawatomie, and a guerrilla war ensued. Even in Congress, violence broke out between politicians.

12. President Pierce supported a Kansas territorial legislature that made _____ a felony. (p. 435)

The Election of 1856

The Democrats, staying with popular sovereignty, nominated the Pennsylvanian James Buchanan to win northern votes. The Republicans, opposing slavery in the territories and favoring federal support for a transcontinental railroad, nominated the free-soiler John C. Frémont, the conqueror of California. Although the Republicans were strong in the North, Buchanan won enough northern votes, along with all of the South, to carry the election. A new party system of Democrats and Republicans had come into being, but the Republicans had support only in the North.

13. The Know-Nothings split into North and South factions over _____ . (p. 437)

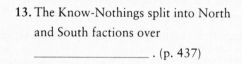

The Democratic Blunders of 1857–1858

In the *Dred Scott* decision, the Supreme Court, at Buchanan's urging, attempted to resolve the question of slavery in the territories. Chief Justice Roger B. Taney ruled that African-Americans could not be citizens of the United States and, therefore, could not sue in a federal court. He also ruled that Congress could not prohibit a citizen from taking his property into any territory and, thus, could not ban slavery in a territory. Republicans denounced the Court as the agent of a "Slave Power" conspiracy.

14. In the *Dred Scott* decision, Chief Justice Taney ruled that the _____ was unconstitutional. (p. 439)

President Buchanan drove northern Democrats under Stephen Douglas to break with him when he supported the admission of Kansas as a slave state under the fraudulent Lecompton constitution, even though the antislavery majority had rejected the constitution in a referendum.

Abraham Lincoln and the Breaking of Union, 1858–1860   pp. 439–445

The violence in Kansas and the *Dred Scott* decision led more northern Democrats and former Whigs to join the Republicans.

Lincoln's Early Career

As a young man, Lincoln worked as a store clerk, a successful corporate lawyer, and finally a state legislator in Illinois during an economic boom in the Ohio River Valley. In the state government Lincoln strongly supported the Whig program of government stimulus for economic development. Entering Congress in 1847, Lincoln opposed the expansion of slavery in the territories and supported African colonization but believed that the federal government lacked the authority to touch slavery in the slave states. He worked to keep the Whig party together, trying to find a satisfactory compromise over slavery. Adamantly opposed to slavery in the territories, Lincoln became a leader in the Republican party. In his 1854 Peoria address, Lincoln condemned slavery because it was based on selfishness; he asked for a return to the Missouri Compromise as a solution to the issue of slavery in the territories. The *Dred Scott* decision convinced him that the Court would one day make slavery legal in all states.

15. After losing reelection to the House of Representatives and going back to private law practice, Lincoln returned to politics because of his opposition to the _____ . (p. 441)

Lincoln versus Douglas

In their battle for an Illinois Senate seat in 1858, Lincoln and Douglas articulated their positions regarding slavery. Lincoln stated that African-Americans were entitled to all the rights listed in the Declaration of Independence. He attacked slavery as a denial of equality of opportunity and believed that the South was attempting to make slavery legal throughout the United States. Douglas, by contrast, enunciated his Freeport doctrine, stating that settlers could keep slavery out of a territory by failing to pass legislation to protect it, an interpretation that alienated southerners in his party. Douglas won the election by a narrow margin.

The Election of 1860

Republican gains in 1858 led southern Democrats to insist that the federal government make a commitment to protect slavery, including reopening the international slave trade, a position that infuriated northern Democrats such as Douglas. Further terrifying southerners was John Brown's attempt at Harpers Ferry, with northern abolitionist support, to arm a slave rebellion and create an African-American state in the South.

16. Stephen Douglas won the Illinois senatorial election of 1858 due to his base of support in _____ . (p. 443)

The Democratic party split over the nomination of a presidential candidate, with northerners choosing Douglas and southerners selecting John C. Breckinridge of Kentucky.

The Republicans selected Lincoln because of his moderate position on slavery. The party platform denied the right of secession, endorsed the old Whig economic program, and ruled out interference with slavery in the states. Douglas campaigned in the South, warning southerners that the North would not tolerate secession. He competed in the South with John Bell of the Constitutional Union party, a residue of southern Whiggery. Lincoln won the election with a plurality of the popular vote. His victory in the Northeast was overwhelming, but he lacked support in the South. Lincoln had rallied the Northeast, Midwest, and Far West around the mission of free soil.

17. To southerners, John Brown's actions at Harpers Ferry seemed the natural result of _____ . (p. 443)

EXPANDED TIMELINE

1845

Polk's inauguration
Polk became a president committed to completing the annexation of Texas and seizing California and New Mexico.

Frémont sets out from St. Louis
On orders of the War Department, Captain Frémont took an exploring party of armed soldiers deep into Mexican territory.

Texas accepts admission to the Union
Democratic congressmen saw the election of James Polk as a national mandate for expansion and moved to annex Texas even before Polk's inauguration. Texas, settled by southern slaveholders, entered the Union as a slave state. Mexico, which had never recognized Texas's independence, broke off diplomatic relations with the United States.

Polk sends Zachary Taylor south of the Nueces River
When the Mexican government refused to listen to John Slidell, President Polk sent General Taylor into disputed territory to provoke an incident hoping for war.

Slidell mission
On President Polk's secret orders, the American emissary to Mexico, John Slidell, offered Mexico $30 million for New Mexico and California. The Mexican government, which believed that the American annexation of Texas was illegal, refused to see Slidell and insisted that the southern border of Texas was the Nueces River, not the Rio Grande.

Frémont reaches the Sacramento Valley
Admitted into California, Frémont defied Mexican authorities by building fortifications near the coast. He fled to Oregon when Mexican authorities threatened to fight.

1846

Polk sends Taylor south of the Rio Grande
Prior to a declaration of war, Polk, on learning of skirmishes near the Rio Grande, sent Taylor and his forces south of the Rio Grande where they occupied Matamoros.

United States declares war on Mexico
When Mexico refused to sell New Mexico and California to the United States, President Polk sent American troops into territory disputed between the United States and Mexico. When skirmishes occurred between the American and Mexican armies, Polk asked for and received a declaration of war from Congress on the basis that United States territory had been invaded.

Oregon treaty ratified
Facing war with Mexico, President Polk decided to compromise with the British over Oregon. On his recommendation, Congress accepted the British proposal to divide Oregon at the 49th parallel.

"Bear Flag Republic" proclaimed; Sloat seizes Monterrey
American settlers in California fomented a rebellion against Mexican rule with the support of United States troops secretly sent by President Polk. Unaware that war had been declared, Americans proclaimed California an independent country, the Bear Flag Republic. A month later the American Navy entered Monterrey and declared California part of the United States.

Walker Tariff passed
To dismantle the American system, Polk and the Democrats significantly reduced tariff rates.

Wilmot Proviso introduced in Congress
Antislavery activists in both parties feared that the acquisition of Mexican land would lead to an expansion of slavery. The Democrat David Wilmot introduced into Congress a resolution prohibiting slavery in any area acquired from Mexico. Although the Wilmot Proviso never passed Congress,

it gained bipartisan support in the North and bipartisan hostility in the South, indicating the divisive power of the slavery issue.

Taylor's victory at Monterrey
After capturing Matamoros, Taylor's troops marched inland and captured Monterrey, establishing a strong American presence in northern Mexico.

1847

Taylor's victory at Buena Vista
General Taylor's troops, although victorious at Buena Vista, suffered heavy casualties at the hands of the Mexican general Santa Anna. Mounting casualties rallied Whig opposition to the war in Congress, which passed a resolution thanking Taylor but criticizing Polk for beginning the war "unconstitutionally and unnecessarily."

Scott captures Mexico City
American troops under General Winfield Scott invaded Mexico from the sea at Veracruz and then marched inland toward Mexico City. While Scott never lost a battle, his victories were costly in terms of human life. When his troops seized Mexico City, the Mexican government surrendered.

1848

Gold discovered in California
Thousands of Americans seeking gold poured into California, whose population increased so rapidly it became a state in 1850. The Americans quickly came to dominate the earlier inhabitants, the *Californios.*

Treaty of Guadalupe Hidalgo
President Polk gave up his hopes of seizing northern Mexico because of some southern Democratic fears that the United States could not absorb large populations of Mexicans. Polk accepted the Treaty of Guadalupe Hidalgo, in which Mexico surrendered New Mexico and Alta California to the United States for $15 million. The United States also agreed to assume the damage claims of American citizens against the Mexican government.

Free Soil party formed
Emerging from the ashes of the Liberty party, the Free Soil party rooted its opposition to slavery in the desire of whites to keep the territories free of slaves. This approach won broad popular support. It appealed to northerners who opposed slavery in the territories because they disliked African-Americans. It also appealed to radical abolitionists who saw the free-soil movement as a way to provoke national confrontation over slavery.

Taylor elected
The Whigs nominated Zachary Taylor, a war hero who, although he owned slaves, was vague on the issue of slavery in the territories. Taylor defeated the Democratic candidate, Lewis Cass, who was selected for his dedication to expansion and commitment to popular sovereignty. Free-soil Democrats deserted Cass and voted for the Free Soil candidate, Martin Van Buren.

1849

Taylor proposes immediate admission of California
As thousands of forty-niners crowded into California in search of gold, President Taylor sought to establish a government there while avoiding the question of whether Congress had jurisdiction over slavery in the territories. Taylor urged the admission of California and New Mexico as free states, bypassing the territorial phase. Southerners delayed this process, fearing the admission of a new free state.

1850

Compromise of 1850
Southerners wanted a federal guarantee of slavery as the price for the admission of California as a free state. Whigs and Democrats forged the Compromise of 1850, which accepted California as a free state and included a Fugitive Slave Act to help slaveowners recapture slaves who fled to the North. The Compromise also organized the rest of the Mexican cession into territories, resolved boundary questions between New Mexico and Texas, and abolished the slave trade in the District of Columbia. Although it staved off a secession crisis, it divided both parties along sectional lines.

1851

Christiana riot
Many northern antislavery activists resisted the Fugitive Slave Act by helping runaway slaves avoid being returned to slavery. In the Quaker city of Christiana, Pennsylvania, African-Americans with white support exchanged gunfire with slave catchers seeking to seize two runaway slaves. President Fillmore sent troops and federal marshals to arrest antislavery supporters for treason. Public support for their cause led the government to drop the case.

American Party formed
Nativist groups united to form a political party whose program focused on opposition to immigrants. It sought to make naturalization more difficult, decreasing the political power of immigrants.

1852

Uncle Tom's Cabin appears in book form
Harriet Beecher Stowe wrote *Uncle Tom's Cabin* in response to the Fugitive Slave Act. Enormously popular in the North, this sentimental novel personalized the horrors of slavery, rallying many northerners around the antislavery cause. Southerners feared this heightened northern concern.

Franklin Pierce elected president
The Democratic party nominated Franklin Pierce, a northerner with proslavery sympathies, to face the Whig Winfield Scott, a war hero. Many southern Whigs deserted their party because of its unenthusiastic support for the Compromise of 1850. Northern Whigs wanted a stronger antislavery candidate. Pierce won by holding the Democratic party together. The Whigs, split over slavery, never again nominated a presidential candidate.

1853

Perry expedition to Japan begins

Perry's arrival in Japan led to the opening of that country to trade with the West.

1854   **Kansas-Nebraska Act**
Settlers moving into the free-soil portion of the Louisiana Purchase demanded territorial organization, as did railroad interests eager to construct a transcontinental railroad with a terminus in Chicago. Southerners, not eager to see new free-soil states, had blocked this, so the Illinois Democrat Stephen Douglas constructed the Kansas-Nebraska Act. This act divided the northern Louisiana Purchase into two territories, Kansas and Nebraska, and voided the Missouri Compromise line by opening the area to slavery through the principle of popular sovereignty.

Republican party formed
Infuriated by the voiding of the Missouri Compromise by the Kansas-Nebraska Act, northern antislavery forces among Whigs, free-soilers, and Know-Nothings united to form a new party, the Republican party, which was committed to free soil in the territories. This new organization quickly gained strength, winning a majority of seats in the House of Representatives in 1854, further infuriating southerners.

Ostend Manifesto
Pierce thought he had found an excuse to seize Cuba when Cuban officials seized an American ship. Northern Democrats refused to support war in order to acquire another slave state, so Pierce then tried to buy Cuba, again with little result. Furious Democrats claimed the rights of Manifest Destiny, that the United States would be justified in taking Cuba from Spain.

Know-Nothing movement peaks
The American party won several congressional seats and some state government positions, attempting to unite northern and southern voters in opposition to immigrants. However, with this election, Know-Nothings reached the height of their influence, declining later in the decade.

1856   **"Pottawatomie massacre"**
Proslavery and antislavery forces in Kansas engaged in open warfare. When proslavery gunmen sacked the antislavery town of Lawrence, the abolitionist John Brown and his party wreaked vengeance by murdering five proslavery settlers. Brown believed himself to be an instrument of God. His activities initiated a guerrilla war in Kansas.

James Buchanan elected president
The Democrats nominated James Buchanan, a northerner with strong southern sympathies. The Republicans, nominating their first presidential candidate, selected John C. Frémont, a war hero and free-soiler. Their platform denounced the Kansas-Nebraska Act, forbade slavery in the territories, and supported the American System. Although Buchanan won, Frémont carried eleven

states in the North. The new party system of Republicans and Democrats was decidedly sectional.

1857   *Dred Scott v. Sandford*
With President Buchanan's encouragement, the Supreme Court declared that African-Americans could not be citizens of the United States, and that the Missouri Compromise was unconstitutional: Slaveowners could take their "property" anywhere in the territories. This decision infuriated northerners, including northern Democrats. Republicans were outraged, and respect for the Court plummeted.

Panic of 1857
Near depression conditions led the Republicans to support the old Whig program of economic development, which won over many midwestern Democrats.

1858   **Buchanan backs Lecompton constitution**
Proslavery forces in Kansas wrote a constitution asking for admission as a slave state even though the majority of Kansans were opposed to slavery and had rejected the constitution in a referendum. President Buchanan supported the proslavery advocates, leading northern congressional Democrats under Stephen Douglas to break with Buchanan and defeat Kansas statehood.

Lincoln-Douglas debates
Competing for an Illinois Senate seat, the Republican Abraham Lincoln and the Democrat Stephen Douglas, in a series of debates, discussed the issue of slavery in the territories. Douglas supported popular sovereignty and asserted his Freeport doctrine, stating that settlers in a particular area could exclude slavery by refusing to adopt legislation to protect it. Southern Democrats were furious that Douglas advocated practices that might not protect slavery. Lincoln declared that slavery attacked equality of opportunity, asserting that African-Americans were included in the Declaration of Independence and entitled to all the Declaration's natural rights. Lincoln said that he feared slaveowners were attempting to have slavery legalized throughout the nation. Douglas won the Senate seat.

1859   **John Brown's raid on Harpers Ferry**
John Brown and heavily armed supporters, both African-American and white, seized the federal arsenal at Harpers Ferry. Brown hoped to incite a slave rebellion that would lead to the creation of an African-American state within the South. Federal troops and local militia caught Brown and his men, who were killed immediately or convicted and hanged. Northern support for Brown further convinced the South that northerners would foment race war in the South. The North idolized Brown as a martyr.

1860   **Abraham Lincoln elected president**

The Democrats split between the northerner Stephen Douglas and the southerner John C. Breckinridge. John Bell, a former Whig from Tennessee, ran with the Constitutional Union party. The Republican Abraham Lincoln swept the Northeast, Midwest, and Far West but won with only a plurality of the popular vote and no support in the South. To southerners, Lincoln's victory meant that both the executive and legislative branches of the federal government were now in antislavery hands.

GLOSSARY

"conscience Whigs"   Although the Whig party officially remained neutral on the question of slavery, a wing of the party, the "conscience Whigs," opposed the Mexican War, believing that its purpose was to acquire more land for the expansion of slavery. As war casualties increased, more Whigs joined this faction in opposing the war and supporting the Wilmot Proviso. (p. 420)

"Slave Power"   Antislavery northerners considered southern politicians to be representatives of a violent "Slave Power" conspiracy determined to subvert the laws of the country in order to spread slavery throughout the nation. As evidence, northerners pointed to the Fugitive Slave Act, the Kansas-Nebraska Act, and the beating of Charles Sumner in the Senate. The *Dred Scott* decision convinced even some northern Democrats that the South was run by a "Slave Power" conspiracy. (pp. 422, 433, 437)

"whitemanism"   William Lloyd Garrison used the term "whitemanism" to describe free-soil supporters who wanted to keep African-Americans out of the territories. He was accusing them of racism. (p. 422)

free soil   The term "free soil" represented the belief that slavery should be kept out of the territories. This was primarily a northern belief, and it became the basis for both the Liberty party and the later Free Soil party. Abraham Lincoln also would adopt it. (pp. 422–423)

popular sovereignty   Michigan senator Lewis Cass, Democratic presidential candidate in 1848, introduced this solution to the problem of slavery in the territories. Popular sovereignty allowed territorial residents to determine the status of slavery in their territory. This policy alienated free-soil Democrats, but it was later adopted by Senator Stephen Douglas of Illinois in the Kansas-Nebraska Act. (pp. 423, 426, 433)

"common property" doctrine   South Carolina senator John C. Calhoun asserted that Congress had no authority to regulate slavery in the territories. This "common property" doctrine claimed that citizens of any state had the right to take their property, especially slaves, into areas owned commonly (the territories) by the states. Proslavery southerners of both parties agreed with Calhoun. (p. 423)

personal liberty laws   The Fugitive Slave Act brought home to northerners some of the cruelties of slavery. The act denied African-Americans accused of being runaway slaves any legal protection whatever. Several state legislatures attempted to provide such protection by passing personal liberty laws to thwart slave catchers and federal marshals. The Supreme Court of Wisconsin ruled that states had the power to declare an act of Congress unconstitutional, but this decision was overturned by the U.S. Supreme Court. (p. 429)

Gadsden Purchase   The Pierce administration inherited a dispute with Mexico over the southern boundary of the New Mexico Territory. Pierce sent James Gadsden, a South Carolinian politician and railroad promoter, to negotiate with the Mexican president, Santa Anna, for a portion of northern Mexico and Baja California. Santa Anna refused even though Gadsden threatened force. Santa Anna did agree to sell about 30,000 square miles of territory in present-day southern Arizona and New Mexico, land that the United States wanted for a railroad route to the Pacific Ocean. (p. 432)

Freeport doctrine   In a debate in Freeport with Abraham Lincoln during the 1858 campaign for an Illinois Senate seat, the Democratic candidate Stephen Douglas claimed that settlers could exclude slavery from their territory by refusing to adopt legislation to support it. This doctrine, resting on the assumption that slavery required favorable laws to protect it, challenged Chief Justice Taney's assertion that slavery could not be regulated in the territories. Although the Freeport doctrine was meant to assuage free-soil Democrats, it alienated proslavery Democrats who wanted assurance that slavery could be taken into the territories. (pp. 442–443)

fire-eaters   Fire-eaters were southern politicians who sought secession. Their demand for relegalization of the international slave trade alienated northern Democrats such as Stephen Douglas and heightened the growing separation between the North and the South. Fire-eaters included men such as Robert Barnwell Rhett and William Lowndes Yancy. They were opposed both by northern Democrats, such as Stephen Douglas, and by more moderate southern Democrats, such as Jefferson Davis, who sought an accommodation with the North. (p. 443)

IDENTIFICATION

Identify by filling in the blanks.

1. During the Mexican War President Polk sent

_____ at the head of an exploring

party of heavily armed troops to California, where they built fortifications near Monterrey. (p. 416)

2. The seizure of _____ led the Mexican government to make peace, bringing the Mexican War to an end. (p. 420)

3. William Lloyd Garrison denounced free-soil doctrine as "_____". (p. 422)

4. The Democratic candidate for president in 1848 was _____ . (p. 422)

5. John C. Calhoun claimed that slaveowners could not be prohibited from taking their slaves into the territories because slaves were _____ . (p. 423)

6. The part of the Compromise of 1850 that was most unacceptable to northerners was the _____ . (p. 429)

7. The election of 1852 was the last national presidential campaign run by the _____ . (p. 431)

8. The _____ stated that the United States was justified in trying to take Cuba from Spain. (p. 433)

9. The Kansas-Nebraska Act led antislavery northerners to create the _____ party. (p. 428)

10. The proslavery author of *Cannibals All: or, Slaves without Masters* was _____ . (pp. 434–435)

11. The militant abolitionist who staged the Pottawatomie massacre as revenge for the sack of Lawrence, Kansas, was _____ . (p. 436)

12. The first Republican candidate for President was _____ . (p. 431)

13. Proslavery settlers attempted to achieve statehood for Kansas under the _____ , which President Buchanan supported. (p. 433)

14. During the Mexican War, Congressman Lincoln voted for the _____ several times. (p. 440)

15. In his _____ , Stephen Douglas claimed that settlers could exclude slavery from a territory by refusing to pass legislation favorable to it. (p. 442)

16. Southerners who demanded relegalization of the international slave trade were called _____ . (p. 443)

17. In the 1860 presidential election the Democrats split between Stephen Douglas and _____ . (p. 444)

SKILL-BUILDING EXERCISE

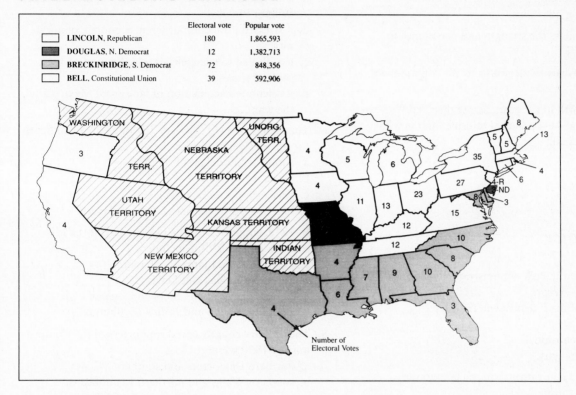

	Electoral vote	Popular vote
LINCOLN, Republican	180	1,865,593
DOUGLAS, N. Democrat	12	1,382,713
BRECKINRIDGE, S. Democrat	72	848,356
BELL, Constitutional Union	39	592,906

Answer the following questions on the Election of 1860.

1. List the six states with the highest number of electoral votes and indicate who won in those states.

2. How many states did each candidate win?

DOCUMENT EXERCISES

American Voices

Behind the Lines in the Mexican War— Captain Franklin Smith

The Mexican War was popular initially as a response to the desire of U.S. citizens for expansion. Thousands of Americans enthusiastically formed volunteer regiments. Americans believed that they had a God-given mission to expand to the Pacific and bring the political, religious, and social systems of the United States to the Mexican people.

As you read "Behind the Lines in the Mexican War," ask yourself the following questions:

1. How does Smith contrast Americans and Mexicans?

2. How does he describe the reactions of Mexicans to the American troops?

3. In what ways does he believe that the war was affecting Americans?

Six Months in "Bleeding Kansas"— Hannah Anderson Ropes

Popular sovereignty sounded like a democratic solution to the question of slavery in the territories, but in reality it led to open warfare between proslavery and antislavery forces for the political future of Kansas. The violence of "Bleeding Kansas" sickened both northerners and southerners; it produced grave doubts that the issue of slavery could be solved without resort to armed conflict.

As you read "Six Months in 'Bleeding Kansas,'" ask yourself the following questions:

1. How does Ropes contrast the proslavery advocates with the citizens of Lawrence?

2. How does Ropes change during her stay in Kansas?

3. In what ways does Ropes relate her experiences in Kansas to national issues?

American Lives

Frederick Douglass: Development of an Abolitionist

Runaway slaves provided some of the most eloquent testimonies against slavery, galvanizing northerners to support abolitionism. Douglass was the most influential of this group.

As you read "Development of an Abolitionist," ask yourself the following questions:

1. What gave Douglass the strength and persistence to escape the South?

2. How did he consistently demonstrate his commitment to education?

3. While in the North in the years before the Civil War, in what ways was he a practical reformer and in what ways was he radical?

SELF-TEST

Multiple Choice

1. The programs of the Polk administration included *all* of the following *except*:
   a. restoration of the Independent Treasury.
   b. lower tariffs.
   c. territorial expansion.
   d. popular sovereignty.

2. Mexico accepted war rather than sell land to the United States because:
   a. the Mexican government wanted to keep the valuable gold fields of California.
   b. the United States did not offer Mexico enough money for the land.
   c. the Mexican government would have fallen if it had not defended its national honor.
   d. Mexican slaveholders feared that the United States would abolish slavery in areas it took over.

3. The Wilmot Proviso did *all* of the following *except*:
   a. win the support of many northern free-soil Democrats.
   b. prohibit slavery in any territory acquired from Mexico.
   c. appease the conscience Whigs.
   d. pass through Congress with the support of an anti-war coalition.

4. The Treaty of Guadalupe Hidalgo ensured:
   a. popular sovereignty in all areas taken from Mexico.
   b. payment by the Mexican government to all American citizens with damage claims resulting from the war.
   c. prohibition of slavery in all areas taken from Mexico.
   d. payment to Mexico of $15 million from the United States.

5. The free-soil concept achieved significant popular support because:

a. southerners saw it as less threatening than the Wilmot Proviso.
   b. it stressed protection of white economic opportunity.
   c. it appealed to evangelicals who focused on the souls of slaves.
   d. it celebrated acquisition of land from Mexico after the war.

6. The Whigs selected Zachary Taylor as their candidate for the presidency because he:
   a. supported popular sovereignty.
   b. was a war hero.
   c. was a supporter of expansion.
   d. had taken a strong stand against slavery.

7. In 1848, supporters of the plan to extend the Missouri Compromise line included:
   a. Lewis Cass and James Buchanan.
   b. Stephen Douglas and Lewis Cass.
   c. James Buchanan and Stephen Douglas.
   d. James Buchanan and John C. Calhoun.

8. The primary congressional supporters of the Compromise of 1850 were:
   a. northern Democrats and southern Whigs.
   b. southern Whigs and northern Republicans.
   c. southern Democrats and northern Whigs.
   d. northern Republicans and Know-Nothings.

9. The direct results of the Fugitive Slave Act included *all* of the following *except*:
   a. the passage of personal liberty laws in northern states.
   b. the formation of the Republican party.
   c. abolitionist attempts to help runaway slaves.
   d. the popularity of *Uncle Tom's Cabin*.

10. The southern conventions considered secession in 1850 and 1851, but southern states did not secede then because:
    a. moderates convinced them to support the Compromise of 1850.
    b. only a small number of southerners were disturbed by northern defiance of the Fugitive Slave Act.
    c. southerners lacked the military readiness to go to war at that point.
    d. they wanted additional time to prepare for war.

11. The Whigs lost the election of 1852 because:
    a. the Liberty party took Whig votes.
    b. many southern Whigs voted Democratic.
    c. the Republican party took many northern votes.
    d. the Democrats found support among northern Know-Nothings.

12. Know-Nothings and free-soilers allied for *all* of the following reasons *except*:
    a. most of their supporters were former Whigs.

b. they both believed that a conspiracy threatened republican institutions.

c. they both emphasized white Protestant control of America.

d. they both supported popular sovereignty.

13. In the 1850s southerners defended slavery with the argument that:

a. agriculture based on slavery was more profitable than the use of free labor.

b. slaves were more obedient than northern wage laborers.

c. slaveowners' life-styles could not have been so opulent without slavery.

d. masters were kinder to their slaves than northern industrialists were to their laborers.

14. Events in Kansas seemed to demonstrate that popular sovereignty would lead:

a. settlers to compromise their differences.

b. to violence.

c. slaveowners to dominate.

d. free-soilers to dominate.

15. The Republican party performed so strongly in its first national campaign in 1856 because:

a. it had broad support in all sections of the country.

b. its candidate, John C. Frémont, was an experienced legislator and politician.

c. it supported expansion into northern Mexico.

d. it had won over former Whigs, Know-Nothings, and free-soil Democrats.

16. The Supreme Court ruled that Dred Scott should remain a slave on the grounds that:

a. Scott's owner had not been paid enough for him.

b. Scott had lived only in the District of Columbia, where slavery was legal.

c. Congress could not prohibit slavery in the territories.

d. Congress could not prohibit slavery in the states.

17. In his Peoria address, Lincoln supported the key tenets of the Republican party, which include *all* of the following *except*:

a. the nation must eventually eliminate slavery.

b. the national government had the right to exclude slavery from the territories.

c. moral opposition to slavery.

d. slavery had to be eliminated even at the cost of the Union.

18. *All* of the following are true about the election of 1860 *except*:

a. Lincoln won a majority of the popular vote but a plurality of the electoral vote.

b. in ten slave states, Lincoln was not even on the ballot.

c. the only northern state Lincoln failed to win was New Jersey.

d. the Republicans won with support in only one section of the country.

Short Essays

Answer the following in a brief paragraph.

1. In the 1840s what evidence did southerners have to support their fear that they were being surrounded by antislavery forces in the West? (pp. 416–417, 422)

2. How successful was Polk's presidency? (pp. 416–422)

3. "Conscience Whigs" declared that the Mexican War had been unconstitutionally begun. Do you agree? Why or why not? (p. 420)

4. What parts of the Compromise of 1850 were designed to appease the North, and what parts to appease the South? (pp. 428–429)

5. Why did Democrats consistently choose northerners as presidential candidates? (pp. 422, 430–431, 437–438)

6. In the long run, was the Fugitive Slave Act beneficial or detrimental to the South? (pp. 429–430)

7. What were the most important effects of the Kansas-Nebraska Act? (pp. 433, 435–436)

8. What evidence did northerners have that there was a "Slave Power" conspiracy to extend slavery throughout the country? (pp. 422, 438–439)

9. What evidence did the South have that the institution of slavery was in danger from the North? (pp. 421–422, 423, 429–430, 432, 433, 445)

10. What events led to the division of the Democratic party in 1860? (p. 444)

ANSWERS

Chapter Précis

1. maintain national honor; protect valuable land

2. Whigs

3. racism

4. defense of slavery

5. legalize or prohibit slavery

6. secession and civil war

7. *Uncle Tom's Cabin*

8. preserve the Union

9. to build a southern railroad

10. it was farther south

11. individualism; republicanism

12. questioning the legitimacy of slavery

13. Kansas-Nebraska

14. Missouri Compromise

15. Kansas-Nebraska Act

16. southern Illinois

17. Republican doctrines

Identification

1. John C. Frémont

2. Mexico City

3. whitemanism

4. Lewis Cass

5. common property

6. Fugitive Slave Act

7. Whig party

8. Ostend Manifesto

9. Republican

10. George Fitzhugh

11. John Brown

12. John C. Frémont

13. Lecompton constitution

14. Wilmot Proviso

15. Freeport doctrine

16. fire-eaters

17. John C. Breckinridge

Skill-Building Exercise

1. New York: 35 electoral votes (Lincoln)
   Pennsylvania: 27 electoral votes (Lincoln)
   Ohio: 23 electoral votes (Lincoln)
   Virginia: 15 electoral votes (Bell)
   Indiana: 13 electoral votes (Lincoln)
   Massachusetts: 13 electoral votes (Lincoln)

2. Lincoln: 17
   Bell: 3
   Breckinridge: 11
   Douglas: 1
   New Jersey split between Lincoln and Douglas.

Self-Test

Multiple Choice

1. d	7. c	13. d
2. c	8. a	14. b
3. d	9. b	15. d
4. d	10. a	16. c
5. b	11. b	17. d
6. b	12. d	18. a

Short Essays

1. The United States was competing with Great Britain for Oregon in the Northwest and Britain had abolished slavery. President Polk also feared that Britain would take California from Mexico in payment for debts. Mexico had abolished slavery, an issue that had led slaveholding settlers in Texas who were from the American South to break away from Mexico and create the Lone Star Republic. The northern portion of the Louisiana Purchase had been closed to slavery by the Missouri Compromise.

2. Polk ran on a platform of expansion, and during his term the United States acquired the Mexican cession and established the boundary of Texas along the Rio Grande. Polk settled, however, for only half of Oregon and was discouraged from seizing northern Mexico. He also attacked the American System by lowering tariffs and restoring the Independent Treasury. Polk's compromise over Oregon alienated free-soil Democrats, who deserted the party in 1848, giving the presidency to a Whig, Zachary Taylor.

3. The Constitution designates the president as commander-in-chief of the military. It assigns to Congress the power to declare war and call out militias to repel invasions. President Polk overstepped his constitutional authority when he provoked war by creating an invasion in an area that may not have been part of the United States: he sent troops into the disputed territory and then responded to gunfire as though it were an invasion. Yet Congress, when it admitted Texas to statehood, claimed the disputed lands as part of Texas and, thus, part of the United States. This gave Congress the responsibility for protecting that area by repelling invasions.

4. The North got another free state in California. Also, the slave state of Texas lost land to the free-soil New Mexico Territory. Finally, the slave trade was ended in the District of Columbia. The South received the Fugitive Slave Act. Further, slavery was not ended in the District of Columbia, only the slave trade. All of

the Mexican cession was opened to slavery on the basis of popular sovereignty.

5. The Democrats could count on the votes of the slave-holding South because southerners distrusted the Whigs, who seemed to be too strongly influenced by abolitionists. To win the presidency, however, Democrats needed some of the northern states' electoral votes in addition to those of the southern states. Cass of Michigan (1848), Pierce of New Hampshire (1852), and Buchanan of Pennsylvania (1856) were selected to pull in northern votes. As non-slaveholders, they were not tainted in the eyes of northerners. This strategy worked in 1852 and 1856.

6. The Fugitive Slave Act was ultimately detrimental to the South because it rallied northern support for the antislavery cause and convinced northerners that the South had made the federal government an instrument of slavery by requiring federal judges and marshals to assist slave catchers. Northerners resisted the act by passing personal liberty laws, and local communities such as Christiana, Pennsylvania, actively thwarted enforcement of the law. Finally, *Uncle Tom's Cabin*, written in response to the act, increased popular sentiment against slavery.

7. The Kansas-Nebraska Act brought out the difficulties inherent in popular sovereignty, which led not to a democratic solution to the slavery issue but to guerrilla warfare. The response of proslavery and antislavery forces to the act demonstrated that both sides would resort to violence rather than compromise. Also, as a result of the act, northern free-soilers united to create the Republican party, which was committed to free-soil principles. Because the issue of Kansas was not resolved in the 1850s, it remained an open wound, agitating sectional differences.

8. Southerners had tried to block California statehood and the territorial organization of the northern Louisiana Purchase because those areas were not considered hospitable to slavery. The South achieved the opening of the Mexican cession and the northern Louisiana Purchase to slavery through popular sover-

eignty, thus voiding the Missouri Compromise. The Fugitive Slave Act put federal officials, even in the North, in the service of slavery. By supporting the Lecompton constitution in Kansas, Buchanan appeared to be supporting fraud for the sake of maintaining slavery. Finally, the *Dred Scott* decision prohibited Congress from making any attempt to restrict slavery in the territories. Lincoln and many others feared that the next step would be to legalize slavery everywhere.

9. The Missouri Compromise had restricted slavery in the Louisiana Purchase to a relatively small area. Northern politicians refused to support southern schemes to acquire areas in Latin America for the expansion of slavery. Free states outnumbered slave states, and by 1856 Republicans dominated the House of Representatives. In response to the Kansas-Nebraska Act, northern abolitionists sent arms to antislavery settlers in Kansas. Stowe's *Uncle Tom's Cabin* stirred popular emotions against slavery. John Brown's actions in Kansas and Virginia were examples of how northerners might put those beliefs into action. Finally, Lincoln's election gave a second branch of government to the Republican party, which had no support in, and thus no reason to appease, the South.

10. Northern Democrats had long shown a tendency to vote for Liberty party or Free Soil party candidates when Democratic candidates appeared to be too favorable to slavery, one of the reasons for Zachary Taylor's victory in 1852. The *Dred Scott* decision and Buchanan's support for the Lecompton constitution in Kansas further alienated northern Democrats. By voiding the Missouri Compromise, the Supreme Court invalidated a long-standing law for the sake of slaveowners. Southern Democrats, in contrast, wanted positive legislative protection for slavery in the territories and even hoped to reopen the international slave trade. Stephen Douglas and other leading northern Democrats broke with Buchanan, who had the support of southern Democrats.

CHAPTER 15

Two Societies at War 1861–1865

★   ★   ★

CHAPTER PRÉCIS

Southern leaders believed that Lincoln would appoint abolitionists and encourage slave revolts in the South. Only secession, they thought, could protect slavery and, in their view, democracy.

Choosing Sides, 1861   pp. 450–455

Southerners thought that by defending states' rights and slavery they were being true to republican ideals. Lincoln and his supporters believed that secession was treasonous.

The Secession Crisis

Led by South Carolina, all the states in the lower South seceded from the Union by February 1862 and proclaimed a new nation—the Confederate States of America—with Jefferson Davis as provisional president. The states of the upper South, where slavery was less prevalent, supported the actions of the new Confederacy but did not move to secede immediately. President Buchanan declared secession illegal but said that the federal government had no authority to force a state to return to the Union.

When, at Buchanan's urging, Congress proposed a plan to prohibit the government from ever abolishing slavery in the states and to extend the Missouri Compromise line to California, Lincoln and other Republicans rejected it. Lincoln reiterated his commitment to free-soil principles and his belief that secession was illegal. When Lincoln sent an armed expedition to reinforce Fort Sumter in Charleston harbor, Confederate forces fired on the fort and forced it to surrender. Lincoln called out state militias in the North to put down the insurrection.

1. Lincoln feared that extending the Missouri Compromise line would encourage southerners to embark on a plan of _____ . (p. 451)

The Contest for the Upper South

Lincoln attempted to keep the upper South from seceding. These states had the bulk of the South's white population, industrial production, food, and fuel, along with many of the nation's best military leaders. The upper South offered important geographic advantages in terms of keeping the Ohio River open to Union troops and protecting Washington, D.C. Virginians seceded quickly after the fall of Fort Sumter, but in northwestern Virginia small farmers resisted, creating the new state of West Virginia. Lincoln quickly secured access to Washington, D.C., and jailed suspected secessionists, keeping Maryland in the Union. He was more cautious in Kentucky, where Confederate troops moved aggressively; Kentuckians were outraged by this and asked for Union protection. Unionist troops composed of German-Americans defeated secessionists in Missouri, although pro-Confederate guerrilla bands fought there throughout the war. Of the eight states of the upper South, Lincoln kept four, as well as West Virginia, in the Union.

2. Control of the upper Mississippi and Missouri rivers was essential to the Union for _____ and _____ . (p. 452)

War Aims and Resources, North and South

Lincoln framed the war as a noble crusade to save democracy and determine its future throughout the world. His lofty concept of the war did much to mobilize the North. Jefferson Davis claimed that the South was fighting to protect self-government against tyranny, recalling the principles of the American Revolution. Southern leaders claimed that slavery made democracy for whites possible by avoiding serfdom, or dependence on economic elites. Confederate leaders stressed that battlefield victories were not necessary; they needed only to make the cost of the war high enough to discourage the North.

3. Lincoln learned that Union troops had to _____ of the southern people in order to win. (p. 453)

The North's advantages included control over the Ohio River, a larger population, most of the nation's railroads and industrial output, and advances in weaponry technology. Several southern states also had important industrial capacity. The South mobilized slaves to provide food for its armies and produce cotton, which could be sold to pay for military supplies. Southern leaders hoped to persuade the British, whose textile factories depended on southern cotton, to support their cause. The South's military advantages included trained military officers, familiar terrain, a difficult coastline to blockade, and the use of the rifle-musket in defensive warfare. Union leaders only slowly decided that they would have to wage a total war against southern society, not just against southern armies.

War Machines, North and South   pp. 455–460

Lincoln quickly consolidated his power by organizing a strong central government. Davis faced greater difficulties because the southern states were suspicious of centralized power.

Mobilizing Armies

The Confederacy imposed the first draft in American history, subjecting all white men up to the age of thirty-five but exempting one white man for each twenty slaves. Draftees could hire substitutes, a policy that infuriated young impoverished farmers. The Union also imposed a draft, with the option of hiring substitutes. Lincoln suppressed rebellion by jailing those who protested the war or the draft. In New York City, urban workers, many of whom were immigrants, protested the Enrollment Act by rioting, and Lincoln used troops to put down their protest. In the Confederacy, which had been organized to protest centralized power, Jefferson Davis had to contend with powerful governors who defied his authority by helping young men resist the draft.

4. In the North, opponents of the war incited rioting by claiming that Lincoln was drafting poor whites in order to _____ and flood the North with _____ . (p. 456)

Mobilizing Money

The war was expensive for both sides. The Union financed the war with taxes (including the nation's first income tax), bond sales, paper money, tariffs, and deficit spending. It also created a national banking system, building the financial foundations of a modern industrial state. In the South, taxation policies fell primarily on middle-class farmers because planters fought taxes on their property or on cotton exports. Planters also resisted pleas that they buy Confederate bonds. Southern monetary policies caused inflation, which increased as the war continued. Food riots broke out in southern cities, and farmers refused to accept Confederate money for their produce. The army had to seize the supplies it needed, further angering southern farmers.

5. The Union's program of public finance tied the interests of _____ to the Union's success in the war. (p. 458)

Economic Programs

The Republicans in Congress enacted the old Whig economic program to increase the effectiveness of northern society and win support from the voters. This program included a national banking system, protective tariffs, the Homestead Act for western settlers, and funding for a transcontinental railroad. Because of its commitment to states' rights, the Confederacy did not attempt to restructure its economic system. The extraordinary demands of the war, however, forced Confederate leaders to build and operate shipyards, armories, textile mills, and mines, and to requisition slaves. Davis justified these actions by telling southerners that they were fighting to expand westward to protect slavery; if they failed, whites would be reduced to the position of African-Americans.

6. The Republicans were able to adopt the old Whig economic program because the war had removed the _____ from Congress. (p.459)

The Home Front: Civilian Support for the War

In the North, the United States Sanitary Commission organized voluntary medical and sanitary services during the war. Although twice as many Union soldiers died from disease as from combat, the Sanitary Commission's heroic efforts led to a level of mortality lower than that of other nineteenth-century wars. Lack of organization made southern health care inferior to that for Union troops. Women on both sides played a major role as nurses, opening that occupation to them. Some also worked as government clerks when men left for war. Far more women took over responsibilities in homes, farms, schools, and factories as men left to join the Union and Confederate armies.

7. The rate of mortality among Union troops was lower than in other nineteenth-century wars primarily because of _____ and _____ . (p. 459)

Military Deadlock, 1861–1863   pp. 460-470

Early Stalemate, 1861–1862

Seeking a quick, early victory, Lincoln ordered Union troops to attack Confederate forces at Bull Run, Virginia. When the Confederates counterattacked, the Union troops panicked and fled, demonstrating to Lincoln that the war would not end soon. Both sides competed to dominate the Tennessee and Mississippi valleys. Ulysses S. Grant led Union forces to victories at Fort Donelson and Shiloh. In concert with Admiral David G. Farragut's capture of New Orleans, Grant's activities won control of the Mississippi River Valley for the Union. In the East, General McClellan's excessive caution allowed General Robert E. Lee to protect Richmond in the Seven Days' battles and to invade the North at the Second Battle of Bull Run. The heavy loss of life at Antietam began to erode popular support for the war in the North, but Lincoln shrewdly declared Antietam to be a northern victory. Lincoln, angered by McClellan's delays, removed him as commander of the Union troops.

8. At the beginning of the war and in response to _____ , Lincoln decided to attack near the Confederate capital, Richmond, Virginia. (p. 460)

Emancipation

Lincoln began to believe that emancipation of the slaves would assist the Union cause. As the war continued, thousands of slaves fled the plantations and followed Union troops, who refused to return them to their owners. Congressional Republicans enacted legislation ending slavery in the District of Columbia and freeing slaves in federal territories. With the Second Confiscation Act, all slaves owned by rebels were declared free. After Antietam, Lincoln declared that slaves in all rebelling states would be free. This left slavery untouched in the border states, which Lincoln wanted to keep loyal to the Union. Although Democrats criticized the Emancipation Proclamation in an appeal to northern racism, Republicans gained Senate seats in the 1862 elections. With emancipation, Lincoln changed the focus of the war.

9. The battle at Shiloh convinced Lincoln and Grant that the war would be _____ . (p. 462)

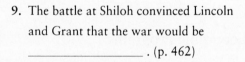

Union Gains in 1863

Grant cut the Confederacy in two by seizing Vicksburg, Mississippi, and gaining complete control of the Mississippi River. Union troops also won control in Tennessee, driving Confederate troops into Georgia. Instead of attacking Vicksburg, Lee chose to invade the North, hoping to threaten Washington. The Union victory at Gettysburg repelled Lee's invasion and increased northern support for the war, helping Lincoln's supporters in the 1863 elections.

10. Congress passed the Thirteenth Amendment so that after the war, the southern states could not _____ . (p. 467)

11. Intervening in the 1862 election campaign Lincoln stressed that opposition to emancipation was opposition to _____ . (p. 470)

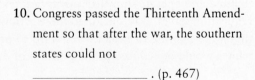

Wartime Diplomacy

Because Britain obtained four-fifths of the cotton for its textile mills from the South, the Confederacy hoped to gain British support for secession. Britain's declaration of neutrality allowed the Confederacy to borrow money and purchase weapons from it. The Union victory at Gettysburg, however, convinced the British to stay out of the war.

12. Lincoln worked to keep Great Britain from formally recognizing the Confederacy's _____ . (p. 470)

The Union Victorious, 1864–1865 pp. 471–479

African-American Soldiers

The northern public and the government came to support the enlistment of African-Americans, and in 1863 the Union War Department began to enlist free blacks in the North and the occupied parts of the South. The gallant performance of African-American troops further transformed public attitudes. African-Americans composed 10 percent of all Union forces, but the army was segregated and paid black soldiers less until pay was equalized in 1864.

13. Black soldiers fought to contribute to the ending of slavery and with the hope that victory would help them achieve _____ . (p. 472)

The New Military Strategy

Lincoln placed Grant in charge of all Union armies because Grant had shown an ability to use modern technology and to direct the war at southern society as well as at Confederate troops. Grant ordered crushing attacks to destroy Lee's troops, regardless of the cost in life. In the Wilderness campaign, the fighting settled into a war of attrition with tremendous loss of life as neither Lee nor Grant succeeded in winning. When Grant tried to seize the railroad center at Petersburg, Lee's forces dug trenches, resulting in a prolonged siege by Union troops. In the Shenandoah Valley, Confederate cavalry raids into Pennsylvania led to Union retaliation against farmers who supplied Confederate troops. Sheridan destroyed the valley's economy and terrified its civilians as part of the Union strategy of demoralizing southern society.

14. Grant sought to overcome the Confederate advantage of interior lines by using railroads and ships to

_____ . (p. 472)

Sherman, Atlanta, and the Election of 1864

While Union troops under General Sherman laid siege to Atlanta, the Republican party prepared for the election of 1864 by renaming itself the National Union party and nominating the Democrat Andrew Johnson for vice-president. Republican criticism of Lincoln led many people to believe that he should abandon emancipation, but Lincoln refused. Individuals who wanted the war to end controlled the Democratic party convention and nominated George McClellan. The fall of Atlanta to Sherman discredited the Democrats, and Lincoln went on to win the election. The votes of Union soldiers contributed significantly to his win.

15. In the presidential election of 1864, opposition to Lincoln was concentrated in the _____ states and in the _____ sections of large northern cities. (p. 476)

Sherman's "March to the Sea"

Union troops marched through Georgia, burning everything in their way and destroying the morale of southerners. Sherman also swept through

South Carolina and burned the capital, Columbia. Internally, the South crumbled as desertions from the army and draft evasion increased. Secret societies of Unionists in the Appalachians, the Ozarks, and parts of Texas resisted Confederate control. At the last moment, the Confederate Congress decided to enlist black soldiers to solve their manpower problems.

The End of the War

Grant forced Lee to surrender at Appomattox Court House, Virginia, allowing Lee's men to return home with their horses for spring planting. General Joseph B. Johnston surrendered nine days later. The Confederate army and government dissolved, with no formal end to the war.

EXPANDED TIMELINE

1861   **Confederate States of America formed (February 4)**
In response to Lincoln's election, seven southern states seceded from the Union and proclaimed a new nation. Their representatives met in Montgomery, Alabama, wrote a provisional constitution, and chose Jefferson Davis to be president.

Abraham Lincoln inaugurated (March 4)
Elected as president with no support from the South, Lincoln used his inaugural speech to welcome back the states that had left the Union and to guarantee the continuation of slavery in those states. He claimed, however, that secession was not legal and that federal property in seceded states still belonged to the Union. Lincoln also stood firm on his commitment to keep slavery out of the territories.

Confederates fire on Fort Sumter (April 12)
Lincoln insisted that federal forts in seceded states continued to belong to the Union. When soldiers at Fort Sumter ran low on supplies, he sent an armed relief force. When Confederate officials learned of this expedition, they fired on Fort Sumter, forcing Major Robert Anderson to surrender. This rallied northern support for Lincoln's actions.

Virginia convention votes to secede (April 17)
In his inaugural address, President Lincoln made clear that he would consider using force as a response to secession. Reversing an earlier vote, the Virginia secession convention voted to secede in response. The non-slaveholding western part of the state opposed secession. Virginia's secession put the Confederacy in easy reach of Washington, D.C.

Lincoln's blockade of southern coast
Lincoln blockaded the southern coast, hoping to cut off southern revenues from food and cotton sales to Europe and its Caribbean colonies, and to keep England from sending arms to the South.

16. By gaining control of a crucial railroad junction near Richmond, Grant was able to cut off _____ . (p. 478)

General Benjamin Butler declares runaway slaves "contraband of war"
Responding to slaves who escaped to Union lines, Butler declared them to be "contraband of war," and refused to return them to their owners.

Lincoln states war aims (July 4)
Lincoln framed the Union war effort as a war to preserve democracy against internal opponents.

First Battle of Bull Run (July 21)
Under Lincoln's direction, the Union army moved to strike General P. G. T. Beauregard's forces at Manassas, near Richmond, Virginia. After receiving this news, Beauregard brought in Confederate reinforcements. Union troops panicked and retreated hastily back toward Washington, D.C. This debacle alerted Lincoln and other Union leaders that the war would be longer and more difficult than they had anticipated.

Lincoln signs First Confiscation Act
Lincoln authorized the seizure of all property used to support the rebellion. This law included slaves and began the move toward emancipation.

Fifty counties in Western Virginia vote to form new state (October)
Non-slaveholding counting in Virginia, after being secured for the Union by McClellan's army, voted to break away from Virginia and form a new state loyal to the Union.

George B. McClellan made general-in-chief of Union Army (November)
McClellan assumed command of all Union armies.

1862   **Congress passes Legal Tender Act (February)**
Congress authorized the issuance of Treasury notes, known as greenbacks, to help finance the Union war effort. The public was required to accept these notes as legal tender.

Congress passes Second Confiscation Act
All captured and fugitive slaves under control of the Union army were declared to be forever free.

This was the first instance when the Union decided to use emancipation as an instrument of war.

Battle of Shiloh (April 6–7)

General Grant moved to exert Union control over the Tennessee and Mississippi rivers. At Shiloh, Union troops began to gain control of the Mississippi Valley. The extensive loss of life at Shiloh convinced Lincoln that the war would be long and difficult.

David G. Farragut takes New Orleans (April 25–29)

Union capture of New Orleans denied the Confederacy a major port, its financial center, and largest city.

Confederacy introduces the first draft

The Confederacy, with its smaller population base than the North, enacted the first draft in American history after the loss at Shiloh. The law extended all enlistments to the end of the war and included all able-bodied men between ages eighteen and thirty-five in the draft.

Seven Days' battles (June 25–July 1)

McClellan led Union troops toward Richmond, but a strong Confederate defense led by Lee made McClellan reluctant to renew his attack. Richmond remained safe from Union attack.

Second Battle of Bull Run (August 29–30)

As part of his plan to embarrass Lincoln's government, Lee, accompanied by Jackson and Longstreet, defeated the Union army under Pope only 20 miles from Washington, D.C. Lee then continued north, invading Maryland.

Homestead Act

This Republican law gave title to any family or individual who lived on and improved 160 acres of public land for five years. Although speculators took much of the land, many small farmers settled on farms through the act.

Battle of Antietam (September 17)

General Lee led Confederate troops on an invasion of the North. His forces met General McClellan's at Antietam Creek, Maryland, and although his troops were outnumbered, Lee forced McClellan back. McClellan's unwillingness to press Lee further allowed the Confederate forces to get away. Although Lincoln publicly declared Antietam a victory, he lost faith in McClellan.

Preliminary Emancipation Proclamation (September 22)

Lincoln declared that on January 1, 1863, slaves in all seceded states would be free. This left untouched slaves in loyal border states and in areas already captured by Union troops, areas whose residents he hoped to keep loyal or win over to the Union cause. This proclamation dramatically changed the nature of the war.

Battle of Fredericksburg (December 13)

Heavy Union losses at Fredericksburg led General Burnside to resign as commander-in-chief of the Army of the Potomac. Lincoln replaced him with Joseph Hooker.

Lincoln signs the Emancipation Proclamation (January 1)

Lincoln declared that on January 1, slaves in areas in rebellion would be free. This left slavery in border states loyal to the Union intact, but encouraged states in rebellion to return to the Union in order to protect slavery.

Enrollment Act establishes draft in the North

This Union law exposed all men between the ages of twenty-five and forty to the draft but encouraged volunteering by assigning quotas for each congressional district. Districts used incentives such as cash bounties to entice volunteers. Men could avoid the draft by paying an exemption (commutation) fee or providing a substitute. The bounties brought in about a million volunteers.

Battle of Chancellorsville (May 2–3)

Lee decisively defeated Hooker, encouraging him to invade the North again.

France sets up Mexican regime

Napoleon III's troops overthrew the republican government in Mexico, replacing it with Archduke Ferdinand Maximilian, Napoleon's puppet, as emperor. The Confederacy hoped France and Mexico would enter the war on the side of the South.

Battle of Gettysburg (July 1–3)

Lee invaded the North to draw Union pressure away from the West and to lower the morale of the northern public by winning a major victory in their territory. From a secure defensive position, Union troops resisted Lee's attacks. The battle cost more lives than any other in the war. The Union victory rallied popular support in the North. Lee was never able to invade the North again. Britain decided against formally supporting the southern cause after this battle.

Fall of Vicksburg (July 4)

After a six-week siege, Grant captured Vicksburg, Mississippi, leading to Union control of the Mississippi River two weeks later. Grant split the Confederacy in two, with Louisiana, Arkansas, and Texas cut off from the rest of the Confederate states.

New York City draft riots

Immigrant Irish workers rioted against the draft, which they believed was subjecting poor whites to military service for the purpose of freeing African-Americans who in the future would compete with them for jobs. Rioters burned offices, sacked the homes of prominent Republicans, and lynched

African-Americans. Lincoln had to bring troops from Gettysburg to stop the violence.

Britain impounds Laird rams
Lincoln's government persuaded the British government to remain neutral, partly by impounding Laird rams, ironclads intended to break the blockade, for which the Confederacy had contracted.

Union forces seize Brownsville, Texas
Capturing Brownsville on the Texas-Mexico border, Union forces effectively warned France and Mexico not to interfere in the war.

1864 Ulysses S. Grant takes command of all Union armies (March 9)
Lincoln had been disappointed with his generals' lack of success on the battlefield. After Grant's victories at Vicksburg and Chattanooga, Lincoln put him in charge of all Union armies. Grant was willing to pursue the enemy even if it meant sustaining heavy casualties. He also was willing to use the North's technological advantages to rapidly deploy troops and maximize force against the Confederacy.

Grant's Wilderness campaign
Grant's troops moved toward Richmond, as Lee fought a stiff defensive campaign. Casualties were high on both sides; however, Grant successfully, if gradually, advanced.

Siege of Petersburg begins (June 15)
Grant attempted to cut Lee's lines of supply by taking Petersburg, Virginia, a major railroad center. Lee, however, had his men dig trenches, a tactic that foiled Grant's plans. The two armies settled into prolonged trench warfare that lasted into the spring of 1865.

Jubal Early's raids
Based in the Shenandoah Valley, Early led Confederate raids into Maryland and Pennsylvania, and close to Washington, D.C.

Atlanta falls to William T. Sherman (September 2)
Lincoln, Grant, and other northern leaders became convinced that southern civilians had to experience the terror of war before they would surrender. General Sherman therefore laid siege to Atlanta, Georgia, and destroyed its rail lines and roads after he captured it. This victory discouraged Lincoln's northern Democratic opponents and led to his victory in the 1864 election.

Shenandoah campaign of Philip H. Sheridan
Punishing residents of the Shenandoah Valley for supplying the Confederate army, Grant ordered Sheridan to destroy Early's forces and to lay waste the farms and homes of people who supported the Confederacy, destroying the valley's economy.

Lincoln's reelection
With the taking of Atlanta, Republican opposition to Lincoln died. With 55 percent of the popular vote, Lincoln won decisively over McClellan. He was weakest in border areas and in the immigrant wards of large cities. Over three-fourths of Union soldiers, who were given leave to return home to vote, voted for Lincoln. This victory expressed northern support for Lincoln's policies.

Sherman's march through Georgia
To demoralize southern civilians, General Sherman marched his troops from Atlanta to Savannah and then north to Columbia, South Carolina. Sherman's troops burned Atlanta and Columbia and destroyed Confederate railroads, property, and supplies along the way. He left southern civilians with little will to continue the war.

1865 Congress approves Thirteenth Amendment
Congress votes to end legal slavery in the United States, primarily to prevent southern states from reestablishing slavery after the war.

Columbia, South Carolina, burns (February 17)
After marching through Georgia, Sherman led Union troops to a sweep through South Carolina, leader of the original secession movement, and burn its capital.

Robert E. Lee surrenders
When Grant cut off Lee's supplies near Richmond, Virginia, Lee fled west. Grant followed him, and with his army shrunk to only 25,000 men, Lee surrendered to Grant at Appomattox Court House, Virginia. This ended the war, although a few Confederate troops did not surrender until the following month.

Ratification of Thirteenth Amendment
Legal slavery was ended in the United States after a sufficient number of states had approved the Thirteenth Amendment.

GLOSSARY

"bushwhackers" These Confederate guerrilla bands in Missouri were led by William Quantrill and Jesse and Frank James. Throughout the war they attacked Union forces to weaken Union control of the Mississippi River. However, they failed to achieve Confederate control of Missouri. (p. 452)

total war Traditionally, armies fought each other and left civilians alone. As the Civil War progressed, Lincoln and Grant realized that to force the Confederacy to surrender, they would have to break the will of the southern people. This required a war against the entire southern society, not just against the Confederacy's troops. (p. 453)

habeas corpus During the war, Lincoln suspended this constitutional right, which protected citizens against arbitrary arrest and detention. His purpose was to stop protests against the draft and other disloyal activities. He also transferred cases of disloyalty from civilian to military jurisdiction, fearing that local juries would have been lenient toward Confederate sympathizers. (p. 456)

greenbacks   To finance the war, the Union issued paper money that was not backed by specie. The Legal Tender Act authorized the issuance of $150 million of these Treasury notes and required people to accept them as legal tender. Paper money financed 13 percent of the cost of the war. (p. 458)

anaconda   The anaconda is a large snake that constricts its prey. At the beginning of the war, the general-in-chief of the Union forces, Winfield Scott, recommended constricting the Confederacy by blockading from the sea and the Mississippi River. Lincoln chose a more aggressive strategy to rally the Union and discredit secession. (p. 460)

"contrabands"   As Union troops entered the South, thousands of slaves fled the plantations for protection behind Union lines. General Benjamin Butler refused to return them to their owners and declared them "contraband of war." Lincoln and Congress regularized this policy in the First Confiscation Act, which authorized Union troops to seize all property, including slaves, used on behalf of the Confederacy. (p. 465)

"scorched earth"   Union commander Philip H. Sheridan led the Army of the Shenandoah on a campaign to punish residents of the Shenandoah Valley who supported Confederate troops with food and other supplies. To wreck the economy and demoralize the people, Sheridan destroyed crops, animals, barns, homes, and agricultural equipment in a campaign that left nothing behind but "scorched earth." General Sherman used this policy successfully on his march through Georgia. (p. 474)

"Copperhead"   This poisonous snake came to represent northerners who sympathized with the South during the war. Many were Democrats who believed that the North should arrange a lenient peace with the South. Southern parts of the Old Northwest and other border regions produced the most "Copperheads." (p. 476)

IDENTIFICATION

Identify by filling in the blanks.

1. The first state to secede from the Union was
   _____ . (p. 450)

2. President Buchanan was reluctant to surrender Fort Sumter because it was _____ .
   (p. 451)

3. In Missouri, William Quantrill and the James brothers _____ led

"_____" in attacks on Unionists. (p. 452)

4. Both the Union and the Confederacy asserted that they were fighting to protect
   _____ . (p. 453)

5. In Virginia, the _____ made Richmond an important industrial center. (p. 454)

6. The _____ encouraged northern states to meet draft quotas by threatening an involuntary draft for those states that failed to meet the quotas. (p. 456)

7. The worst riots in U.S. history occurred in _____ over the draft. (p. 456)

8. The Confederacy financed most of the war with _____ . (p. 458)

9. The _____ gave 160 acres of public lands to settlers after five years of residence and improvement. (p. 459)

10. _____ worked as a nurse during the Civil War and later founded the American Red Cross. (p. 460)

11. In 1862 Admiral _____ took New Orleans, opening the Mississippi River to Union control. (p. 461)

12. Due to General McClellan's reluctance to fight Lee to a finish, after _____ Lincoln replaced him with Ambrose Burnside. (p. 464)

13. General _____ was one of the first Union officials to refuse to return runaway slaves to their masters. (p. 465)

14. Two days before the Battle of Gettysburg, Lincoln put General _____ in charge of Union troops. (p. 467)

15. French control of _____ threatened Union power west of the Mississippi should Great Britain and France have recognized the Confederacy. (p. 470)

16. The heroic but tragic attack on _____ by black troops won northern sympathy for African-American soldiers. (p. 472)

17. In 1864, Grant sent troops under _____ to punish Shenandoah Valley residents for supplying Confederate troops. (p. 474)

18. In the presidential election campaign of 1864, Peace Democrats were also called _____ by their opponents. (p. 476)

19. Sherman's "March to the Sea" resulted in his presentation of the city of _____ to Lincoln as a Christmas present. (p. 474)

20. Lee surrendered to Grant at _____ . (p. 478)

SKILL-BUILDING EXERCISE

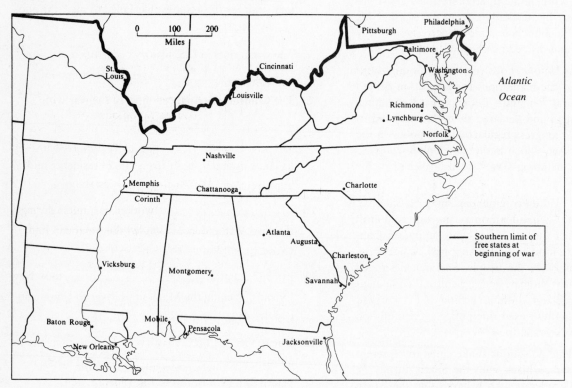

1. Identify the eight states of the upper South.
2. Identify the states that remained loyal to the Union.
3. Identify the states that joined the Confederacy.

DOCUMENT EXERCISES

American Voices

Elizabeth Mary Meade Ingraham— A Vicksburg Diary

The Civil War split many families as members were forced to choose sides, often against their loved ones. Here, Ingraham demonstrates to what degree she had adopted the South and all its attitudes although her brother was the Union General George Meade.

As you read "A Vicksburg Diary," ask yourself the following questions:

1. What is Ingraham's relationship with the slaves like?
2. Why do you think so many of them still took care of her?
3. In what ways do the slaves' attitudes change and why?
4. How does Ingraham attempt to maintain her position and control over them?

The Diary of a Union Soldier—Elisha Hunt Rhodes

Young men flocked to Union regiments at the beginning of the war. Their experiences in the following years transformed their perspectives on the war and their roles in it.

Many felt the cynicism that war often brings, but many others, such as Elisha Hunt Rhodes, gained a deeper sense of mission.

As you read "The Diary of a Union Soldier," ask yourself the following questions.

1. At the beginning of the war, how did Rhodes and his mother see their responsibilities in regard to the conflict?

2. What were Rhodes's primary impressions of the battles?

3. In what ways did Rhodes disagree with Union strategy at Antietam?

4. How did Rhodes describe the purpose of the war?

New Technology

The Rifle-Musket

When the war began, neither side was well equipped, most soldiers carrying old smooth-bore muskets. Northern manufacturers produced two million rifle-muskets during the war, whereas the South, lacking similar manufacturing capacity, relied on British imports and captured Union rifles. By 1863 soldiers on both sides carried the new rifle-muskets. It was such a successful defensive weapon that commanders came to believe that attacking forces had to have a numerical superiority of three to one to prevail in battle.

As you read "The Rifle-Musket," ask yourself the following questions:

1. Why was the United States military so slow to adopt the rifle-musket?

2. In what ways were soldiers carrying rifle-muskets still vulnerable?

3. Explain how the use of the rifle-musket affected the results of the Battle of Gettysburg.

4. How did Grant and Lee alter their strategies to adapt to the rifle-musket?

American Lives

William Tecumseh Sherman: An Architect of Modern War

General William Tecumseh Sherman was a hero to the Union cause and at the same time, reviled in the South. His "March to the Sea" left scars on the southern memory for generations to come.

As you read "William Tecumseh Sherman," ask yourself the following questions:

1. What does Sherman's life story prior to 1860 tell you about life in the United States during this period?

2. In what ways did family play a role in his career?

3. In what ways did Sherman's actions demonstrate the concept of total war?

4. Why do you think that Sherman was more receptive than other military leaders to newer ideas about how to conduct war?

SELF-TEST

Multiple Choice

1. Secession came earliest in states:
   a. closest to the North.
   b. farthest from the North.
   c. with the highest concentration of slaves.
   d. with the lowest concentration of slaves.

2. The Crittenden Plan of compromise included *all* of the following *except*:
   a. the abolition of slavery in Southern states would be prohibited.
   b. a tougher fugitive slave law would be enacted.
   c. the Missouri Compromise line would be extended to the California border.
   d. slavery would be protected in any territories acquired in the future.

3. One reason Kentucky stayed in the Union was that:
   a. Confederate troops infuriated Kentuckians by seizing several cities.
   b. as the home of Henry Clay, Kentucky was committed to working out a compromise rather than seceding.
   c. it had stronger economic ties with the North than with the South.
   d. Lincoln sent troops into Kentucky right away to put down secessionist sentiment.

4. Lincoln was successful in keeping *all* of the following states in the Union *except*:
   a. Missouri.   c. Tennessee.
   b. Maryland.   d. West Virginia.

5. Confederate advantages included *all* of the following *except*:
   a. cotton as a diplomatic weapon.
   b. greater iron production.
   c. self-sufficiency in food.
   d. well-trained military officers.

6. The Union's early conscription program was more successful than the Confederacy's because:

a. it did not include a provision for the hiring of substitutes.
b. it permitted the enlistment of African-Americans.
c. draft evaders were efficiently caught and prosecuted.
d. it focused on voluntary enlistment.

7. The Confederacy did not achieve a more effective economic program primarily because:
a. planters refused to contribute to the war effort.
b. the South resisted establishing a national bank.
c. states' rights philosophy left most power with the state governments.
d. planters simply did not have the financial resources to support the war.

8. In the South women worked as civil servants in the:
a. War Department.
b. Treasury.
c. Tredegar Iron Works.
d. postal service.

9. At the beginning of the war Lincoln's strategy was:
a. to delay while the Union built up its troops.
b. aggressive assault.
c. a "scorched earth" policy to demoralize southern civilians.
d. to blockade the South from the sea and the Mississippi River.

10. Lincoln's generals-in-chief included *all* of the following *except*:
a. Joseph E. Johnston   c. Ambrose Burnside
b. Winfield Scott   d. Joseph Hooker

11. Both Union and Confederate forces fought to gain control of the Tennessee and Mississippi river valleys because:
a. they were vital to the South's communication with its western areas.
b. they controlled access to major agricultural areas that supplied the South with much of its food.
c. through these valleys, Confederate troops could invade the North.
d. crucial railroads that allowed troops to mobilize quickly ran through these valleys.

12. Moderate Republicans feared immediate emancipation of the slaves for *all* of the following reasons *except*:
a. border states might leave the Union.
b. areas conquered by federal troops might resist Union control.
c. there would be a racist backlash in the North.
d. recently freed African-Americans would want to enlist in the Union army.

13. In 1863, General Robert E. Lee argued for permission to invade the North in the campaign that resulted in

the battle at Gettysburg for *all* of the following reasons *except*:
a. he hoped eventually to capture Washington, D.C.
b. his troops outnumbered disorganized Union troops in Pennsylvania.
c. he wished to relieve Union pressure on Vicksburg.
d. he was feeling overly confident after his victory at Chancellorsville.

14. The South was not completely successful in winning British support for *all* of the following reasons *except*:
a. Britain found other sources of cotton.
b. British manufacturers had stockpiled textiles.
c. southern diplomats insulted the British.
d. Britain imported grain supplies from the North.

15. Northern public opinion came to accept the enlistment of African-Americans for *all* of the following reasons *except*:
a. white resistance to the draft increased.
b. if a major war aim was emancipation, then blacks should take part in the fighting.
c. blacks were known to be particularly tough fighters.
d. the north needed the additional troops.

16. The siege of Petersburg was noteworthy for the use, by both Union and Confederate forces, of:
a. trench warfare.
b. ironclad ships.
c. the rifle-musket.
d. a scorched-earth policy.

Short Essays

Answer the following in a brief paragraph.

1. In what ways did the strategic location of the upper South affect Union war policies in regard to military strategy? (p. 452)

2. Compare and contrast the ways in which Lincoln and Davis viewed the reasons for and the purpose of the war. How and why did these views change over the course of the war? (pp. 453, 465–466, 478)

3. What effects did the Confederacy's commitment to states' rights have on the way its leaders managed the war? (pp. 456, 458–459)

4. How did the Union emphasize voluntary compliance with its war financing and conscription policies? (pp. 457–459)

5. In what ways did class conflict pose difficulties for both the Union and Confederate governments? (pp. 456–459)

6. In what ways did the war permit African-Americans and women to break through some barriers of racism

and sexism? What were the limits on that break-
through? (pp. 460, 471–472)

7. Where did the major campaigns of the war take place,
and why did those areas attract most of the fighting?
(pp. 460–464, 467–470, 473–478)

8. Explain how and why the Union's policy toward slavery evolved during the war. (pp. 451, 465–467)

9. How did Lincoln and his supporters evolve the new
concept of total war? (pp. 453, 460–461, 474–478)

ANSWERS

Chapter Précis

1. imperialist expansion
2. communications; trade
3. break the will
4. free slaves; black workers
5. taxpayers, bondholders, and those holding paper
money
6. southern Democrats
7. sanitation; quality of food
8. northern public opinion
9. long and protracted
10. reestablish slavery
11. northern victory
12. declaration of independence
13. full equality in American society
14. rapidly move troops
15. border; immigrant
16. Lee's supplies

Identification

1. South Carolina
2. federal property
3. bushwhackers
4. democracy
5. Tredegar Iron Works
6. Militia Act of 1862
7. New York City
8. unbacked paper money
9. Homestead Act

10. Clara Barton
11. David G. Farragut
12. Antietam
13. Benjamin Butler
14. George G. Meade
15. Mexico
16. Fort Wagner, South Carolina
17. Philip H. Sheridan
18. copperheads
19. Savannah
20. Appomattox Court House

Skill-Building Exercise

1. Arkansas, Delaware, Kentucky, Maryland, Missouri,
North Carolina, Tennessee, Virginia
2. Delaware, Kentucky, Maryland, Missouri, West Virginia
3. Arkansas, North Carolina, Tennessee, Virginia

Self-Test
Multiple Choice

1. c   7. c   13. b
2. b   8. d   14. c
3. a   9. b   15. a
4. c   10. a   16. c
5. b   11. a
6. d   12. d

Short Essays

1. The upper South had much of the South's population
and accounted for most of its industrial production.
Maryland and Virginia surrounded the nation's capital, Washington, D.C. For these reasons and because
of its control of the crucial Ohio and Mississippi
rivers, the Union wanted to keep the states of the
upper South from seceding. Lincoln was cautious
with Fort Sumter, not wanting to turn these states
away from the North. After Sumter fell, Lincoln
quickly moved troops into Virginia to protect Washington; these troops put down secessionist sympathies
among Maryland residents. In Missouri, a small
Union force defeated Confederate sympathizers and
kept that area of the Mississippi River open to the
Union. In Kentucky, where sympathy was more

divided, Confederate troops alienated the public, winning that state for the Union.

2. Lincoln saw the war as a crusade to preserve the Union. If democracy could not maintain itself against internal foes, the nation would not survive and the fate of democracy worldwide would be poor. Davis explained the war as a fight against tyranny and for self-government. The Confederate vice-president declared that democracy for whites was made possible by African-American slavery. Davis emphasized that slavery had to expand and, thus, the Confederacy was fighting to expand westward and avoid containment. With emancipation, Lincoln broadened the purpose of the war; he saw it as an act of justice to revolutionize southern society and end slavery. While Davis's views may not have changed significantly, by the end of the war he was willing to enlist and free slaves who would agree to fight for the Confederacy.

3. The Confederacy experienced difficulty securing compliance with its draft laws. Southern governors and state judges did not want the central government to have much power and thus resisted President Davis's policies. Health care similarly lacked central organization. The Confederacy did not attempt to manage the economy centrally, leaving this to the states. When the war went badly, Davis's government had to intervene directly, building and operating its own shipyards, armories, and mills. It also had to seize property when farmers would not sell sufficient supplies to the troops. Thus, because the Confederacy believed in less central control and had fewer mechanisms for governmental coordination, it was forced into extremely oppressive measures in the last war years.

4. The Union sought voluntary enlistments in its conscription program by assigning quotas to states and districts; the draft would take place only when an area failed to meet its quota. The federal government also offered bounties for enlistment and permitted men to hire substitutes or pay a commutation fee. The Union financed the war by attracting investment money to its cause. It marketed bonds successfully by appealing to the public in the United States and Britain, by passing laws that encouraged state banks to purchase bonds, and by paying bondholders in gold.

5. Draft policies created class conflict in both the North and the South. Both governments allowed drafted men to hire substitutes, angering poor young farmers in the South and urban laborers in the North. A substantial proportion of southern men became draft-evaders and deserters. Inflation and food shortages in the South infuriated southerners, some of whom felt they were fighting the war to protect the planters' interests. In the North, the New York City draft riots were expressions of both racism and workers' resentment toward men who could afford to buy their way out of the draft.

6. Both the Union and Confederacy finally enlisted African-Americans as soldiers. In the Confederacy, this was due to a severe personnel shortage at the end of the war. The Union needed additional men, but northern whites also came to believe that African-Americans deserved to be able to fight against slavery. In the Union army, African-Americans received lower pay and fewer supplies and were kept in segregated regiments, restricted to manual labor. The Union government did not insist that African-Americans captured by the Confederacy be treated as prisoners of war, leaving these soldiers vulnerable to Confederate retaliation.

   Women were crucial to the cause on both sides. As men left home for the war, women assumed responsibilities on farms and plantations and in schools and factory work. Nursing opened to women because both governments needed people to care for the injured. Government jobs also were made available to women as male clerks joined the armies. Women, however, were restricted to the poorest paying jobs in government work and were not able to become doctors.

7. Fighting centered on three areas: the corridor between Richmond and Washington, D.C.; the Mississippi and Tennessee rivers; and across Georgia. The Union and the Confederacy each hoped to protect its own capital and attack the other's. From this area, both armies tried to invade the other's territory, with Lee moving into Pennsylvania and Grant moving into Virginia. The Tennessee and Mississippi river valleys were crucial to the South to maintain communication with its western states; the North hoped to cut the Confederacy in two, which it succeeded in doing. Union troops moved across Georgia to demoralize southern civilians, taking the war deep into the Confederacy. Sherman attacked and seized Atlanta and Savannah and then moved on to burn Columbia, South Carolina, the capital of the first state to secede. By striking so deeply into the South, Union troops made it clear that the Confederacy could not survive.

8. Initially, Lincoln was willing to guarantee that the federal government would not ban slavery in the southern states, although he insisted that slavery should not expand into the territories; this was his basis for rejecting the Crittenden Plan. He did not wish to alienate the slaveholding states of the upper South. As Union troops moved into the South, officers had to decide what to do with slaves who escaped to their lines. The First Confiscation Act authorized troops to seize this "property," while the second

declared such slaves "forever free." As casualties mounted, public enthusiasm for emancipation increased. Congress abolished slavery in Washington, D.C., and then in the federal territories. Lincoln freed slaves in areas still in rebellion when he announced the Emancipation Proclamation in September 1862. He still feared alienating slaveholders in states in the upper South that had remained loyal to the Union. Finally, the Thirteenth Amendment, which ended slavery, was passed by Congress in January 1865.

9. The Union's strategy at the beginning of the war was to attack Confederate troops aggressively. When this was not successful at the First Battle of Bull Run, Lincoln began to realize that the war would be longer than anyone had expected. His generals then avoided direct attacks, hoping to build up overwhelming numbers before waging any battles. Lincoln grew impatient with McDowell, McClellan, Hooker, Burnside, and Meade, desiring a more aggressive strategy. In Grant, Lincoln found a general who was determined to use technology and the Union's superiority in numbers to make crushing attacks on Confederate troops, pursuing them until they were defeated. Grant also understood that southern civilians had to realize that their cause could not be pursued endlessly; he forced them to accept their situation by bringing the war to them. Sheridan terrorized the Shenandoah Valley, which supplied Confederate troops. Finally, Sherman's march through Georgia and into South Carolina devastated southern morale as Sherman destroyed everything in his path. This application of total war brought the fighting to an end as southern civilians realized that they could not continue their resistance against Union troops.

CHAPTER 16

The Union Reconstructed 1865–1877

★   ★   ★

CHAPTER PRÉCIS

Presidential Restoration   pp. 486–494

Believing that the southern states had never legally seceded from the Union, Presidents Abraham Lincoln and Andrew Johnson attempted to install loyal state governments quickly.

Restoration under Lincoln

During the war Lincoln initiated a lenient plan to organize new state governments in the South, hoping to appeal to former southern Whigs. Many congressional Republicans wanted a harsher program, treating the South as conquered territory under congressional rule. Although some radical Republicans supported the redistribution of southern plantations to freedmen and loyal white farmers, most agreed on a more moderate program in which Confederate leaders would not return to power, the Republican party would be established as a major political force in the South, and the federal government would protect the voting rights of freedmen. The Wade-Davis bill would have deprived ex-Confederates of political power permanently, but Lincoln used a "pocket" veto to defeat it.

Lincoln's assassination convinced northerners that harsher policies toward the South were necessary. Vice-President Andrew Johnson became president.

Restoration under Johnson

President Johnson quickly restored the southern state governments, offering a generous amnesty and the return of all property except slaves to

1. Lincoln's plan required that only _____ percent of the number of voters in 1860 would have to take an oath of loyalty before a state could form a new state government. (p. 486)

2. Lincoln believed that a policy of moderation and generous reconciliation terms would encourage Confederates to _____ . (p. 486)

most former Confederates who took an oath of allegiance to the Union. These new southern state governments, which were controlled by former Confederates, passed laws oppressing the freedmen, and violent attacks by ex-Confederates on freedmen became frequent. Johnson had already alienated radical Republicans, and as their distrust of him grew, he attempted to build a coalition of white southerners, northern Democrats, and conservative Republicans. Johnson foiled his Republican opponents by restoring the southern states under generous terms while Congress was not in session. Once Congress convened, Republicans moved to look into the situation in the South.

Acting on Freedom: African-Americans in the South

During the war, freedmen, with the support of Union troops and the Freedmen's Bureau, often took possession of plantations after the owners had fled. President Johnson's amnesty plan returned the land to its white owners, frustrating freedmen's hopes of owning their own land. Planters, who wanted the freedmen to work as wage laborers on their fields, were frustrated by the freedmen's determination to resist the gang system. Federal troops, desiring stability in the South and a return to productive agriculture, encouraged freedmen to return to work for their former masters. Southern legislatures responded to the need of planters for a disciplined labor force by passing Black Codes designed to keep freedmen in conditions close to slavery.

Congressional Initiatives

Congressional Republicans, determined to protect the civil rights of freedmen, passed a civil rights bill and later the Fourteenth Amendment. Johnson vetoed the bill and encouraged former Confederate states to turn down the amendment. When Johnson's supporters fared poorly in the congressional elections of 1866, Republicans won an overwhelming majority in Congress.

3. Johnson required that the former Confederate states only revoke their ordinances of secession and ratify the _____ to be restored fully to the Union. (p. 488)

4. During hearings of the _____, Republicans investigated violence in the South under Johnson's restored state governments. (p. 489)

5. Land seized by Union troops from southerners and then distributed to freedmen became known as _____ . (p. 491)

6. The Fourteenth Amendment assigned to _____ the power to enforce its provisions. (p. 493)

Radical Reconstruction   pp. 494–507

Moderate and radical Republicans joined to take charge of Reconstruction.

The Congressional Program

With the Reconstruction Act of 1867, Congress divided the South into five military districts to supervise the writing of new constitutions for the states, in preparation for their return to the Union and to protect African-American suffrage. Congress passed the Tenure of Office Act to prevent Johnson from dismissing Republican officials who were opposed to him. When he dismissed Secretary of War Edwin M. Stanton, Congress attempted to impeach Johnson, failing to convict him by only one

7. Union army commanders in the five military districts had orders to _____ all adult black men. (p. 494)

vote. In 1868 the nation elected Ulysses S. Grant, a war hero and supporter of the radical Republicans, to the presidency. The Republicans attempted to guarantee African-American male suffrage by passing the Fifteenth Amendment and making its ratification a condition for the readmission to the Union of southern states that were still unreconstructed.

The Issue of Suffrage for Women

Radical Republicans, believing that the public was not ready for woman suffrage, abandoned suffrage leaders, many of whom had worked for decades for the end of slavery and African-American voting rights. One branch of the woman suffrage movement focused on working for universal suffrage at the state level. Another group allied themselves with the Republicans and supported the Fifteenth Amendment.

The South during Radical Reconstruction

Southern state governments under Republican control included African-Americans, white southerners who hoped to attract northern capital or rid the South of the planter aristocracy, and northerners who moved to the South to settle. African-American leaders, some of whom were army veterans, included those who had been free before the war and came to hold state executive offices, as well as some of the many freedmen who entered state legislatures. These legislatures repealed the Black Codes, modernized and democratized state governments, and used taxes for public works such as schools, hospitals, and roads. African-Americans strengthened their family life by building their own social institutions, creating new communities, and founding their own churches.

The Planters' Counterrevolution

Former slaveowners united under the Democratic party to regain political control of the South. Using appeals to racial solidarity and southern patriotism, they gained the allegiance of poorer whites. They also terrorized African-American voters through the violence of secret societies.

Limited prosecutions and Grant's unwillingness to risk rekindling the war allowed ex-Confederates to regain control of all but three southern states by 1877. As federal help diminished, Republican governments were overwhelmed by former Confederates who had regained control of southern states.

The Economic Fate of the Former Slaves

Radical Reconstruction failed to give freedmen substantial land ownership. With diminishing political power and limited land distribution, freedmen became sharecroppers, working land owned by whites and paying for it with a share of their crops. They sank deeply into debt to their landlords and to the merchants who provided their supplies. As Democrats won control of southern state governments, they passed laws supporting landlords and merchants, keeping the freedmen in a situation of debt peonage.

8. By allowing states to deny suffrage to women, the _____ split the woman suffrage movement. (p. 497)

9. The Republican party looked to the _____ as the center of its political support in the South. (p. 497)

10. Republicans who controlled southern state governments emphasized _____ as the basis for the new democratic order in the South. (p. 500)

11. In 1870 and 1871, Congress and President Grant passed the Force Acts to assert federal authority against the _____ . (p. 502)

12. Southern state legislatures under control of the Democratic party passed laws permitting lenders to take _____ on crops when sharecroppers fell behind on loan payments. (p. 507)

The North during Reconstruction   pp. 507–513

Congressional Republicans transformed the northern economy with an aggressive program of government assistance to industrial capitalism.

A Dynamic Economy

Heavy capital investment in northeastern industry created the era of big business, which was marked by the development of giant corporations. The Republican economic program included high tariffs to protect industry from foreign competition, taxes on alcohol and tobacco to pay for infrastructure construction and Civil War pensions, and the Homestead Act to appeal to western settlers, although it benefited primarily the wealthy. The Republicans also reassured investors by exercising greater control over national banking. The war made northerners less suspicious of government and concentrations of power.

13. The age of capital was a period marked by increased investment in
_____ . (p. 508)

Republican Foreign Policy

In foreign policy, Republicans sought to acquire colonies as trading bases for expanding American commerce. President Johnson and Secretary of State William H. Seward threatened force in Mexico to compel French troops to leave. The United States also convinced the British to submit to arbitration American claims for damages caused by British aid to the Confederacy. Congress refused to expand in the Caribbean but did annex the Midway Islands in the Pacific and buy Alaska from Russia.

14. Alaska's value to the United States included natural resources such as
_____ , _____ ,
_____ , and
_____ . (p. 509)

The Politics of Corruption and the Grant Administration

Democrats charged that Republican programs had created special privileges and increased concentrations of wealth and power, thus corrupting the republic. They were joined by dissident Republicans, including radicals on Reconstruction policy and those who sought civil service reform. These Liberal Republicans formed a new party and challenged Grant in 1872 with their candidate, Horace Greeley, whom the Democrats also nominated. This coalition failed to oust Grant. In his second term, various examples of corruption came to light, including the Crédit Mobilier, which was a dummy corporation allowing railroad stockholders to defraud the corporation and the federal government, and whiskey distillers who were defrauding the government of tax revenues. These scandals discredited the Grant administration. A depression, started by a panic over a railroad bankruptcy, led to severe and prolonged unemployment. Actions by the Grant administration decreased the money supply and worsened the situation.

15. Liberal Republicans hoped to replace the spoils system with a(n)
_____ . (p. 510)

16. With the _____ the government was determined to decrease the nation's money supply by exchanging gold for greenbacks, thus increasing the length and severity of the 1873–1877 depression. (p. 511)

The Political Crisis of 1877

In 1876 both parties nominated candidates noted for honesty and commitment to reform. Although the Democrat, Samuel J. Tilden, won the most popular votes, electoral votes were contested in three southern states still under Republican control. Congress appointed a commission, which gave all the contested electoral votes to the Republican, Rutherford B. Hayes. Congressional Democrats accepted the commission's decision. Historians are uncertain whether they struck a deal with the Republicans for the confinement to barracks of troops in the South, the appointment of Democrats to major offices, and federal support for a railroad across the South—all of which occurred during Hayes's presidency. This brought Reconstruction to an end, leaving African-Americans without further northern support.

17. During his campaign for the presidency, the Republican nominee Hayes appealed to Democratic voters by promising to end _____ . (p. 513)

EXPANDED TIMELINE

1863 **Lincoln announces his restoration plan**
Lincoln's plan, based on moderation, was designed to encourage Confederates to surrender. He offered a general amnesty to most Confederates, asked only that southern citizens take an oath of loyalty to the Union, and accept Union proclamations concerning slavery. When ten percent of the number of voters in 1860 had taken the loyalty oath, those individuals could organize a new state government.

1864 **Wade-Davis bill passed by Congress**
Lincoln gives Wade-Davis bill a "pocket" veto
Radical and moderate congressional Republicans proposed this harsher alternative to Lincoln's Reconstruction plan. It would have permitted only those southerners who could swear that they had not taken up arms against the Union or aided the Confederacy to participate in the creation of new state governments. President Lincoln used a "pocket" veto to prevent the bill from becoming law.

1865 **Freedmen's Bureau established**
Congress created the Freedmen's Bureau to help feed and clothe refugees of both races in the aftermath of war. To try to return the South quickly to productive agriculture, the Bureau established labor contracts between freedmen and landowners. It also sponsored missionaries and teachers from the North who set up schools to educate freedmen.

Lincoln supports limited suffrage for freedmen
Lincoln began to suggest that he would agree to establish federal control over the South to protect freedmen's suffrage rights. He was first concerned with African-Americans who had served in the Union army.

Lincoln assassinated; Andrew Johnson succeeds as president
While attending the theater, President Lincoln was shot by John Wilkes Booth, an actor and Confederate supporter. Union troops killed Booth, and eight people were convicted as his accomplices. Vice-President Andrew Johnson, a Democrat who

had supported the Union, became president. He was easily manipulated by ex-Confederates.

Johnson implements his restoration plan
Johnson's plan offered amnesty and a return of all property excluding slaves to southerners who took loyalty oaths to the Union. High-ranking Confederate officials and military leaders had to appeal personally to the president for amnesty.

Joint Committee on Reconstruction formed
In response to President Johnson's lenient treatment of former Confederates, his movement toward the Democrats, and violence in the South toward the freedmen, Republicans in the House and Senate created a committee to hold hearings on conditions in the South. Their findings of terrorism against African-Americans shocked northerners, who came to believe that southerners were trying to get around the Thirteenth Amendment.

1866 **Republicans fail to override Johnson's veto of Freedmen's Bureau bill**
President Johnson vetoed a bill to extend the life of the Freedmen's Bureau on grounds that the Constitution did not authorize aid to the indigent and that the affected states were not represented in Congress. With this act, Johnson claimed that any reconstruction legislation would be unconstitutional without southern representation in Congress.

Civil Rights Act passed over Johnson's veto
President Johnson vetoed this attempt by Congress to define the citizenship rights of freedmen, including the rights to rent and own property, make contracts, and have access to the courts. Johnson based his veto on the lack of southern representation in Congress. He also said that the bill discriminated against whites by granting freedmen immediate citizenship, whereas immigrants had to wait five years. Congress overrode the veto and was determined to take control of Reconstruction away from Johnson.

Memphis and New Orleans riots
Riots against blacks in Memphis and white mobs who attacked delegates to a black suffrage convention in New Orleans demonstrated to the North the violence of white southerners and their determination to circumvent African-American suffrage.

Occurring right before the congressional elections of 1866, these riots hindered Johnson's attempts to campaign for politicians who would support his lenient policies toward white southerners.

Johnson makes disastrous "swing around the circle"
President Johnson toured major cities personally campaigning against the Fourteenth Amendment and radical Republicans, claiming that they were traitors. Moderates responded by siding with the radicals. Johnson's candidates lost decisively, giving his critics control of both houses of Congress.

American Equal Rights Association founded
When the Fourteenth Amendment did not extend suffrage to women, women leaders were disappointed but accepted defeat at the federal level. They formed the American Equal Rights Association to focus on winning woman suffrage at the state level.

Johnson defeated in Congressional elections
Republicans won wide margins in the Senate and House as voters rejected candidates who supported President Johnson and his lenient Reconstruction policies. During the campaign Johnson further alienated Republicans by calling them traitors. With greater numbers in Congress, Republicans took control of Reconstruction.

1867   Reconstruction Acts
Congress passed the Reconstruction Acts to eliminate Johnson's new southern state governments and divide the South into five military districts where Union officers would supervise the creation of new state governments and protect African-American suffrage.

Tenure of Office Act
Congress passed the Tenure of Office Act to prohibit President Johnson from removing federal officials without congressional approval. Congress wanted to protect Secretary of War Stanton, a radical Republican, from being fired by Johnson. When Johnson dismissed Stanton, Congress based its bill of impeachment on this law.

Purchase of Alaska
Secretary of State William H. Seward persuaded Congress to purchase Alaska from Russia for $7.2 million. Although critics ridiculed the idea, Alaska was rich in fish, fur, timber, and minerals. The purchase of Alaska blocked any potential British plans to expand in North America.

1868   Impeachment crisis
The House of Representatives impeached President Johnson on the grounds that he had violated the Tenure of Office Act, but in reality the dispute was over how to handle Reconstruction. The Senate failed to convict Johnson by only one vote, as some moderate Republicans refused to use the impeachment process for political purposes.

Fourteenth Amendment ratified
In the Fourteenth Amendment, Congress granted citizenship to freedmen and prohibited the states from depriving any citizen of his or her civil rights. It provided for penalties if a state denied suffrage to any adult male citizen. The Fourteenth Amendment was the first to put the word *male* in the Constitution, clearly excluding women from suffrage. Congress required reconstructed state governments to ratify this amendment before they could be readmitted to the Union.

Ulysses S. Grant elected president
As the North's greatest war hero, Ulysses S. Grant easily won both the Republican nomination and the presidency. The Democratic candidate, Horatio Seymour of New York, wanted to let southern governments reorganize on their own, an unpopular idea in the North.

1869   *Texas v. White*
The Supreme Court ruled that secession was unconstitutional, in agreement with Lincoln and Johnson.

1870   Ku Klux Klan at peak of power
Begun in Tennessee by ex-Confederate general Nathan Bedford Forrest, the Klan spread throughout the South. Young ex-Confederate soldiers, smarting under the South's defeat, flocked to join this paramilitary organization. The Klan used violence and terrorism to keep freedmen from voting and intimidate them into submitting to white rule.

First Force Act passed by Congress
Responding to the violence of the Klan-led counterrevolution in the South, Congress authorized the president to use federal prosecutions, martial law, and military force to end terrorism designed to deprive citizens of the right to vote, hold office, serve on juries, and equal protection of the law. This was followed by the Ku Klux Klan Act in 1871.

Fifteenth Amendment ratified
The Fifteenth Amendment prohibited states from denying any citizen the right to vote on the grounds of race, color, or previous condition of servitude. The intention of Congressional Republicans had been to guarantee full suffrage to African-American men, but that intention was not realized. More radical Republicans had wanted to forbid the use of property ownership or literacy tests to disqualify voters, but moderates did not want to prohibit states from using such tactics to prevent immigrants from voting. Congress required the remaining

unreconstructed states to accept this amendment before they could be readmitted to the Union.

1871 **Ku Klux Klan Act passed by Congress**
Treaty of Washington
Negotiated by Hamilton Fish, this treaty resolved all outstanding issues, including Civil War claims, between Britain and the United States, strengthening ties between the two nations.

1872 **Grant's reelection as president**
Grant won overwhelmingly with 56 percent of the popular vote, defeating Horace Greeley who had been the nominee of both the Democrats and the Liberal Republicans.

1873 **Panic of 1873 ushers in depression of 1873–1877**
When the Northern Pacific Railroad went bankrupt, a financial panic developed. When Grant administration policies contracted the money supply, a severe depression set in, the worst the nation had seen to that point. Unemployment reached 15 percent, and thousands of farmers went bankrupt. Many people blamed the hardship on the financial manipulations of the Republicans.

Crédit Mobilier scandal breaks
This scandal implicated high-ranking Republicans in a scheme to defraud the government through federal subsidies for railroad construction.

1874 **Democrats win majority in House of Representatives**
Playing on the scandals of the Grant administration and supporting a bill to alleviate the exigencies of the depression by increasing the circulation of greenbacks, the Democrats won a majority in the House of Representatives and gains in the Senate, for the first time since 1860.

1875 **Whiskey Ring scandal undermines Grant administration**
Whiskey distillers defrauded the government with the collusion of Treasury agents who helped them avoid paying millions of dollars in taxes. When President Grant's private secretary was implicated and Grant tried to protect him, public confidence in the administration declined.

1877 **Compromise of 1877**
Rutherford B. Hayes becomes president
Although Samuel Tilden won the most popular votes, contested electoral votes in southern states still controlled by Republicans threw the election into question. A commission appointed by Congress voted strictly along party lines, giving the election to the Republican, Rutherford B. Hayes. Southern Democratic congressmen accepted the commission's determination because they felt that Hayes would restrict the activities of federal troops in the South, appoint Democrats to major offices, and support the construction of a major railroad across the South.

Reconstruction ends
By 1877 all the southern states had returned to the Union, and federal troops ceased to control southern politics. White southerners had regained control of state governments. Although slavery had ended and the three amendments to the Constitution had granted freedmen national citizenship and suffrage, support for further improvements in the conditions of life for African-Americans would not come soon.

GLOSSARY

restoration At the end of the war moderate Republicans wanted to rebuild the Union by establishing loyal governments in southern states and restoring those states' representation in Congress. Restoration required little change in the southern way of life. (p. 485)

reconstruction Freedmen, abolitionists, and more radical Republican politicians wanted reconstruction—a change in the South that would ensure political equality for the freedmen and grant them greater economic rights. (p. 485)

redemption Ex-Confederates and their northern supporters sought redemption—the return of political and economic control in the South to white southerners. They believed that Union support of the freedmen had deprived the South of democratic self-government. (p. 485)

ironclad oath This oath of allegiance to the Union was part of the Wade-Davis bill, in which Congress required southerners to swear they had never carried arms against the Union or aided the Confederacy before they could vote or serve as delegates in conventions to establish new state governments. This would have eliminated most southern whites from participating in these conventions. President Lincoln used a "pocket" veto to keep the Wade-Davis bill from becoming law. (p. 487)

"pocket" veto When congressional Republicans passed the Wade-Davis bill, a harsher alternative to President Lincoln's restoration plan, Lincoln used a "pocket" veto to kill it. Avoiding a formal veto, Lincoln did not sign the bill, letting it expire after Congress adjourned. (p. 487)

Black Codes After the war, southern states passed laws to keep African-Americans in conditions close to slavery.

These Black Codes required freedmen to sign restrictive labor contracts that were little different from slavery. They also controlled African-Americans' activities through curfews, vagrancy laws, requirements to obtain passes, and restrictions on meetings. (p. 492)

scalawags   These southern whites joined the Republicans during Reconstruction and were ridiculed by ex-Confederates as worthless traitors. They included wealthy ex-Whigs and yeomen farmers who had not supported the Confederacy and who believed that an alliance with the Republicans was the best way to attract northern capital to the South. (pp. 497–498)

carpetbaggers   These northerners moved to the South during Reconstruction to develop its economic potential. Carpetbaggers included former Union army officers who had learned to love the South, as well as educated professionals. Former Confederates despised them as transient exploiters. (p. 498)

sharecropping   Freedmen agreed to work the land and pay a share (between one-half and two-thirds) of their harvested crops to the landowners. Sharecropping developed because freedmen wanted to work their own land but lacked the money to buy it, and because white landowners did not have the cash to pay wages. This agricultural system increased freedmen's control over their own time and activities but made it difficult for them to save enough money to buy land. (p. 506)

debt peonage   Country merchants took advantage of freedmen who needed to buy seed, fertilizer, and equipment but were unable to borrow from established banks. Merchants gave them credit, but at high rates of interest, and freedmen often found it difficult to get out of debt. By passing laws granting merchants liens on their debtors' crops and requiring criminal prosecution of farmers who could not pay their debts, southern state governments institutionalized this system. (p. 507)

age of capital   During the era that lasted from the end of the Civil War until World War I, northeastern industries expanded, leading to the growth of huge corporations. Capital investment in railroads and factories created the era of big business. (p. 508)

Grantism   Under the system of party patronage during the Grant administration, Republican politicians gave government positions to their supporters, requiring them to donate part of their salaries to the party. As the government bureaucracy grew, filled with these party men, some Republicans began to criticize Grantism as corrupt. (p. 510)

merit system   Liberal Republicans and other reformers sought to replace the system of awarding government jobs on the basis of party affiliation with a merit system. They advocated the creation of a civil service commission that

would appoint people to jobs on the basis of their capabilities as determined by competitive examinations. (p. 510)

IDENTIFICATION

Identify by filling in the blanks.

1. Radical Republicans argued that the states of the former Confederacy had left the Union and were now _____ . (p. 486)

2. In _____ the Supreme Court ruled that secession was illegal under the Constitution. (p. 486)

3. The majority of Republicans refused to support the confiscation of southern plantations and the redistribution of land to freedmen because they believed it would violate constitutional protection of _____ . (p. 487)

4. President Johnson believed that Reconstruction was an issue that should be handled by the _____ and attempted to bypass Congress in reunifying the country. (p. 488)

5. Southern state legislatures passed laws known as _____ , which were designed to ensure that African-Americans would remain a cheap, controlled labor force. (p. 492)

6. The _____ gave 80-acre grants of public lands to settlers who cultivated the land for five years but barred ex-Confederates and their supporters from receiving these grants. (p. 492)

7. In 1866 race riots in Memphis and New Orleans convinced moderate Republicans to support radical efforts to pass the _____ . (p. 493)

8. The _____ divided the South into five military districts. (p. 494)

9. Seeking to protect Secretary of War Edwin M. Stanton from dismissal by President Johnson, Congress passed the _____ , requiring congressional consent for the removal of any official

whose appointment had required Senate confirmation. (p. 494)

10. When the Fourteenth Amendment failed to give the vote to women, woman suffrage leaders began a new campaign to win universal suffrage at the _____ level. (p. 497)

11. Democratic former Confederates called northerners who participated in rebuilding the South _____ . (p. 498)

12. A former Confederate general, _____ , was the first leader of the Ku Klux Klan. (p. 501)

13. With the _____ , Congress authorized the president to use federal prosecutions and military force to put down violence against freedmen. (p. 502)

14. Sharecroppers and tenant farmers found themselves tied to the land and in debt to landlords and merchants in a system known as _____ . (p. 507)

15. Military spending, including funds to support the cavalry against native Americans on the Great Plains,

amounted to _____ percent of the federal budget by 1880. (p. 508)

16. The most popular Republican economic program was the _____ , which was expanded virtually every year. (p. 508)

17. Senator Charles Sumner hoped to acquire _____ from Britain as payment for damages caused by British support for the Confederacy during the Civil War. (p. 509)

18. The _____ was a dummy corporation that allowed railroad stockholders to defraud their corporation and the federal government. (p. 510)

19. In the _____ scandal, President Grant appeared to have perjured himself to protect Orville Babcock, his private secretary, from conviction. (p. 511)

20. An electoral commission's selection of Rutherford B. Hayes to be president is known as the _____ . (p. 513)

SKILL-BUILDING EXERCISE

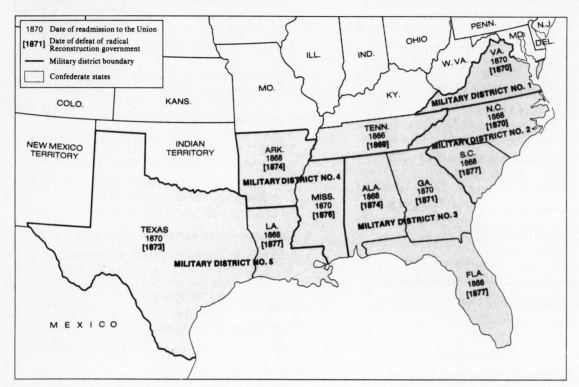

1. List the southern states in the order in which they returned to the Union. Explain the lags in time.

2. List the southern states in the order in which Democrats defeated radical Reconstruction governments. Explain why the dates range from 1869 in Tennessee to 1877 in Florida, Louisiana, and South Carolina.

3. How does Whittlesey describe the situation of the freedmen and their responses to freedom?

4. How does Whittlesey describe southern whites?

5. What accomplishments of the Freedmen's Bureau does Whittlesey report?

DOCUMENT EXERCISES

American Voices

Report on the Freedmen's Bureau— Eliphalet Whittlesey

Many northern idealists, including missionaries and women teachers, joined the Freedmen's Bureau and went south to assist war refugees. Their own racism, however, made it difficult for them to empathize with the plight of the freedmen. Their inclinations and respect for private property led them to side with the planters against the freedmen in conflicts over land and conditions of labor.

As you read "Report on the Freedmen's Bureau," ask yourself the following questions:

1. What does Whittlesey believe was his role as a representative of the Freedmen's Bureau?

The Intimidation of Black Voters— Harriet Hernandes

During Congressional Reconstruction, Union troops attempted to protect the voting rights of African-Americans whose exercise of the suffrage had led to Republican-controlled state governments. Ex-Confederates struck back by trying to prevent freedmen from voting, using violence and intimidation to drive freedmen from the polls.

As you read "The Intimidation of Black Voters," ask yourself the following questions:

1. What had the Hernandeses done that attracted the attention of the Klan?

2. How did Hernandes and her husband try to protect themselves?

3. Why was Harriet Hernandes particularly vulnerable?

4. What impact did the Klan's activities have on the Hernandeses' neighborhood?

American Lives

Nathan Bedford Forrest: A Violent Defender of Honor

Nathan Bedford Forrest's life tells us much about the South before and after the Civil War. He became a leader in the South because of his business success in the booming Old Southwest in the 1850s and his military victories during the war. After the war Forrest used President Johnson's amnesty program to his advantage. He also used the loyalty to him of former Confederate soldiers to strengthen the Klan. He tried to take advantage of the new business opportunities created during the war, but the depression of the 1870s brought him, like many others, financial grief.

As you read about Nathan Bedford Forrest, ask yourself the following questions:

1. What personality traits did Forrest have that seem characteristic of the Old South?

2. What does Forrest's business career in the 1840s and 1850s tell you about the antebellum South?

3. What types of men joined Forrest in the Klan, and why did they join?

4. What does Forrest's business career after the war indicate about the postwar South?

SELF-TEST

Multiple Choice

1. Lincoln hoped to gain support for his restoration plan from:
   a. freedmen.
   b. former southern Whigs.
   c. scalawags.
   d. carpetbaggers.

2. The Wade-Davis bill required *all* of the following for a former Confederate state to rejoin the Union *except*:
   a. the ironclad oath.
   b. the prohibition of slavery.
   c. the permanent disfranchisement of former Confederate civil and military leaders.
   d. ten percent of the 1860 voters to have pledged their future loyalty to the Union.

3. Under President Andrew Johnson, high-ranking Confederate military officers could regain their property and win amnesty by:
   a. taking an oath of allegiance to the Union.
   b. accepting the Union's wartime acts, including the abolition of slavery.
   c. petitioning the president personally.
   d. supporting African-American suffrage.

4. General Sherman gave African-American settlers "possessory title" to land:
   a. because he felt they had earned it.
   b. to relieve the pressure for food from refugees who followed his troops.
   c. to punish plantation owners.
   d. all of the above.

5. Freedmen resisted the gang system of labor for *all* of the following reasons *except* they:
   a. wanted greater control over their pace of work.
   b. wanted to work individually.
   c. wanted more free time.
   d. hated to be supervised.

6. Congress passed the Fourteenth Amendment to:
   a. end slavery.
   b. forbid the states from denying any citizen the right to vote.
   c. embarrass President Johnson.
   d. provide constitutional protection for African-American suffrage.

7. The Reconstruction Act of 1867 included *all* of the following provisions *except*:
   a. division of the South into five military districts.
   b. military supervision of voter registration.
   c. distribution of land to former slaves.
   d. the requirement that new state legislatures approve the Fourteenth Amendment.

8. Moderate Republicans who voted to acquit President Johnson of criminal misconduct did so for *all* of the following reasons *except*:
   a. Johnson was clearly not guilty of the charge.
   b. removal of a president over a policy dispute would be a dangerous precedent.
   c. they believed that the country needed a strong presidency.
   d. a powerful executive was necessary to conduct foreign policy.

9. When the Fifteenth Amendment was ratified, Elizabeth Cady Stanton claimed that:
   a. woman suffrage leaders should support it to maintain their alliance with the Republicans.
   b. woman suffrage supporters should unite in opposition to it.
   c. women should try to vote under its provisions.
   d. women would continue to be oppressed because the amendment would create an "aristocracy of sex."

10. Freedmen asserted their independence by doing *all* of the following *except*:
    a. building schools.

b. recording marriages that had been unrecognized under slavery.

c. keeping women out of field work.

d. insisting on becoming part of white churches.

11. The Ku Klux Klan was most effective in:
    a. forcing freedmen to accept restrictive labor contracts.
    b. chasing carpetbaggers out of the South.
    c. keeping African-American women working at field labor.
    d. returning the Democratic party to power.

12. The Force Acts were not effective in suppressing the Ku Klux Klan because:
    a. federal agents were not able to identify Klan members.
    b. the Justice Department lacked the resources to prosecute effectively.
    c. federal agents were not able to get freedmen to testify against Klansmen.
    d. federal agents made no arrests.

13. Sharecropping was introduced into the South by:
    a. the Freedmen's Bureau.
    b. Union army troops.
    c. southern landlords.
    d. southern merchants.

14. The Republican economic program included *all* of the following *except*:
    a. crop lien laws.
    b. redistribution of wealth from the poor to the rich.
    c. railroad construction subsidies.
    d. high tariffs.

15. The experience of working within the modern bureaucracies of Civil War armies and agencies taught Americans:
    a. to distrust government bureaucrats because of war profiteering.
    b. to accept the federal government as the central agency of national economic development.
    c. that a civil service system was needed to get more competent people into government jobs.
    d. that better education was necessary to prepare men and women for government jobs.

16. Liberal Republicans challenged Grant in 1872:
    a. to win greater support for freedmen's rights in the South.
    b. to achieve civil service reform.
    c. with the support of northern African-Americans.
    d. to enact higher tariffs for the protection of northern industries.

17. Secretary of State William H. Seward was able to acquire _____ for the United States.
    a. Santo Domingo   c. the Midway Islands
    b. Hawaii   d. the Virgin Islands

18. The Specie Resumption Act of 1875 did *all* of the following *except*:
    a. require the federal government to exchange gold for greenbacks.
    b. cause a general deflation and ease the burden of debts.
    c. put the nation's money on the gold standard.
    d. encourage foreign investors to put their money in the U.S. economy.

Short Essays

Answer the following in a brief paragraph.

1. Compare and contrast Lincoln's and Johnson's restoration plans. (pp. 486–489)

2. How did President Johnson try to get his restoration plan accomplished without congressional support? (pp. 488–489)

3. What issues did freedmen consider most important during congressional Reconstruction? (pp. 491–493)

4. How did northern racism influence the work of the Freedmen's Bureau? (p. 492)

5. What were the successes and failures of the Congressional Reconstruction period? (pp. 491, 503, 506–509)

6. How did southern whites attempt to regain control of the freedmen, first during Presidential Reconstruction and then during Congressional Reconstruction? (pp. 492, 499–501)

7. How did the Republicans attempt to appeal to all segments of northern society with their economic program? (p. 508)

8. Was the Democrats' decision to accept the Compromise of 1877 a wise one? Explain your answer. (pp. 511–513)

ANSWERS

Chapter Précis

1. 10

2. abandon the rebellion

3. Thirteenth Amendment

4. Joint Committee on Reconstruction

5. "Sherman" land

6. Congress

7. register to vote

8. Fifteenth Amendment

9. freedmen

10. education

11. Ku Klux Klan

12. liens

13. factories and railroads

14. fish; furs; timber; minerals

15. merit system

16. Specie Resumption Act of 1875

17. military occupation of the South

Identification

1. conquered territory

2. *Texas v. White* in 1869

3. property rights

4. executive branch

5. Black Codes

6. Southern Homestead Act of 1866

7. Fourteenth Amendment

8. Reconstruction Act of 1867

9. Tenure of Office Act

10. state

11. carpetbaggers

12. Nathan Bedford Forrest

13. Force Acts of 1870 and 1871

14. debt peonage

15. 60

16. Civil War pension program

17. Canada

18. Crédit Mobilier

19. Whiskey Ring

20. Compromise of 1877

Skill-Building Exercise

1. Tennessee: 1866; Arkansas: 1868; North Carolina:

1868; South Carolina: 1868; Florida: 1868; Alabama: 1868; Louisiana: 1868; Georgia: 1870; Mississippi: 1870; Texas: 1870; Virginia: 1870.

Tennessee was readmitted to the Union under President Johnson's Reconstruction plan. It had been controlled by Union forces since 1862 and its new state government was dominated by former Whigs. When Congress took over Reconstruction, it accepted Tennessee's new state constitution, but the other southern states were placed under military rule and only later formed state governments acceptable to Congress.

2. Tennessee: 1869; Virginia: 1870; North Carolina: 1870; Georgia: 1871; Texas: 1873; Alabama: 1874; Arkansas: 1874; Mississippi: 1876; Florida: 1877; Louisiana: 1877; South Carolina: 1877.

Tennessee returned to Democratic control quickly; it had never been under military rule. In other southern states, former Confederates were determined to return Democrats to political control, but military officials supported Republicans. Radical Republicans held control in Mississippi until 1876 and in Louisiana and South Carolina until 1877 because in these states whites were a minority of the population.

Self-Test

Multiple Choice

1. b	5. b	9. a	13. a	17. c
2. d	6. d	10. d	14. a	18. b
3. c	7. c	11. d	15. b	
4. d	8. a	12. b	16. b	

Short Essays

1. Both Lincoln and Johnson believed that secession had been illegal and that the southern states never actually left the Union. Both also believed that restoration should be handled by the executive branch of the federal government. Lincoln offered amnesty to all ex-Confederates except high-ranking civil and military leaders. To participate in the reconstitution of state governments, citizens had only to pledge future loyalty to the Union. Johnson's requirements were similar, including amnesty and the return of all property to those who would swear allegiance to the Union. Johnson, however, allowed high-ranking civil and military ex-Confederates to petition the president (himself) for amnesty and then permitted them to participate in the new state governments. Johnson required the new state governments to ratify the Thirteenth Amendment, abolishing slavery; Lincoln had not in-

cluded such a requirement. Lincoln had hoped to base his restoration plan on former southern Whigs, whereas Johnson appealed to small farmers.

2. Johnson believed that restoration was a matter for the executive branch exclusively. He had the southern states form new governments during the summer of 1865, while Congress was not in session. He planned to build a coalition of white southerners, northern Democrats, and conservative Republicans who would acknowledge senators and congressmen from the new state governments.

3. The freedmen's primary goal was economic independence as well as control over their own time and family life. They hoped to receive the land they had worked as slaves, looking forward to land distribution by the Union army and then the federal government. When this did not materialize, they emphasized control over their time, forcing white landowners to accept sharecropping or tenancy arrangements rather than the gang system of paid agricultural labor. Freedmen felt that suffrage and education were crucial to their hopes for economic independence. African-American women left the fields whenever they could, preferring to work in their own homes. Freedmen created their own communities, which included churches and civic organizations.

4. When Freedmen's Bureau agents entered the South they sought first to establish stability. Accepting the lack of land distribution, these agents supported the private property interests of the white landowners and helped them arrange for labor contracts with freedmen. They discouraged violence and encouraged the freedmen to be content with agricultural labor.

5. For a time, freedmen voted and participated in state and local governments. They established their own families and communities, independent of white southerners. State governments and local communities established public schools for many African-American children. Freedmen avoided working in the gang system and acquired the ability to cultivate land through sharecropping or tenancy. They did not acquire title to much land because the federal government did not support land redistribution; many, there-

fore, fell into debt peonage, owing landlords and merchants for their supplies. They lost political power quickly when Union troops could not put down the Klan's violence, and without political power their economic independence was continually threatened.

6. During presidential Reconstruction, southern whites used the Black Codes and other restrictive legislation to force freedmen to accept labor contracts with planters. Such laws allowed state and local governments to control the lives of the freedmen. During Congressional Reconstruction, the northern military presence tilted the balance of power in favor of the freedmen. In addition, state governments included freedmen and those supportive of their interests. White southerners then resorted to violence and secret societies to terrorize and intimidate the freedmen, trying to keep them from voting and forcing them into accepting disadvantageous labor arrangements.

7. The Republican economic program appealed to manufacturers with its tariff protection against cheap imports. This also appealed to factory workers, who wanted their wages kept up. Subsidies for a national transportation network also appealed to businessmen who needed effective, inexpensive transportation for their products. The Homestead Act appealed to people who wanted to move west. "Sin taxes" appealed to the religious community as well as bringing in money for transportation projects. Finally, the Civil War pension system was generous to Union veterans and their survivors, a group that included most northerners.

8. The Democrats could have challenged the decision of the electoral commission to select Hayes as president, but that would have led to a contested presidency and an investigation that might have dragged on for years without necessarily ending in their favor. By accepting the compromise, they were able to restrict military influence in the South and obtain major offices for Democrats. A southern railroad was constructed with federal financial support, whether or not this was part of the compromise. The Democrats obtained all these benefits and solidified their control over the white South.